Test Item File

INTEGRATED ADVERTISING, PROMOTION, AND MARKETING COMMUNICATIONS

Third Edition

Kenneth E. Clow *University of Louisiana*
Donald Baack *Pittsburg State University*

PEARSON

Prentice
Hall

Upper Saddle River, New Jersey 07458

VP/Editorial Director: Jeff Shelstad
Acquisitions Editor: Katie Stevens
Product Development Manager: Ashley Santora
Associate Director, Manufacturing: Vincent Scelta
Production Editor & Buyer: Carol O'Rourke
Printer/Binder: Offset Paperback Manufacturing

Pearson Prentice Hall™ is a trademark of Pearson Education, Inc.

10 9 8 7 6 5 4 3 2 1
ISBN 0-13-186625-7

Contents

INTRODUCTION

Welcome to the *Test Item File* for the third edition of the Clow and Baack text, ***Integrated Advertising, Promotions, and Marketing Communications***. This test bank was designed with both the student and the instructor in mind. All of the questions contained in the manual are taken from the text. The instructor and the student should find it easy to locate the source of any question.

The test bank for this third edition contains over 3, 300 questions, which is more than twice as many as in the previous editions. This increase is based on requests by an increasing number of instructors who wish to post some questions on the Internet for quizzes and yet have a sufficient number left to choose from for the exams. The larger number of items provides instructors with numerous questions that can be used without repeating items.

Each chapter in the *Test Item File* contains three types of questions: True/False, Multiple Choice, and Short Answer. Each question is formatted with the question number, possible answers, the correct answer, a difficulty scale, and the page number from the textbook from which the question was derived. The questions in the *Test Item File* begin at the first of the chapter and follow a page-by-page sequence to the end of the chapter.

The Short Answer Questions address primary components of each chapter. A brief answer using text materials is provided for each question. The instructor may notice that student responses may have more information or slightly different responses than the exact text.

As noted, each question includes a difficulty scale. This is intended to help the instructor choose the degree of difficulty of questions to place on an examination. The *Test Item File* provides a mixture of these difficulty levels for each chapter, however there are more (easy) and (moderate) questions and fewer (challenging) questions.

Students taking examinations drawn from the *Test Item File* should be encouraged to carefully read the materials in the text and should be instructed to choose the "best answer" from the available options. Some questions are drawn from the Figures, Tables, and other exhibits in the textbooks, so students should be advised to review those elements.

Good luck with your course and subsequent evaluation of student learning. Should you have any difficulty with the question content, please send an e-mail to **Clow@ulm.edu**. We sincerely hope you find this supplemental material useful. Thank you for using the Clow/Baack text.

Kenneth E. Clow, Ph.D., Professor of Marketing, University of Louisiana at Monroe.
Donald Baack, Ph.D., Professor, Management and Marketing Department, Pittsburg State University.

CHAPTER 1
INTEGRATED MARKETING COMMUNICATIONS

True-False Questions

1) Ron Jon's Surf Shop's logo has helped increase brand recall.
   (True; Easy; p. 2)

2) Ron Jon's Surf Shop's failure to effectively create cooperative advertising tie-ins hurt the company's sales in the 1990s.
   (False; Moderate; p. 3).

3) In recent years, the nature of the job of account executive has changed due to new pressures for accountability.
   (True; Easy; p. 5)

4) A brand manager is the individual who oversees a line of products on behalf of an advertising agency.
   (False; Easy; p. 5)

5) The people who develop advertisements and promotional campaigns are called creatives.
   (True; Easy; p. 5)

6) The person who directs the filming of a television commercial is normally the brand manager.
   (False; Moderate; p. 5)

7) Brand managers, creatives, and account executives all have new tasks associated with creating strategies to send a unified message in today's marketing environment.
   (True; Moderate; p. 5)

 8) Communication is defined as transmitting, receiving, and processing information.
   (True; Easy; p. 5)

 9) Companies using advertisements to send messages to customers are the senders in a communications model.
   (True; Easy; p. 6)

10) When an advertising creative takes an idea and transforms it into an ad, the process is known as encoding in a communications model
    (True; Moderate; p. 7)

11) Television commercials, print ads, and retail coupons are examples of encoding.
   (True; Moderate; p. 7)

12) Televisions carrying advertisements or billboards that are available for new ads are examples of transmission devices.
   (True; Moderate; p. 7)

13) Decoding occurs when the message is interpreted by the receiver.
   (True; Easy; p. 7)

14) When a customer smells a perfume sample in a magazine while reading an ad, decoding is taking place
   (True, Challenging; p. 7)

15) Typically, advertising messages are decoded in exactly the same way by large numbers of consumers because of the standard nature of the decoding process.
   (False; Challenging; p. 7)

16) The large number of marketing messages consumers are exposed to daily is an example of noise and is also called clutter.
   (True; Moderate; p. 7)

17) The actual purchase of a product or a complaint about a good or service is feedback in the communications model
   (True; Moderate; p. 8)

18) The most common form of noise in the marketing communication process occurs when viewers are multitasking, which is doing something else at the same time the ad is viewed.
   (False; Challenging; p. 8)

19) In today's marketplace, advertising alone is often enough to sustain sales.
   (False; Easy; p. 8)

20) An integrated marketing communications program should be viewed as an overall organizational process rather than a marketing plan or marketing function.
   (True; Moderate; p. 8)

21) Coca-Cola's consistent use of the same logo, theme, and colors on packages and in advertisements is an example of an integrated marketing communications approach.
   (True; Challenging; p. 8)

22) Some marketing scholars argue that the integrated marketing communications (IMC) approach is a recent phenomenon while others suggest the name is new, but the concept has been around for a long time.
(True; Moderate; p. 8)

23) In addition to the traditional elements of advertising, direct marketing, and personal selling - promotions now also includes activities such as database marketing, sponsorship marketing, sales promotions, Internet marketing, and public relations.
(True; Moderate; p. 9)

24) The first step to preparing a marketing plan is a situational analysis in which the marketing team identifies problems and opportunities.
(True; Moderate; p. 9)

25) The budget preparation stage of a marketing analysis focuses on finding company strengths and weaknesses and environmental opportunities and threats.
(False; Moderate; p. 9)

26) Marketing tactics apply to all the ingredients of the marketing mix plus any positioning, differentiation, or branding strategies the marketing team wishes to add.
(False; Challenging; p. 10)

27) Knowing how to reach purchasing managers and other decision makers within target businesses is a critical element in the development of a totally integrated communications plan.
(True; Challenging; p. 11)

28) Effective advertising is based on a foundation of understanding consumer and business buyer behaviors.
(True; Moderate; p. 11)

29) Promotional tools include trade promotions, sales promotions, database marketing, personal selling, and advertising.
(True; Moderate; p. 11)

30) Trade promotions include contests, incentives, vendor support programs, and other fees and discounts that help the manufacture push the product through the channel.
(True; Moderate; p. 12)

31) The integration tools presented in Chapter 1 include Internet marketing, direct marketing, database marketing, and sponsorship marketing.
(False; Moderate; p. 12)

32) The "We Understand" marketing theme at Hewlett Packard is part of the company's overall emphasis of having a unified message
(True; Challenging; p. 13)

33) According to the American Productivity & Quality Center, the first stage in developing an integrated marketing communications system is to identify, coordinate, and manage all forms of marketing communication.
(True, Moderate; p. 13)

34) A study by the American Productivity & Quality Center notes that successful IMC programs require cross-functional communication.
(True; Moderate; p. 13)

35) One of the major challenges for marketers is gathering information about potential customers and product sales.
(False; Moderate; p. 14)

36) With the advancement of the World Wide Web and information technology, channel power has shifted to the consumer.
(True; Moderate; p. 16)

37) Susan researches car stereos on the Internet and by visiting Best Buy. This is an example of a shift in power to the retailer.
(False; Challenging; p. 16)

38) One new marketing challenge is that consumers can now purchase goods and services from anywhere in the world, which increase competitive forces.
(True; Moderate; p. 17)

39) Nike has gained the greatest amount of market share in the past decade at the expense of Reebok, Adidas, and other athletic shoe companies.
(True; Moderate; p. 18)

40) Reebok has moved from emphasizing the fashion element of the company's shoes in response to competitive pressures to focusing on the female outdoor enthusiast.
(False; Challenging; p. 18)

41) Brand parity is the belief that multiple brands consist of or offer the same set of attributes and benefit and are of equal quality.
(True; Moderate; p. 19)

42) In the past Bruce bought Kleenex brand tissues, but has now decided that all of tissues brands are pretty much the same. This is an example of brand parity.
(True; Challenging; p. 19)

43) Brand loyalty has steadily increased over the last decade.
(False; Moderate; p. 19)

44) Today's consumers have a variety of choices regarding where they can obtain information about a brand.
(True; Easy; p. 19)

45) A Web site is not considered a contact point because both the consumer and the company employee talking to the consumer can remain anonymous.
(False; Challenging; p.19)

46) Television is becoming a more effective mass media outlet for advertising because so many more people own sets and have access to cable as well as satellite.
(False; Challenging; p.10)

47) A Globally Integrated Marketing Communications plan creates a standard message across all cultures.
(False; Moderate; p. 20)

48) Adaptation in a global advertising campaign means rewriting an advertisement to fit the nuances of a given language and culture.
(True; Moderate; p. 21)

49) Standardization would be an effective GMIC tactic in the Middle East because of the variety of religions and cultures.
(False; Challenging; p. 21)

50) Standardization and adaptation are the same thing.
(False; Moderate; p. 21)

Multiple Choice Questions

51) Ron Jon's Surf Shop sales increased when the company became involved in:
    a) snow skiing
    b) cooperative programs with others swimwear and beach sport companies
    c) eliminating unprofitable locations
    d) surf board manufacturing
(b; Challenging; p. 3)

52) Ron Jon's Surf Shop used each of the following marketing strategies *except:*
    a) sponsorship of professional surfing contests with beachwear manufacturers
    b) sponsorship of "End of Summer Skateboard Contest" in Florida
    c) developing an 11-page advertisement in Sports Illustrated swimsuit issue
    d) developing a cooperative agreement with Chrysler Corporation to create a limited edition of the Ron Jon PT Cruiser
(c; Difficult; p. 3)

53) Marketing account executives are facing increasing pressures related to:
    a) accountability
    b) affordability
    c) accessibility
    d) applicability
(a; Easy; p. 4)

54) An advertising agency is told a campaign should result in a 20% increase in sales. This is an example of:
    a) marketing myopia
    b) standardization
    c) adaptation
    d) accountability
(d; Moderate; p. 4)

55) An account executive's duties include:
    a) preparing a database
    b) strategic development of a marketing plan and ad campaign
    c) preparing the actual advertisements
    d) product development and applications
(b; Challenging; p. 5)

56) The individual who is responsible for a specific brand or line of products is the:
   a) agency account executive
   b) brand manager
   c) media buyer
   d) media planner
(b; Easy; p. 5)

57) The individual is most likely to work for the company that produces the product is a(n):
   a) agency account executive
   b) brand manager
   c) media buyer
   d) media planner
(b; Moderate; p. 5)

58) The individual in charge of Tide, Bold, and Cheer at Procter & Gamble would be the:
   a) agency account executive
   b) brand manager
   c) media buyer
   d) media planner
(b; Challenging; p. 5)

59) The individuals who develop the actual advertisements for promotional campaigns are called:
   a) account executives
   b) brand managers
   c) creatives
   d) receivers
(c; Easy; p. 5)

60) A creative's main responsibility is to:
   a) compile a database regarding consumer behavior
   b) evaluate of the marketing plan
   c) develop advertisements and campaigns
   d) receive marketing messages from various sources
(c; Moderate; p. 5)

61) Susan just developed a new slogan to use in a company's advertising. Her main job is to think up these ideas and put them into the company's advertising. Susan is a(n):
   a) account manager
   b) brand manager
   c) creative
   d) media manager
(c; Challenging; p. 5)

62) One of the more common trends in promotions is:
   a) a decline in accountability
   b) an emphasis on print media
   c) a more integrated approach
   d) greater reliance on network advertising
(c; Challenging; p. 5)

63) The person or group who wishes to convey a message plays which role in a communications model?
   a) sender
   b) encoder
   c) decoder
   d) receiver
(a; Easy; p. 6)

64) In terms of a communications model, the sender is:
   a) the company seeking to sell a product
   b) a television set
   c) sales data following a campaign
   d) a consumer ignoring an ad in a newspaper
(a; Moderate; p. 6)

65) When Sean shops for an automobile, the most likely to be communications senders are:
   a) Honda and Toyota
   b) NBC and CSPAN
   c) The New York Times and the Chicago Sun Times
   d) The Internet and the Web
(a; Challenging; p. 6)

66) The verbal and nonverbal cues that are part of a communication message take place in which stage of a communications model?
   a) sending
   b) encoding
   c) transmission
   d) filtering out noise
(b; Moderate; p. 7)

67) In preparing an ad, a creative is most likely going to be involved in:
   a) encoding
   b) transmission
   c) decoding
   d) noise or clutter
   (a; Moderate; p. 7)

68) Preparing ad copy is which part of the communication process?
   a) decoding
   b) situational analysis
   c) encoding
   d) filtering out noise
   (c; Moderate; p. 7)

69) In terms of communication, encoding is:
   a) a sales pitch recited by a salesperson
   b) database management finding a statistical oddity
   c) a chat room on the Internet
   d) a purchase decision
   (a; Challenging; p. 7)

70) The items that carry the message from the sender to the receiver are:
   a) encoding processes
   b) decoding processes
   c) transmission devices
   d) feedback devices
   (c; Easy; p. 7)

71) A consumer sees a billboard while driving. The billboard is a:
   a) creative
   b) decoding device
   c) transmission device
   d) form of feedback
   (c; Moderate; p. 7)

72) When a message is being heard or seen, what is taking place?
   a) encoding
   b) transmission
   c) decoding
   d) feedback
   (c; Moderate; p. 7)

73) A person smells the fragrance of a perfume attached to a magazine advertisement. What is taking place?

    a) encoding
    b) transmission
    c) decoding
    d) feedback

(c; Moderate; p. 7)

74) The person reading a magazine advertisement plays which role in the communications model?

    a) sender
    b) decoder
    c) receiver
    d) object

(c; Easy; p. 7)

75) Kodak identifies a group of people who are most likely to use the company's new digital photo technology and creates advertisements specifically for them. In a communication model, these individuals are:

    a) senders
    b) decoders
    c) receivers
    d) subjects

(c; Challenging; p. 7)

76) Noise is:

    a) anything which carries a message from a sender to a receiver
    b) changing a message to match the specific needs of a target audience
    c) a verbal or nonverbal cue delivered by the sender
    d) anything that distorts the sender's message

(d; Easy; p. 7)

77) Michelle is trying to tutor George, but a stereo is playing loudly in the room next door, making it difficult to concentrate. This is an example of:

    a) feedback disruption
    b) noise
    c) encoding design
    d) a contact point

(b; Moderate; p. 7)

78) In which of the following situations has noise disrupted the transmission of a message created by Reebok?
   a) the creative working on the assignment was working on several assignments at the same time and did a poor job of translating Reebok's desires into an ad
   b) the account executive was not clear about what Reebok wanted to accomplish with the ad
   c) the Reebok ad that was designed was in the middle of a sequence of television ads; as a result, few people watched or paid attention to it
   d) The person looking at the ad was also playing cards
(c; Challenging; p. 7)

79) While browsing the Internet, a consumer encounters a new pop-up ad every time a new page is opened. This is an example of:
   a) advertising effectiveness
   b) perceptual distortion
   c) clutter
   d) brand parity
(c; Moderate; p. 7)

80) Which is an example of clutter?
   a) watching six hours of television per day, the family average
   b) not paying attention to the only billboard within a 10-mile stretch of highway
   c) hearing a radio advertisement while reading one for a different company in a magazine
   d) a miscommunication between an ad agency and a brand manager
(c; Challenging; p. 7)

81) Which would be an example of feedback in a marketing channel?
   a) new product development
   b) a customer complaint
   c) a decision to begin international operations
   d) removing a product from the market
(b; Moderate; p. 8)

82) Julie is explaining an integrated marketing communications program to Michael. In this situation:
   a) Julie is a sender and Michael is an encoder
   b) Julie is a receiver and Michael is providing feedback
   c) Julie is a sender and Michael is a receiver
   d) Julie is a transmission device and Michael is a decoder
(c; Moderate; pp. 5-7)

83) The coordination and integration of all marketing communication tools, avenues, and sources within a company into a seamless program that maximizes the impact on consumers and other end users at a minimal cost is:
   a) the marketing plan
   b) the marketing mix
   c) integrated marketing communications
   d) marketing strategy

(c; Easy; p. 8)

84) Of the four "P's" of marketing, where does integrated marketing communications belong?
   a) pricing decisions
   b) product design
   c) promotion
   d) distribution

(c; Easy; p. 8)

85) The four "P's" of marketing are also called:
   a) marketing management
   b) marketing myopia
   c) marketing design
   d) the marketing mix

(d; Easy; p. 8)

86) The marketing mix consists of the product, the price, the distribution system, and:
   a) emotions
   b) promotions
   c) delivery systems
   d) services

(b; Easy; p. 8)

87) Which is ordinarily *not* considered part of the promotions mix?
   a) advertising
   b) product design
   c) personal selling
   d) sales promotions

(b; Easy; p. 9)

88) The first element of an IMC marketing plan is a(n):
   a) situational analysis
   b) set of marketing objectives
   c) analysis of human resources
   d) statement of marketing strategies and tactics

(a; Easy; p. 9)

89) Which is *not* a component of an IMC marketing plan?
   a) situational analysis
   b) marketing objectives
   c) sales promotions
   d) marketing strategies and tactics
(c; Moderate; p. 9)

90) In this text, an integrated marketing communications program is compared to:
   a) a pyramid of marketing activities
   b) the parts of a computer
   c) the government of a state
   d) a car traveling at a high speed
(a; Easy; p. 11)

91) The foundation of an integrated marketing communications program consists of managing the corporation image, understanding buyer behaviors, and a(n):
   a) analysis of the organization
   b) promotions opportunity analysis
   c) advertising management program
   d) company assessment program
(b; Moderate; p. 11)

92) The two types of buyer behaviors the marketing team must understand are business-to-business behaviors and:
   a) local community activities
   b) governmental purchase
   c) consumer buyer behaviors
   d) competitive actions
(c; Easy; p. 11)

93) Promotions that help the manufacture push the product through the channel are:
   a) consumer promotions
   b) rebate programs
   c) direct marketing programs
   d) trade promotions
(d; Moderate; p. 12)

94)   Promotions directly oriented to end users and include coupons, contests, premiums, refunds, rebates, free samples, and price-off offers are:
        a) consumer promotions
        b) rebate programs
        c) direct marketing programs
        d) trade promotions
(a; Easy; p. 12)

95)   Programs that can help the marketing team connect with consumers in positive and socially responsible ways are included in:
        a) consumer promotions
        b) public relations
        c) database marketing
        d) customer relationship management
(b; Moderate; p. 13)

96)   Hewlett-Packard's use of the phrase "We Understand" is an example of:
        a) marketing myopia
        b) franchise development
        c) an IMC umbrella designed to create a clear voice
        d) an effective marketing tactic due to the vagueness of the statement
(c, Moderate; p. 13)

97)   Part of the process of refining an IMC program is:
        a) reducing all forms of external communications
        b) viewing communications from the perspective of the customer
        c) limiting technology to mandated programs
        d) making sure it only pertains to the marketing department
(b; Moderate; p. 13)

98)   Refining an IMC program is to identify, coordinate, and manage all forms of marketing communication is which step?
        a) first
        b) second
        c) third
        d) last
(a; Challenging; p. 13)

99)   The final stage in refining an IMC program occurs when an organization:
        a) identifies and coordinates all forms of external communications
        b) extends the scope of communication to include everyone in the organization
        c) puts technology at the forefront
        d) uses the IMC program to help drive corporate strategic planning
(d; Challenging; p. 14)

100) The major force compelling firms to seek greater integration of advertising and marketing communications is:
   a) developments in information technology
   b) changes in channel power
   c) increased global competition
   d) decline in effectiveness of mass-media advertising
(a; Challenging, p. 15)

101) What gives consumers and businesses access to an abundance of marketing information?
   a) the nightly news
   b) database management programs
   c) word of mouth
   d) increases in information technology
(d; Easy; p. 15)

102) Bank of America has recently started analyzing the features customers use with ATM cards. This is an example of:
   a) coordinating communication cross-functionally
   b) applying information technology
   c) a price and distribution system
   d) developing interpersonal communications
(b; Moderate; p. 15)

103) Predicting purchasing behavior of customers is more accurate today because of:
   a) increased use of credit cards
   b) the UPC bar coding system and point-of-purchase systems
   c) the shift of power to retailers and consumers
   d) the ability of advertisers to accurately measure how many people watch or see advertisements
(b; Challenging; p. 15)

104) A typical marketing channel is:
   a) producer-wholesaler-retailer-consumer
   b) consumer-producer-retailer-wholesaler
   c) producer-consumer-retailer-wholesaler
   d) business agent-retailer-producer-business merchant
(a; Easy; p. 16)

105) Members of a typical marketing channel include producers, wholesalers, retailers, and:
    a) consumers
    b) competitors
    c) business agents
    d) business merchants
(a; Easy; p. 16)

106) Many marketing experts agree channel power has shifted from:
    a) the producer to the wholesaler
    b) the ad agency to the marketing department
    c) the retailer to the wholesaler
    d) from all other groups to the consumer
(d; Easy; p. 16)

107) Buying on-line from Amazon.com rather than a record store is an example of:
    a) a power shift to the consumer
    b) a power shift to the producer
    c) decline in the effectiveness of mass media
    d) a new form of wholesaling
(a; Moderate; p.16)

108) In terms of global Internet retail sales, the category with the highest percentage of the sales, at approximately 29% of the total sales, is:
    a) CDs, music, and videos
    b) computers, electronics, and software
    c) tickets and travel
    d) household goods
(c; Challenging; p. 16)

109) The competitive environment is now more:
    a) local
    b) global
    c) concentrated
    d) benign
(b; Easy; p. 17)

110) Which athletic shoe company gained the most market share in the 1990s?
    a) Adidas
    b) Nike
    c) Reebok
    d) New Balance
(b; Moderate; p. 17)

111) Which athletic shoe company lost the most market share in the 1990s?
   a) Adidas
   b) Nike
   c) Reebok
   d) New Balance
(c; Challenging; p. 17)

112) The loss of market share led Reebok to refocused company marketing strategies on which market?
   a) amateur athlete market
   b) female outdoor enthusiast
   c) hip-hoppers, hipsters, and other fashion-forward urbanites
   d) teenagers and college-aged students
(c; Challenging; p. 18)

113) Brand parity is the:
   a) perception that there are no real differences between major brands
   b) feeling that most advertising is false
   c) belief that all advertisers say essentially the same thing
   d) idea that brands are distinct and easy to identify
(a; Moderate; p. 19)

114) Michael buys a CD player from the closest store because he doesn't think there is much of a difference between brands. This is an example of:
   a) a poor quality IMC program
   b) standardization
   c) marketing integration
   d) brand parity
(d; Moderate; p. 19)

115) Within the marketing channel, manufacturers are having to invest more money in trade promotions because:
   a) consumers expect them
   b) retailers control the merchandise that is on the store's shelves
   c) advertising is not enough to get consumers to purchase products
   d) the brand parity issue makes it necessary
(d; Challenging; p. 19)

116) To combat brand parity, IBM's advertisements might claim the company:
   a) is developing additional products
   b) has found new customers to buy products
   c) has new locations
   d) sells superior products
(d; Challenging; p. 19)

117) A contact point is:
   a) the place where a marketer reaches the production team
   b) the place where the product is packaged or sold
   c) a description of the effects of an advertisement
   d) a place in which a consumer interacts with a company
(d; Easy; p. 20)

118) The following are examples of a customer contact points, *except:*
   a) barnes&noble.com
   b) the white pages in a phone book
   c) a receptionist at Microsoft
   d) a sales clerk at a retail store
(b; Challenging; p. 20)

119) Web sites, phone lines, and advertisements that present the same message and theme are:
   a) contact points
   b) marketing plans
   c) account executives
   d) marketing objectives
(a; Moderate; p. 20)

120) Mass media advertising:
   a) is as effective as ever
   b) has risen in the past decade
   c) has not been assessed effectively
   d) is declining in effectiveness
(d; Easy; p. 20)

121) The following are causes of the decline in mass media advertising, *except:*
   a) satellite television offering more channels
   b) technologies that make it possible to "zap" commercials
   c) greater Internet use
   d) a greater number of new product introductions
(d; Moderate; p. 20)

122) A survey by Roper Starch Worldwide revealed the most common negative response to a television commercials is to:
   a) become annoyed with all of the ad
   b) get up and do something else
   c) switch channels
   d) talk to others in the room
(b; Challenging, p. 20)

123) GIMC stands for:
    a) Globally Integrated Marketing Communications
    b) Global and Institutional Marketing Concepts
    c) Generic and Institutionalized Marketing Creations
    d) Generating Ideas for Marketing Control
(a; Easy; p.   )

124) In terms of marketing communications, standardization is:
    a) using the same message across national boundaries
    b) a form of adaptation
    c) new product development
    d) a new form of the promotions mix
(a; Easy; p. 20)

125) Coca Cola runs the same advertisement in all French-speaking countries. This is an example of:
    a) a diversified IMC theme
    b) standardization
    c) customization
    d) integration
(b; Moderate; p. 21)

126) An example of standardization is:
    a) using the "Generation Next" theme in all of global Pepsi markets
    b) using women with their faces covered in ads for Islamic countries
    c) developing a Web site in several languages
    d) using local salespeople
(a; Challenging; p. 21)

127) In terms of marketing communications, adaptation is:
    a) not used in international environments
    b) a form of e-commerce
    c) advertising in unusual media
    d) adjusting a message to local conditions
(d; Easy; p. 21)

128) An example of adaptation is:
    a) Ford's One-World Ford Contour car
    b) not selling the McRib sandwich in Israel
    c) printing ads only in English for European countries
    d) using direct mail
(b; Challenging; p. 21)

Short-Answer Questions

129) What are the components of the communications model?

The sender is the person(s) attempting to deliver a message or idea. Encoding is creating verbal and nonverbal cues that the sender uses to dispatch a message. A transmission device is any item that carries the message from the sender to the receiver. Decoding takes places when the receiver employs any set of his or her senses to capture the message. The receiver is the intended audience for a message.
(Moderate; p. 5-8)

130) What are the components of the marketing mix? The promotions mix?

The components of the marketing mix are: product, price, promotion, and distribution. The components of the promotions mix are: advertising, personal selling, sales promotions, direct marketing, and public relations.
(Easy; p. 8)

131) Define IMC. What makes it different from traditional promotions programs?

IMC is the coordination and integration of all marketing communication tools, avenues, and sources within a company into a seamless program. IMC maximizes the impact on consumers and other end-users at minimal cost; it also affects all of the firm's business-to-business, customer-focused, and internally-oriented communications.

IMC is different because it is a more sweeping or strategic approach to marketing communications, designed to incorporate the entire company into the program.
(Moderate; pp. 8-9)

132) What are the steps in preparing a marketing plan?

The steps of preparation for a marketing plan are: 1) situational analysis; 2) establishing marketing objectives; 3) creating marketing budget; 4) devising the marketing strategy; 5) creating marketing tactics; and 6) marketing evaluation.
(Moderate; p. 9)

133) The writers of this text describe an IMC plan as similar to a pyramid. Describe this approach.

The foundation is the IMC concept and:
- firm and brand image
- understanding buyer behaviors
- promotions opportunity analysis

A second layer consisting of the advertising tools, including:
- advertising management
- advertising design: appeals
- advertising design: executional frameworks
- media selection

A third level containing other elements of the promotional mix, including:
- trade promotions
- consumer promotions
- direct marketing programs
- legal, social, and regulatory issues

Integration tools, consisting of:
- Internet marketing and e-commerce
- IMC for small businesses and entrepreneurial ventures
- evaluation

(Challenging; p. 9-12)

134) What elements form the foundation of an IMC program?

Corporate image and brand management, understanding buyer behaviors, and a promotions opportunity analysis.
(Moderate; p. 11)

135) What are the advertising tools presented in this chapter?

- advertising management
- advertising design: appeals
- advertising design: executional frameworks
- media selection
(Moderate; p. 11)

136) What are the promotional tools presented in this chapter?

- trade promotions
- consumer promotions
- database marketing programs
- personal selling
- public relations
(Challenging; pp. 11-12)

137) What recent trends make an IMC approach valuable to companies in the marketplace?

The development of information technology.
Changes in channel power.
Increases in global competition.
Maturing markets.
Integration of information by consumers.
Brand parity.
The decline in the effectiveness of mass media advertising.
(Challenging; pp. 15-20)

138) Describe the brand parity problem.

Brand parity is the problem that all products are basically equal in terms of the benefits they deliver.
(Easy; p. 19)

139) Describe contact points.

A contact point is any place in which the customer may interact with or acquire information about a firm. This would include advertising, service departments, personal selling situations, and phone calls or Internet inquiries to the company.
(Easy; p. 19-20)

140) Why is mass media advertising less effective?

Inventions, such as the VCR, make it possible to fast forward through commercials. Remotes can turn down the sound while commercials run. Cable offers more outlets and fewer viewers per outlet. Mass media outlets, including television, newspapers, radio, and magazines, carry a large number of ads, which creates clutter. This makes it difficult for any one ad to standout and be noticed.
(Moderate; p. 20)

141) Define GMIC. What makes it a quality GMIC program crucial in the twenty-first century marketplace?

GMIC is globally integrated marketing communications. It is important because most companies compete in an international arena.
(Easy; p. 20-21)

CHAPTER 2
BRAND AND CORPORATE IMAGE MANAGEMENT

True-False Questions

1) Gucci is not a strong brand, because the company has changed advertising campaigns too many times.
    (False; Easy; p. 28)

2) Gucci has the image of being a seductive, high fashion brand.
    (True; Moderate; p. 29)

3) A firm's image is based on the feeling consumers and businesses have about the overall organization and its individual brands.
    (True; Easy; p. 30)

4) Effective marketing communications are based on a clearly defined corporate image.
    (True; Easy; p. 30)

5) What a firm's employees believe about the company's image is far more important than what consumers think.
    (False; Moderate; p. 30)

6) Perceptions of a corporation's image are based solely on price and quality.
    (False; Moderate; p. 30)

7) A corporate image contains both ~~visible~~ tangible and intangible elements.
    (True; Easy; p. 31)

8) An organizational policy to actively recruit minority employees would be an element of a company's image.
    (True; Moderate; p. 31)

9) From the consumer's perspective, corporate image provides psychological reinforcement and social acceptance of a purchasing decision.
    (True; Easy; p. 32)

10) A positive corporate image can reduce search time when a consumer is making a buying decision.
    (True; Easy; p. 32)

11) While a corporation's image plays a key role in marketing to consumers, it is not significant when selling to other businesses.
    (False; Moderate; p. 33)

12) Brand image is especially valuable to a company that is expanding internationally because it reduces risk and uncertainty on the part of the buyer.
(True; Moderate; p. 33)

13) A strong corporate image does not affect the firm's ability to charge a higher price.
(False; Moderate; p. 34)

14) A well-developed, favorable image creates loyal customers who will generate positive word-of-mouth endorsements about the company and its products.
(True; Easy; p. 34)

15) A corporation's image has little or no effect on other business activities, such as recruiting employees.
(False; Moderate; p. 34)

16) The image a firm tries to project should accurately portray the firm and coincide with the goods and services being offered.
(True; Easy; p. 35)

17) Reinforcing or rejuvenating a current image is more difficult to accomplish than changing a well-established image.
(False; Moderate; p. 35)

18) In some cases, modifying the current image or trying to create an entirely new image for a firm is not possible.
(True; Moderate; p. 35)

19) Reestablishing or rebuilding the firm's image that has been hurt by bad press is usually not a difficult task if the firm admits the mistake.
(False; Challenging; p. 35)

20) In each industry, the right image is one that sends a clear message about the unique nature of an organization and its products.
(True; Moderate, p. 35)

21) The key to successfully rejuvenating a corporation's image is to remain consistent with the previous image while adding new elements.
(True; Easy; p. 36)

22) It is impossible to change a corporation's image.
(False; Easy; p. 36)

23) Rejuvenating an image is more related to raising prices than to finding new customers or selling new products.
(False; Challenging; p. 36)

24) Changing a corporation's image requires both internal programs and external promotions.
(True; Moderate; p. 37)

25) An overt corporate name reveals what the company does.
(True; Moderate; p. 37)

26) An overt corporate name tends to be conceptual in nature.
(False; Moderate; p. 37)

27) Krispy Kreme is an example of an overt corporate name.
(False; Challenging; p. 37)

28) An implied corporate name contains recognizable words or word parts that suggest what the company does.
(True; Easy; p. 37)

29) Google is an example of an implied corporate name.
(False; Challenging; p. 37)

30) A conceptual corporate name seeks to capture the essence of the idea behind the brand.
(True; Easy; p. 37)

31) Krispy Kreme is an example of a conceptual corporate name seeking to suggest the idea of a tasty creme-filled pastry.
(True; Challenging; p. 37)

32) Quality corporate logos should be easily recognizable and elicit a consensual meaning among those in the target market.
(True; Easy; p. 38)

33) The notion that a logo can elicit a consensual meaning among customers is known as stimulus codability.
(True; Moderate; p. 38)

34) Quality logos and corporate names should meet four tests. They should be 1) easily recognizable, 2) elicit a consensual meaning among those in the firm's target market, 3) be familiar, and 4) evoke positive feelings.
(True; Challenging; p. 38)

35) Nike has spent considerable resources developing stimulus codability related to its "Swoosh."
(True; Challenging; p. 39)

36) Brands are names generally assigned to individual goods or services or to sets of products in a line.
(True; Easy; p. 39)

37) A brand name has salience when consumers are aware of a brand but have mostly negative feelings about the name.
(False; Moderate; p. 39)

38) Using a standardized global branding strategy reduces marketing costs.
(True; Easy; p. 40)

39) With an adaptation global marketing strategy, the same brand name, advertising, and promotion communications are used in all countries.
(False; Moderate; p. 40)

40) Standardized global brands allow a firm to transfer the best practices from one country to another.
(True; Challenging; p. 40)

41) A family brand is a situation in which a series of companies produce one brand in a co-operative venture.
(False; Moderate; p. 40)

42) One goal of branding is to set a product apart from its competitors.
(True; Moderate; p. 41)

43) The secret to a long brand life is finding what influences consumers to purchase a particular brand.
(False; Challenging; p. 41)

44) Brand parity is the perception that most products are relatively similar or have no distinct differences.
(True; Easy; p. 41)

45) Brand equity is the perception that most products are relatively similar or have no distinct differences.
(False; Easy; p. 41)

46) Brand equity is a set of characteristics that are unique to a brand that make it seem different and better.
(True; Easy; p. 41)

47) Brand equity is not important in business-to-business markets.
(False; Moderate, p. 41)

48) Brand equity is not as important in international markets because fewer brands are available.
(False; Moderate; p. 41)

49) Brand parity is a strong weapon that might dissuade consumers from looking for a cheaper product or for special deals or incentives to purchase other brands.
(False; Moderate; p. 41)

50) Brand recognition is the first phase of the marketing program to develop brand equity for a product.
(True; Challenging; p. 42)

51) Brand equity is weakened by continuous innovation.
(False; Easy; p. 42)

52) Brand equity is strengthened when a company does not rely too heavily on a single customer.
(True; Moderate p. 42)

53) Domination is a negative force in brand equity because it suggests poor publicity has affected the brand.
(False; Moderate; p. 43)

54) To develop brand equity in today's competitive markets, companies must always be on the cutting edge, create new products, move faster then the competition, and effectively reach consumers.
(True; Moderate; p. 43)

55) Brand metrics measure returns on branding investments.
(True; Easy; p. 43)

56) Another name for domain squatting is cyber squatting.
(True; Easy; p. 44)

57) Brand infringement can be created by cyber squatting.
(True; Moderate; p. 44)

58) A brand extension is the use of a new brand name to identify an old product.
(False; Easy; p. 44)

59) A flanker brand is the use of a new brand name to identify an old product.
(False; Easy; p. 44)

60) When Proctor & Gamble adds new laundry detergents to help dominate the market, it is an example of using flanker brands.
   (True; Challenging; p. 45)

61) A flanker brand can be introduced when company leaders think that offering the product under the current brand name may adversely affect the overall marketing program.
   (True; Challenging; p. 45)

 62) Ingredient branding is the placement of one brand within another, such as NutraSweet as part of Diet Coke.
   (True; Moderate; p. 45)

63) Oreo milkshakes sold in a Dairy Question is an example of complementary branding.
   (True; Challenging; p. 45)

64) Ingredient branding is the joint venture of two or more brands into a new good or service.
   (False; Moderate; p. 45)

65) Co-branding succeeds when it builds the brand equity of both brands involved.
   (True; Easy; p. 45)

66) Private brands and private label programs diminished greatly in the 1990s, due to increasing levels of consumer affluence.
   (False; Moderate; p. 47)

67) In recent years, loyalty toward retail stores has been declining, while loyalty toward individual brands has been increasing.
   (False; Moderate; p. 47)

68) Many retailers are treating private labels more like national brands and investing more money into marketing, advertising, and in-store displays.
   (True; Moderate; p. 47)

69) A product's package is the last opportunity for a brand to make an impression on a consumer before a purchase is made.
   (True; Moderate; p. 49)

70) Marketing surveys have revealed that only about one-third of purchases are planned prior to reaching a store.
   (True; Challenging, p. 49)

71) Positioning is the process of creating a perception in the consumer's mind regarding the nature of a company and its products relative to the competition.
   (True; Easy; p. 51)

72) In positioning products, it is important to be sure that the positioning strategy chosen is relevant to consumers and provides them with a benefit that consumers consider to be useful in decision making.
   (True; Challenging; p. 51)

73) Consumers ultimately determine the position a product holds.
   (True; Moderate; p. 51)

74) Using an attribute positioning strategy would involve emphasizing a particular trait or characteristic of the product.
   (True; Moderate; p. 52)

75) A product user positioning strategy is creating a new or unusual product class that the brand can dominate.
   (False; Challenging; p. 52)

76) When orange juice producers promote the idea that orange juice can be consumed at any time during the day, it is an attempt to reposition orange juice using the product class positioning strategy.
   (True; Challenging; p. 53)

Multiple-Choice Questions

77) The Gucci company is an example of:
   a) advertising success based on building greater brand awareness
   b) an advertising program based on stimulus codability
   c) a strong and identifiable corporate image
   d) an advertising failure
   (c; Moderate; p. 29)

78) The feelings consumers and business have about an organization and its brand is the corporation's:
   a) advertising program impact
   b) flanker brand
   c) image
   d) persona
   (c; Easy; p. 30)

79) Company leaders study the firm's image during as part of:
   a) the development of a mission statement
   b) the development of the marketing plan
   c) a target market analysis
   d) a promotion opportunity analysis
   (d; Challenging; p. 30)

80) A strong corporate image can be combined with which factor in external environment to create a major strategic advantage for the firm?
   a) strength
   b) weakness
   c) opportunity
   d) threat
   (c; Challenging; p. 30)

81) The following items are tangible components of a corporate image, *except:*
   a) goods and services sold
   b) retail outlets where the product is sold
   c) advertising, promotions, and other forms of communication
   d) competing businesses
   (d; Moderate; p. 31)

82) Which is an intangible element of a corporate image?
   a) the corporate name and logo
   b) ideals and beliefs of corporate personnel
   c) the employees
   d) the package and label
   (b; Challenging; p. 31)

83) In the mind of the consumer, a strong corporate image is linked to:
   a) perceptions of economic conditions
   b) ratings by financial advisors
   c) reduction of search time in purchase decisions
   d) finding substitute goods when making purchases
   (c; Moderate; p. 32)

84) From a consumer's perspective, a strong corporate image provides each of the following functions, *except:*
   a) provides assurance regarding purchase decisions in unfamiliar settings
   b) provides purchase alternatives
   c) reduces search time
   d) provides social acceptance of purchases
   (b; Moderate; p. 32)

85) Feeling good after making a purchase from a company with a strong and positive image is an example of:
   a) an impulse buy
   b) psychological reinforcement
   c) cognitive dissonance
   d) brand metrics
   (b; Challenging; p. 32)

86) When you know other people have purchased the same brand that you are buying, the feeling is called:
   a) social acceptance
   b) reliability
   c) cognitive dissonance
   d) brand recognition
   (a; Moderate; p. 32)

87) From a business-to-business perspective, a strong corporate image provides each of the following functions, *except:*
   a) provides assurance regarding purchase decisions in unfamiliar settings
   b) provides purchase alternatives
   c) reduces search time
   d) provides social acceptance of purchases
   (b; Moderate; p. 33)

88) From the perspective of the corporation, a strong brand image is related to each of the following, *except:*
   a) being able to charge a higher price
   b) psychological reinforcement and social acceptance
   c) more frequent purchases by customers
   d) more favorable ratings by financial observers
   (b; Moderate; p. 34)

89) From the company's perspective, a quality corporate image enhances the introduction of a new product because:
   a) the company can charge a lower price for the new product
   b) a new distribution channel can be established
   c) customers normally transfer their trust in and beliefs about the corporation to a new product
   d) the competition does not know how to respond
   (c; Challenging; p. 34)

90) In the early 2000s, Wal-Mart's corporate image was negatively affected by:
   a) new competitors
   b) positive word-of-mouth endorsements
   c) lawsuits, governmental actions, and unionization attempts
   d) ineffective advertising
   (c; Easy; p. 35)

91) Which of the following statements about image is *false*?
   a) Reinforcing or rejuvenating a current image that is consistent with the view of consumers is easier to accomplish than changing a well-established image that is not consistent with the image the company wants to project.
   b) It is relatively easy to change the image people hold about a given company.
   c) Any negative or bad press can quickly destroy an image that took years to build.
   d) The image being projected must accurately portray the firm and coincide with its goods and services.
   (b, Challenging, p. 35)

92) In making decisions about the image to be projected, it will be the easiest for marketers to:
   a) rejuvenate an image that is consistent with consumer's current view of the company
   b) reinforce an image that is not consistent with a consumer's current view of the company
   c) develop a new image for a new company
   d) revert to an earlier image of the company
   (a; Challenging; p. 35)

93) It is important that the image being projected by a company's marketing messages:
   a) reinforce the competition's concept of the image
   b) accurately portray the firm and coincide with the goods and services being offered
   c) be consistent with what consumers already believe about the firm
   d) coincide with what competitors are doing
   (b; Challenging; p. 35)

94) The right image is one that:
   a) coincides with the majority of companies within the industry
   b) highlights the quality of products being sold by the company
   c) is consistent with the views of management of each company
   d) sends a clear message about the unique nature of an organization and its products
   (d; Challenging; p. 35)

95) Keeping a consistent image while incorporating new elements is an example of:
   a) developing a new image
   b) image positioning
   c) rejuvenating an image
   d) completing an image
(c; Moderate; p. 36)

96) Hewlett-Packard (HP)'s move from being viewed as a staid company run by engineers to an ultimate lifestyle technology company in tune with pop culture is an example of:
   a) brand development
   b) reinforcing a current image
   c) image positioning
   d) rejuvenating an image
(d; Challenging; p. 36)

97) When Thrifty's became Bluenotes, the goal was to:
   a) eliminate an image
   b) enhance the image
   c) rejuvenate the image
   d) change the image
(d; Moderate; p. 36)

98) Changing an image is most necessary:
   a) every few years
   b) when the company is ready for a change
   c) when target markets shrink or disappear
   d) when a competitor enters the market
(c; Moderate; p. 36)

99) In promoting a desired corporate or brand image, the most difficult would be to:
   a) create a new image for a new product
   b) reinforce a current image that is consistent with consumers' views
   c) rejuvenate a current image that is consistent with consumers' views
   d) modify a current image because it is not consistent with what the company wants to project
(d; Moderate; p. 36)

100) Changing an image requires more than one well-made ad or press release--it begins with:
   a) hiring a public relations firm to plan the image change
   b) designing a series of advertisements that take customers through the rationale for the image change
   c) selling the idea internal company personnel and then moving outward to suppliers, other businesses, and customers
   d) selling the idea to customers and then working inward to company personnel
(c; Moderate; p. 37)

101) Which type of corporate name reveals what a company does?
   a) overt
   b) implied
   c) conceptual
   d) iconoclastic
(a; Easy; p. 37)

102) American Airlines and BMW Motorcycles are examples of:
   a) overt names
   b) implied names
   c) conceptual names
   d) iconoclastic names
(a; Moderate; p. 37)

103) Which type of corporate name contains recognizable words or word parts that imply what the company is about?
   a) overt
   b) implied
   c) conceptual
   d) iconoclastic
(b; Moderate; p. 37)

104) Federal Express and International Business Machines (IBM) are examples of:
   a) overt names
   b) implied names
   c) conceptual names
   d) iconoclastic names
(b; Challenging; p. 37)

105) Which type of corporate name captures the essence of the idea behind the brand?
   a) overt
   b) implied
   c) conceptual
   d) iconoclastic
   (c; Moderate; p. 37)

106) Lucent Technologies and Google are examples of:
   a) overt names
   b) implied names
   c) conceptual names
   d) iconoclastic names
   (c; Challenging; p. 37)

107) Which type of corporate name does not reflect the company's goods or services?
   a) overt
   b) implied
   c) conceptual
   d) iconoclastic
   (d; Easy; p. 38)

108) Which type of corporate name is unique, different, and memorable without suggesting the company's goods or services?
   a) overt
   b) implied
   c) conceptual
   d) iconoclastic
   (d; Easy; p. 38)

109) Monstor.com and Apple Computers are examples of:
   a) overt names
   b) implied names
   c) conceptual names
   d) iconoclastic names
   (d; Challenging; p. 38)

110) Overt names:
   a) reveal what the company does
   b) capture the essence of the idea behind the brand
   c) contain recognizable words or word parts that imply what the company is about
   d) do not reflect the company's good or services, but instead something that is unique, different, and memorable
   (a; Moderate; p. 37)

111) Implied names:
    a) reveal what the company does
    b) capture the essence of the idea behind the brand
    c) contain recognizable words or word parts that imply what the company is about
    d) do not reflect the company's good or services, but instead something that is unique, different, and memorable
(c; Moderate; p. 37)

112) Conceptual names:
    a) capture the essence of the idea behind the brand
    b) contain recognizable words or word parts that imply what the company is about
    c) do not reflect the company's good or services, but instead something that is unique, different, and memorable
    d) reveal what the company does
(b; Moderate; p. 37)

113) Iconoclastic names:
    a) reveal what the company does
    b) capture the essence of the idea behind the brand
    c) contain recognizable words or word parts that imply what the company is about
    d) do not reflect the company's good or services, but instead something that is unique, different, and memorable
(d; Moderate; p. 38)

114) Logos help with in-store shopping because:
    a) corporate logos are more readily recognized by shoppers
    b) logos move traffic past goods which are not being purchased
    c) they are a form of clutter
    d) consumers have made up their minds prior to arrival
(a; Easy; p. 38)

115) Stimulus codability is:
    a) a form of brand name
    b) the perception that the brand is known
    c) consensually held meanings among customers
    d) another name for product positioning
(c; Moderate; p. 38)

116) A logo with a consensually held meaning, such as the Prudential Rock, displays:
   a) brand prominence
   b) stimulus codability
   c) brand parity
   d) product positioning
   (b; Moderate; p. 39)

117) The Nike Swoosh is an example of a:
   a) brand
   b) package
   c) label
   d) logo
   (d; Moderate; p. 39)

118) Corporate logos:
   a) are unrelated to image but are related to positioning
   b) help with recall of advertisements and brands
   c) usually are inexpensive to develop
   d) increase search time in product purchase decisions
   (b; Challenging; p. 38)

119) Quality logos and corporate names should pass each of the following tests, *except:*
   a) be easy to pronounce
   b) be familiar
   c) elicit a consensual meaning among those in the firm's target market
   d) evoke positive feelings
   (a; Challenging; p. 38)

120) Names assigned to individual goods or services or to groups of products in a line are:
   a) brands
   b) logos
   c) metrics
   d) designs
   (a; Easy; p. 39)

121) When a brand name has attributes consumers desire and they are aware of the name, it has:
   a) communicability
   b) salience
   c) metrics
   d) momentum
   (b; Easy; p. 39)

122) A particular brand is salient for consumers under all of the following situations *except* when they:
   a) are aware of the brand
   b) regard the product and brand as a good value
   c) recommend it to others
   d) position it against the market leader
   (d; Challenging; p. 39)

123) Two approaches to international branding are standardization and:
   a) communication
   b) identification
   c) adaptation
   d) notification
   (c; Easy; p. 40)

124) Using a standardized global brand offers a company all of the following advantages *except:*
   a) reduces costs
   b) allow for the transference of best practices from one country to another
   c) can be viewed by buyers as a better choice than purchasing a local brand
   d) allows a company to modify the communication approach to better fit each target market
   (d; Moderate; p. 40)

125) Global brands enjoy the most success in:
   a) high-profile, high-involvement product categories
   b) low-involvement, everyday products
   c) low income households
   d) developing countries
   (a; Challenging, p. 40)

126) Of the following list of product categories, the ones that have done the best as global brands are:
   a) soft drinks and snack foods
   b) computers and automobiles
   c) candy and other food items
   d) fast food restaurants
   (b; Challenging; p. 40)

127) Local brands enjoy the most success in:
   a) high-profile, high-involvement product categories
   b) low-involvement, everyday products
   c) low income households
   d) developing countries
   (b; Challenging, p. 40)

128) Of the following list of product categories, the ones that have done the best as local brands are:
   a) soft drinks and snack foods
   b) computers and automobiles
   c) electronics
   d) financial and banking services
   (a; Challenging; p. 40)

129) Developing a strong brand begins with:
   a) a SWOT analysis
   b) developing a product positioning strategy
   c) discovering why consumers buy a brand and why they rebuy the brand
   d) understanding how a brand compares with competing brands
   (c; Moderate; p. 40)

130) In developing a strong brand name, the following are good questions to ask, *except:*
   a) How long has the brand name been in existence?
   b) What are the brands most compelling benefits?
   c) What one word best describes the brand?
   d) What is important to consumers when purchasing the product?
   (a; Moderate, p. 40)

131) A family brand is:
   a) one in which a company offers a series or group of products under one brand name
   b) a type of extension or flanker brand
   c) a logo or theme
   d) a brand for a substitute good
   (a; Easy; p. 40)

132) Black and Decker's line of power tools is an example of a(n):
   a) adaptation
   b) family brand
   c) flanker brand
   d) private label brand
   (b; Moderate; p. 40)

133) When Black and Decker introduced a new form of wrench with the name "Black and Decker Adjustable Wrench," which was being used?
   a) family brand
   b) cooperative brand
   c) flanker brand
   d) complementary brand
   (a; Challenging; p. 40)

134) The goal of branding is to:
   a) be able to charge a higher price than the competition
   b) gain the largest market share
   c) set a product apart from its competitors
   d) have a trademark that is easily identifiable
   (c; Moderate; p. 41)

135) The secret to a long brand life is:
   a) developing a unique brand name
   b) having the largest market share within an industry
   c) having a high level of product quality and high margins
   d) finding one unique selling proposition and sticking with it
   (d; Challenging, p. 41)

136) The perception that all brands are mostly the same is called:
   a) brand equity
   b) brand parity
   c) flanker branding
   d) the private label problem
   (b; Easy; p. 41)

137) The perception a brand is different and better is called:
   a) brand equity
   b) brand parity
   c) flanker branding
   d) the private label advantage
   (a; Easy; p. 41)

138) When a customer believes Black and Decker makes the best and most reliable tools, this is an example of:
   a) brand parity
   b) brand equity
   c) brand cooperation
   d) brand decision
   (b; Moderate; p. 41)

139) Which is *not* true concerning brand equity?
   a) it allows the company to charge a higher price
   b) it reduces name retention
   c) it is helpful in business-to-business markets
   d) it is helpful in international markets
   (b; Moderate; p. 41)

140) Brand equity offers the following benefits, *except:*
    a) allows manufacturers charge more for their brands
    b) creates higher gross margins
    c) provides retailers and wholesalers with greater power
    d) captures additional shelf space in retail stores
(c: Challenging; p. 41)

141) Brand equity offers the following benefits, *except:*
    a) serves as a weapon against consumers switching to another brand due to sales promotions or other competitors' deals
    b) prevents erosion of market share
    c) allows wholesalers and retailers to have a greater profit margin
    d) provides power with wholesalers and retailers
(c; Challenging, p. 42)

142) Which is true concerning brand name recognition and brand equity?
    a) they are unrelated
    b) they are synonymous
    c) to gain brand equity, it is not essential to have a high level of brand recognition
    d) recognition is the first phase of developing brand equity
(d; Challenging; p. 42)

143) Brand equity includes all of the following concepts, *except:*
    a) brand name recognition
    b) brand name recall
    c) domination
    d) exaggeration
(d; Moderate; p. 42)

144) Brand equity can be built using each of the following, *except:*
    a) integrating old and new media
    b) innovation
    c) domination
    d) exaggeration
(d; Moderate; p. 42)

145) The strongly held view that a brand is number one in its product category is:
    a) recognition
    b) recall
    c) domination
    d) moderation
(c; Moderate; p. 43)

146) If consumers believe that Crest is the number one toothpaste for fighting cavities, this is an example of:
   a) corporate image
   b) brand domination
   c) brand recognition
   d) brand evaluation
   (b; Challenging; p. 43)

147) Which measures returns on branding investments?
   a) brand infringement
   b) brand parity
   c) brand equity
   d) brand metrics
   (d; Easy; p. 43)

148) When a company creates a brand name that closely resembles a popular or successful brand, it is called:
   a) brand identification
   b) brand placement
   c) brand infringement
   d) brand association
   (c; Moderate; p. 44)

149) When someone buys Web site names that are valuable to specific people or businesses, it is called:
   a) cyber squatting
   b) brand copying
   c) brand infringement
   d) name association
   (a; Moderate; p. 44)

150) In measuring brand equity companies can use a method called revenue premium, which compares a branded product's revenue to:
   a) the industry's average
   b) a private label brand
   c) a firm's primary competitors
   d) the industry leader
   (b; Challenging; p. 44)

151) Energizer would like to measure the brand equity using the revenue premium method, which involves comparing Energizer's revenues to:
   a) the industry average
   b) a private label brand
   c) Energizer's primary competitors
   d) the industry leader
   (b; Challenging; p. 44)

152) A brand extension is:
   a) a group of related core products sold under one name
   b) the creation of a logo which further explains the brand
   c) the design of a public relations campaign to support a brand
   d) using an established brand name on goods or services not related to the core brand
   (d; Easy; p. 44)

153) American Express Traveler's Cheques are a form of:
   a) flanker brand
   b) brand extension
   c) cooperative brand
   d) complementary brand
   (b; Challenging; p. 44)

154) Which is a flanker brand?
   a) the offering of two or more brands in a single marketing offer
   b) the joint venture of two or more brands into a new product or service
   c) development of a new brand by a company in a good or service category where it currently has an offer
   d) a brand with the same name in a different industry
   (c; Moderate; p. 45)

155) When Procter and Gamble introduces a new laundry detergent with a different brand name, it is an example of creating a:
   a) family brand
   b) cooperative brand
   c) co-brand
   d) flanker brand
   (d; Moderate; p. 45)

156) When Procter and Gamble adds a new laundry detergent called "Reach" to its current line of laundry detergents, Reach is a:
   a) brand extension
   b) brand fabrication
   c) flanker brand
   d) complementary brand
   (c; Moderate; p. 44)

157) If a company feels that offering a new product under the current brand name may adversely affect the current brand, the best strategy would be to introduce the product as a(n):
a) brand extension
b) ingredient brand
c) flanker brand
d) co-brand
(c; Challenging; p. 44)

158) Which involves using an established brand name on goods or services that are not related to the core brand?
a) brand extension
b) private brand
c) flanker brand
d) complementary brand
(a: Moderate; p. 44)

159) When a company develops a new brand in the same category in which the firm already has a branded product, it is a:
a) brand extension
b) private brand
c) flanker brand
d) complementary brand
(c; Moderate; p. 45)

160) When a company's marketing team introduces a new brand within a product category where it already has brands in an effort to appeal to target markets the team believes is not being reached by the company's main brand, which is being used?
a) brand extension
b) private brand
c) flanker brand
d) complementary brand
(c; Challenging; p. 45)

161) Which strategy is used to develop a complete product line within a product category in order to create barriers to entry for new and competing firms?
a) brand extension
b) private brand
c) flanker brand
d) complementary brand
(c; Challenging; p. 45)

162) A firm that is expanding to international markets often adds additional brands to current brands in order to strengthen an international presence, reflecting which strategy?
    a) brand extension
    b) private brand
    c) flanker brand
    d) complementary brand
(c; Moderate; p. 45)

163) Co-branding can take the following forms, *except:*
    a) flanker brand
    b) ingredient brand
    c) cooperative brand
    d) complementary brand
(a; Moderate; p. 45)

164) Ingredient branding involves:
    a) placing one brand within another
    b) developing a new brand to be sold in a category where the firm already has a brand
    c) a joint venture of two brands in one product
    d) marketing two brands together to encourage co-consumption
(a; Easy p. 45)

165) Intel Pentium processors placed inside computers is a form of:
    a) ingredient branding
    b) flanker brand
    c) cooperative branding
    d) complementary branding
(a; Moderate; p. 45)

166) Cooperative branding is:
    a) private labeling with a major brand
    b) placing one brand in another as a form of cooperation
    c) the joint venture of two or more brands in one product
    d) the marketing two brands together to encourage co-consumption
(c; Easy; p. 45)

167) Co-branding works the best when:
    a) the two brands are unrelated
    b) a well-known brand is attached to a lesser-known brand
    c) a private label is co-branded with a manufacturer's brand
    d) it builds the brand equity of both brands
(d; Challenging; p. 45)

168) Complementary branding is:
- a) using a private label to complement the main brand
- b) placing one brand within another brand
- c) the joint venture of two or more brands in one product
- d) marketing two brands together to encourage co-consumption

(d; Easy; p. 45)

169) Selling Reese's Peanut Butter Cup milkshakes at the DQ is an example of:
- a) flanker branding
- b) extension branding
- c) cooperative branding
- d) complementary branding

(d; Moderate; p. 45)

170) A Pillsbury cake mix featuring Hershey's Chocolate is a form of:
- a) flanker brand
- b) cooperative brand
- c) ingredient brand
- d) complementary brand

(c; Challenging; p. 45)

171) The placement of one brand within another brand is:
- a) ingredient branding
- b) cooperative branding
- c) complementary branding
- d) flanker branding

(a; Moderate; p. 45)

172) The joint venture of two or more brands into a new good or service is:
- a) ingredient branding
- b) cooperative branding
- c) complementary branding
- d) flanker branding

(b; Moderate; p. 45)

173) The marketing of two or more brands together to encourage co-consumption or co-purchases is:
- a) ingredient branding
- b) cooperative branding
- c) complementary branding
- d) flanker branding

(c; Moderate; p. 45)

174) A proprietary brand marketed by an organization and normally distributed within the organization's outlets is a:
   a) private label
   b) flanker brand within another brand
   c) joint venture of two brands
   d) complementary brand
(a; Easy; p. 47)

175) Private brands are:
   a) new brands sold in the same category
   b) the joint venture of two or more brands in a new good or service
   c) the use of established brand names on goods and services not related to the company's core brand
   d) proprietary brands marketed by an organization and normally distributed exclusively within the organization's outlets.
(d; Easy; p. 47)

176) Over the past few years, each of the following are changes that have occurred in the area of private branding, *except:*
   a) priced equal to national brands
   b) improved quality
   c) increased advertising of private brands
   d) increased quality of in-store displays of private brands
(a; Challenging; p. 47)

177) Private labels are attractive to retail stores because:
   a) they are priced higher than national brands
   b) they do not require any advertising
   c) they tend to have higher margins than national brands
   d) consumers are becoming more loyal to private brand
(c; Challenging, p. 47)

178) Private brands are becoming more successful because of each one of the following trends, *except:*
   a) loyalty toward retail stores has been increasing, while loyalty toward individual brands has been declining
   b) retailers are treating private labels more like national brands and investing marketing dollars into promoting them
   c) retailers are investing more money into in-store displays of private brands to make them as attractive as national brands
   d) retailers are pricing private brands equal to or higher than national brands
(d; Moderate; p. 47)

179) One reason private labels have been successful is:
    a) they are manufactured by generic manufacturing firms
    b) because they do not have to spend any money on advertising
    c) loyalty towards stores is rising while loyalty toward brands is declining
    d) they are sold only in discount stores
(c; Moderate; p. 47)

180) The following statements about private labels are true, *except:*
    a) quality levels of many private label products have improved
    b) prices for private labels are going up in many markets
    c) consumers still perceive private labels as being inferior to manufacturer's brands
    d) some firms have begun advertising private labels
(c; Moderate; p. 47)

181) A package provides each of the following functions, *except:*
    a) creates an new image when the label is modified
    b) contribute to the overall marketing program
    c) protect the contents
    d) help make the product identifiable, even when the label is missing
(a; Easy; p. 49)

182) New trends in packaging include the following, *except:*
    a) disguise the product
    b) meet consumer needs for speed, convenience, and portability
    c) contemporary and striking design
    d) designed for ease of use
(a; Moderate; p. 50)

183) Which is positioning?
    a) a form of logo
    b) a form of extension brand
    c) creating a perception in the consumer's mind regarding the nature of a brand relative to the competition
    d) creating the impression that the company is from a particular industry
(c; Easy; p. 51)

184) Creating a perception in the consumer's mind regarding the nature of a company and its products relative to the competition is called:
    a) product positioning
    b) brand management
    c) stimulus codability
    d) changing a corporate image
(a; Easy; p. 51)

185) Positioning a product using the attribute positioning strategy would involve promoting:
   a) a product trait or characteristic which sets the product apart from its competitors
   b) the product in relation to the competition
   c) an extension of a brand name
   d) the price of the product in relation to its best attribute
(a; Moderate; p. 52)

186) A brand that is compared to competitors is using which type of product positioning strategy?
   a) attribute
   b) competitor
   c) use or application
   d) price-quality relationship
(b; Moderate; p. 52)

187) When Arm & Hammer advertises that baking soda can be used as a deodorizer in refrigerators, which product positioning strategy is being used?
   a) attribute
   b) competitor
   c) use or application
   d) price-quality relationship
(c; Challenging; p. 52)

188) When Hallmark advertises cards that are for those who "want to send the best," which product positioning strategy is being used?
   a) attribute
   b) competitor
   c) use or application
   d) price-quality relationship
(d; Challenging; p. 52)

189) Distinguishing a product from its competitors based on who uses it is a positioning strategy based on:
   a) product user
   b) product class
   c) use or application
   d) competitors
(a; Easy; p. 52)

190) When V8 Vegetable Soup is promoted as having less sodium for individuals on a low-sodium diet, the positioning strategy is based on:
   a) attributes
   b) use or application
   c) product user
   d) product class
   (c; Challenging; p. 51)

191) Which has the smallest effect on a product's positioning strategy?
   a) price/quality relationship
   b) economic conditions
   c) competitive activities
   d) consumer beliefs
   (b; Challenging; p. 51)

Short-Answer Questions

192) What functions are related to corporate image from a consumer's perspective?

   1. Assurance regarding purchase decisions of familiar products in unfamiliar settings
   2. Assurance concerning purchases where there is little previous experience
   3. Reduction of search time in purchase decisions
   4. Psychological reinforcement and social acceptance of purchase decisions
   (Moderate, p. 32)

193) What are the benefits of a strong corporate image in the eyes of the company?

   1. Extension of positive consumer feelings to new products
   2. The ability to charge a higher price or fee
   3. Consumer loyalty leading to more frequent purchases
   4. Positive word-of-mouth endorsements
   5. The ability to attract quality employees
   6. More favorable ratings by financial observers and analysts
   (Challenging, p. 33)

194) When should a company consider rejuvenating its image and how should it be done?

A company should consider rejuvenating its image when sales have declined or a competitor has taken a strong market position in the industry. Any time the brand has suffered a decline in brand equity is a good time to consider rejuvenating an image. Rejuvenating an image requires developing a campaign that is consistent with the current image while at the same time incorporating new elements into the image to expand the firm's target market and to reconnect with previous customers.
(Challenging, pp. 36)

195) When are the four types of corporate names?

Overt names, implied names, conceptual names, iconoclastic names.
(Moderate, p. 37)

196) What four tests should quality logos and corporate names pass?

1. They should be easily recognizable.
2. They should be familiar.
3. They should elicit a consensual meaning among those in the firm's target market.
4. They should evoke positive feelings.
(Moderate, p. 38)

197) When developing a strong brand name, what are some typical questions that should be asked?

1. What are the most compelling benefits?
2. What emotions are elicited by the brand either during or after the purchase?
3. What one word best describes the brand?
4. What is important to consumers in the purchase of the product?
(Challenging, p. 40)

198) Identify the steps in building a high level of brand equity.

1. Research and analyze what it would take to make the brand distinctive.
2. Engage in continuous innovation.
3. Move fast.
4. Minimize reliance on any one customer.
5. Integrate new and old media.
6. Focus on domination.
(Challenging, p. 42)

199)   What are brand metrics?

They are used to measure returns on branding investments.
(Easy, p. 43)

200)   Describe brand extensions and flanker brands.

Brand extensions use an established brand name on goods or services not related to a core brand. Flanker brands are brands used by a company in a category in which the company currently has an offering.
(Easy, p. 44)

201)   What three forms of co-branding are there? Define each one.

1. Ingredient branding is placement of one brand within another brand.
2. Cooperative branding is the joint venture of two brands or more into a new product or service.
3. Complementary branding is marketing of two brands together to encourage co-consumptions or co-purchases.

(Moderate, p. 45)

202)   Why have private brands or private labels been more successful in recent years?

1. Quality levels have improved.
2. Higher prices can be charged.
3. Loyalty toward stores is higher than loyalty to brands.
4. Increased advertising of private labels.

(Challenging, p. 47)

203)   What traditional elements should be incorporated into packaging design and what are the new trends that impact packaging?

Traditional elements of packaging include:
1. Protect the product inside
2. Provide for ease in shipping, moving, and handling
3. Provide for easy placement on store shelves
4. Prevent or reduce the possibility of theft
5. Prevent tampering
New trends in packaging include:
1. Meet consumer needs for speed, convenience, and portability
2. Must be contemporary and striking
3. Must be designed for ease of use

(Challenging, pp. 49)

204) What are the types of product positioning?

1. Attributes
2. Competitors
3. Use or application
4. Price/quality relationship
5. Product user
6. Product class
7. Cultural symbol positioning

(Moderate, p. 51)

CHAPTER 3
BUYER BEHAVIORS

True-False Questions

1) Starbucks was able to build market share due to low prices and quality service.
   (False; Easy; p. 60)

2) A major reason for the success of Starbucks was the nonchalance of major competitors.
   (True; Moderate; p. 60)

3) The first step of the consumer buying decision-making process is identification of alternatives.
   (False; Easy; p. 63)

4) Upon recognizing a need, if a particular brand that was chosen in the past met that need and result in a positive experience, the consumer is likely to purchase the same brand again and will not engage in further search for information.
   (True; Moderate; p. 63)

5) An internal search for purchasing alternatives takes place when a consumer thinks about the brands he or she is willing to consider.
   (True; Easy; p. 63)

6) During the initial internal search, a consumer considers all of the brands that he or she has used in the past.
   (False; Challenging; p. 63)

7) If a consumer has sufficient information from an internal search, he or she moves on to the next step of the decision-making process, evaluating alternatives, without engaging in an external search for additional information.
   (True; Moderate; p. 64)

8) An external search for purchasing alternatives and information may begin with dissatisfaction with the last purchase.
   (True; Easy; p. 64)

9) The amount of time a consumer spends on an external search depends on the four factors of 1) ability, 2) motivation, 3) costs, and 4) brand name.
   (False; Challenging; p. 64)

10) An individual who has an extensive knowledge of a product category will likely spend more time in the external search process than someone with just a moderate level of product category knowledge.
   (False; Challenging; p. 65)

11) The motivation to search for purchase alternatives is largely determined by the individual's age and social status.
   (False; Moderate; p. 65)

12) The greater the motivation, the greater the extent of external search for information in a buying decision making process.
   (True; Easy; p. 65)

13) A person's ability to search and level of motivation partly determine how much time will be spent on an external search of purchasing alternatives.
   (True; Moderate; p. 65)

14) The level of involvement a consumer displays during the external information search process is determined by such factors as cost and the product's importance.
   (True; Moderate; p. 65)

15) Involvement is the degree of ability a person holds in an external search of purchasing alternatives.
   (False; Moderate; p. 65)

16) The need for cognition is a personality characteristic that links the drive to consider alternatives with the drive to take action quickly.
   (False; Challenging; p. 65)

17) People with a high need for cognition will gather more information and spend more time searching for information prior to a purchase than individuals with a low need for cognition.
   (True; Moderate; p. 65)

18) The higher the perceived benefit a consumer perceives from an external search for information, the more likely he or she will be to spend time searching for information.
   (True; Easy; p. 65)

19) The cost of conducting an external search for information consists of the actual cost of the product, subjective costs associated with the search, and the opportunity cost of foregoing other activities.
   (True; Moderate; p. 65)

20) The cognitive component of an attitude is a person's mental image, understanding, and interpretation of the product.
(True; Easy; p. 66)

21) The affective part of an attitude is the part most directly related to making the actual purchase.
(False; Moderate; p. 66)

22) The cognitive component of an attitude is the part most directly connected to taking action.
(True; Moderate; p. 66)

23) Most of the time, the consumer first develops an understanding or cognitive belief about an idea or object, followed by affective feelings.
(True; Challenging; p. 66)

24) Consumer values are loosely held attitudes about various topics or concepts.
(False; Easy; p. 67)

25) Values tend to be enduring and normally form during adulthood and can change as person ages and experiences life.
(False; Moderate; p. 67)

26) Factors that affect a person's values include the individual's personality, temperament, environment, and culture.
(True; Challenging; p. 68)

27) Marketing communications are considerably more effective in changing a person's attitude about a product than they are in changing a consumer's value structure.
(True; Moderate; p. 68)

28) Cognitive maps are simulations of the knowledge structures and memories embedded in an individual's brain.
(True; Easy; p. 68)

29) A cognitive map explains search motives using ability, time, and how much the individual likes shopping.
(False; Moderate; p. 69)

30) Cognitive maps explain the importance of repetition, because most marketing messages are quickly lost in short term memory.
(True; Challenging; p. 69)

31) Cognitive maps can be altered to incorporate situations in which a message or idea currently has no current linkages within a person's current knowledge structure.
(True; Challenging; p. 69)

32) From a marketing perspective it is easier to strengthen a linkage that already exists than to create a new linkage or modify a current linkage.
(True; Challenging; p. 70)

33) The evoked set in a purchase decision consists of brands that have been purchased previously.
(False; Moderate; p. 70)

34) An evoked set consists of the inept set and the inert set.
(False; Moderate; p. 70)

35) An inept set consists of brands that are not considered because they elicit negative feelings.
(True; Easy; p. 70)

36) An inert set is a series of brands that are viewed as being negative because of past buying experiences.
(False; Easy; p. 70)

37) A person considering only Coke, Pepsi, and Royal Crown Cola at a vending machine is employing his or her evoked set.
(True; Challenging; p. 70)

38) The multiattribute model of purchase evaluation is best suited for low involvement purchase decisions.
(False; Moderate; p. 71)

39) The multiattribute model of purchase evaluation suggests the consumers consider both product characteristics and the importance of those characteristics as they make purchases.
(True; Moderate; p. 71)

40) The key to understanding the multiattribute model to evaluate alternatives is being aware that consumers examine sets of product attributes across an array of brands.
(True; Moderate, p. 71)

41) The affect referral model of evaluating alternatives suggests that consumers will buy products they used and liked in the past.
(True; Easy; p. 71)

42) The affect referral model of evaluating alternatives is not used for high involvement purchase situations.
(False; Moderate; p. 71)

43) The affect referral model of evaluating alternatives suggests that consumers tend to buy products when they are emotionally detached.
(False; Moderate; p. 71)

44) One reason consumers use the affect referral model of evaluating alternatives is that it saves mental energy.
(True; Moderate, p. 72)

45) One reason consumers may use the affect referral model of evaluating alternatives is that they may have already used the multiattribute approach to evaluate the alternatives for a previous purchase situation.
(True; Challenging, p. 72)

46) Age complexity involves children growing up at a younger age as well as older Americans wanting to act and feel younger than they are.
(True; Moderate; p. 72)

47) Women attending college, delaying marriage, and waiting to start families are characteristics of the consumer buyer behavior trend of age complexity.
(False; Moderate; p. 73)

48) Gender complexity and increased individualism in purchasing preferences are two new trends in the consumer buying environment.
(True; Easy; p. 73)

49) Because of the consumer buyer behavior trend of active, busy lifestyles, Levi Strauss has developed personalized jeans where consumers can provide Levi with their exact measurements over the Internet.
(False; Challenging, p. 74)

50) As a result of active, buys lifestyles, many consumers now spend less on material possessions and more on experiences such as vacations, entertainment, and dining out.
(True; Moderate; p. 74)

51) Spending on home purchases such as expensive sound systems, satellite television systems, swimming pools, and saunas is the result of the consumer buyer behavior trend of cocooning.
(True; Moderate; p. 75)

52) Divorcees or second-chancers usually have lower household incomes and are between the ages of 40 and 59.
(False; Challenging; p. 75)

53) Second-chancers or divorcees exhibit higher levels of cocooning and place greater emphasis on the family and the home.
(True; Challenging, p. 75)

54) One recent trend in purchasing decisions is a greater emphasis on indulgences and pleasure binges, even after the events of September 11, 2001.
(True; Challenging; p. 75)

55) Some people handle stress caused by a hectic, busy lifestyle through occasional indulgences or pleasure binges such as an expensive dinner out or a cruise.
(True; Easy; p. 75)

56) A greater emphasis on health is part of the new consumer buying environment.
(True; Easy; p. 75)

57) The business buying center is the group of people who make purchasing decisions on behalf of a company.
(True; Easy; p. 76)

58) An influencer always serves as the gatekeeper in the business buying center.
(False; Moderate; p. 76)

59) The gatekeeper is the individual in the business buying center who makes the eventual purchasing decision.
(False; Easy; p. 76)

60) In the business buying center, buyers are given formal responsibility for making the purchase while deciders are the individuals who authorize those decisions.
(True; Moderate; p. 76)

61) Individuals within the buying center who shape the purchasing decision by providing information or criteria that should be used in evaluating alternatives are called influencers.
(True; Moderate; p. 76)

62) Individuals can perform more than one role in the buying center and more than one individual can be involved in any particular role.
(True; Moderate; p. 76)

63) The behaviors of each member of the buying center are influenced by both organizational and individual factors.
(True; Easy; p. 77)

64) Organizational factors that impact individuals in the buying center include the company's goals, its operating environment, and personalities of the buying center members.
(False; Moderate; p. 77)

65) Heuristics that are used in purchase decision-making are created by company goals, budgets, and other organizational factors.
(True; Moderate; p. 77)

66) A decision rule often employed by organizations is satisficing, which means that when the buying center has identified the best possible solution, it is chosen and the search is complete.
(False; Moderate; p. 77)

67) Most buying center members are able to avoid personalities from affecting decisions by using decision rules called heuristics.
(False; Challenging; p. 77)

68) Individuals that have extroverted personalities tend to become more involved in the b-to-b buying process than someone who is an introvert.
(True; Moderate, p. 78)

69) Roles within the buying center are socially constructed, which means people define how they intend to play roles as part of the negotiation process with others nearby.
(True; Challenging, p. 78)

70) Power relationships and personal objectives can affect business buying decisions.
(True; Moderate; p. 78)

71) When a particular purchase decision directly affects an employee, that person may try to gain more power in the buying process.
(True; Moderate; p. 78)

72) Various members of a buying center will have different degrees of cognitive involvement, depending on which role is being played.
(True; Moderate; p. 78)

73) A straight rebuy is a reorder from the same vendor.
(True; Easy; p. 79)

74) The straight rebuy is normally a routine process involving only a few members of the buying center and may even be done electronically with little human involvement.
(True; Moderate; p. 79)

75) A modified rebuy may occur when someone in the buying center believes the current vendor should be reevaluated.
(True; Moderate; p. 79)

76) A new task purchase situation exists when a new, potential vendor offers a company what is perceived to be a better buy than the company is getting now from the current vendor, and members of the buying center want to reconsider the purchase decision.
(False; Challenging; p. 79)

77) If bids are taken at the end of each year's contractual agreement with a company's vendors, then each time the company engages in this activity, it is in a straight rebuy purchase.
(False; Challenging; p. 79)

78) A new task purchase is the easiest, since new specifications will be developed.
(False; Moderate; p. 79)

79) Typically, the new task purchase would involve the most members of the buying center and take the longest amount of time to complete.
(True; Moderate; p. 79)

80) In new task purchasing situations, members of the buying center tend to go through all of the steps of the b-to-b buying process.
(True; Moderate; p. 79)

81) In modified rebuy and in straight rebuy situations; one or more steps of the b-to-b buying process may be eliminated.
(True; Moderate; p. 79)

82) The first step in the business-to-business buying process is the identification of needs.
(True; Easy; p. 80)

83) Derived demand is based on, linked to, or generated by the production of raw materials within a country.
(False; Moderate; p. 80)

84) In the modified rebuy situation, once a need has been recognized buyers will skip intervening steps in the b-to-b buying process and go directly to making a purchase.
(False; Challenging; p. 80)

85) In the new task purchase situation, potential vendors are often involved in helping the buyer develop clear specifications of what is needed.
(True; Moderate, p. 80)

86) In the b-to-b buying process, once specifications have been identified, potential vendors are identified and notified to find out if they are interested in submitting bids.
(True; Moderate, p. 81)

87) Bribes are unethical in every culture.
(False; Easy; p. 81)

88) Vendor evaluation consists of an initial screening of proposals, a vendor audit, and sharing audit information internally.
(True; Moderate; p. 81)

89) As the dollar value of a purchase increases, the number of individuals in the buying center that will be involved in the vendor evaluation stage also increases.
(True; Easy; p. 81)

90) The goal of the vendor audit is to evaluate potential suppliers in terms of cost and quality of merchandise.
(False; Challenging; p. 81)

91) When selection criteria are used in the vendor selection decision, the most common criteria includes quality delivery, performance history, warranties, facilities and capacity, geographic location, and technical capability.
(True; Moderate; p. 82)

92) Purchase terms following the selection of a vendor are often only a formality because in most cases the agreement has been worked out during the selection process.
(True; Challenging; p. 82)

93) An emphasis on accountability has affected business-to-business marketing programs.
(True; Easy; p. 82)

94)	Brand equity is a major concern for many business-to-business vendors, especially since global competition has increased dramatically.
	(True; Challenging; p. 83)

95)	Database mining is one of the future trends in the business-to-business buying environment.
	(True; Easy; p. 83)

96)	Internet firms, such as Google, have changed the landscape of business-to-business vending since these companies allow for totally new purchasing approaches.
	(True; Challenging; p. 83)

97)	Focusing on internal communications is important for long-term success.
	(True; Easy; p. 84)

98)	Selling to both consumers and businesses is known as dual-channel marketing.
	(True; Moderate; p. 84)

99)	Dual-channel marketing can create image problems for some organizations due to the transfer of image between markets.
	(True; Challenging; p. 84)

Multiple-Choice Questions

100)	Starbucks created an advantage in the gourmet coffee market based on:
	a)	low demand
	b)	offering a pleasant coffee-drinking experience
	c)	lower prices
	d)	extensive advertising
	(b; Moderate; p. 60)

101)	Each of the following factors was instrumental in Starbuck's success, *except:*
	a)	unique coffee blends and products
	b)	locations that are easily accessible and on commuter routes
	c)	pricing
	d)	an effective marketing communications program
	(c; Moderate; p. 61)

102) The two components of the consumer decision-making process that are most critical to developing an integrated marketing communications program are:
   a) problem recognition and information search
   b) information search and evaluation of alternatives
   c) evaluation of alternatives and purchase decision
   d) problem recognition and evaluation of alternatives
   (b; Challenging; p. 63)

103) An information search typically begins with:
   a) an internal search
   b) an external search
   c) a combination of internal and external searching
   d) a review of the brands available
   (a; Easy; p. 63)

104) An internal information search is when:
   a) a consumer experiences uneasiness
   b) a consumer thinks about brands he/she is willing to consider
   c) the consumer buying process is nearly complete
   d) advertisements are being ignored
   (b; easy; p. 63)

105) During a search for purchase information, what factor will increase the probability that a brand will be considered?
   a) brand parity
   b) brand equity
   c) product viability
   d) brand ambiguity
   (b; Moderate; p. 64)

106) During the consumer internal search process, a key objective for creatives and brand managers is to:
   a) have information readily available to consumers
   b) make sure the company's brand is part of the consumer's inert set
   c) have the brand in the person's cognitive map
   d) make sure the company's brand is part of the consumer's set of potential alternatives
   (d; Moderate; p. 64)

107) When a person conducts an internal search and has sufficient information, the next step will be to:
   a) search for additional information
   b) make the purchase decision
   c) evaluate the alternatives
   d) identify the need or problem the choice will meet
   (c; Moderate; p. 64)

108) An external search of purchasing information occurs when:
   a) the consumer is uncertain about which brand to purchase
   b) the internal search has been successful
   c) the evaluation of alternatives has been completed
   d) a purchase has been finalized and the buyer is looking for reassurance
   (a; Moderate; p. 64)

109) The amount of time a consumer spends on an external search depends on each of the following factors below, *except:*
   a) ability
   b) motivation
   c) benefit
   d) brand name
   (d; Challenging; p. 64)

110) A person's educational level combined with specific knowledge about a product category determines the:
   a) ability to search
   b) desire to search
   c) need for cognition
   d) involvement level
   (a; Moderate; p. 64)

111) The individual that has the greatest ability to conduct an external search for information is the consumer that has:
   a) a low level of knowledge about the product category
   b) an extensive knowledge of the product category
   c) some knowledge of the product category, but not enough to make an intelligent decision
   d) a low educational level
   (b; Challenging; p. 64)

112) The individual that is most likely to spend the greatest amount of time in an external search for information is the consumer that has:
   a) a low level of knowledge about the product category
   b) an extensive knowledge of the product category
   c) some knowledge of the product category, but not enough to make an intelligent decision
   d) a low educational level
   (c; Challenging; p. 65)

113) Motivation to conduct an external search for information depends on all of the following *except:*
   a) level of brand parity within a product category
   b) level of involvement
   c) need for cognition
   d) level of shopping enthusiasm
   (a; Moderate; p. 65)

114) In terms of the external information search process, the extent to which a stimulus or task is relevant to a consumer's existing needs determines the:
   a) ability to search
   b) need for cognition
   c) search methods
   d) level of involvement
   (d; Moderate; p. 65)

115) In terms of an external search for information in a purchasing decision, involvement is:
   a) the extent to which a stimulus or task is relevant to a consumer's existing needs, wants, or values
   b) a personality characteristic an individual displays when he or she engages in and enjoys mental activities
   c) the mental position a person takes on a topic, person, or event that influences the holder's feelings, perceptions, learning processes, and subsequent behaviors
   d) simulations of the knowledge structure embedded in an individual's brain
   (a; Moderate; p. 65)

116) During the external information search process, consumers with high levels of involvement tend to spend:
   a) more time searching for external information
   b) less time searching for external information
   c) rely on external information more than internal information
   d) more time shopping in retail stores
   (a; Moderate; p. 65)

117) Individuals who engage in and enjoy mental activities have a:
   a) low need for cognition
   b) high need for cognition
   c) low level of shopping enthusiasm
   d) high level of shopping enthusiasm
   (b; Moderate; p. 65)

118) In terms of external search for information in a purchase decision, need for cognition is:
   a) the extent to which a stimulus or task is relevant to a consumer's existing needs, wants, or values
   b) a personality characteristic an individual displays when he or she engages in and enjoys mental activities
   c) the mental position a person takes on a topic, person, or event that influences the holder's feelings, perceptions, learning processes, and subsequent behaviors
   d) simulations of the knowledge structure embedded in an individual's brain
   (b; Moderate; p. 65)

119) People who like to be involved in extensive searches for goods and services have a:
   a) low need for cognition
   b) high need for cognition
   c) low level of shopping enthusiasm
   d) high level of shopping enthusiasm
   (d; Challenging; p. 65)

120) The perceived cost of a purchase decision includes each of the following, *except:*
   a) the actual price or cost of the product
   b) the subjective costs associated with the search
   c) the economic conditions of the area
   d) the opportunity costs of foregoing other activities to make the search
   (c; Moderate; p. 65)

121) The motivation to search externally for a purchase option includes each of the following, *except:*
   a) specific product knowledge
   b) enduring involvement
   c) cognitive consistency
   d) costs and benefits
   (c; Challenging; p. 65)

122) The mental position a person takes about a topic, person, or event is called a(n):
   a) value
   b) attitude
   c) level of involvement
   d) cognition
   (b; Easy; p. 66)

123) Which component of an attitude contains the feelings or emotions a person has about a product?
   a) affective
   b) cognitive
   c) conative
   d) rational
   (a; Easy; p. 66)

124) Which component of an attitude refers to a person's mental images, understanding, and interpretation of a product?
   a) affective
   b) cognitive
   c) conative
   d) rational
   (b; Easy; p. 66)

125) Which component of an attitude displays the individual's intentions, actions, or behavior?
   a) affective
   b) cognitive
   c) conative
   d) rational
   (c; Easy; p. 66)

126) The affective component of attitude:
   a) contains the feelings or emotions a person has about an object, person, or idea
   b) refers to a person's mental images, understanding, and interpretations of an object, person, or idea
   c) is an individual's intentions, actions, or behavior
   d) is the mental picture a person has of an object, person, or idea
   (a; Easy; p. 66)

127) The cognitive component of attitude:
   a) contains the feelings or emotions a person has about an object, person, or idea
   b) refers to a person's mental images, understanding, and interpretations of an object, person, or idea
   c) is an individual's intentions, actions, or behavior
   d) is the mental picture a person has of an object, person, or idea
   (b; Easy; p.66)

128) The conative component of attitude:
   a) contains the feelings or emotions a person has about an object, person, or idea
   b) refers to a person's mental images, understanding, and interpretations of an object, person, or idea
   c) is an individual's intentions, actions, or behavior
   d) is the mental picture a person has of an object, person, or idea

(c; Easy; p. 66)

129) In terms of attitude formation, the most common sequence is:
   a) affective → conative → cognitive
   b) conative → cognitive → affective
   c) conative → affective → cognitive
   d) cognitive → affective → conative

(d; Challenging; p. 66)

130) A person who reasons that a Kenmore refrigerator has the best price/quality relationship is using which component of an attitude?
   a) affective
   b) cognitive
   c) conative
   d) value

(b; Challenging; p. 66)

131) If an ad appeals to a person's emotions first, the ad is addressing which component of an attitude?
   a) affective
   b) cognitive
   c) conative
   d) value

(a; Moderate; p. 67)

132) A person who is swayed by an ad that incites fear is being influenced by which component of an attitude?
   a) affective
   b) cognitive
   c) conative
   d) value

(a; Challenging; p. 67)

133) A low price, low involvement purchase is likely to begin with which component of an attitude?
   a) affective
   b) cognitive
   c) conative
   d) value
   (c; Moderate; p. 67)

134) An impulse buy probably means that the consumer acted on which component of an attitude?
   a) affective
   b) cognitive
   c) conative
   d) value
   (c; Moderate; p. 67)

135) An advertisement that encourages consumers to call a toll free number or access a Web site to purchase a product at a discount price focuses on which part of an attitude?
   a) affective
   b) conative
   c) cognitive
   d) the inert set
   (b; Challenging; p. 67)

136) Strongly held beliefs about various topics or concepts are:
   a) attitudes
   b) cognitive maps
   c) values
   d) mental images
   (c; Easy; p. 67)

137) A simulation of the knowledge structures embedded in an individual's brain is called a:
   a) value
   b) affect referral
   c) cognitive map
   d) component of an attitude
   (c; Easy; p. 68)

138) A cognitive map consists of the following components, *except:*
   a) levels
   b) layers
   c) linkages
   d) behaviors
   (d; Moderate; p. 69)

139) When an individual considers all the ideas that come to mind when the name of a product is mentioned, which best explains the thinking?
   a) maps of attitudes
   b) value models
   c) a cognitive map
   d) affect referral
   (c; Challenging; p. 69)

140) In terms of cognitive mapping, if most consumers have not considered Sunkist oranges as a substitute for salt, then an advertisement that conveys such a message to consumers is attempting to:
   a) strengthen a linkage that already exists
   b) modifying a current linkage
   c) create a new linkage
   d) create a new layer
   (c; Challenging; p. 69)

141) The brands a person considers in a purchasing situation is called the buyer's:
   a) evoked set
   b) inept set
   c) inert set
   d) feasible set
   (a; Easy; p. 70)

142) An evoked set does *not* contain:
   a) brands a person considers
   b) brands linked to a positive experience
   c) brands which have been previously purchased
   d) brands the consumer knows little about
   (d; Moderate; p. 70)

143) The set of brands a person will not consider due to negative feelings is the:
   a) inept set
   b) inert set
   c) negative set
   d) evoked set
   (a; Moderate; p. 70)

144) The set of brands a consumer knows about but has neither positive nor negative feelings is the:
   a) inept set
   b) inert set
   c) cognitive set
   d) evoked set
   (b; Moderate; p. 70)

71

145) An evoked set is the set of brands:
   a) that are part of a person's memory, but not considered because they elicit negative feelings
   b) the consumer has awareness of, but has neither negative or positive feelings toward
   c) that a person would consider as potential solutions to meet a need
   d) that viewed by a consumer as being approximately equal in terms of quality

   (c; Easy; p. 70)

146) The inept set is the set of brands:
   a) that are part of a person's memory, but not considered because they elicit negative feelings
   b) the consumer has awareness of, but has neither negative or positive feelings toward
   c) that a person would consider as feasible solutions to meet a need
   d) that viewed by a consumer as being approximately equal in terms of quality

   (a; Moderate; p. 70)

147) The inert set is the set of brands:
   a) that are part of a person's memory, but not considered because they elicit negative feelings
   b) the consumer has awareness of, but has neither negative or positive feelings toward
   c) that a person would consider as feasible solutions to meet a need
   d) that viewed by a consumer as being approximately equal in terms of quality

   (b; Moderate; p. 70)

148) Derek eliminated New Balance shoes because he doesn't know anything about them. Derek used which type of evaluation process to make this decision?
   a) evoked method
   b) multiattribute
   c) affect referral
   d) attitude formation

   (a; Challenging; p. 70)

149) In deciding on a place to eat dinner tonight, Donna thought about all of her favorite places and finally chose Red Lobster because she loves the food and it has been a while since she ate there. In making this decision, Donna used which method to evaluate the possible choices?
   a) evoked method
   b) multiattribute
   c) affect referral
   d) attitude formation
   (a; Challenging; p. 70)

150) Using the multi-attribute approach, an individual considers:
   a) beliefs about product attributes and the importance of those attributes
   b) layers, levels, and linkages of the cognitive map
   c) cognitive, conative, and affective reactions to the product
   d) the evokes, inert, and inept sets
   (a; Moderate; p. 71)

151) Didi carefully considers price, sound quality, and space taken by a new stereo system. The sound quality is the most important factor, followed by the price. The evaluation model being used by Didi is:
   a) cognitive mapping
   b) evoked set
   c) multi-attribute
   d) affect referral
   (c; Moderate; p. 71)

152) Which model of evaluation of alternatives suggests consumers buy brands they like best or connect with emotionally?
   a) cognitive mapping
   b) multiattribute
   c) affect referral
   d) evoked-set
   (c; Moderate; p. 71)

153) In using the affect referral approach to decision-making, the person considers:
   a) product attributes and the importance of attributes
   b) the brand he or she likes the best
   c) cognitive and conative cues
   d) all of the above
   (b; Easy; p. 71)

154) Carrie buys a Honda Accord without considering other brands because she really likes the Accord and feels it is the best automobile on the market. Carrie's evaluation of alternatives is best explained by which model?
a) cognitive mapping
b) evoked set
c) multi-attribute approach
d) affect referral
(d; Challenging; p. 71)

155) Fred thinks about buying lunch and quickly decides to go to Long John Silver's because they have his favorite shrimp. Fred's evaluation of alternatives is best explained by which model?
a) cognitive mapping
b) evoked set
c) multi-attribute approach
d) affect referral
(d; Challenging; p. 71)

156) A teenager is taking forever to buy a pair of jeans because he or she is considering all the factors involved, such as price, color, and style. Which method is being used to evaluate the various brands?
a) cognitive mapping approach
b) evoked set
c) multi-attribute approach
d) affect referral
(c; Challenging; p. 71)

157) The following are reasons consumers use the affect referral method to evaluate alternatives, *except:*
a) consumers have already eliminated the inert and inept sets from consideration
b) the affect referral method saves time and mental energy
c) the consumer may have already used the multiattribute approach in a previous purchase situations
d) the consumer has developed an emotional bond with the particular brand
(a; Challenging; p. 72)

158) The following are trends in consumer buyer behavior discussed in the textbook, *except:*
a) age complexity
b) gender complexity
c) information overload
d) individualism
(c; Moderate; p. 72)

159) Many older adults are refusing to grow old, wearing fashions of college students and driving sports cars. This is an example of the consumer buyer behavior trend of:
   a) age complexity
   b) gender complexity
   c) active, busy lifestyles
   d) individualism
   (a; Moderate; p. 72)

160) Which consumer buyer behavior trend suggests that the traditional roles, lifestyles, and interests of both men and women are becoming blurred?
   a) age complexity
   b) gender complexity
   c) active, busy lifestyles
   d) individualism
   (b; Easy; p. 73)

161) Advertisements for food products and cleaning supplies once directed exclusively to women now must also be geared towards men. This is an example of the consumer behavior trend of:
   a) age complexity
   b) gender complexity
   c) active, busy lifestyles
   d) individualism
   (b; Moderate; p. 73)

162) Through the Internet, Nike now offers consumers the opportunity to custom design own shoes. This approach reflects the consumer buyer behavior trend of:
   a) age complexity
   b) gender complexity
   c) active, busy lifestyles
   d) individualism
   (d; Challenging; p. 74)

163) The consumer buyer behavior trend of individualism has resulted in consumers wanting:
   a) new products developed at a faster pace then ever before
   b) companies to design products just for them, that meet their individual needs
   c) companies to develop time-saving products
   d) gender neutral products
   (b; Moderate; p. 74)

164) The consumer demand for convenience and time-saving devices is the result of which consumer buyer behavior trend?
   a) age complexity
   b) cocooning
   c) active, busy lifestyles
   d) pleasure pursuits
   (c; Easy; p. 74)

165) Each of the following would be examples of the consumer buyer behavior trend of cocooning, *except:*
   a) buying an elaborate home
   b) building a gourmet kitchen
   c) taking a pleasure cruise
   d) purchasing expensive television and stereo sound systems
   (c; Moderate; p. 75)

166) Spending more money on homes and making the home environment pleasurable is a result of which consume buyer behavior trend?
   a) health emphasis
   b) cocooning
   c) active, busy lifestyles
   d) pleasure pursuits
   (b; Moderate; p. 75)

167) Pleasure cruises and exotic vacations take advantage of which consumer behavior trend?
   a) health emphasis
   b) cocooning
   c) active, busy lifestyles
   d) pleasure pursuits
   (d; Moderate; p. 75)

168) Spending money you don't have on a designer outfit to reward yourself for hard work would be an example of the consumer buyer behavior trend of:
   a) health emphasis
   b) cocooning
   c) active, busy lifestyles
   d) pleasure pursuits
   (d; Challenging; p. 75)

169) Two outcomes of the aging U.S. population are
   a) increased interest in health and maintaining one's youthful appearance
   b) cocooning and occasional pleasure pursuits
   c) active, busy lifestyles and pleasure pursuits
   d) cocooning and age complexity
   (a; Moderate; p. 75)

170) The group of people who make a purchasing decision on behalf of a company is called the:
a) decision-makers
b) marketing team
c) institutional buyers
d) buying center
(d; Easy; p. 76)

171) The member of the buyer center who actually utilizes items after they are purchased is the:
a) user
b) influencer
c) decider
d) gatekeeper
(a; Easy; p. 76)

172) In a buying center, who would say, "Since I'm the one who actually has to use this product, you should listen to me."
a) a user
b) a buyer
c) a decider
d) a gatekeeper
(a; Moderate; p. 76)

173) In a buying center at a large company, the purchasing agent is often the:
a) user
b) buyer
c) decider
d) gatekeeper
(b; Challenging; p. 76)

174) The member of the buying center who is most likely to negotiate the price is the:
a) user
b) influencer
c) buyer
d) gatekeeper
(c; Challenging; p. 76)

175) The members of the buying center who shape purchasing decisions by providing information and criteria are called:
   a) users
   b) influencers
   c) deciders
   d) buyers
   (b; Easy; p. 76)

176) In a buying center, who would most likely say, "We need to limit our choices to local vendors."
   a) a user
   b) a buyer
   c) an influencer
   d) the gatekeeper
   (c; Moderate; p. 76)

177) The members of the buying center who authorize purchasing decisions are called:
   a) users
   b) influencers
   c) deciders
   d) buyers
   (c; Easy; p. 76)

178) The members of the buying center who control the flow of information and keep vendors in or out of the process are called:
   a) users
   b) influencers
   c) deciders
   d) gatekeepers
   (d; Easy; p. 76)

179) The member of the buying center who is most likely to let the group know that some alternative companies have already been rejected is the:
   a) user
   b) influencer
   c) decider
   d) gatekeeper
   (d; Challenging, p. 76)

180) The owner of a small company asks his secretary to call some of the local office supply stores and locate two that would offer a good deal on a new copy machine. In performing this task, the secretary is assuming which roles within the buying center?
a) user and gatekeeper
b) user and buyer
c) user, decider, and influencer
d) buyer and gatekeeper
(a; Challenging; p. 76)

181) Two of the factors that affect members of the buying center are individual factors and:
a) perceptual factors
b) ideological factors
c) recreational factors
d) organizational factors
(d; Easy; p. 77)

182) Decision rules that help employees make quick decisions regarding purchases are called:
a) heuristics
b) satisficing
c) methodologies
d) role playing
(a; Easy; p. 77)

183) When an acceptable purchasing alternative has been identified and it is taken, the process is called:
a) decision maximization
b) satisficing
c) utilization
d) standardization
(b; Easy; p. 77)

184) An organizational factor that impacts the manner in which a purchase decision is made includes the:
a) norms members of the buying center are expected to follow
b) risk involved in switching vendors
c) personalities of the sales staff and members of the buying center
d) capital assets a firm has available
(d; Challenging; p. 77)

185) The following are individual factors that might influence a member of the buying center, *except:*
    a) personality features
    b) roles and perceived roles
    c) levels of cognitive involvement
    d) capital assets a firm has available
(d; Moderate; p. 77)

186) In terms of personality, an extrovert is likely to display each of the following characteristics within the buying center, *except:*
    a) spends more time talking within the buying center
    b) becomes more involved in the buying process
    c) will not ask important questions
    d) will not listen to others in the group
(c; Challenging, p. 78)

187) In terms of personality, an introvert is likely to display each of the following characteristics within the buying center, *except:*
    a) spends less time talking within the buying center
    b) becomes more involved in the buying process
    c) will not ask important questions because of timidity
    d) will listen carefully to others in the group
(b; Challenging, p. 78)

188) Roles and perceived roles, motivational levels, and attitudes toward risk are examples of which factor that affects members of business buying centers?
    a) organizational
    b) individual
    c) cultural
    d) economic
(b; Easy; p. 78)

189) The level of motivation displayed by a member of a buying center depends on:
    a) how well the individual's goals match the organization's goals
    b) how well the individual's goals match his or her career goals
    c) the tendency to overanalyze things
    d) the level of power the individual has in the buying center as well as in the company itself
(a; Challenging; p. 78)

190) A person's level of power in the buying process depends on each of the following, *except:*
   a) his or her role in the buying center
   b) his or her official position in the company
   c) the impact of the purchase decision on a his or her job
   d) the level of cognitive involvement
   (d; Challenging; p. 78)

191) Buying center members with higher levels of cognitive involvement will:
   a) use the purchasing process to further personal power goals
   b) ask more questions during the purchasing process
   c) have no opinion about purchasing risk
   d) be most inclined to base a purchase decision on nepotism
   (b; Challenging; p. 78)

192) Individuals with a high level of cognitive involvement will display the following characteristics, *except:*
   a) want more information prior to making a decision
   b) ask more questions during the purchase process
   c) spend less time deliberating prior to making a decision
   d) want clear message arguments
   (c; Challenging; p. 78)

193) A straight rebuy involves:
   a) re-ordering raw materials from the same vendor
   b) buying materials from a new vendor
   c) seeking bids from a new vendor because of dissatisfaction with the current supplier
   d) purchasing a new building for an expansion project
   (a; Moderate; p. 79)

194) The purchase decision that requires the least effort and is often made quickly is a(n):
   a) straight rebuy
   b) modified rebuy
   c) new task
   d) accelerated buy
   (a; Moderate; p. 79)

195) A straight rebuy purchase decision occurs:
   a) when the firm has previously chosen a vendor and intends to place a reorder
   b) when a company is dissatisfied with their current vendor and want to consider new options
   c) when a new company makes an offer that appears to be more attractive than what is currently being supplied by their current vendor
   d) at the end of a contractual relationship and the company wants to evaluate competitive bids
   (a; Moderate; p. 79)

196) There is no evaluation of vendor alternatives or information in which situation?
   a) modified rebuy
   b) straight rebuy
   c) new task
   d) high-involvement
   (b; Moderate; p. 79)

197) A modified rebuy purchase decision occurs in each of the following situations, *except:*
   a) when the firm has previously chosen a vendor and intends to place a reorder
   b) when a company is dissatisfied with their current vendor and wants to consider new options
   c) when a new company makes an offer that appears to be more attractive than what is currently being supplied by their current vendor
   d) at the end of a contractual relationship and the company wants to evaluate competitive bids
   (a; Moderate; p. 79)

198) A modified re-buy is most likely to occur when:
   a) the company becomes dissatisfied with a vendor and wants to examine new options
   b) re-ordering raw materials from the same vendor
   c) buying a new computer system
   d) purchasing a new building for an expansion project
   (a; Moderate; p. 79)

199) A company that buys a product but only has limited or infrequent experience with that product will be involved in a:
   a) straight rebuy
   b) modified rebuy
   c) new task purchase
   d) joint demand purchase
   (b; Challenging; p. 79)

200) If a potential vendor offers what is perceived by a member of the buying center to be a better buy, the company may want to revisit their purchase decision. This type of situation is typically a:
a) straight rebuy
b) modified rebuy
c) new task purchase
d) joint demand purchase
(b; Challenging; p. 79)

201) A company has reached the end of a contractual agreement with a vendor and wants to open it up for bid again before signing a new contract. This type of purchase situation is a:
a) straight rebuy
b) modified rebuy
c) new task purchase
d) joint demand purchase
(b; Challenging; p. 79)

202) A new task purchasing decision involves:
a) re-ordering from the same vendor
b) ordering new materials from the same vendor
c) upgrading the computer system
d) buying an expensive good or service for the first time
(d; Moderate; p. 79)

203) Which takes the most time to complete and involves the highest number of people in the buying process?
a) straight rebuy
b) modified rebuy
c) new task purchase
d) identifying a need
(c; Challenging; p. 79)

204) Kimberly-Clark is going to place an additional order for plastic because of a larger order it has received from a customer for products the company manufacturers. The additional order for plastic would be a:
a) straight rebuy purchase
b) modified rebuy purchase
c) new task purchase
d) none of the above
(a; Challenging; p. 79)

205) In the business-to-business buying process, the first step is:
   a) identification of a need
   b) establishment of specifications
   c) identification of alternatives
   d) appointing a committee
   (a; Easy; p. 80)

206) Derived demand is demand:
   a) from consumers for new goods and services
   b) from manufacturers to find new customers
   c) linked to the production and sale of some other item
   d) as specified by governmental orders
   (c; Moderate; p. 80)

207) The linkage between the demand for steel and sales automobiles is an example of:
   a) derived demand
   b) co-demand
   c) joint demand
   d) fabricated demand
   (a; Moderate; p. 80)

208) In the business-to-business buying process, the step the follows need identification is:
   a) identification of a problem
   b) establishment of specifications
   c) identification of alternatives
   d) appointing a committee
   (b; Moderate; p. 80)

209) When a firm's buying center agrees that defect rates for a purchased component part should be less than .01% of items received, the team is:
   a) identifying needs
   b) establishing specifications
   c) evaluating vendors
   d) negotiating purchase terms
   (b; Easy; p. 80)

210) In the business-to-business buying process, the step that follows establishing specifications is:
   a) identification of a need
   b) identifying additional complicating circumstances
   c) identification of vendors
   d) vendor evaluation
   (c; Moderate; p. 81)

211) When members of the buying center agree to consider IBM, Compac, and Hewlett-Packard in purchasing new computers because they are the firms that expressed interest, which stage of the b-to-b buying process is taking place?
a) vendor selection
b) identification of alternatives
c) identification of vendors
d) vendor evaluation
(c; Moderate; p. 81)

212) The fees paid to Olympic Committee members to place the 2002 games in Salt Lake City are an example of:
a) an ethical concern regarding bribes
b) social concern related to purchasing decisions
c) an economic concern based on risk versus return
d) an example of intrabusiness selling
(a; Easy; p. 81)

213) When the buying center members find out that leasing a fleet from one car rental company has the advantage of a better repair service contract than other companies provide, they are in which stage of the b-to-b buying process?
a) identification of vendor
b) establishment of specifications
c) vendor selection
d) vendor evaluation
(d; Challenging; p. 81)

214) In the business-to-business buying process, evaluation of vendors normally occurs at three levels, which include each of the following, *except:*
a) vendor audit
b) initial screening of proposals
c) sharing of vendor audit information
d) vendor identification
(d; Challenging, p. 81)

215) In the business-to-business buying process evaluation of vendors normally occurs at three levels. The first level is:
a) a vendor audit
b) an initial screening of proposals
c) a sharing of vendor audit information
d) vendor identification
(b; Challenging, p. 81)

216) An audit team is utilized in which stage of the b-to-b buying process?
   a) identification of vendors
   b) vendor evaluation
   c) vendor selection
   d) negotiating of terms
   (b; Challenging; p. 81)

217) In the business-to-business buying process evaluation of vendors normally occurs at three levels. The second level is:
   a) a vendor audit
   b) an initial screening of proposals
   c) a sharing of vendor audit information
   d) vendor identification
   (a; Challenging, p. 81)

218) In the business-to-business buying process evaluation of vendors normally occurs at three levels. The third level is:
   a) a vendor audit
   b) an initial screening of proposals
   c) a sharing of vendor audit information
   d) vendor identification
   (c; Challenging, p. 81)

219) In the business-to-business buying process evaluation of vendors normally occurs at three levels. Company leaders will normally share production schedules to ensure a constant supply can be met and that the two companies can develop a long-term relationship in which stage?
   a) vendor audit
   b) initial screening of proposals
   c) sharing of vendor audit information
   d) vendor identification
   (c; Challenging, p. 81)

220) Once a firm has carefully studied all of the vendors, bids have been considered, and the vendor audit has been conducted, the next step in the business-to-business buying process is:
   a) the vendor screening
   b) vendor selection
   c) negotiation of purchase terms
   d) postpurchase evaluation
   (b; Moderate; p. 82)

221) In the business-to-business arena, the post-purchase phase is critical because:
    a) businesses are more critical of quality than are consumers
    b) of the high cost involved in purchase decisions
    c) of the critical importance of supplying a continual supply of a product
    d) a positive evaluation may result into a straight rebuy situation or an advantage in a modified rebuy situation
    (d; Challenging; p. 82)

222) The following are business-to-business buyer behavior trends, *except:*
    a) greater reliance on advertising
    b) emphasis on accountability
    c) importance of Web sites and Internet marketing
    d) global branding
    (a; Challenging; p. 82)

223) The following are business-to-business buyer behavior trends, *except:*
    a) database mining
    b) increased emphasis on direct marketing
    c) changes in methods of communications
    d) focus on internal marketing communications
    (b; Challenging; p. 82)

224) Acme brick is able to sell products at prices that are 10% higher than competitors due to strong:
    a) marketing myopia
    b) Internet integration
    c) brand equity
    d) perceptions of brand parity
    (c; Challenging; p. 83)

225) The role and importance of a strong brand name is dramatically important in today's global market because of:
    a) the emphasis on accountability
    b) importance of consumer E-commerce
    c) brand parity in the business-to-business sector
    d) database mining capabilities of business firms
    (c: Challenging; p. 83)

226) New database mining programs allow businesses to:
   a) customize messages to individual customers, based on a customer's needs and past purchase behavior
   b) customize message to individual customers, based on that customers demographic and psychographic profile
   c) locate the most feasible businesses to market
   d) locate the person in the buying center that should be contacted

(a; Moderate; p. 84)

227) The following are alternative methods that being used to communicate with customers, *except:*
   a) telephone calls
   b) personal sales calls
   c) interactive Web sites
   d) E-mail

(b; Moderate; p. 84)

228) Of the following venues, the best to reach most CEOs with an advertisement is:
   a) sports programs
   b) lifestyle magazines such as New Yorker
   c) Wall Street Journal
   d) NCAA basketball tournament

(c; Challenging, p. 84)

229) Internal marketing communications are messages sent to:
   a) employees
   b) vendors
   c) buyers
   d) the government

(a; Easy; p. 84)

230) Selling virtually the same goods or services to consumers and businesses is called:
   a) relationship marketing
   b) double vending
   c) dual-channel marketing
   d) marketing extension

(c; Easy; p. 84)

231) Selling personal computers to both retail stores and other businesses is an example of:
   a) multi-outlet marketing
   b) merchant distribution
   c) quantity enhancement marketing
   d) dual channel marketing
   (d; Moderate; p. 84)

232) It is typical for dual-channel marketing to begin with:
   a) sales to businesses and later to consumers
   b) manufacturer demand for better component parts
   c) retailer demand for new products
   d) consumer demand for more purchasing options
   (a; Challenging; p. 85)

233) Spin-off sales occur when:
   a) a person likes a business product so well he or she buys one for personal use
   b) advertising is combined with consumer promotions
   c) retailing is combined with wholesaling
   d) two related business buyers are identified by the vendor
   (a; Moderate; p. 85)

234) A sales rep who likes his company car so well that he buys one for personal use is creating:
   a) joint demand
   b) derived demand
   c) a spin-off sale
   d) vendor audit sale
   (c; Moderate; p. 85)

235) Starbucks would be an example of a company involved in dual channel marketing because the company sells coffee:
   a) in retail stores only
   b) to businesses such as United Airline, Holland America cruise line, and Chicago's Wrigley Field
   c) using integrated channels
   d) to both consumers and the government
   (d; Moderate; p. 85)

Short-Answer Questions

236) Name the steps of the consumer buying decision-making process.

1. problem recognition
2. information search
3. evaluation of alternatives
4. purchase decision
5. post-purchase evaluation

(Easy; p. 63)

237) The amount of time a consumer spends on an external information search depends on four factors. What are they?

1. ability
2. motivation
3. costs
4. benefits

(Moderate; p. 64)

238) A consumer's level of motivation in making an external search depends on three factors. What are they?

1. level of involvement
2. need for cognition
3. level of shopping enthusiasm

(Moderate; p. 65)

239) An attitude consists of three components. Name and describe each one.

1) The affective component is the feelings or emotions a person holds regarding a topic, object, or idea. 2) The cognitive component is the person's mental images, understanding, and interpretations of the person, object, or idea. 3) The conative component is an individual's intentions, actions, or behavior.

(Moderate; p. 66)

240) What are the three components of the evoked set method of evaluating purchase alternatives? Describe each.

1) The evoked set, which are the brands a consumer will consider on their next purchase. 2) The inept set, which consists of brands that will not be considered because they elicit negative feelings. 3) The inert set, which holds the brands the consumer is aware of but has neither negative nor positive feelings about those products.

(Moderate; p. 70)

241) What new trends are affecting consumer buyer behavior?

    1. Age complexity
    2. Gender complexity
    3. Individualism
    4. Active, busy lifestyles
    5. Cocooning
    6. Pleasure binges
    7. Health

(Challenging; p. 72)

242) Name and describe the members of a business buying center.

Users are the members of the organization who will actually use the good or service. Buyers are the individuals given the formal responsibility of making the purchase. Influencers are people who shape purchasing decisions by providing the information or criteria utilized in evaluating alternatives. Deciders are the individuals who authorize decisions. Gatekeepers control the flow of information to members of the buying center, keep people informed about potential alternatives and decision rules, and let people know when certain alternatives have been rejected.

(Moderate; p. 76)

243) What factors affect members of the buying center?

Organizational and individual factors.

(Easy; p. 77)

244) What individual factors affect members of the buying center?

    1. Personality features
    2. Roles and perceived roles
    3. Motivational levels
    4. Levels of power
    5. Attitudes toward risk
    6. Levels of cognitive involvement
    7. Personal objectives

(Challenging; p. 77)

245) What are the three categories of business-to-business purchase decisions? Define each one.

1) A straight rebuy occurs when the firm has previously chosen a vendor and wishes to make a re-order. 2) A modified rebuy occurs when the company considers and evaluates alternatives on infrequent purchases. 3) A new task occurs when the company is buying a good or service for the first time and the company has no experience with the product.
(Moderate; p. 79)

246) What are the steps of the business-to-business buying process?

1. Identification of needs
2. Establishment of specifications
3. Identification of vendors
4. Vendor evaluation
5. Vendor selection
6. Negot1ation of terms
7. Postpurchase evaluation
(Challenging; p. 80)

247) What recent trends are present in the business-to-business buying environment?

1. Emphasis on accountability
2. Importance of E-commerce
3. Global branding
4. Database mining
5. Alternative methods of communication
6. Focus on internal communications
(Moderate; p. 82)

248) What is dual-channel marketing?

Selling virtually the same product to both consumer and business-to-business customers.
(Easy; p. 84)

CHAPTER 4
PROMOTIONS OPPORTUNITY ANALYSIS

True-False Questions

1) Hallmark targets only the high-end card buyers with its "very best" theme.
(False; Easy; p. 94)

2) Hallmark has consistently taken advantage of its primary strength – a lower price that appeals to both consumers and retailers.
(False; Moderate; p. 94)

3) Hallmark entered the international arena with its first foreign location in China.
(False; Challenging; p. 95)

 4) A promotions opportunity analysis is the process of identifying target audiences for a company's products and the communication strategies needed to reach these audiences.
(True; Moderate; p. 96)

5) One of the objectives of a promotions opportunity analysis is to identify the characteristics of each target audience so that precise marketing communications messages can be designed.
(True; Moderate; p. 96)

6) The first step of a promotions opportunity analysis is the creation of a communications budget.
(False; Moderate; p. 96)

7) A communications market analysis is the process of discovering the company's strengths and weaknesses in the area of marketing communications, along with an analysis of the opportunities and threats in the firm's external environment.
(True; Easy; p. 97)

8) When conducting a communication market analysis, an examination of competitors is used to identify major suppliers for the firm.
(False; Easy; p. 97)

9) A communication market analysis examines five areas: competitors, opportunities, threats, target markets, and customers.
(False; Challenging; p. 97)

10) Primary research involves searching the library for literature about the competition.
(False; Moderate; p. 98)

11) Reading a magazine article about a competitor is a form of secondary research.
(True; Moderate; p. 98)

12) Visiting a competitor's store to see how salespeople deal with customers is a form of secondary research.
(False; Moderate; p. 98)

13) When examining competitors for a communications market analysis, it is essential to identify domestic competitors, but not foreign or international competitors.
(False; Easy; p. 98)

14) Considering whether or not the competition is ignoring a set of customers is part of the search for opportunities in the communication market analysis.
(True; Moderate; p. 98)

15) In the communication market analysis, opportunities include an unfilled market niche or when the competition is doing a poor job of meeting the needs of some customers.
(True; Moderate; p. 98)

16) In the communication market analysis, opportunities exist when the company has a distinct competence to offer customers or when a market niche is not being targeted with effective marketing communications.
(True; Moderate; p. 98)

17) When searching for opportunities in the communication market analysis, a company's marketing team should examine all available data and information about the market.
(True; Challenging; p. 98)

18) In examining target markets during the communications market analysis, the goal is to divide the total market into smaller market segments.
(True; Easy; p. 99)

19) In conducting a communications market analysis, an examination of customers should include current company customers as well as potential new customers.
(True; Moderate; p. 99)

20) In conducting a communications market analysis, an examination of customers involves understanding how people in each customer group think, why they buy, when they buy, where they buy, and how they evaluate a product after a purchase.
(True; Moderate; p. 99)

21) Product positioning is the perception created in the consumer's mind regarding the nature of the competition and the external environment.
(False; Easy; p. 99)

22) The quality of products, prices charged, methods of distribution, image, and communication tactics create a product's position and, in turn, affected by the product's position.
(True; Moderate; p. 99)

23) Communication objectives are derived from marketing objectives.
(True; Easy; p. 101)

24) Marketing objectives typically include target sales volume, market share, and profits.
(True; Moderate; p. 101)

25) Benchmark measures are often used to study whether or not a promotional campaign has been successful.
(True; Moderate; p. 101)

26) Managers make unrealistic assumptions about communications budget when they assume there is a direct relationship between expenditures on advertising and subsequent sales revenues.
(True; Moderate; p. 101)

27) Business-to-business companies spend a greater percentage of marketing communication dollars on telephone marketing than do consumer markets.
(True; Challenging; p. 102)

28) In terms of the hierarchy of effects model, advertising expenditures during the awareness stage should generate higher sales revenue than advertising expenditures during the liking or preference stage.
(False; Challenging; p. 102)

29) A threshold effect occurs when repeated exposures to a message cause a consumer to lose interest in the company.
(False; Moderate; p. 103)

30) When a company introduces a new product under a strongly established brand name, the length of time to reach the threshold point where advertising is effective is normally shorter.
(True; Moderate; p. 103)

31) A sales-response function curve shows when diminishing returns on advertising expenditures are present.
(True; Moderate; p. 103)

32) A marginal analysis is used to portray how returns on additional advertising expenditures are related to incremental increases in advertising expenditures.
(True; Challenging; p. 103)

33) A "carryover effect" means that an ad has been shown often enough so that the consumer will remember the company when it is time to buy a product.
(True; Moderate; p. 103)

34) Decay effects occur when a company's advertisements have become old or boring.
(False; Moderate; p. 103)

35) In terms of developing a communications budget, the percentage of sales method is similar to the objective and task approach.
(False; Easy; p. 104)

36) The primary reason so many companies use the percentage of sales method to prepare communications budget is its simplicity.
(True; Moderate; p. 104)

37) The percentage of sales method for communication budgeting tends to allocate funds for advertising in the opposite direction from when they are needed.
(True; Challenging; p. 104)

38) Meet--the-competition budgeting is the most efficient form of developing a marketing communications budget.
(False; Moderate; p. 105)

39) Meet-the-competition method of developing a marketing communications budget is often used in highly competitive markets where rivalries between competitors are intense.
(True; Moderate; p. 105)

40) The primary goal of meet-the-competition method of developing a marketing communications budget is to prevent the loss of market share.
(True; Challenging; p. 105)

41) The "what we can afford" method of budgeting for marketing communications is the most difficult form of communications budget that a company can prepare.
(False; Easy; p. 105)

42) The "what we can afford" method of developing a marketing communications budget suggests that managers do not see the benefits of marketing.
(True; Moderate; p. 105)

43) The objective and task method of budgeting marketing communications links dollars to specific marketing or communication goals.
(True; Easy; p. 105)

44) Many marketers believe that the objective and task method of developing marketing communications budgets is the best method of budgeting.
(True; Moderate; p. 105)

45) Payout planning is a form of consumer market segmentation.
(False; Easy; p. 105)

46) The payout planning method of developing a marketing communications budget establishes a ratio of advertising to sales or market share, then reduces the ratio as the product reaches the threshold level and diminishing returns begin occurring.
(True; Challenging; p. 105)

47) In using the payout planning method of developing a marketing communications budget, a higher percentage is allocated to marketing communications in the products early years and when the product is building brand awareness and brand equity.
(True; Challenging; p. 106)

48) Quantitative methods of developing a marketing communications budget rely on computer models or simulations.
(True; Easy; p. 106)

49) The United States leads the world in annual advertising expenditures.
(True; Easy, p. 106)

50) Company product manufacturers spend more money on media advertising, while service companies tend to spend more money on trade promotions.
(False; Challenging; p. 106)

51) In terms of business-to-business advertisements, about 20 percent promote the corporate image, while 80 percent focus on specific goods or services.
(True; Challenging; p. 106)

52) On average, companies spend about 10 percent of a total communications budget on marketing to other businesses.
(False; Challenging; p. 106)

53) Strategies are sweeping guidelines concerning the essence of the firm's short-term marketing activities and efforts.
(False; Easy; p. 107)

54) It is critical that the company's communications strategies mesh with its overall message and be carefully linked to opportunities identified by a communication market analysis.
(True; Challenging; p. 107)

55) Tactics are activities performed to support strategies.
     (True; Easy; p. 108)

56) A holiday promotion featuring a company's products with a unique design is a form of marketing tactic.
     (True; Moderate; p. 108)

57) One ethical criticism of marketing is that using segmentation tactics is the same thing as stereotyping consumers.
     (True; Moderate; p. 109)

58) Segmentation is an effective method to identify target markets.
     (True; Easy; p. 109)

59) A market segment is a general approach which differentiates products to all customers in a geographic area.
     (False; Moderate; p. 109)

60) The two most general forms of market segments are current customers and potential customers.
     (False; Challenging; p. 109)

61) Consumers within a market segment tend to be homogenous, which means they are similar.
     (True; Moderate; p. 109)

62) A market segment must be financially viable to be useful.
     (True; Moderate; p. 110)

63) Demographics, or population characteristics, can be used to identify market segments.
     (True; Easy; p. 110)

64) Selling a product to women is a form of demographic market segmentation.
     (True; Easy; p. 109)

65) Because a high percentage of women work, goods and services that offer convenience, flexibility, and independence are in demand.
     (True; Moderate; p. 110)

66) Marketing products that are purchased by both genders with different types of appeals are not usually successful.
     (False; Moderate; p. 111)

67) When marketing to children, a company is using generations as the segmentation variable.
(False; Moderate; p. 111)

68) Lower-level income families spend money primarily on luxury-type products.
(False; Easy; p. 112)

69) Selling to various ethnic groups is a form of demographic market segmentation.
(True; Easy; p. 112)

70) By the year 2010, most Americans will be nonwhite.
(True; Moderate; p. 112)

71) The ethnic group in the United States with the highest economic buying power is Hispanics.
(False; Moderate; p. 113)

72) Ethnic consumers tend to be more brand loyal than their Caucasian counterparts.
(True; Challenging; p. 113)

73) In ethic marketing it is important to present one overall message theme, but it should then be tailored to fit the needs and values of each ethnic group.
(True; Moderate; p. 113)

74) Psychographics, or patterns that reflect attitudes, interests, and opinions, can be used for demographic market segmentation.
(False; Moderate; p. 113)

75) Psychographic information is often combined with demographic profiles to provide marketers with a more complete understanding of a target market.
(True; Moderate; p. 113)

76) Generation Y focuses on family and children and spend more on food, housing, transportation, and personal services than other generation segments.
(False; Challenging; p. 115)

77) For Generation Y, clothes, automobiles, and college are big ticket items. They also spend substantial amounts on televisions, stereo systems, and products that enhance their personal appearance.
(True; Challenging; p. 115)

78) For younger boomers, the focus is on home and family.
(True; Challenging, p. 113)

79) The priorities of the older boomers is on upgrading homes, ensuring education and independence of their children, buying luxury items, and taking more exotic vacations.
(True; Challenging; p. 116)

80) In terms of generation segmentation, seniors spend heavily on home mortgages, new furniture, new automobiles, and personal indulgence items.
(False; Challenging; p. 116)

81) Geographic segmentation is especially useful for retailers that want to limit their marketing communications to specific areas.
(True; Easy; p. 116)

82) Geodemographic segmentation is a combination of census data with psychographic information.
(True; Moderate; p. 116)

83) Benefit segmentation is a combination of census data with psychographic information.
(False; Moderate; p. 117)

84) Benefit segmentation is more valuable if it can be combined with demographic and psychographic information.
(True; Moderate; p. 117)

85) The NAICS code helps in geodemographic segmentation programs.
(False; Challenging; p. 118)

86) The NAICS coding system allows marketing teams to examine specific industries.
(True; Easy; p. 118)

87) One method of business-to-business market segmentation utilizes company size as a factor.
(True; Easy; p. 119)

88) Geodemographics can be used to segment business markets as well as consumer markets.
(True; Moderate; p. 119)

89) Product usage is not normally used as a method of business-to-business market segmentation.
(False; Easy; p. 119)

90) A successful GIMC program utilizes market segmentation adapted to countries and cultures.
(True; Easy; p. 120)

Multiple-Choice Questions

91) Hallmark was able to widen the company's base of customers by:
   a) adapting various lines of cards to different target markets
   b) standardizing all products with the Hallmark brand
   c) standardizing cards within the United States, customizing internationally
   d) avoiding computer databases that would overcomplicate the selling process
(a; Easy; p. 94)

92) Hallmark's "Touch Screen Greeting" card is designed to reach which target market?
   a) females, ages 20 to 35
   b) men and younger consumers in their teens and early 20s
   c) middle-age consumers, 30 to 50
   d) higher income consumers, primarily female
(b; Challenging; p. 95)

93) A primary factor in Hallmark's success is the ability to consistently take advantage of one major strength, which is a:
   a) lower prices
   b) broad distribution
   c) image of high quality
   d) multiple brands
(c; Challenging; p. 96)

 94) A promotions opportunity analysis is:
   a) the process of identifying audiences for the goods and services the company sells and the communication strategies needed to reach these audiences
   b) the process of discovering the organization's strengths and weaknesses in the area of marketing communications and combining the information with an analysis of the opportunities and threats in the firm's external environment
   c) an analysis of the potential market for new goods and services
   d) a series of attempts to improve the promotion of the company through effective public relations
(a; Easy; p. 96)

95) The process of identifying audiences for the goods and services the company sells and the communication strategies needed to reach these audiences is which of the following?
    a) communication marketing analysis
    b) competitive analysis
    c) target market analysis
    d) promotions opportunity analysis
(d; Moderate; p. 96)

96) A promotions opportunity analysis should:
    a) be concerned with product differentiation
    b) determine the promotional opportunities that exist for the company
    c) be the basis for the development of a marketing plan
    d) focus on short-range tactics
(b; Moderate; p. 96)

97) The first step in a promotional opportunity analysis is to:
    a) establish communication objectives
    b) create a communications budget
    c) conduct a communications market analysis
    d) prepare promotional strategies
(c; Moderate; p. 97)

98) After conducting a communications market analysis, the next step in a promotional opportunity analysis is to:
    a) establish communication objectives
    b) create a communications budget
    c) conduct a communications market analysis
    d) prepare promotional strategies
(a; Moderate; p. 97)

99) After establishing communication objectives, the next step in a promotional opportunity analysis is to:
    a) establish communication objectives
    b) create a communications budget
    c) match tactics with strategies
    d) prepare promotional strategies
(b; Challenging; p. 97)

100) A communication market analysis is:
   a) the process of identifying audiences for the goods and services the company sells and the communication strategies needed to reach these audiences
   b) the process of discovering the organization's strengths and weaknesses in the area of marketing communications and combining the information with an analysis of the opportunities and threats in the firm's external environment
   c) an analysis of the potential for new products and services
   d) a series of attempts to improve the promotion of the company through effective public relations
(b; Easy; p. 97)

101) A communication market analysis consists of the following ingredients, *except:*
   a) threats
   b) competitors
   c) opportunities
   d) target markets
(a; Moderate; p. 97)

102) A communication market analysis consists of the following ingredients, *except:*
   a) company strengths
   b) product positioning
   c) customers
   d) target markets
(a; Moderate; p. 97)

103) An examination of competitors during the communication market analysis involves:
   a) identifying a firm's major competitors
   b) an examination of domestic competitors in terms of their product portfolios
   c) identifying all of a firm's competitors and what they are doing in marketing communications
   d) identifying the pricing and distribution strategies of all competitors
(c; Moderate; p. 97)

104) Listing all of a firm's competitors and what they are doing in the area of marketing communications would occur in which area of the communication market analysis?
   a) competitors
   b) opportunities
   c) target markets
   d) customers
(a; Easy; p. 97)

105) The second component of a communication market analysis is the search for opportunities, which involves:
   a) watching for new marketing communication opportunities by examining all of the available data and information about the market
   b) examination of various target markets to determine the various needs of each target market
   c) an in-depth analysis of customers in terms of why, where, when and how they buy
   d) an in-depth analysis of competitors, what they offer, and how they communicate with their customers
(a; Easy; p. 98)

106) In the communications market analysis, watching for new marketing communication opportunities by examining all of the available data and information about the market would occur in the examination of:
   a) competitors
   b) opportunities
   c) target markets
   d) customers
(a; Easy; p. 98)

107) In terms of searching for opportunities in a communications market analysis, a new communication opportunity exists in each of the following situations, *except:*
   a) there is an unfilled market niche
   b) the competition is doing a poor job of meeting needs of some customers
   c) competitors have a distinct competence to offer customers
   d) a market niche is not being targeted with effective marketing communications
(c; Challenging; p. 98)

108) In conducting a communication market analysis, Digital Lifestyles discovered that most computer companies treated teens like all other market segments. This finding would likely occur during the examination of:
   a) competitors
   b) opportunities
   c) threats
   d) customers
(b; Challenging; p. 98)

109) During a communications market analysis, an inventory software producer found that no one was producing software to handle inventory for salvage yards. This information would have mostly likely been gathered during an analysis of:
   a) competitors
   b) governmental customers
   c) opportunities
   d) customers
(c; Challenging; p. 98)

110) A communication market analysis is the examination of various target markets, which involves:
   a) watching for new marketing communication opportunities by examining all of the available data and information about the market
   b) determining the various needs of each target market
   c) an in-depth analysis of customers in terms of why, where, when and how they buy
   d) an in-depth analysis of competitors, what they offer, and how they communicate with their customers
(a; Easy; p. 99)

111) During a communication market analysis, Foot Locker has determined that the company is not effectively reaching Generation Y. This information would have most likely been gathered during the analysis of:
   a) competitors
   b) threats
   c) target markets
   d) customers
(c; Challenging; p. 99)

112) A component of a communication market analysis is the examination of customers, which involves:
   a) watching for new marketing communication opportunities by examining all of the available data and information about the market
   b) determining the various needs of each target market
   c) an in-depth analysis of customers in terms of why, where, when and how they buy
   d) an in-depth analysis of competitors, what they offer, and how they communicate with their customers
(c; Easy; p. 99)

113) The goal of examining customers in the communications market analysis is to:
   a) measure the impact of market segmentation
   b) determine products are not being made by the competition
   c) understand they think, why they buy, when they buy, where they buy, and how they evaluate a product after a purchase
   d) differentiate the various customer groups and how much market share each competitor has
   (c; Easy; p. 99)

114) The perception created in the consumer's mind regarding a company's products relative to the competition is:
   a) opportunity analysis
   b) a product's position
   c) competitive analysis
   d) communication analysis
   (b; Easy; p. 100)

115) Mountain Dew might learn that the soft drink is considered more hip and trendy than Coke during an analysis of:
   a) primary data
   b) market segments
   c) the company or product's position
   d) secondary data
   (c; Moderate; p. 100)

116) The following are possible product positioning strategies, *except:*
   a) attributes
   b) competitors
   c) use or application
   d) by-products
   (d; Moderate; p. 100)

117) The following are possible product positioning strategies, *except:*
   a) for governmental customers
   b) cultural symbols
   c) product users
   d) product class
   (a; Moderate; p. 100)

118) During a communication market analysis, a company learned that its brand is viewed as being of high quality. This information would have most likely been gathered during the analysis of:
   a) competitors
   b) product positioning
   c) target markets
   d) customers
(b; Challenging; p. 100)

119) A local video rental store looking to increase customer traffic in the summer would be an example of a:
   a) target market analysis
   b) product positioning
   c) communications analysis
   d) communications objective
(d; Moderate; p. 100)

120) The following are examples of typical communication objectives, *except:*
   a) identify competitors
   b) encourage repeat purchases
   c) enhance firm image
   d) change customer beliefs or attributes
(a; Challenging; p. 101)

121) The following are examples of typical marketing communications objectives, *except:*
   a) increase market share
   b) increase the number of products offered
   c) increase profits
   d) increase return on investment
(b; Challenging; p. 101)

122) The starting point that is studied in relation to the degree of change following a promotional campaign is called a:
   a) post-hoc analysis
   b) marginal analysis
   c) benchmark measure
   d) standardized measure
(c; Easy, p. 101)

123) In terms of communication spending, the highest business-to-business expenditures are typically for:
   a) television
   b) magazines
   c) telephone marketing
   d) direct mail
(c; Challenging; p. 101)

124) In terms of communication spending, the highest expenditures on consumer markets are typically made for:
   a) television
   b) magazines
   c) telephone marketing
   d) direct mail
(a; Challenging; p. 101)

125) In terms of the relationship between expenditures on advertising communications and subsequent sales revenues, too many marketing managers assume that there is:
   a) a direct relationship
   b) an indirect relationship
   c) inverted U-shaped relationship
   d) an inverse relationship
(a; Moderate; p. 101)

126) The following factors have an impact on the relationship between expenditures on marketing communications and sales revenue, *except:*
   a) the goals of the promotion, advertisement, or marketing communications program
   b) marginal costs
   c) threshold effects
   d) carryover effects
(b; Moderate; p. 102)

127) The following factors have an impact on the relationship between expenditures on marketing communications and sales revenue, *except:*
   a) decay effects
   b) wear out effects
   c) moderating events
   d) random events
(c; Moderate; p. 102)

128) In terms of the hierarchy of effects model, ads targeted at which stage will have the least impact on consumers, in terms of generating sales revenues?
   a) awareness
   b) knowledge
   c) liking
   d) preference
(a; Challenging; p. 103)

129) As consumers see advertisements over time they become more likely to recall a message and purchase a product. This demonstrates:
   a) diminishing returns
   b) decay effects
   c) threshold effects
   d) purchase simulation
(c; Moderate; p. 103)

130) The early effects of an advertising campaign may be minimal, but over time gain momentum. This phenomena is called:
   a) diminishing returns
   b) threshold effects
   c) the sales-response curve
   d) carryover effect
(b; Moderate; p. 103)

131) When BMW Motorcycles first began targeting some advertisements toward females, the impact was minimal at first, but after awhile began to have an impact on inquiries by females and later on sales revenue. This illustrates the concept of:
   a) impact of communication goals on sales revenues
   b) threshold effects
   c) sales-response function curve
   d) carryover effect
(b; Challenging; p. 103)

132) Pepsi and Coke both have reached the point that investing more dollars in advertising yields lower and lower increases in sales. This illustrates the concept of:
   a) decay effects
   b) threshold effects
   c) sales-response function curve
   d) carryover effect
(c; Challenging, p. 103)

133) The sales-response function curve models the:
   a) diminishing returns of advertising
   b) threshold effects of advertisements
   c) carryover effects of advertising
   d) decay effects of advertisements
(a; Moderate; p. 103)

134) When a concave downward function is present, increasing advertising expenditures result in:
   a) greater sales
   b) diminishing returns
   c) average returns
   d) further advertising expenditures
(b; Moderate; p. 103)

135) Which is a model that shows when further advertising and promotion expenditures may result in adverse effects on profits?
   a) a sales-response function
   b) a marginal analysis
   c) average return on investment curve
   d) promotions opportunity curve
(b; Moderate; p. 103)

136) Which concept explains that consumers may recall an ad and make a purchase because they have seen the ad several times?
   a) a sales-response curve
   b) a marginal analysis
   c) decay effects
   d) carryover effects
(d; Moderate; p. 103)

137) Even though Montgomery Wards went out of business, a few consumers still recall the company when thinking about making a new washing machine purchase due to:
   a) carryover effects of previous ads
   b) wear out effects of ads of competitors
   c) threshold effects of former ads
   d) decay effects of former ads
(a; Moderate; p. 103)

138) Manufacturers of appliances, such as GE and Whirlpool, advertise on a continuous basis since appliances are purchased infrequently and only when they are needed. To ensure the brand name is remembered when the need arises, these manufacturers are relying on:
   a) threshold effects
   b) sales-response function curve
   c) wear out effects
   d) carryover effects
   (d; Challenging; p. 103)

139) Automobile manufacturer ads result in about 15 percent of all magazine advertising revenue. One reason auto manufactures spend so much on advertising is that consumers do not purchase vehicles on a regular basis. When they do make decisions to purchase new cars, the auto companies want to make sure consumers remember the right brand. This illustrates the concept of:
   a) decay effects
   b) wear out effects
   c) carryover effects
   d) threshold effects
   (c; Challenging; p. 103)

140) When consumers begin to think of an advertisement as old or stale, the concept being illustrated is:
   a) a sales-response curve
   b) wear out effects
   c) decay effects
   d) carryover effects
   (b; Moderate; p. 103)

141) When consumers begin to forget a brand name because advertising message have stopped, it is a sign of:
   a) a sales-response curve
   b) wear out effects
   c) decay effects
   d) carryover effects
   (c; Moderate; p. 103)

142) S.O.S. soap pads were advertised on television for many years. When the company discontinued advertising, sales slowly began to decline and consumers gradually forgot the brand name. This illustrates the concept of:
   a) decay effects
   b) wear out effects
   c) carryover effects
   d) threshold effects
   (a; Challenging; p. 103)

143) The following are methods of determining marketing communications budgets, *except:*
    a) percentage of sales
    b) sales approximation
    c) meet the competition
    d) what we can afford
   (b; Easy; p. 104)

144) The following are methods of determining marketing communications budgets, *except:*
    a) objective and task
    b) payout planning
    c) sales-response function curve
    d) quantitative methods
   (c; Easy; p. 104)

145) Basing a communications budget on sales from the previous year or anticipated sales for the next year is which method?
    a) percentage of sales
    b) meet the competition
    c) what we can afford
    d) payout planning
   (a; Easy; p. 104)

146) One of the problems with the percentage of sales budgeting method is:
    a) deciding on the percentage level
    b) finding a benchmark figure to use
    c) the budget tends to change in the opposite direction of what may be needed
    d) the competition knows how much the company will spend on advertising
   (c; Moderate; p. 104)

147) The primary reason companies develop a communications budget using the percentage of sales method is:
    a) it tends to be more accurate than the other methods
    b) the budget tends to change with sales so as sales increases there is more money available for communications
    c) money is available for unique marketing opportunities that arise
    d) it is simple to prepare
   (d; Moderate; p. 104)

148) Basing a budget on what other companies are spending on advertising and communication is which method?
   a) percentage of sales
   b) meet the competition
   c) what we can afford
   d) payout planning
   (b; Easy; p. 105)

149) The primary disadvantage of the meet-the-competition method of marketing communication budgeting is:
   a) marketing dollars may not be spent efficiently
   b) there is little flexibility in how the marketing dollars can be spent
   c) when sales go down, so does spending
   d) it shows a lack of commitment to marketing
   (a; Moderate; p. 105)

150) If Burger King decides to match McDonald's dollar-for-dollar in advertising expenditures, which type of advertising budget is being used?
   a) objective and task
   b) meet the competition
   c) what we can afford
   d) the percentage of share method
   (b; Moderate; p. 105)

151) The primary objective of the meet-the-competition method for developing a marketing communications budget is to:
   a) match the communication budget with sales
   b) ensure marketing dollars are invested where it is most needed
   c) prevent the loss of market share
   d) ensure marketing dollars are allocated appropriately
   (c; Challenging; p. 105)

152) Which method of developing marketing communications budget is often used in highly, competitive markets where rivalries between competitors is intense?
   a) percentage of sales
   b) meet the competition
   c) what we can afford
   d) objective and task
   (b; Moderate; p. 105)

153) Managers who do not recognize the benefits of marketing may be most inclined to use which method of communications budgeting?
   a) percentage of sales
   b) meet the competition
   c) what we can afford
   d) payout planning
(c; Easy; p. 105)

154) Newer and smaller companies are inclined to use which method when developing marketing communications budgets?
   a) percentage of sales
   b) meet the competition
   c) what we can afford
   d) payout planning
(c; Easy; p. 105)

155) Which method of developing the marketing communications budget suggests management does not recognize the benefits of marketing?
   a) percentage of sales
   b) meet the competition
   c) what we can afford
   d) objective and task
(c; Challenging; p. 105)

156) Which method for developing a marketing communications budget links dollars to defined goals?
   a) percentage of sales
   b) meet the competition
   c) what we can afford
   d) objective and task
(d; Easy; p. 105)

157) If a company rejects a communications budgeting method because it would take too long to prepare, odds are the budgeting method is:
   a) percentage of sales
   b) meet the competition
   c) what we can afford
   d) objective and task
(d; Challenging; p. 105)

158) Which approach to developing a marketing communications budget is often viewed as being the most effective?
   a) objective and task
   b) percentage of sales
   c) what we can afford
   d) payout planning
(a; Moderate; p. 105)

159) Which method of developing a marketing communications budget establishes a ratio of advertising dollars to sales or market share then reduces the percentage as sales build and the product obtains market share?
   a) arbitrary allocation
   b) meet-the-competition
   c) payout planning
   d) quantitative models
(c; Moderate; p. 105)

160) In using the payout planning method of developing a marketing communications budget, the larger amounts of dollars would be spent on marketing communications:
   a) in the early years to build brand awareness and brand equity
   b) in the middle years to build brand equity and brand preference
   c) in the later years to maintain market share
   d) when the market share is the lowest
(a; Challenging; p. 105)

161) In using the payout planning method of developing a marketing communications budget, the marketing budget would be reduced:
   a) at the product's introduction, then increased when brand acceptance occurs
   b) after the brand gains market acceptance
   c) when the brand reaches the point at which additional dollars invested in communications yields diminishing returns
   d) when the market becomes saturated
(c; Moderate; p. 106)

162) Which method of developing a marketing communications budget is used when the marketing budget is reduced as the brand reaches the point that additional dollars invested in communications yields diminishing returns?
   a) percentage of sales
   b) objective and task
   c) payout planning
   d) quantitative methods
(c; Challenging; p. 106)

163) Which method of developing a marketing communications budget uses computer simulations to model the relationship between advertising and marketing communications and sales, profits, and other factors?
    a) meet the competition
    b) objective and task
    c) payout planning
    d) quantitative models
(d; Moderate; p. 106)

164) In terms of marketing expenditures, consumer product manufacturers tend to spend thee most on which of the following?
    a) media advertising
    b) trade promotions
    c) consumer promotions
    d) direct marketing
(b; Challenging; p. 106)

165) In terms of marketing expenditures, service companies tend to spend more on which of the following than companies in general?
    a) media advertising
    b) trade promotions
    c) consumer promotions
    d) direct marketing
(a; Challenging; p. 106)

166) Which country has the highest level of annual advertising expenditures?
    a) the United States
    b) Japan
    c) Germany
    d) United Kingdom
(a; Challenging; p. 106)

167) Sweeping guidelines that direct the essence of a company's marketing efforts are called:
    a) strategies
    b) tactics
    c) incentives
    d) objectives
(a; Easy; p. 107)

168) If Tang breakfast drink focuses on changing its image to a more current and "hip" image, it is an example of a:
   a) reallocating the percentage-of-sales budget
   b) communications strategy
   c) competitive analysis
   d) communications tactic
   (b; Moderate; p. 107)

169) Activities that support strategies are called:
   a) enticements
   b) tactics
   c) incentives
   d) objectives
   (b; Easy; p. 108)

170) Coupon programs are an example of:
   a) a marketing strategy
   b) a marketing tactic
   c) geo-demographic analysis
   d) collecting secondary data
   (b; Moderate; p. 108)

171) Which of the following is not an example of a communication tactic?
   a) selling gift certificates
   b) creating purchase bonus programs
   c) changing prices
   d) presenting a young, trendy image
   (d; Challenging; p. 108)

172) Some marketing critics say that segmentation is the same thing as:
   a) stereotyping
   b) puffery
   c) discrimination
   d) marketing myopia
   (b; Moderate; p. 109)

173) A set of businesses or groups of individual consumers with distinct characteristics is a:
   a) differentiated group
   b) production department
   c) market segment
   d) manufacturing system
   (c; Easy; p. 109)

174) Market segments should be internally:
   a) heterogeneous
   b) high frequency
   c) variable
   d) homogenous
(d; Easy; p. 109)

175) For a market segment to be viable, it should meet each of the following tests, *except:*
   a) the members of the market segment should be ambiguous
   b) the market segment must be large enough to be financially viable to market with a separate marketing campaign
   c) the market segment must differ from the population as a whole
   d) the market segment must be reachable through some type of media or marketing communications
(a; Moderate; p. 109)

176) Market segmentation efforts should each of the following activities, *except:*
   a) help marketers identify company strengths and weaknesses as well as opportunities in the marketplace
   b) assist marketers in clarifying marketing objectives associated with individual target markets
   c) identifying governmental customers
   d) work toward the goal of matching what the firm offers with the most lucrative market segments
(c; Challenging; p. 109)

177) The following are methods of segmenting consumer markets, *except:*
   a) demographics
   b) industry size
   c) psychographics
   d) generations
(b; Easy; p. 110)

178) The following are methods of segmenting consumer markets, *except:*
   a) geographic
   b) geodemographics
   c) distribution channel
   d) benefits
(c; Easy; p. 110)

179) The method of consumer segmentation that is based on population characteristics is:
   a) demographics
   b) psychographics
   c) geographic
   d) polygraphic
(a; Easy; p. 110)

180) The following are types of demographic segmentation variables, *except*:
   a) gender
   b) lifestyles
   c) age
   d) income
(b; Easy; p. 110)

181) Level of educational is an example of segmentation by:
   a) psychographics
   b) generations
   c) demographics
   d) geodemographics
(c; Moderate; p. 110)

182) Analysis of buying patterns by gender is an example of segmentation by:
   a) psychographics
   b) generations
   c) demographics
   d) usage
(c; Moderate; p. 110)

183) Which group is most likely to express concerns about balancing family and work?
   a) females
   b) Generation X
   c) Generation Y
   d) males
(a; Challenging; p. 110)

184) Many professional sports teams have started targeting ads to females because:
   a) women now watch sports as much as men
   b) men will attend more sporting events if the wife is also a sports fan
   c) ads to men have declined in effectiveness
   d) it is easier to influence women to attend a sporting event than men
(b; Challenging; p. 111)

185) In an effort to attract more fans to baseball games, the Houston Astros have developed an advertising campaign that is targeted to females. This is an example of the demographic segmentation variable of:
    a) gender
    b) age
    c) income
    d) ethnicity
(a; easy; p. 111)

186) If a company chooses to focus marketing efforts on children, which demographic variable is being used to segment the market?
    a) gender
    b) age
    c) generations
    d) benefits
(b; Easy; p. 111)

187) In an effort to attract more fans to baseball games, the St. Louis Cardinals have developed an advertising campaign that is targeted to teenagers. This is an example of the demographic segmentation variable of:
    a) gender
    b) age
    c) income
    d) ethnicity
(b; easy; p. 111)

188) Consumer goods that are related to basic, everyday needs are:
    a) necessities
    b) sundries
    c) luxuries
    d) demographic items
(a; Easy; p. 112)

189) Consumer goods that are "nice to own" are:
    a) necessities
    b) sundries
    c) low-priced
    d) demographic items
(b; Easy; p. 112)

190) Consumer goods that are "once in a lifetime" purchases due to the expense involved are:
    a) necessities
    b) sundries
    c) luxuries
    d) demographic items
(c; Easy; p. 112)

191) A commercial showing the luxury and quality of a Lexus is based on:
    a) geographic segmentation
    b) income segmentation
    c) ethnic segmentation
    d) geo-demographic segmentation
(b; Challenging; p. 112)

192) African American and Hispanic ethnic groups tend to:
    a) be less brand loyal than Asian Americans
    b) put less value on quality than Caucasians
    c) value relationships with companies that serve them
    d) be primarily concerned with price
(c; Moderate; p. 112)

193) By the year 2010, most Americans will be:
    a) Caucasian
    b) African American
    c) Hispanic
    d) nonwhite
(d; Moderate; p. 112)

194) Successful ethnic marketing requires:
    a) hiring ethnically-owned marketing and advertising agencies
    b) translating English speaking ads into Spanish or native language of the ethnic group
    c) understanding the various ethnic groups and writing marketing communications that speak to their specific values and cultures
    d) using ethnically-owned media outlets
(c; Moderate; p. 112)

195) Attitudes, interests, and opinions are reflected in:
    a) demographic market segments
    b) geographic market segments
    c) psychographic market segments
    d) product differentiation programs
(c; Easy; p. 113)

196) The VALS typology is based on which type of segmentation?
   a) demographic
   b) psychographic
   c) generations
   d) geodemographic
(b; Moderate; p. 113)

197) Marketing to individuals who are successful, sophisticated, receptive to new technologies, enjoy sports, and are liberal in their political views is an example of which type of segmentation?
   a) demographic
   b) psychographic
   c) generations
   d) geodemographic
(b; Challenging; p. 113)

198) In terms of the VALS2 typology, members of which group are successful, sophisticated receptive to new technologies?
   a) innovators
   b) thinkers
   c) achievers
   d) experiencers
(a; Challenging; p. 113)

199) Which method of segmenting markets is based on the idea that people experience significant external events during their late adolescence and early adulthood that impact their social values, attitudes, and preferences?
   a) demographic
   b) psychographic
   c) generations
   d) geodemographics
(c; Moderate; p. 115)

200) The following are components of the generations segmentation method, *except:*
   a) children
   b) Generation Y
   c) empty nesters
   d) seniors
(a; Challenging; p. 115)

201) In terms of generation segmentation, which groups contribute 5 percent of total spending power to clothes, automobiles, and college and other high-ticket items?
   a) Generation Y
   b) Generation X
   c) Younger boomers
   d) Older boomers
(a; Challenging; p. 115)

202) In terms of generation segmentation, which group spends substantial amounts on televisions, stereo systems, and products to enhance their personal appearance?
   a) Generation Y
   b) Generation X
   c) Younger boomers
   d) Older boomers
(a; Challenging; p. 115)

203) In terms of generation segmentation, which group focuses on family and children with food, housing, transportation, and personal services being important categories?
   a) Generation Y
   b) Generation X
   c) Younger boomers
   d) Older boomers
(b; Challenging; p. 115)

204) In terms of generation segmentation, which group allocates a large portion of family income to the home mortgage, home furnishings, and home renovations? The rest of their disposable income is spent on pets, toys, playground equipment, or large recreational items.
   a) Generation Y
   b) Generation X
   c) Younger boomers
   d) Older boomers
(c; Challenging; p. 115)

205) In terms of generation segmentation, which group allocates a large portion of family income to upgrading homes, ensuring education and independence of their children, buying luxury items, and taking exotic vacations? Insurance and investments are also important to this generation group.
   a) Generation Y
   b) Generation X
   c) Younger boomers
   d) Older boomers
(d; Challenging; p. 116)

206) In terms of generation segmentation, over 80 percent of which of these groups own their homes as they spend heavily on new furniture, new automobiles, and personal indulgence items they could not afford earlier because of children?
   a) empty nesters
   b) Generation X
   c) Younger boomers
   d) Older boomers
(a; Challenging; p. 116)

207) When Skechers targets California with a special advertising and promotional campaign, which type of segmentation is being used?
   a) psychographics
   b) demographics
   c) geographic area
   d) geodemographics
(c; Easy; p. 116)

208) Geodemographics:
   a) combines census data with psychographic data
   b) segments populations by generations
   c) is a form of global marketing
   d) groups consumers by region
(a; Easy; p. 116)

209) Geodemographic segmentation combines all of the following, *except:*
   a) census demographic information
   b) geographic information
   c) product usage information
   d) psychographic information
(c; Challenging; p. 116)

210) If a company sends direct mail to only the zip codes of communities that match the firm's best customer profiles, it is using which type of segmentation?
   a) demographic
   b) psychographic
   c) geographic
   d) geodemographic
(d; Moderate; p. 116)

211) PRIZM is a company that specializes in which type of segmentation?
   a) product differentiation
   b) geodemographic
   c) geographic
   d) psychographic
(b; Challenging; p. 116)

212) A shift in advertising that shows the benefits of the product rather than a focus on the customers is called:
   a) demographic segmentation
   b) psychographic segmentation
   c) benefit segmentation
   d) usage segmentation
   (c; Moderate; p. 117)

213) A firm that has a database containing consumer purchasing histories and uses the information to create market segments is using:
   a) demographic segmentation
   b) psychographic segmentation
   c) benefit segmentation
   d) usage segmentation
   (d; Challenging; p. 117)

214) In terms of market segmentation, the usage segmentation approach offers each of the following advantages, *except:*
   a) a meaningful classification scheme based on the benefits each segment desires
   b) ability to reduce a large volume of customer data to a few, concise clusters
   c) ability to measure the growth of each cluster and the migration of customers from one cluster to another
   d) ability to compare a firm's customers with customers from competing firms
   (d; Challenging; p. 117)

215) The following are methods of segmenting business-to-business markets, *except:*
   a) demographics
   b) NAICS/SIC code
   c) geographic location
   d) size of business
   (a; Easy; p. 118)

216) The following are methods of segmenting business-to-business markets, *except:*
   a) product usage
   b) psychographics
   c) geographic location
   d) customer value
   (b; Easy; p. 118)

217) The most common method of segmenting business markets by industry is to use:
    a) the NAICS code system
    b) geographic location
    c) business characteristics
    d) customer value measures
(a; Moderate; p. 118)

218) If Microsoft's marketing team wanted to use a different communications approach when designing mailings for various business industries, they could utilize:
    a) the NAICS code
    b) demographics
    c) competitive analysis
    d) opportunity analysis
(a; Challenging; p. 118)

219) Applied Microbiology used which method to segment the business market by combining geographic area data for dairy farmers with demographic and psychographic information?
    a) product usage
    b) NAICS/SIC code
    c) geodemographics
    d) size of business
(c; Moderate; p. 119)

220) Marketing to companies that use the same good or service, but in different ways is segmentation based on:
    a) the NAICS code
    b) demographics
    c) geographic location
    d) product usage
(d; Moderate; p. 119)

221) When the Edgewater Hotel & Resort develops a marketing campaign aimed to attract business customers, institutions, and organizations who need a location to hold 2 to 4 day conferences, the type of segmentation approach being used was:
    a) demographics
    b) product usage
    c) type of business
    d) customer value
(b; Challenging; p. 119)

222) A quality global marketing communications analysis includes the following activities, *except:*
    a) identification of strengths and weaknesses of local competitors
    b) segmentation programs
    c) literal translations of ads
    d) studies of norms, beliefs, and laws
    (c; Moderate; p. 120)

223) Stopping an ad which appears to be funny in one culture but offensive in another is probably performed by:
    a) a creative
    b) a bilingual
    c) a cultural assimilator
    d) the local government
    (c; Challenging; p. 121)

Short-Answer Questions

224) What are the steps in a promotions opportunity analysis?

    1. Complete a communications marketing analysis
    2. Establish objectives
    3. Create a budget
    4. Prepare a strategy
    5. Match tactics with strategy
    (Moderate; p. 97)

225) What are the five components of a communications market analysis?

    1. competitors
    2. opportunities
    3. target markets
    4. customers
    5. positioning
    (Moderate; p. 97)

226) What is an opportunity analysis? What are some typical questions that should be asked during an opportunity analysis?

This is an analysis to see what type of communications' opportunities may exist for a particular product. Typical questions that can be asked include:
1. Are there customers that the competition is ignoring or not serving?
2. Which markets are heavily saturated and have intense competition?
3. Are the benefits of our goods and services being clearly articulated to our customers?
4. Are there opportunities, using a slightly different marketing approach, to build relationships with customers?
5. Are there opportunities that are not being pursued or is our brand positioned with a cluster of other companies in such a manner that it cannot stand out?
(Challenging; p. 98)

227) What customer groups should be considered during the customer analysis?

1. Current company customers
2. The competition's customers
3. Potential new customers
(Moderate: p. 99)

228) Identify the various methods that can be used to develop a communications budget?

1. Percentage of sales
2. Meet-the-competition
3. What we can afford
4. Objective and task
5. Payout planning
6. Quantitative models
(Moderate; pp. 104)

229) Describe the difference between strategies and tactics.

Strategies are sweeping guidelines concerning the essence of a company's long-term marketing efforts. Tactics are the things companies do to support strategies in the shorter term.
(Moderate; p. 107)

230) What are the characteristics of a viable market segment?

1. The individuals within the segment should be similar, i.e. homogenous.
2. The segment should differ from the population as a whole.
3. The segment must be large enough to be financially viable when targeted by a separate marketing campaign.
4. The segment must be reachable through some type of media or marketing communications method.

(Challenging; p. 109)

231) What are the major consumer market segments?

1. Demographics
2. Psychographics
3. Generations
4. Geographic
5. Geodemographic
6. Benefit
7. Usage

(Moderate; p. 110)

232) What are the methods of segmenting business-to-business markets?

1. Industry
2. Business size
3. Geographic location
4. Product usage
5. Customer value

(Moderate; p. 118)

CHAPTER 5
ADVERTISING MANAGEMENT

True-False Questions

1) Marketing to women over the age of forty is not likely to be profitable.
(False; Easy; p. 130)

2) For women over 40, affluence, self-indulgence, and comfort characterize typical buying habits.
(True; Challenging; p. 131)

3) The message theme is an outline of the key idea(s) that an advertising program is supposed to convey.
(True; Moderate; p. 133)

4) The leverage point is how the design of the ad will attract attention or presents information to the consumer or business viewing the ad.
(False; Moderate; p. 133)

5) An appeal is the key element in the advertisement that taps into, or activates, a consumer's personal value system.
(False; Moderate; p. 133)

6) The executional framework explains how the message in an advertisement will be delivered.
(True; Easy; p. 133)

7) Advertising management is the process of preparing and integrating a company's advertising efforts with the overall IMC message.
(True; Easy; p. 134)

8) Advertising is separate from the traditional promotions mix since it focuses on the end user.
(False; Moderate; p. 134)

9) One important choice in advertising management is between an in-house and an external advertising agency.
(True; Easy; p. 134)

10) Consistency is ordinarily not a major concern in advertising management.
(False; Easy; p. 134)

11) Advertising is a major component of integrated marketing communications.
(True; Easy; p. 134)

12) In business-to-business communications, advertising is often the primary promotion method with the other components of the promotional mix, such as trade promotions, consumer promotions, and personal selling supporting the advertising.
(False; Moderate; p. 134)

13) In the consumer sector, advertising is usually the primary communication vehicle with the other promotional tools (trade promotions, consumer promotions, and personal selling) designed to back the advertising campaign.
(True; Moderate; p. 134)

14) Part of the reasoning for using an in-house advertising department is that internal organization members have a better sense of the company's mission and message.
(True; Moderate; p. 135)

15) One of the disadvantages of an external advertising agency is that the client company can go "stale" in terms of generating new ideas.
(False; Easy; p. 135)

16) An external advertising agency is likely to be more objective than an in-house advertising department.
(True; Easy; p. 135)

17) An external advertising agency is more likely to understand a complex product than an in-house advertising department.
(False; Easy; p. 135)

18) When the majority of a company's advertising budget is spent on media buys, rather than producing the advertisement, the company should be inclined to do the work in-house.
(False; Moderate; p. 136)

19) In terms of the 75/15/10 rule, 75 percent of the money spent on advertising should be spent for media buys.
(True; Moderate; p. 136)

20) In terms of the 75/15/10 rule, the 15 represents the amount of money that is spent on producing the advertisements.
(False; Challenging; p. 136)

21) In terms of the 75/15/10 rule, the 10 represents the amount of money that is spent on creating or designing the ads.
(False; Challenging; p. 136)

22) To be effective in terms of using an external agency, at least 75 percent of the advertising budget should be spent on media buys.
(True; Moderate; p. 136)

23) An external advertising agency is likely to be more creative in designing ads than an in-house department.
(True; Easy; p. 137)

24) A media service company negotiates and purchases media packages, which are also known as media buys.
(True; Easy; p. 137)

25) A boutique agency is one that provides a full range of advertising services.
(False; Moderate; p. 137)

26) The "whole egg theory" was introduced by professors at Texas A & M University.
(False; Challenging; p. 137)

27) The concept of the whole egg theory is to move from selling a client's products to helping a client attain total success in the marketplace.
(True; Moderate; p. 137)

28) The first step in selecting an advertising agency is to set and prioritize goals.
(True; Easy; p. 138)

29) In terms of selecting an advertising agency, requesting client references should occur before the initial list of applicants is screened, since the client list can be used to eliminate agencies where there is a conflict of interest.
(False; Challenging; p. 141)

30) The request for a creative pitch would occur after the list of candidate agencies is reduced to only two or three agencies.
(True; Moderate; p. 141)

31) In terms of selecting an advertising agency, without clearly understood goals, it is virtually impossible to choose an agency because company leaders may not have a clear idea of what they want to accomplish.
(True; Moderate; p. 138)

32) Matching the size of an advertising agency to the size of the client company is typically not a key issue in agency selection.
(False; Easy; p. 138)

33) If an agency has relevant experience in a particular product category, then it will create a conflict of interest.
   (False; Easy; p. 139)

34) If an agency had represented a dine-in restaurant in the past, but no longer has the account, it would be conflict of interest for another dine-in restaurant to hire the agency.
   (False; Challenging; p. 139)

35) One method to measure the creative reputation and capability of an advertising agency is to look at a list of awards the company has received for past campaigns.
   (True; Moderate; p. 139)

36) Winning a variety of advertising awards for creativity assures a company that the agency can be objective in developing a campaign.
   (False; Challenging; p. 140)

37) In selecting an advertising agency, it is important to assess the agency's production capabilities and media purchasing capabilities, even if these services will not be a part of the contract with the agency.
   (False; Moderate; p. 140)

38) Reference requests are not usually made during the selection of an advertising agency, especially for finalist companies.
   (False; Easy; p. 140)

39) Discovering an advertising agency's client retention rate helps reveal how effective the agency has been in working with various clients.
   (True; Easy; p. 140)

40) In terms of selecting an advertising agency, a creative pitch is a formal presentation addressing a specific problem, situation, or set of questions.
   (True; Easy; p. 141)

41) When two or more companies compete for a contract with creative pitches, the process is sometimes called a "shootout."
   (True; Moderate; p. 141)

42) Normally every company that asks to be considered for an advertising campaign will prepare a creative pitch as part of the application.
   (False; Moderate; p. 141)

43) Chemistry is the feeling that an advertising agency and a client company will work well together.
   (True; Easy; p. 141)

44) If a company's marketing manager says, "I have a good feeling about working with this advertising agency," chemistry is probably present.
    (True; Moderate; p. 141)

45) It is important to visit an agency's office if at all possible in order to meet the actual people who will be working on the account.
    (True; Moderate; p. 141)

46) The first ingredient in advertising planning and research is gathering general pre-planning input.
    (True; Easy; p. 142)

47) "Reading up" on a company is part of the first ingredient in advertising planning and research, which is gathering general pre-planning input.
    (True; Moderate; p. 142)

48) During the product-specific research phase of advertising planning and research, an agency asks consumers if there are any problems or difficulties with the product.
    (True; Moderate; p. 142)

49) It is important to spell out the major selling idea that will be used in the ad campaign during the advertising planning and research stage.
    (True; Easy; p. 142)

50) During the advertising planning and research stage, qualitative research can be used to assist the vendor company and its advertising agency to better understand consumers and why the product is purchased.
    (True; Moderate; p. 142)

51) Qualitative advertising research is typically based on statistics.
    (False; Moderate; p. 142)

52) Qualitative advertising research includes using methods from disciplines such as anthropology and sociology.
    (True; Easy; p. 142)

53) Qualitative research using methods from anthropology often includes direct observation of consumer behaviors or activities.
    (True; Moderate; p. 143)

54) Qualitative research using methods from sociology often includes the study of mental value systems and personal drives.
    (False; Moderate; p. 143)

55) An advertising account executive is the key go-between for the advertising agency and the client company.
(True; Easy; p. 143)

56) A stewardship report is an update on the work performed on an advertising campaign and is prepared by the advertising agency.
(True; Moderate; p. 143)

57) An advertising account executive is the person who actually develops and produces the advertisement.
(False; Easy; p. 144)

58) A traffic manager is the person who schedules media for advertising.
(False; Easy; p. 144)

59) Creatives are the people who actually develop and produce advertisements.
(True; Easy; p. 144)

60) The first step in managing an advertising campaign is preparing a creative brief.
(False; Easy; p. 144)

61) The final step in managing an advertising campaign is to select the media that will be used.
(False; Moderate; p. 144)

62) A communication market analysis is the stage in which communication objectives are established.
(False; Moderate; p. 144)

63) By reviewing the communication market analysis, the advertising agency can understand where best to focus the advertising and promotional efforts.
(True; Moderate; p. 146)

64) In reviewing the communication market analysis, it is important to examine the media usage habits of the people in the target market as well as the media being utilized by the competition.
(True; Moderate; p. 146)

65) The second step in advertising planning is to establish the advertising goals, which are derived from the communication objectives.
(True; Moderate; p. 147)

66) Building a strong global brand and corporate image is one of the most important advertising goals.
(True; Moderate; p. 147)

67) Successful brands have two characteristics: top of mind and top choice.
   (True; Easy; p. 147)

68) A top-of-mind brand is the brand that creates the impression that it is the easiest to buy.
   (False; Easy; p. 147)

69) A top-choice brand is the one that the customer ordinarily prefers in his or her evoked set when making a purchase decision.
   (True; Moderate; p. 147)

70) When a consumer is asked which brand of razor he is most inclined to buy, the individual will respond with a top-choice brand.
   (True; Challenging; p. 147)

71) Part of building brand image and brand equity is developing brand awareness.
   (True; Moderate; p. 148)

72) Providing information in an advertisement is most useful in the business-to-business buying situation when members of the buying center are in the information search stage of the purchasing process.
   (True; Challenging; p. 148)

73) Providing information in an advertisement is most useful in the business-to-business sector for low-involvement purchase decisions.
   (False; Challenging; p. 148)

74) Deception and puffery are the same because they both rely on exaggeration.
   (False; Moderate; p. 148)

75) Puffery uses terms such as "greatest," "best," and "finest," and is legal to use in an advertisement.
   (True; Moderate, p. 148)

76) Persuasion is one of the most common advertising goals.
   (True; Moderate; p. 149)

77) Persuasive advertising is used more in the business-to-business sector than in consumer marketing.
   (False; Challenging; p. 149)

78) Persuasive advertising is used more frequently in the broadcast media, such as television and radio, than in print advertising.
   (True; Challenging; p. 149)

79) When advertising is combined with other marketing efforts into a larger, more integrated effort revolving around a theme; it is known as a promotional campaign.
(True; Moderate; p. 149)

80) Advertisements designed to meet the goal of encouraging action are often used in the business-to-business sector.
(True; Moderate; p. 149)

81) A pulsating schedule of advertising distribution involves continuous advertising with bursts of higher intensity during specific periods of the year.
(True; Moderate; p. 150)

82) A flighting approach to advertising distribution is a year-round level budget method.
(False; Easy; p. 150)

83) A continuous campaign approach to advertising distribution involves advertising only during certain times of the year with no advertising between.
(False; Moderate; p. 150)

84) Toy companies and diet food companies have one thing in common: they are likely to use continuous campaign schedules in terms of advertising distribution.
(False; Challenging; p. 150)

85) In terms of the ad agency personnel, the creative brief is typically prepared by the creatives.
(False; Challenging; p. 151)

86) The first step in preparing a creative brief is to identify the target audience of the ad.
(False; Moderate; p. 151)

87) In preparing a creative brief, the only information that is needed in terms of the target audience is demographic characteristics. The creative can research the other information as he or she designs the ad.
(False; Moderate; p. 151)

88) In a creative brief, the message theme is the benefit or promise the advertiser wants to use to reach consumers or businesses.
(True; Easy; p. 152)

89) In terms of the creative brief, legal and mandatory restrictions placed on advertisements are also called constraints.
(True; Easy; p. 153)

90) A "left-brain" advertisement is oriented towards emotion and feelings.
(False; Moderate; p. 153)

91) A "left-brain" advertisement is logical, factual, and rational.
(True; Moderate; p. 153)

92) In terms of the creative brief, the support takes the form of facts that substantiate the message theme.
(True; Moderate; p. 153)

93) A disclaimer warranty describes the shelf life of a product.
(False; Moderate; p. 154)

94) The Surgeon General's warning on a pack of cigarettes is an example of an advertising constraint component of the creative brief.
(True; Challenging; p. 154)

Multiple-Choice Questions

95) The buying power of women over 40 is:
   a. declining
   b. steady
   c. larger than the buying power of women under 40
   d. smaller than the buying power of women under 40
(c; Moderate; p. 130)

96) Women over the age of 40:
   a. have less buying power than women under 40
   b. tend to have a lower level of self-assurance than women under 40
   c. are a key focus for most advertising campaigns directed at females
   d. are inclined to make purchases that reflect affluence, self-indulgence and comfort
(d; Challenging p. 131)

97) The average consumer sees about how many advertisements per day?
   a. 100
   b. 300
   c. 600
   d. 1,000
(c; Challenging; p. 132)

98) A message theme is:
   a. a form of leverage point
   b. the media choices a company makes
   c. the key idea(s) an advertisement conveys
   d. the type of appeal that is used in an advertisement

(c; Easy; p. 133)

99) The key idea or ideas contained in an advertisement are referred to as a(n):
   a. message theme
   b. appeal
   c. executional framework
   d. leverage point

(a; Easy; p. 133)

100)   The element of an advertisement that taps into or activates a person's value system is a(n):
   a. message theme
   b. appeal
   c. executional framework
   d. leverage point

(d; Easy; p. 133)

101)   The leverage point is the:
   a. key idea or ideas that an advertisement is to convey
   b. key element in that advertisement that taps into or activates a consumer's personal value system
   c. design of the advertisement that attracts attention or presents information
   d. theme that explains how the message will be delivered

(b; Moderate; p. 133)

102)   The design of an advertisement that attracts attention or presents information is called the:
   a. message theme
   b. appeal
   c. executional framework
   d. leverage point

(b; Moderate; p. 133)

103)   The device used to deliver a message in an advertisement is the:
   a. message theme
   b. appeal
   c. executional framework
   d. leverage point

(c; Easy; p. 133)

104) An advertising appeal is the:
   a. key idea or ideas that an advertisement is to convey
   b. key element in that advertisement that taps into or activates a consumer's personal value system
   c. design of the advertisement that attracts attention or presents information
   d. theme that explains how the message will be delivered
   (c; Moderate; p. 133)

105) The executional framework is the:
   a. key idea or ideas that an advertisement is to convey
   b. key element in that advertisement that taps into or activates a consumer's personal value system
   c. design of the advertisement that attracts attention or presents information
   d. theme that explains how the message will be delivered in an advertisement
   (d; Easy; p. 133)

106) The process of preparing and integrating a company's advertising efforts with the overall IMC message is the:
   a. message theme
   b. advertising management program
   c. executional framework
   d. communication analysis
   (b; Easy; p. 134)

107) The first step of an advertising management program is to:
   a. review the company's activities in light of advertising management
   b. select an in-house or external advertising agency
   c. develop an advertising campaign management strategy
   d. prepare a creative brief
   (a; Moderate; p. 134)

108) After reviewing the company's activities in light of advertising management, the second step of an advertising management program is to:
   a. choose an advertising agency
   b. deciding to use either an in-house or external advertising agency
   c. develop an advertising campaign management strategy
   d. prepare a creative brief
   (b; Moderate; p. 134)

109) After deciding to use either an in-house or external advertising agency, the third step of an advertising management program is to:
   a. review the company's activities in light of advertising management
   b. select the actual advertising agency
   c. develop an advertising campaign management strategy
   d. prepare a creative brief
   (c; Moderate; p. 134)

110)   After all other activities have been completed, including selecting the agency, the final step of an advertising management program is to:
   a. review the company's activities in light of advertising management
   b. select an in-house or external advertising agency
   c. develop an advertising campaign management strategy
   d. prepare a creative brief
(d; Moderate; p. 134)

111)   A major principle guiding any advertising program should be:
   a. personality
   b. complexity
   c. conversation
   d. consistency
(d; Easy; p. 134)

112)   An advertising program should be:
   a. the basis of the IMC program
   b. one of many promotional efforts
   c. a stand-alone program
   d. the same thing as a public relations program
(b; Easy; p. 134)

113)   In the business-to-business sector, advertising tends to:
   a. support other promotional tools such as personal selling, trade promotions, consumer promotions, direct marketing, and trade shows
   b. be the primary vehicle for communicating to customers
   c. be performed in-house to prevent competitors from learning about the company's products and communication approach
   d. identify key new target markets
(a; Moderate; p. 134)

114)   In the consumer sector, advertising tends to:
   a. support other promotional tools such as personal selling, trade promotions, consumer promotions, direct marketing, and trade shows
   b. be the primary vehicle for communicating to customers
   c. be done in-house to prevent competitors from learning about the company's products and communication approach
   d. be used to support consumer promotions and personal selling efforts
(b; Moderate; p. 134)

115) One disadvantage of an in-house advertising department is:
   a. the ads created may become stale or the staff fails to recognize new opportunities
   b. higher cost because of outsourcing components of the ad process
   c. morale within the marketing department may be lower
   d. greater potential for lawsuits

   (a; Moderate; p. 135)

116) The following are disadvantages of using an in-house advertising department, *except:*
   a. the company can go stale and fail to recognize other promotional or advertising opportunities
   b. the internal department may lack the expertise to carry out all of the necessary functions
   c. the internal department may not have a good understanding of the firm's mission and message
   d. the internal department may lack objectivity in creating advertisements

   (c; Challenging; p. 135)

117) In deciding between an external advertising agency and creating advertisements in-house, each of the following variables should be considered, *except:*
   a. the objectivity factor
   b. the spokesperson factor
   c. the complexity of the product
   d. the creativity issue

   (b; Moderate; p. 135)

118) With regard to the account size in determining whether to use an external agency or perform the work in-house, the following statements are true, *except:*
   a. a small account is not usually attractive to a large agency
   b. if 75% of the money cannot be used to buy media time and space, it is better to do the work in-house
   c. if the agency charges more than 25% of the money to design and create the ads, then the account is too small to use an external agency
   d. a small agency is not a viable choice, even for a small account, because the agency will lack the necessary resources to do the work

   (d; Challenging; p. 136)

119) In terms of the 75/15/10 rule, the 75% represents the:
   a. money spent on media time or space
   b. money spent on ad production
   c. money spent for the creative work
   d. percentage of the work that must be completed before the client can be billed

   (a; Moderate; p. 136)

120)   In terms of the 75/15/10 rule, the 15% represents the:
   a. money spent on media time or space
   b. money spent on ad production
   c. money spent for the creative work
   d. fee for the media planner
(c; Challenging; p. 136)

121)   In terms of the 75/15/10 rule, the 10% represents the:
   a. money spent on media time or space
   b. money spent on ad production
   c. money is spent for the creative work
   d. fee for the media buyer
(b; Moderate; p. 136)

122)   If a company's media budget numbers are 85-10-5 and uses an external ad
agency, this means the company:
   a. is spending too much money on creative work
   b. should continue using an external advertising agency
   c. should discontinue using an external agency and perform the work in-
       house
   d. is spending too much money on media buys
(b; Challenging; p. 136)

123)   In terms of money spent on developing an advertising campaign, a
company should spend at least what percent of the money on buying media time
or space?
   a. 25
   b. 40
   c. 50
   d. 75
(d; Challenging; p. 136)

124)   Which is probably best for creating an advertisement for a complex
product?
   a. an in-house advertising department
   b. an external advertising agency
   c. the public relations department
   d. a media buyer
(a; Moderate; p. 136)

125)   A boutique-type advertising agency:
   a. is the largest form of agency
   b. are designed to handle smaller accounts
   c. serves in-house clients

d. offers one specialized service or works with one type of client

(d; Moderate; p. 137)

126) A media service company:
   a. negotiates contract rates between the agency and the client
   b. negotiates pay rates for creatives and advertising performers
   c. negotiates and purchases media packages
   d. handles direct marketing efforts

(c; Easy; p. 137)

127) Media buys are normally made by:
   a. the creative
   b. the account executive
   c. the traffic manager
   d. a media service company

(d; Easy; p. 137)

128) If a company wanted to use a boutique agency for developing a special contest or sweepstakes event, who should be contacted?
   a. a media service agency
   b. a consumer promotion agency
   c. a direct marketing agency
   d. a trade promotion agency

(b; Challenging; p. 137)

129) If a company received negative press, the marketing department may hire a:
   a. boutique specialty agency
   b. media service company
   c. public relations firm
   d. direct-marketing agency

(c; Easy; p. 137)

130) The "whole egg theory" developed by Young and Rubicam:
   a. heavily utilizes boutique agencies
   b. is only offered to small clients
   c. is designed to help the client achieve total success
   d. is a new type of public relations program

(c; Moderate; p. 137)

131) If a company's leaders decided to use the "whole egg theory," they would:
   a. hire a full-service agency
   b. hire a boutique agency
   c. retain a media service company to buy media time, but do the creative with free lancers
   d. utilize different companies for each aspect of the advertising campaign

(a; Challenging; p. 137)

132)   If a company wanted to make sure in integrated approach is used in marketing communications, then the best approach would be to:
   a. hire a full-service agency
   b. use a boutique agency
   c. use a media service company to buy media time, but do the creative with free lancers
   d. utilize different companies for each aspect of the advertising campaign

(a; Challenging; p. 137)

133)   The first step of selecting an advertising agency is:
   a. set goals
   b. screen initial list of applicants
   c. request client references
   d. select the process to be used and the criteria for selection

(a; Moderate; p. 138)

134)   In selecting an advertising agency, after corporate goals are set, the next step in the process is to:
   a. request a creative pitch
   b. screen initial list of applicants
   c. request client references
   d. select the process to be used and the criteria for selection

(d; Moderate; p. 138)

135)   In selecting an advertising agency, client references should not be requested until each of the following have been completed, *except:*
   a. set goals
   b. screen initial list of applicants
   c. reduce the list to two or three viable candidates
   d. select the process to be used and the criteria for selection

(c; Challenging; p. 138)

136)   In selecting an advertising agency, the request for a creative pitch should occur after:
   a. goals have been set
   b. the initial list of applicants have been screened
   c. the list has been reduced to only two or three viable candidates
   d. the selection process to be used and the criteria for selection have been decided

(c; Challenging; p. 138)

145

137)   In terms of selecting an advertising agency, company leaders at Atco Electronics do not have a clear idea of what want to accomplish and therefore disagree as to what type of agency should be hired. This situation occurred because the company failed to:
   a. develop selection criteria to be used in the ad selection process
   b. set goals before starting their search for an agency
   c. solicit client references before discussing what type of agency they want
   d. ask for a creative pitch
(b; Challenging; p. 138)

138)   The following are important evaluation criteria that should be considered in selecting an advertising agency, *except:*
   a. size of the agency
   b. relevant experience of the agency
   c. governmental regulations
   d. conflicts of interest
(c; Moderate; p. 139)

139)   The following are evaluation criteria that should be considered in selecting an advertising agency, *except:*
   a. creative reputation and capabilities
   b. industry regulations
   c. production capabilities
   d. media purchasing capabilities
(b; Challenging; p. 139)

140)   An agency representing convenience stores that has previously created ads for a grocery stores would have:
   a. relevant experience
   b. a conflict of interest
   c. interpersonal chemistry
   d. company complexity
(a; Challenging; p. 139)

141)   Which situation below would be considered as a conflict of interest in the selection of an advertising agency?
   a. the advertising agency is owned by a larger company
   b. the advertising agency already represents a similar product or company
   c. the advertising agency outsources creative work
   d. the creative works for more than one client
(b; Easy; p. 139)

142)   A conflict of interest would be present if:
   a.   the client company's leaders cannot decide which ad agency to select
   b.   the ad agency already represents a similar product
   c.   the client company employs several former members of the ad agency
   d.   the ad agency employs several former members of the client company
(b; Moderate; p. 139)

143)   One simple method used to judge an advertising agency's creative reputation is to:
   a.   contact the company's competition
   b.   ask for a list of awards the company has won
   c.   conduct a shootout
   d.   review the most recent media buys the agency made
(b; Moderate; p. 139)

144)   Questions that company leaders should ask about an ad agency's production capabilities and media purchasing capabilities include each of the following, *except:*
   a.   Does the agency buy efficiently?
   b.   Is the agency able to negotiate special rates and publication positions?
   c.   Does the agency routinely get "bumped" by higher-paying firms so ads do not run at highly desirable times?
   d.   Does the agency use a media service company to purchase television time?
(d; Challenging; p. 140)

145)   Personal chemistry is a selection factor that should:
   a.   be examined early in the selection process
   b.   never affect the choice, which should only be made rationally
   c.   determine if an in-house agency should be chosen
   d.   be considered in the final stages of selection
(d; Moderate; p. 140)

146)   From the list below, the task that is most likely to be a part of the reference request step in selecting an ad agency is:
   a.   studying past media purchases
   b.   conducting a shootout
   c.   studying the firm's client retention rate
   d.   offering the contract
(c; Moderate; p. 140)

147) Asking two or more advertising companies to make a creative pitch is sometimes called:
    a. studying past media purchases
    b. conducting a shootout
    c. studying the firm's client retention rate
    d. switching the contract
(b; Moderate; p. 141)

148) In terms of an advertising agency selection process, a shootout includes viewing:
    a. goal setting processes
    b. selection criteria
    c. references
    d. creative pitches
(d; Moderate; p. 141)

149) A creative pitch by an advertising agency seeking a new client should:
    a. reveal how the agency would deal with specific issues in preparing a campaign
    b. nearly always be presented by a heavy hitter
    c. be refused because the client company has not clarified its selection criteria
    d. be the first step in the selection process
(a; Challenging; p. 141)

150) In choosing an advertising agency, Lycra asked three different agencies to make a presentation about how each would enhance the unique position of the Lycra brand. Who do people in the advertising industry call this process?
    a. unique selling proposition presentation
    b. shootout
    c. creative exposure
    d. creative presentation
(b; Moderate; p. 141)

151) The member of an advertising agency who focuses on winning contracts, but will not be involved in doing any of the actual work, is sometimes called a:
    a. mind bender
    b. interpersonal expert
    c. heavy hitter
    d. creative pitcher
(c; Moderate; p. 141)

152)   When an advertising agency uses a "heavy hitter" to solicit an account, the agency is utilizing:
   a. the creatives who will actually be working on the account
   b. a corporate executive
   c. all of the personnel who will be working on the account
   d. agency personnel trained to sell their services
(b; Challenging; p. 141)

153)   When an advertising agency "reads up" on a client before developing the advertising campaign, the process is called:
   a. agency selection
   b. general pre-planning input
   c. product-specific research
   d. the major selling idea
(b; Moderate; p. 142)

154)   Discovering if there are problems associated with a given good or service takes place during which component of advertising planning and research?
   a. major selling point
   b. general pre-planning input
   c. product-specific research
   d. quantitative research
(c; Moderate; p. 142)

155)   The "Got milk?" campaign emerged after consumers were deprived of milk for a week. What form of research was used?
   a. product specific
   b. market specific
   c. consumer specific
   d. quantitative
(a; Moderate; p. 142)

156)   Discovering the major selling idea for a good or service is part of which component of advertising planning and research?
   a. agency selection
   b. general pre-planning input
   c. product-specific research
   d. quantitative research
(c; Moderate; p. 142)

157) When conducting qualitative research during advertising planning and research, each of the following perspectives can be used, *except:*
   a. anthropology
   b. sociology
   c. psychology
   d. statistics
(d; Moderate; p. 142)

158) Using anthropological methods for advertising research often includes:
   a. a statistical analysis
   b. a sociological study
   c. direct observation
   d. secondary research
(c; Moderate; p. 143)

159) If Ralph Lauren marketing team is trying to determine if the brand will appeal to a cohort group that is rich, elite, and distinct, which method would reveal such a trend?
   a. product specific research
   b. personal drive analysis
   c. assessment of the major selling idea
   d. a sociological approach assessing social class
(d; Challenging; p. 143)

160) Predicting consumer behavior by concentrating on self-orientation and resources is a(n):
   a. type of statistical analysis
   b. application of the values and life style model (VALS)
   c. personal drive analysis (PDA)
   d. form of secondary research
(b; Challenging; p. 143)

161) Someone who believes he or she is always on the cutting edge of fashion can be identified using which advertising planning and research technique?
   a. product specific research
   b. a major selling idea
   c. the Values and Life Style Model (VALS)
   d. quantitative research
(c; Challenging; p. 143)

162)   Someone who believes he or she expresses individuality with brand choices can be identified using which advertising planning and research technique?
   a. product specific research
   b. a major selling idea
   c. the values and life style model (VALS)
   d. personal drive analysis (PDA)
(d; Challenging; p. 143)

163)   An individual's desire to drink high quality wine as an expression of individuality and taste is discovered using which type of advertising planning and research program?
   a. product specific research
   b. direct observation (anthropology)
   c. mood assessment techniques
   d. a personal drive analysis approach
(d; Challenging; p. 143)

164)   The key go-between for the advertising agency and a client company is usually the:
   a. account executive
   b. creative
   c. media planner
   d. traffic manager
(a; Easy; p. 143)

165)   A stewardship report describes:
   a. how an advertising agency is selected
   b. how the client has developed its advertising budget
   c. the nature of a company's public relations program
   d. the status of an advertising campaign for the client
(d; Moderate; p. 143)

166)   The account executive normally performs all of the following functions, *except:*
   a. helping prepare the creative brief
   b. serves as a liaison between the client and the agency
   c. prepares ad copy
   d. negotiate contracts
(c; Challenging; p. 143)

167) Which individual works closely with the account executive to schedule the various aspects of the agency's work to ensure the work is completed by the target deadline?
   a. creative
   b. traffic manager
   c. media buyer
   d. media planner
(b; Moderate; p. 144)

168) The person who develops and produces the actual advertisement is the:
   a. account executive
   b. creative
   c. media buyer
   d. media planner
(b; Easy; p. 144)

169) Who is in charge of maintaining project history, creating schedules, managing resources, setting up team meetings, prioritizing projects, training new employees about agency processes, setting up new clients, routing proofs, proofreading material, and whatever else needs to be done to ensure deadlines are met?
   a. account executive
   b. creative
   c. traffic manager
   d. media planner
(c; Easy; p. 144)

170) A communications market analysis includes all of the following, *except:*
   a. a competitive analysis
   b. a target market analysis
   c. an economic forecasting analysis
   d. an analysis of customers
(c; Moderate; p. 146)

171) In developing an advertising campaign, studying the media usage habits of the people in the target market should be part of the:
   a. communication market analysis
   b. advertising planning and research
   c. pitch made by the agency candidates
   d. creative brief
(a; Challenging; p. 146)

172)   Finding out that a company's advertisements are viewed negatively by a large portion of its business buyers results from examining during which part of the communications market analysis?
   a. product positioning
   b. competitors
   c. target market
   d. customers
(d; Challenging; p. 146)

173)   Advertising goals are derived from:
   a. communications market analysis
   b. goals in the marketing plan
   c. communication objectives
   d. mission statement of the company
(c; Moderate; p. 147)

174)   The following are examples of advertising goals, *except:*
   a. building brand image
   b. defending against lawsuits
   c. to inform
   d. to persuade
(b; moderate; p. 147)

175)   A top-of-mind brand is:
   a. the company's chief competitor, as identified by a competitive analysis
   b. the brand that comes to mind in a product category when asked to name the first brands a person can think of
   c. the most expensive good or service in a product category
   d. a purchasing alternative when the primary product is not available
(b; Easy; p. 147)

176)   A customer who reports that Lexus is the first car he thinks of in the "luxury automobile" category is describing a:
   a. top-of-mind brand
   b. top-choice brand
   c. quality choice brand
   d. top-of-industry brand
(a; Moderate; p. 147)

177)   When a customer prefers a specific brand, that brand is called:
   a. top-of-mind
   b. top-choice
   c. quality choice
   d. top-of-industry
(b; Easy; p. 147)

178) A customer who buys Coke and Dr. Pepper all the time, and no other brands, holds these two products as:
   a. quality brands
   b. price brands
   c. top-choice brands
   d. continuous choices

(c; Moderate; p. 147)

179) A brand that is both top of mind and top choice reflects:
   a. a high degree of brand parity
   b. a high level of brand equity
   c. brand availability
   d. distinct private branding

(b; Challenging; p. 147)

180) In business-to-business situations, being top of mind or top choice is most important in:
   a. modified rebuy situations
   b. straight rebuy situations
   c. new task purchases
   d. contract review situations

(a; Challenging; p. 148)

181) For a brand to have a high level of brand equity, it must have all of the following, *except:*
   a. high level of brand awareness
   b. top-of-mind status
   c. top choice status
   d. brand parity status

(d; Challenging; p. 148)

182) From the methods listed below, the best method for building brand awareness is:
   a. consumer promotions
   b. advertising
   c. trade promotions
   d. personal selling

(b; Challenging; p. 148)

183) Most of the time, brand equity is developed through:
   a. consumer and trade promotions
   b. public relations and personal selling
   c. advertising and product quality
   d. advertising and consumer promotions

(c; Challenging; p. 148)

184) A Campbell's Soup print advertisement shows a young family enjoying a bowl of soup with the Campbell's name and logo prominently displayed in the ad. No other information or copy is in the ad. The advertising goal of this advertisement is most likely to:
   a. build brand image
   b. inform
   c. persuade
   d. support other marketing efforts
(a; Challenging; p. 148)

185) Providing a retail store's location and operating hours to the public in an advertisement is an example of ad designed to meet the advertising goal to:
   a. build brand image
   b. persuade
   c. encourage action
   d. inform
(d; Challenging; p. 148)

186) An advertisement for an Applebee's restaurant provides information about its location, operating hours and different types of food it offers. The goal of this advertisement is most likely to be:
   a. build brand image
   b. inform
   c. persuade
   d. support other marketing efforts
(b; Challenging; p. 148)

187) Puffery is:
   a. the use of exaggerated claims about a product with an overt attempt to mislead or deceive
   b. the use of exaggerated claims about a product without making an overt attempt to deceive or mislead
   c. illegal in most states in the United States
   d. illegal in the United States, but not most other countries of the world
(b; Moderate; p. 148)

188) Using words such as "greatest," "finest," and "best" in an advertisement is considered:
   a. deceptive advertising
   b. deceptive advertising, but legal
   c. puffery and is legal to use
   d. puffery and is illegal to use
(c; Moderate; p. 148)

189)   Of the following advertising goals, the most common goal is to:
     a. build brand image
     b. inform
     c. persuade
     d. support other marketing efforts
   (c; Challenging; p. 149)

190)   When advertising is combined with other marketing efforts into an integrated effort around a theme, it is called a:
     a. promotional campaign
     b. deception program
     c. persuasion campaign
     d. comparison campaign
   (a; Moderate; p. 149)

191)   A Campbell's Soup advertisement is designed to support the launch of a new type of soup and to tell consumers about a special sweepstakes that is tied into the launch. The advertising goal of this advertisement is most likely to:
     a. encourage action
     b. inform
     c. persuade
     d. support other marketing efforts
   (d; Challenging; p. 149)

192)   When an television advertisement makes a special offer on a piece of luggage, encouraging viewers to call a toll-free number to take advantage of the special, the ad is designed to meet the goal of:
     a. building brand image
     b. informing
     c. persuading
     d. encouraging action
   (d; Challenging; p. 149)

193)   An advertisement by 1st Source Mortgage provides information about a fall special in which a consumer can obtain a free mortgage analysis by calling or e-mailing 1st Source Mortgage. The advertising goal of this advertisement is most likely to:
     a. encouraging action
     b. inform
     c. persuade
     d. support other marketing efforts
   (a; Challenging; p. 148)

194) In terms of the method of distribution of the advertising budget, the following are methods commonly used, *except:*
   a. pulsating
   b. flighting
   c. continuous campaign
   d. sporadic
(d; Easy; p. 150)

195) A pulsating schedule of advertising:
   a. involves continuous advertising with bursts of higher intensity
   b. involves advertising during certain times of the year with no advertising at other times
   c. is level throughout the year
   d. involves alternating levels of advertising from high to low amount
(a; Moderate; p. 150)

196) A flighting schedule of advertising:
   a. involves continuous advertising with bursts of higher intensity
   b. involves advertising during certain times of the year with no advertising at other times
   c. is level throughout the year
   d. involves alternating levels of advertising from high to low amount
(b; Moderate; p. 150)

197) A continuous campaign schedule of advertising:
   a. involves continuous advertising with bursts of higher intensity
   b. involves advertising during certain times of the year with no advertising at other times
   c. is level throughout the year
   d. involves alternating levels of advertising from high to low amount
(a; Moderate; p. 150)

198) In terms of advertising allocation, a pulsating schedule is best for products that have:
   a. steady sales throughout the year
   b. peak seasons but do sell throughout the entire year
   c. peak seasons at certain times in the year and are not purchased at all during other times of the year
   d. a high level of fluctuating demand
(b; Moderate; p. 150)

199)   In terms of advertising allocation, a flighting schedule is best for products that have:
   a.   steady sales throughout the year
   b.   peak seasons but do sell throughout the entire year
   c.   peak seasons at certain times in the year and are not purchased at all during other times of the year
   d.   a high level of fluctuating demand
(c; Challenging; p. 150)

200)   In terms of advertising allocation, a continuous campaign schedule is best for products that have:
   a.   steady sales throughout the year
   b.   peak seasons but do sell throughout the entire year
   c.   peak seasons at certain times in the year and are not purchased at all during other times of the year
   d.   a high level of fluctuating demand
(a; Moderate; p. 150)

201)   In terms of the communications budget schedule, diet services, such as Jenny Craig and Weight Watchers, would ordinarily use:
   a.   continuous advertising schedules
   b.   a pulsating schedule
   c.   a derivative advertising schedule
   d.   a flighting schedule
(b; Challenging; p. 150)

202)   In terms of advertising budget distribution, a flighting campaign is best suited to products with:
   a.   one key peak season and an off season
   b.   a series of small seasons and no off seasons
   c.   a series of customers who buy at different times during the year
   d.   services
(a; Moderate; p. 150)

203)   Which company is most likely going to use a continuous campaign schedule of advertising?
   a.   a lawn mower manufacturer
   b.   a Christmas decoration supplier
   c.   a beer distributor
   d.   a space heater manufacturer
(c; Challenging; p. 150)

204) The following are components of a creative brief, *except:*
    a. stating which media will be used in the campaign
    b. the objective of the campaign
    c. the target market for the campaign
    d. outlining the message theme
(a; Moderate; p. 151)

205) A creative brief may include all of the following, *except:*
    a. an objective of building brand image
    b. specifying the target audience
    c. describing the public relations program
    d. a clear message theme
(c; Moderate; p. 151)

206) In terms of the advertising agency, the creative brief is typically prepared by the:
    a. traffic manager
    b. brand manager
    c. creative
    d. account executive
(d; Challenging; p. 151)

207) The first step in preparing a creative brief is to identify the:
    a. target audience
    b. support
    c. objective
    d. message theme
(c; Moderate; p. 151)

208) For a creative brief, the target audience information should contain:
    a. only basic demographic information, such as gender and age
    b. information about the users of a particular product
    c. not only demographic information, but also psychographic information and any other information that will help the creative better understand the target audience
    d. past purchase behavior of every company or consumer that has purchased the product in addition to the demographic information
(c; Challenging; p. 152)

209) In the creative brief, the message theme is the:
    a. rationale behind a unique selling point
    b. benefit or promise the advertiser wants to convey
    c. written or verbal component of the ad
    d. information provided in the ad to support the key idea
(b; Moderate; p. 152)

210)   A "left-brain" advertisement is:
      a. oriented towards the logical, rational side of the brain
      b. oriented towards the emotional or feeling side of the brain
      c. used primarily for consumer advertisements
      d. used with pulsating distribution schedules
   (a; Moderate; p. 153)

211)   A "right-brain" advertisement is:
      a. oriented towards the logical, rational side of the brain
      b. oriented towards the emotional or feeling side of the brain
      c. used primarily for business-to-business advertisements
      d. used with pulsating distribution schedules
   (b; Moderate; p. 153)

212)   The advertising support component of the creative brief includes:
      a. media selection and media buys
      b. the creative brief's constraint component
      c. the nature of the advertising appeal
      d. the facts which substantiate a unique selling point
   (d; Easy; p. 153)

213)   In terms of the creative brief, an endorsement by eight out of 10 doctors recommending a product is a form of:
      a. disclaimer
      b. message theme
      c. support
      d. constraint
   (c; Challenging; p. 153)

214)   Which product is most likely to include a disclaimer warranty?
      a. medicine
      b. shirt
      c. hammer
      d. scotch tape
   (a; Moderate; p. 154)

215)   Which product is least likely to require a disclaimer warranty?
      a. automobile
      b. airline travel
      c. athletic socks
      d. chewing tobacco
   (d; Moderate; p. 154)

216) A disclaimer warranty typically specifies each of the following, *except:*
   a. the conditions under which a warranty will be honored
   b. statements about past legal actions regarding the product
   c. potential hazards associated with products
   d. the terms of financing agreements, bonuses, and discounts

(b; Moderate; p. 154)

217) For a creative brief, constraints include all of the following, *except:*
   a. left-brained appeals
   b. disclaimers
   c. copyright registrations
   d. trademarks

(a; Challenging; p. 154)

Short-Answer Questions

218) What is a message theme? What does it reflect?

A message theme is an outline of the key idea(s) that the advertising program is supposed to convey. It should reflect the overall IMC theme.
(Easy; p. 133)

219) Name and describe the five most common decision variables in the selection of an in-house versus external advertising agency.

   1. The size of the account, which should match the client to the agency.
   2. The money that can be spent on media, which should be 75% of the budget.
   3. The objectivity factor, recognizing that an agency can be more objective.
   4. The complexity of a product, where more complex products are better understood internally.
   5. The creativity issue, agencies are usually more creative in their approach.

(Challenging; p. 136)

220) Name and describe other types of agencies that serve client firms, besides advertising agencies.

Media service companies negotiate and purchase media packages or media buys. Direct marketing agencies handle direct marketing campaigns. Sales or trade promotions companies provide assistance in creating attention-getting mechanisms. Public relations firms help companies develop positive images and deal with negative publicity.

(Moderate; p. 137)

221)   Name the steps involved in selecting an advertising agency.

1.	Set goals
2.	Select criteria
3.	Request references
4.	View oral and written presentations
5.	Meet key personnel
6.	Make the selection and finalize the contract
7.	Notify all parties

(Moderate; p. 138)

222)   What roles do advertising account executives play in developing campaigns?

The advertising account executive is the key go-between for the agency and the client company. The executive solicits the account, finalizes the details of the contract, works with the creative department that will prepare the campaign, and helps the client company refine and define its major message.
(Moderate; p. 143)

223)   Describe the work of the creative in creating an advertising campaign.

Creatives are the persons who actually develop and produce advertisements.
(Easy, p. 144)

224)   Name the steps of advertising campaign management.

1.Review the communications market analysis.
2. Establish advertising objectives consistent with those developed in a Promotions Opportunity Analysis program.
3.Review the advertising budget.
4.Select the media in conjunction with the advertising agency.
5.Review the information with the advertising creative in the creative brief.
(Challenging; p. 144)

225)   Discuss the difference between deception and puffery.

Puffery is the use of an exaggerated claim about a product without making an overt attempt to deceive or mislead. A deceptive advertisement gives a typical person a false impression or presents false information that results in a favorable

attitude towards the product and the purchase or intent to purchase the product being advertised.
(Moderate: p. 148)

226)   Name the elements of a creative brief.

- The objective
- The target audience
- The message theme
- The support
- The constraints

(Moderate; p. 151)

227)   For the creative brief, name the most common objectives of an advertisement.

- Increase brand awareness
- Build brand image
- Increase customer traffic
- Increase retailer or wholesaler orders
- Increase inquiries from end-users and channel members
- Provide information

(Challenging; p. 151)

CHAPTER 6
ADVERTISING DESIGN
THEORETICAL FRAMEWORKS AND TYPES OF APPEALS

True-False Questions

1)   White space is used effectively in every print advertisement.
        (False; Easy; p. 162)

2)   Creatives know that white space is a crucial ingredient in an inviting, easy to read ad.
        (True; Easy; p. 162)

3)   In magazine ads, white space is used, but does not necessarily need to frame the ad because the page is already differentiated from the one next to it.
        (True; Challenging; p. 162)

4)   The secret to effective use of color is to make sure it matches the product and current market trends.
        (True; Moderate; p. 163)

5)   The same base colors have been consistently popular since the 1980s.
        (False; Easy; p. 163)

6)   A leverage point moves the consumer from understanding a product's benefits to linking those benefits with personal values.
        (True; Easy; p. 165)

7)   There is a sequential set of steps that leads to a purchase, according to the hierarchy of effects model.
        (True; Easy; p. 165)

8)   The first stage in the hierarchy of effects model is awareness.
        (True; Easy; p. 165)

9)   The second stage in the hierarchy of effects model is awareness, which follows liking.
        (False; Moderate; p. 165)

10)   The third stage in the hierarchy of effects model is liking, which follows awareness.
        (True; Moderate; p. 165)

11) The fourth stage in the hierarchy of effects model is preference, which follows awareness and liking.
    (True; Moderate; p. 166)

12) The final stage in the hierarchy of effects model is the actual purchase.
    (True; Moderate; p. 166)

13) The final stage in the hierarchy of effects model is liking and/or preference.
    (False; Moderate; p. 166)

14) A shopper who sees an item in a store, becomes intrigued, asks for information, and then makes a purchase is following the sequence of the hierarchy of effects model.
    (True; Moderate; p. 166)

15) One criticism of the hierarchy of effects model is that when making purchases, consumers and businesses do not always follow the six steps in a sequential order.
    (True; Moderate; p. 166)

16) The major benefit of the hierarchy of effects model is that it is one method to identify the typical steps consumers and businesses take when making purchases.
    (True; Moderate; p. 166)

17) To achieve brand loyalty, advertisers must achieve all six stages of the hierarchy of effects model.
    (True; Challenging; p. 166)

18) The attitude sequence of cognitive → affective → conative is based on the hierarchy of effects model sequence.
    (True; Challenging; p. 166)

19) Based on the hierarchy of effects model, affective-oriented advertisements are superior in developing liking, preference, and conviction for a product.
    (True; Challenging; p. 166)

20) Based on the hierarchy of effects model, cognitive-oriented advertisements are superior in developing brand awareness, brand knowledge, and brand preference.
    (False; Challenging; p. 166)

21) Based on the hierarchy of effects model, conative-oriented advertisements are superior in facilitating product purchases and other consumer actions.
    (True; Challenging; p. 167)

22) In a means-ends chain, the message should be the means that leads the consumer to a desired end state.
    (True; Moderate; p. 167)

23) MECCAS stand for Means-End Conceptualization of Components of Advertising Strategy.
(True; Moderate; p. 167)

24) A means-end chain stresses the linkage between a product's attributes and its price.
(False; Easy; p. 167)

25) Means-end theory is the basis of the MECCAS approach to advertising.
(True; Easy; p. 167)

26) Executional frameworks are a key part of a MECCAS model.
(True; Moderate; p. 167)

27) Personal values are not part of a MECCAS model but are part of a means-ends chain.
(False; Moderate; p. 167)

28) Both the hierarchy of effects model and the means-end chain model are associated with the use of a leverage point.
(True; Moderate; p. 168)

29) The leverage point in an advertisement is the message or concept that links the product's attributes and benefits to the consumer end-state values.
(True; Moderate; p. 168)

30) Creatives spend considerable time designing ads with powerful leverage points.
(True; Moderate; p. 169)

31) A leverage point is associated with an attitudinal change, especially when the sequence used is cognitive--affective--conative.
(True; Challenging; p. 169)

32) Visual images tend to be more difficult to remember than verbal copy.
(False; Moderate; p. 169)

33) Visual elements in an advertisement are stored in the brain as both pictures and words.
(True; Moderate; p. 169)

34) A message is more likely to be effective when it has both visual and verbal elements, since these components will be dual-coded into the person's memory.
(True; Moderate; p. 170)

35) Verbal images are usually stored in both the left and right sides of the brain, while visual elements tend to be stored in the left side of the brain only.
   (False; Challenging; p. 170)

36) Abstract pictures have a higher level of recall than do concrete pictures because of the dual-coding process whereby the image is stored in the brain as both a visual and a verbal representation.
   (False; Challenging; p. 170)

37) Ads with concrete images tend to lead to more favorable attitudes than ads with no pictures or abstract pictures.
   (True; Challenging; p. 170)

38) In terms of a radio ad that does not have a visual component, if consumers can see the image created by the ad in their minds, the effect may be greater than seeing an actual visual portrayal.
   (True; Challenging; p. 170)

39) *Visual esperanto* is the development of an image that readily translates across cultures, but only with certain languages, such as Spanish.
   (False; Moderate; p. 170)

40) *Visual esperanto* advertising recognizes that visual images are more powerful than verbal descriptions.
   (True; Moderate; p. 170)

41) The most difficult aspect of creating *visual esperanto* is finding the right verbal message to transcend across various cultures.
   (False; Moderate; p. 170)

42) In the past, creatives designing business-to-business advertisements relied heavily on the verbal element rather than on visuals. In recent years, there has been a shift to using stronger visual elements in b-to-b advertisements.
   (True; Challenging; p. 170)

43) The particular type of appeal that should be used in an advertisement should be based on a review of the creative brief, the objective of the advertisement, and the means-end chain to be conveyed.
   (True; Moderate; p. 171)

44) Using a fear appeal in an advertisement increases both the viewer's interest in the ad and the persuasiveness of the ad.
   (True; Challenging; p. 171)

45) Fear is an ineffective form of advertising appeal that has been largely abandoned.
   (False; Easy; p. 171)

46) In using a fear appeal, severity is the degree of potential physical, social, or psychological harm.
    (True; Moderate; p. 171)

47) In using a fear appeal, vulnerability is the likelihood the probability that the consequence will occur.
    (True; Moderate; p. 171)

48) Severity and vulnerability are key elements in rational advertisements.
    (False; Moderate; p. 171)

49) An advertisement using a fear appeal that discusses how good a person will feel about losing weight is an example of highlighting extrinsic rewards.
    (False; Challenging; p. 172)

50) In using a fear appeal, an advertisement designed to convince viewers that if they do not use a particular brand of deodorant they will be social outcasts is an example of addressing the severity of the negative consequence.
    (True; Challenging; p. 172)

51) In using a fear appeal, self-efficacy deals with the concept that the viewer believes he or she can take the required action necessary to prevent the negative consequences.
    (True; Moderate; p. 172)

52) Low levels of fear in an ad may not create feelings of severity or vulnerability.
    (True; Challenging; p. 172)

53) A fear level that is too high is impossible to create, because viewers have become immune to fear tactics in advertising.
    (False; Challenging; p. 172)

54) Humor is a rarely-used form of advertising appeal.
    (False; Easy; p. 172)

55) Humor has proven to be one of the best appeals for cutting through advertising clutter.
    (True; Easy; p. 172)

56) In the Clio Awards for radio ads, ads using a sex appeal are normally the most likely to win.
    (False; Challenging; p. 173)

57) To be successful, humor used in ads should be connected directly to the product's benefits.
    (True; Challenging; p. 174)

58) When humor in an ad is remembered, the product or brand is almost always easily recalled.
(False; Challenging; p. 174)

59) Sarcastic humor is an effective advertising appeal, especially with older consumers.
(False; Moderate; p. 174)

60) While some evidence exists that humor may be universal, other research indicates that particular executions of humor appeals may not be universal and that humor is often based in one's culture.
(True; Challenging; p. 174)

61) Although using sex in advertising no longer sells the way it used to and no longer has the shock value it had in the past, advertising in the United States and other countries contain more visual sexual themes than ever before.
(True; Challenging; p. 175)

62) Truly subliminal sexual messages are highly effective advertising techniques.
(False; Easy; p. 175)

63) Nudity and partial nudity in advertisements are most effective when the product has some form of sexual connotation.
(True; Easy; p. 176)

64) Using overt sexuality in ads for products that are sexually-oriented is normally accepted, but it often become controversial when used for other types of products.
(True; Moderate; p. 176)

65) A major ethical issue that has risen from using sex in advertising is the concern over the use of nudity and sexuality featuring children and teenagers.
(True; Easy; p. 177)

66) Sexually suggestive ads tend to work well with personal products such as perfume or cologne.
(True; Easy; p. 177)

67) Women tend to respond more favorably to the use of overt sexuality in advertisements than they do to the use of sensuality.
(False; Easy; p. 177)

68) Sex appeals and nudity tend to increase attention to advertisements, but only for males.
(False; Easy; p. 177)

69) Although sexually-oriented ads attract attention, brand recall for ads using a sex appeal is lower than ads using some other type of appeal.
(True; Challenging; p. 177)

70) Controversial sexual ads are interesting to viewers, but sometimes fail to transmit key information that will be recalled.
(True; Moderate; p. 178)

71) Advertisements using overt sexual stimuli or containing nudity produce higher levels of physiological arousal responses in males, but not for females.
(False; Challenging; p. 178)

72) The cognitive impression made on viewers of a sexually-oriented ad depends on whether the viewer feels the advertisement is pleasant or offensive.
(True; Challenging; p. 178)

73) A decorative model is a person who adorns a product as a sexual or attractive stimulus, but has nothing to actually do with the product.
(True; Easy; p. 178)

74) In determining the level of sex appeal to use in an advertisement, it is important to consider society's view and level of acceptance at the time the ad is to run.
(True; Moderate; p. 178)

75) Just as economies go through cycles, attitudes towards sex in advertising experiences acceptance changes.
(True; Moderate; p. 178)

76) Many researchers believe that society is becoming more liberal and that youth are returning to more liberal open views of sex.
(False; Challenging; p. 179)

77) Religion, cultures, and value systems determine the level of nudity, sexual references, and gender-specific issues that are permitted in sexually-oriented advertising in a country.
(True; Moderate; p. 179)

78) In France, humor and sexuality are often used together in advertising.
(False; Challenging; p. 180)

79) In many Middle East countries, sex and gender issues are taboo subjects.
(True; Moderate; p. 180)

80) One major criticism of sexually-based advertising is that it perpetuates dissatisfaction with one's body. This is true for both males and females.
(True; Challenging; p. 180)

81) In Saudi Arabia and Malaysia, women used in an advertisement must be shown in a family setting and they cannot be depicted as being carefree or desirable to the opposite sex.
(True; Challenging; p. 181)

82) While a musical appeal is very good at gaining a viewer's attention, it often decreases the retention of information in the ad.
(False; Challenging; p. 181)

83) In terms of music used in advertisements, the most common method is to use a song that has already been written or a jingle that already exists.
(False; Moderate; p. 182)

84) The primary benefit of using a well-known song in a musical appeal is that consumers have already developed an affinity for a song, which normally is then transferred to the product or brand.
(True; Moderate; p. 182)

85) Brand awareness, brand equity, and brand loyalty are easier to develop when consumers are already familiar with the music used in an advertisement than when a new song, music, or jingle is written.
(True; Moderate; p. 182)

86) Musical artists in the United Kingdom are positive about using their songs in advertisements because they believe that using the songs will capture the kind of attention that will lead radio disc jockeys to play the song on the air.
(True; Challenging; p. 183)

87) Rational appeals are most effective when consumers have high levels of involvement and are willing to pay attention to the ad.
(True; Moderate; p. 183)

88) A rational appeal is closely tied to the stages of visual and verbal imagining, moving viewers from the cognitive to the conative component of attitude.
(False; Challenging; p. 183)

89) Print media offer the best outlets for rational appeals.
(True; Moderate; p. 183)

90) Rational appeals are superior to other appeals in developing and changing attitudes and establishing brand beliefs when a consumer has interest in a product or brand.
(True; Challenging; p. 184)

91) Emotional appeals are designed to capture a viewer's attention and foster an attachment between the consumer and the brand.
    (True; Challenging; p. 184)

92) Most creatives view emotional advertising as the key to developing brand loyalty.
    (True; Challenging; p. 184)

93) Visual and peripheral cues are important in developing effective emotional appeals.
    (True; Challenging; p. 184)

94) Emotional appeals are not useful for business-to-business advertisements because they do not incorporate cognitive elements.
    (False; Challenging; p. 185)

95) The underlying principle for using more emotional appeals in b-to-b advertising is that emotions can be a part of every type of decision, even in the b-to-b environment.
    (True; Moderate; p. 186)

96) Scarcity appeals are designed to build brand awareness and a positive attitude towards the brand.
    (False; Moderate; p. 186)

97) The promise of a benefit is normally part of an advertisement's headline.
    (True; Moderate; p. 187)

98) An advertisement's headline is usually the same as the ads' tag line.
    (False; Moderate; p. 188)

99) Amplification is an advertisement's body or text.
    (True; Moderate; p. 188)

Multiple-Choice Questions

100) White space in an ad is:
    a) not used by most companies
    b) rejected by most magazine publishers
    c) the absence of copy in a printed text
    d) the opposite of a mostly subliminal ad
    (c; Easy; p. 162)

101) The use of white space in an ad may be:
    a) a unique method for overcoming clutter
    b) rejected by most magazine publishers
    c) similar to a "cluttered" ad, in terms of attracting attention
    d) the opposite of a mostly subliminal ad
(a; Easy; p. 162)

102) The use of color in advertising is:
    a) unaffected by changes in consumer preferences
    b) largely irrelevant because most consumers ignore ads
    c) designed to attract attention and build favorable feelings
    d) declining due to the costs of four-color printing
(c; Easy; p. 163)

103) Over the years, certain colors were more common. In the early 2000s, the most common colors were:
    a) mauve, dusty teal, and blue
    b) jewel tones such as ruby red, sapphire, and emerald
    c) natural colors including green, gold, and umber
    d) optimistic colors such as red, yellow, and orange
(d; Challenging; p. 163)

104) The popular colors in the early 2000s were red, yellow, and orange, which would be considered:
    a) jewel tones
    b) natural colors
    c) optimistic colors
    d) cool, professional colors
(c; Moderate; p. 163)

105) The creative brief directs the work of which individual in developing advertisements?
    a) media planner
    b) creative
    c) account executive
    d) traffic manager
(b; Easy; p. 165)

106) What moves a consumer from understanding a product's benefits to linking those benefits with personal values is called:
    a) awareness
    b) liking
    c) preference
    d) a leverage point
(d; Easy; p. 165)

107) A leverage point is the feature of the ad that moves the viewer from understanding the product's benefits to linking those benefits with:
   a) a liking for the product
   b) personal values
   c) the visual element into both a mental picture and words
   d) some type of action or change in attitude
(b; Moderate; p. 165)

108) The first step in a purchase decision according to the hierarchy of effects model is:
   a) awareness
   b) liking
   c) preference
   d) conviction
(a; Easy; p. 165)

109) The second step in a purchase decision, which follows awareness in the hierarchy of effects model, is:
   a) recognition
   b) liking
   c) preference
   d) knowledge
(d; Moderate; p. 165)

110) The third step in a purchase decision, which follows the knowledge stage in the hierarchy of effects model, is:
   a) awareness
   b) liking
   c) preference
   d) conviction
(b; Moderate; p. 165)

111) The fifth step in a purchase decision, which follows both liking and preference in the hierarchy of effects model, is:
   a) the actual purchase
   b) recognition
   c) knowledge
   d) conviction
(d; Moderate; p. 166)

112) The final step of the hierarchy of effects model is:
   a) the actual purchase
   b) liking
   c) preference
   d) conviction
(a; Easy; p. 166)

113) In the hierarchy of effects model, preference for a particular product only occurs after each of the following occurs, *except:*
    a) awareness
    b) liking
    c) knowledge
    d) conviction
    (d; Moderate; p. 166)

114) According to the hierarchy of effects model, before Sandra will develop a preference for K-Swiss shoes, she must first:
    a) have a knowledge of K-Swiss shoes and also must like the K-Swiss brand
    b) have a conviction that the K-Swiss brand is superior to other brands
    c) have a knowledge of the K-Swiss shoes and belief it is the best
    d) be aware of the K-Swiss brand and develop a conviction about the brand
    (a; Moderate; p. 166)

115) In terms of the hierarchy of effects model, to obtain brand loyalty:
    a) all six steps must be present
    b) knowledge and preference is essential, the other steps are not
    c) liking, preference, and conviction are essential, the other steps are not
    d) awareness, knowledge, and conviction are essential, the other steps are not
    (a; Moderate; p. 166)

116) The sequence which matches the typical steps in the hierarchy of effects model is:
    a) cognitive-affective-conative
    b) affective-conative-cognitive
    c) liking-decision-discovery
    d) discovery-liking-decision
    (a; Moderate; p. 166)

117) The hierarchy of effects model:
    a) only works in the correct sequence of the model
    b) is designed to build recall more than an actual purchase decision
    c) clarifies the advertising approach to use by showing what to emphasize during each stage of the model
    d) leads to impulse buying decisions if applied correctly
    (c; Challenging; p. 166)

118) The cognitive component of attitude matches the hierarchy of effects model's components of:
    a) awareness and knowledge
    b) liking, preference, and conviction
    c) conviction and action
    d) the actual purchase
    (a; Moderate; p. 166)

119) The affective component of attitude matches the hierarchy of effects model's components of:
   a) awareness and knowledge
   b) liking, preference, and conviction
   c) conviction and action
   d) the actual purchase
(b; Moderate; p. 166)

120) The conative component of attitude matches the hierarchy of effects model's element of:
   a) knowledge
   b) preference
   c) conviction
   d) the actual purchase
(d; Moderate; p. 166)

121) In an advertisement for Curves for Women, consumers are encouraged to "join now" by offering them the rest of the summer free. This portion of the ad corresponds to which step in the hierarchy of effects model?
   a) awareness
   b) knowledge
   c) conviction
   d) the actual purchase
(d; Challenging; p. 166)

122) In an advertisement for Curves for Women, consumers are encouraged to "join now" by offering them the rest of the summer free. This statement in the ad corresponds to which component of an attitude?
   a) cognitive
   b) affective
   c) conative
   d) verbal
(c; Challenging; p. 166)

123) The means-ends chain approach suggests that an advertisement should contain a message or means that:
   a) leads the consumer to a desired end state
   b) changes a consumer's attitude
   c) modifies a consumer's beliefs
   d) stimulates some type of behavior
(a; Moderate; p. 167)

124) In a means-ends chain, end states include:
   a) the components of attitude
   b) personal values
   c) the purchase of a product
   d) either a change in beliefs or a change in attitude
(b; Moderate; p. 167)

125) A means-ends chain is the basis for the:
   a) hierarchy of effects model
   b) MECCAS model
   c) visual and verbal cue consistency approach
   d) components of attitudes
(b; Easy; p. 167)

126) The theory that emphasizes leverage points and personal values is:
   a) hierarchy of effects
   b) MECCAS
   c) visual and verbal cues
   d) conative and cognitive models
(b; Moderate; p. 167)

127) In the means-ends chain for milk, the calcium content of milk leads to healthier bones, which leads to a display of wisdom and a comfortable life free of osteoporosis. The healthier bones component of the means-ends chain is the:
   a) product attribute
   b) consumer benefit
   c) leverage point
   d) personal value
(b; Challenging; p. 167)

128) In the means-ends chain for milk, the calcium content of milk leads to healthier bones, which leads to a display of wisdom and a comfortable life free of osteoporosis. The fact that milk has calcium represents which component of the means-ends chain?
   a) product attribute
   b) consumer benefit
   c) leverage point
   d) personal value
(a; Challenging; p. 167)

129) In the means-ends chain for milk, the calcium content of milk leads to healthier bones, which leads to a display of wisdom and a comfortable life free of osteoporosis. The display of wisdom and a comfortable life component of the means-ends chain is the:
   a) product attribute
   b) consumer benefit
   c) leverage point
   d) personal value
(d; Challenging; p. 167)

130) To construct a quality leverage point, the creative needs to build a pathway that connects a:
   a) product attribute to the product benefit
   b) product attribute to the potential buyer's value system
   c) product benefit to the potential buyer's value system
   d) personal value to the potential buyer's value system
(b; Moderate; p. 168)

131) In an advertisement, which part is the plot or scenario that used to convey a message?
   a) leverage point
   b) product benefit
   c) executional framework
   d) personal value
(c; Easy; p. 169)

132) Visual elements of an advertisement are stored in the brain as:
   a) forms of verbal cues
   b) images or pictures
   c) abstractions
   d) both pictures and words
(d; Moderate; p. 169)

133) Each of the following statements about the visual element in ads is true, *except:*
   a) visual elements are stored only in the left side of the brain
   b) visual elements tend to be more easily remembered than verbal copy
   c) visual elements are stored in the brain as both pictures and words
   d) visual images often lead to more favorable attitudes toward both the advertisement and the brand
(a; Challenging; p. 169)

134) Visual elements of an advertisement are stored in:
   a) the left side of the brain
   b) the right side of the brain
   c) both sides of the brain
   d) the left side of the brain if the visual is abstract and right side if the visual is concrete
(c; Moderate; p. 170)

135) In terms of the visual element of an advertisement, an abstract image has a:
   a) higher level of recall than a concrete image
   b) lower level of recall than a concrete image
   c) greater impact on the affective component of attitude than a concrete image
   d) greater impact on the cognitive component of attitude than on the affective component
(b; Challenging, p. 170)

136) In terms of the visual element of an advertisement, a concrete image has a:
   a) higher level of recall than an abstract image
   b) lower level of recall than an abstract image
   c) lesser impact on the affective component of attitude than an abstract image
   d) lesser impact on the cognitive component of attitude than on the affective component
(a; Challenging, p. 170)

137) In terms of a radio advertisement, if consumers can see the image in the mind, then the effect is:
   a) greater than if the consumer could see the actual visual
   b) greater only if the image is concrete
   c) greater only if the image is abstract
   d) greater than an ad with an abstract image, but less effective than an ad with a concrete image
(a; Moderate; p. 170)

138) *Visual esperanto* is:
   a) an application of the hierarchy of effects model
   b) a universal language for global advertising
   c) a technique for Spanish-speaking advertisers and consumers
   d) the application of a rational leverage point
(b; Easy; p. 170)

139) Which is an example of *visual esperanto*?
    a) showing a shared family moment
    b) using a decorative model
    c) tailoring ad copy to a particular region
    d) showing the Rocky Mountains
(a; Moderate; p. 170)

140) Which is an example of *visual esperanto*?
    a) a photo of a Saturn automobile
    b) a child enjoying a snack
    c) a description of an office machine
    d) a decorative model
(b; Challenging; p. 170)

141) The key to creating a successful *visual esperanto* is creating something that transcends cultures, through a(n):
    a) effective verbal message
    b) brand name
    c) visual image
    d) leverage point
(c; Moderate; p. 170)

142) The most difficult task for a creative in developing an advertisement with *visual esperanto* is finding:
    a) the right tagline to use
    b) the right words
    c) the right colors
    d) the right image
(d; Moderate; p. 170)

143) In the past, creatives designing business-to-business ads relied heavily on:
    a) a blend of visual and verbal elements
    b) the visual component of the ad
    c) the verbal component of the ad
    d) the leverage point and terminal values
(c; Challenging; p. 170)

144) In recent years, more business-to-business advertisements have incorporated:
    a) stronger verbal elements to persuade business buyers
    b) stronger visual elements to heighten the emotional aspect of making a purchase
    c) leverage points to move business buyers from knowledge to purchases
    d) more rational appeals to create stronger affinities for particular brands
(b; Challenging; p. 170)

145) The following are types of appeals that can be used in designing ads, *except*:
   a) fantasy
   b) fear
   c) humor
   d) sex
(a; Easy; p. 171)

146) The following are types of appeals that can be used in designing ads, *except:*
   a) music
   b) cognitive
   c) rationality
   d) emotion
(b; Easy; p. 71)

147) Although almost any type of appeal can be used to create an advertisement, it is the key responsibility of the marketer to make sure, to whatever degree possible, that the appeal is the right choice for the:
   a) advertising agency and creative that will be working on the ad
   b) product, media planner, and media buyer
   c) brand and the target audience
   d) account executive and creative
(c; Challenging; p. 171)

148) In a fear appeal, showing the potential for a devastating injury when seat belts are not used is an example of:
   a) cognition
   b) severity
   c) vulnerability
   d) self-efficacy
(b; Moderate; p. 171)

149) In the business-to-business advertisement for Service Metrics where the man is blindfolded and about ready to step into a manhole, the manhole illustrates which component of the behavioral response model?
   a) severity
   b) vulnerability
   c) response cost
   d) negative consequence
(b; Challenging; p. 172)

150) Which level of fear is most likely to succeed in an advertisement?
   a) a low, non-threatening level
   b) a moderate level
   c) high levels
   d) it's not the level of fear that matters, it's the type
(b; Easy; p. 172)

151) The appeal that has proven to be one of the best for cutting through clutter is:
   a) fear
   b) humor
   c) emotions
   d) music
(b; Moderate; p. 172)

152) In terms of a fear approach, one reason teenagers who smoke do not quit is because they are afraid they will lose their friends. The social aspect of their lives is more important than the health aspects. In their minds, losing their friends is which component of the behavioral response model?
   a) intrinsic reward
   b) severity
   c) vulnerability
   d) response cost
(d; Challenging; p. 173)

153) According to the behavioral response model, an example of intrinsic reward in drug use would be the:
   a) internal feeling created by the use of drugs
   b) acceptance by peers who use drugs
   c) possibility of serious health concerns or jail time if caught
   d) probability that police or someone else in authority will catch them using drugs
(a; Challenging; p. 173)

154) According to the behavioral response model, an example of extrinsic reward in drug use would be the:
   a) internal feeling created by the use of drugs
   b) acceptance by peers who use drugs
   c) possibility of serious health concerns or jail time if caught
   d) probability that police or someone else in authority will catch them using drugs
(b; Challenging; p. 173)

155) According to the behavioral response model, an example of severity in drug use would be the:
   a) internal feeling created by the use of drugs
   b) acceptance by peers who use drugs
   c) possibility of serious health concerns or jail time if caught
   d) probability that police or someone else in authority will catch them using drugs
(c; Challenging; p. 173)

156) According to the behavioral response model, an example of vulnerability in drug use would be the:
   a) internal feeling created by the use of drugs
   b) acceptance by peers who use drugs
   c) possibility of serious health concerns or jail time if caught
   d) probability that police or someone else in authority will catch them using drugs

(d; Challenging; p. 173)

157) The appeal that often wins awards and tends to be favorites among judges is:
   a) fear
   b) humor
   c) sex
   d) emotions

(b; Challenging; p. 173)

158) At the Clio Awards ceremony for radio ads, the appeal that wins the most awards tends to be:
   a) fear
   b) sex
   c) humor
   d) emotions

(c; Challenging; p. 173)

159) Humor overcomes clutter by:
   a) making the person laugh
   b) frequently repeating the company's name
   c) capturing attention
   d) making other products less memorable

(c; Moderate; p. 173)

160) The goal of a humorous ad is to have consumers:
   a) pause, remember, and act
   b) watch, laugh, and remember
   c) concentrate on the funny part
   d) ignore the musical element

(b; Easy; p. 174)

161) To be successful, the humor in a humor appeal should be:
   a) directed at the target audience of the ad
   b) of a low level since humor that is too heavy tends to interfere with message recall
   c) directed to the audience's value system
   d) connected directly to the product's benefits

(d; Challenging; p. 174)

162) Research indicates that humor will:
   a) get a person's attention, but adversely affects recall of the product's benefits
   b) get a person's attention, but interferes with brand recall
   c) cut through clutter if the humor is tied closely to the product's attributes
   d) elevate a person's mood, which will then be transferred to the product being advertised
   (d; Moderate; p. 174)

163) In terms of the use of humor internationally, humor is:
   a) used less frequently in other countries
   b) often based in one's culture
   c) normally transferable to other cultures
   d) equally effective in all cultures
   (b; Challenging; p. 174)

164) In terms of using a sex appeal, many advertisers are shifting to:
   a) subliminal advertising techniques
   b) nudity and partial nudity
   c) subtle sexual cues, suggestions, and innuendos
   d) overt sexual themes
   (c; Challenging; p. 175)

165) Sexuality has been employed in advertising in each of the following ways, *except:*
   a) subliminal techniques
   b) nudity or partial nudity
   c) overt sexuality
   d) pornographic
   (d; Easy; p. 176)

166) Attempting to place a sexual cue in an ad to affect a viewer's subconscious mind is:
   a) seductive advertising
   b) subliminal advertising
   c) partial instead of full nudity
   d) sexual suggestiveness
   (b; Easy; p. 176)

167) Subliminal sexual messages are:
   a) often ignored by viewers
   b) highly effective with teenage viewers
   c) increasingly used instead of humor
   d) used to advertise children's products
   (a; Easy; p. 176)

168) Television and print advertisements by Victoria Secret's of models wearing only underwear are using which sexual appeal?
   a) subliminal technique
   b) nudity or partial nudity
   c) overt sexuality
   d) sexual suggestiveness
(b; Easy; p. 176)

169) Clothing, perfume, and cologne have sexual connotations, so they are more likely to be advertised using
   a) rational appeals
   b) subliminal approaches
   c) sexual suggestiveness
   d) scarcity appeals
(c; Easy; p. 177)

170) A television ad that uses a lesbian or gay theme of two individuals meeting for a date would be an example of the sex appeal of:
   a) subliminal techniques
   b) sexual suggestiveness
   c) sensuality
   d) overt sexual
(b; Challenging; p. 177)

171) Clairol's "yes, yes, yes!" campaign is an example of which type of sex appeal?
   a) overt sexuality
   b) subliminal sexuality
   c) sexual suggestiveness
   d) sensuality
(c; Challenging; p. 177)

172) Using sensuality as a type of sex appeal in advertising:
   a) requires both visual and verbal cues
   b) requires viewer imagination
   c) is based on subliminal cues
   d) works only with female viewers since they are more romantic then men
(b; Moderate; p. 177)

173) Although sexually-oriented advertisements attract attention, which is lower for ads using a sex appeal than for ads using some other type of appeal?
   a) the interest level
   b) the level of physiological response
   c) brand recall
   d) the level of sexual arousal
(c; Moderate; p. 177)

174) The following statements are true about sexually-oriented ads, *except:*
    a) sexually-oriented ads increases the level of brand recall
    b) sexually-oriented ads attract attention
    c) sexually-oriented ads are rated as more interesting
    d) sexually-oriented ads produce higher levels of physiological arousal responses
(a; Challenging; p. 177)

175) Ads that were rated as highly controversial in terms of sexual content by both males and females:
    a) were also rated as most interesting
    b) had the lowest level of brand recall
    c) were the best at relaying product information
    d) produced the best results
(a; Challenging; p. 177)

176) The types of sexually-oriented ads that will produce the highest level of physiological responses are:
    a) nudity and overt sexuality
    b) nudity and sexual suggestiveness
    c) sensuality and sexual suggestiveness
    d) nudity and partial nudity
(a; Challenging; p. 178)

177) The cognitive impression made on viewers of a sexually-oriented ad depends on:
    a) the level of nudity in the ad
    b) the level of sensuality in the ad
    c) the type of product being advertised
    d) whether the viewer feels the advertisement is pleasant or offensive
(d; Challenging; p. 178)

178) Placing a female wearing a bikini in advertisement for power tools is an example of:
    a) a subliminal sexual cue
    b) a decorative model
    c) overt sexuality
    d) sexual suggestiveness
(b; Easy; p. 178)

179) Decorative models are people who:
    a) are key product spokespersons
    b) are nude models in television ads
    c) adorn a product as a sexual stimulus
    d) design attractive products
(c; Easy; p. 178)

180) A nude male on a calendar for household furniture is a(n):
    a) source or spokesperson
    b) decorative model
    c) example of subliminal advertising
    d) example of overt sexuality
(b; Moderate; p. 178)

181) Each of the following statements about the use of decorative models is true, *except:*
    a) the presence of a decorative model improves ad recognition, but not brand recognition
    b) attractive models produce higher levels of attention than do less attractive models
    c) the presence of an attractive model produces higher purchase intentions
    d) the presence of a decorative model influences the affective component of attitude
(c; Challenging; p. 178)

182) In determining the level of sex appeal to use in an advertisement, it is important to consider:
    a) the amount of sexually-oriented advertising that is being used by competitors
    b) how decorative models are being used
    c) society's view and level of acceptance at the time the ad is to run
    d) the target audiences view of sexuality
(c; Challenging; p. 178)

183) In terms of advertising internationally, the levels of nudity, sexual references, and gender-specific issues that are permitted in a country are determined by all of the following, *except:*
    a) religions
    b) culture
    c) value systems
    d) personal preferences
(d; Moderate; p. 180)

184) In terms of using sexually-oriented ads, each of the following statements about Moslem countries is true, *except:*
    a) Moslem nations permit the advertising of personal products, such as female hygiene products
    b) Moslem nations tend to reject any kind of nudity and any reference to sexuality
    c) Moslem nations forbid any hint of sexuality or display of the female body
    d) Moslems tend to reject gender-related issues
(a; Moderate; p. 180)

185) Using "regular person" models in advertisements are being used by companies like Wal-Mart in response to:
   a) the decrease in the use of fear advertising tactics
   b) the ineffectiveness of rational advertising tactics
   c) the criticism of sexually-oriented advertising perpetuating a dissatisfaction with one's body
   d) the need to reach female audiences, who do most of the buying in the household

(c; Challenging; p. 181)

186) Music can be intrusive, which means it will:
   a) gain the attention of someone who previously was not listening or watching a program
   b) be the most important aspect of an advertisement
   c) be effective if the listener recognizes the tune
   d) lead to a greater level of brand recall and create positive emotions in listeners

(a; Moderate; p. 181)

187) Of the following types of appeals, the one that has the greatest intrusion ability typically would be:
   a) fear appeal
   b) music appeal
   c) sex appeal
   d) emotional appeal

(b; Challenging; p. 181)

188) Music is very good at gaining a viewer's attention:
   a) but often interferes with the person's ability to retain the information in the ad
   b) but interferes with brand and product recall
   c) and increases the retention of information in the ad
   d) and increasing the viewer's propensity to action

(c; Challenging; p. 181)

189) Using a popular song in an advertisement:
   a) does not have as much of an effect as writing a new tune
   b) transfers the emotional affinity for the song to the product
   c) creates brand parity
   d) interferes with brand recall ability

(b; Easy; p. 182)

190) Using songs from popular musicians is:
   a) popular because musicians seek greater exposure of their songs
   b) popular because the affinity for the song normally transfers to the product
   c) not popular because the songs typically overwhelm the message
   d) not popular because people remember the musician and the song, not the message

(b; Challenging; p. 182)

191) In the United Kingdom, musicians are:
   a) more likely to agree to let their songs be part of ads than in the U.S.
   b) less likely to agree to let their songs be part of ads than in the U.S.
   c) cannot receive royalties for songs used in advertisements
   d) banned by law from using songs that are released in advertisements

(a; Challenging; p. 183)

192) Which type of appeal follows the hierarchy of effects model?
   a) sexual
   b) emotional
   c) rational
   d) scarcity

(c; Easy; p. 183)

193) Rational appeals:
   a) match the traditional steps of the hierarchy of effects model
   b) often include some other type of appeal to gain attention
   c) are focused on brand image rather than product benefits
   d) are used more in consumer advertising than in business-to-business advertising

(a; Easy; p. 183)

194) Rational appeals:
   a) are best for low-involvement products
   b) are best for hedonic-type purchases
   c) are most effective when viewers are highly involved and willing to pay attention
   d) are often used for consumer products

(c; Moderate; p. 183)

195) Which is the best outlet for a rational appeal?
   a) broadcast media
   b) Internet and magazines
   c) print media
   d) non-traditional media

(c; Moderate; p. 183)

196) Rational appeals work best when:
   a) there is low involvement and the product is simple
   b) there is high involvement, but no emotion
   c) there is high involvement and the viewer is willing to pay attention to the ad
   d) they are related more to the product than the amount of involvement
(c; Moderate; p. 183)

197) Byron has an interest in purchasing a motorcycle and is now looking at the different models, gathering information about each one. Which type of appeal would be the most effective in developing or changing Bryon's attitude and in establishing specific brand beliefs?
   a) sex appeal
   b) emotional appeal
   c) humor appeal
   d) rational appeal
(d; Challenging; p. 183)

198) Emotional appeals are based on each of the following ideas, *except:*
   a) humor and sex appeals are being overused and therefore not as effective as in the past
   b) consumers ignore most advertisements
   c) rational appeals go unnoticed unless the consumer is in the market for the particular product at the time it is advertised
   d) emotional advertising can capture a person's attention and foster an attachment between the consumer and the brand
(a; Challenging; p. 183)

199) Emotional appeals are popular because:
   a) they are better at getting a viewer's attention than humor or sexuality
   b) rational appeals are often ignored
   c) they emphasize product features
   d) they often contain subliminal messages
(b; Moderate; p. 184)

200) Most creatives view which type of advertising appeal as the key to developing brand loyalty?
   a) rational
   b) humorous
   c) emotional
   d) sex-oriented
(c; Challenging; p. 184)

201) Which type of appeal reaches the more creative right side of the brain?
   a) rational
   b) sex
   c) humor
   d) emotional
(d; Challenging; p. 184)

202) In the Effie Awards, sponsored by the New York chapter of the American Marketing Association, the most common approach used by winners was:
   a) to combine humor with emotions
   b) sexually-oriented appeals
   c) using a humor appeal
   d) using an emotional appeal combined with rationality
(a; Challenging; p. 185)

203) The priceless campaign of MasterCard is based on a(n):
   a) humor appeal
   b) emotional appeal
   c) rational appeal
   d) fear appeal
(b; Challenging; p. 185)

204) A description of how a search engine can help the web specialist at an e-business feel good about its website's ability to handle the e-commerce traffic is an example of an advertisement using a(n):
   a) rational appeal
   b) emotional appeal
   c) scarcity appeal
   d) fear appeal
(b; Challenging; p. 185)

205) Emotional appeals:
   a) have been used more frequently in business-to-business ads in the past decade
   b) are designed to evoke cognitive responses
   c) primarily describe product attributes
   d) are difficult to create on television
(a; Moderate; p. 185)

206) Business-to-business ads have tended to use the rational advertising appeals almost exclusively. In recent years, there has been a move to use more:
   a) sex appeals
   b) emotional appeals
   c) fear appeals
   d) scarcity appeals
(b; Challenging; p. 185)

207)   The best medium for using an emotional appeal is probably:
       a) magazines
       b) radio
       c) television
       d) newspapers
(c; Moderate; p. 186)

208)   Scarcity appeals:
       a) only work in children's advertising because adults are aware of the ploy
       b) do not work for children because they cannot process the information
       c) urge consumers to buy a product because of some kind of limitation
       d) urge consumers to save money to buy a product later
(c; Easy; p. 186)

209)   From the list below, the product that best fits a scarcity appeal would be:
       a) a television
       b) black dress socks
       c) deodorant
       d) a musical compilation CD from one artist
(d; Moderate; p. 186)

210)   The primary benefit of using a scarcity appeal is that it:
       a) increases brand awareness
       b) encourages consumer action
       c) is an excellent method of conveying product information
       d) is an excellent method of gaining attention
(b; Moderate; p. 187)

211)   Which type of appeals tends to work well on the Super Bowl?
       a) humor and emotion
       b) humor and music
       c) humor and rational
       d) fear and sex
(a; Challenging; p. 187)

212)   According to research studies, the worst type of appeal to use in the Super Bowl
       is:
       a) sex
       b) fear
       c) music
       d) rational
(d; Challenging; p. 187)

213) Most print ads begin with a(n):
   a) headline
   b) proof of claim
   c) amplification
   d) unique selling proposition
   (a; Easy; p. 187)

214) For print ads, the most crucial element is the:
   a) headline or promise of a benefit
   b) proof of claim
   c) amplification
   d) unique selling proposition
   (a; Challenging; p. 187)

215) An advertising headline:
   a) makes the promise of a benefit
   b) proves an advertising claim
   c) amplifies an advertising claim
   d) suggests a unique selling proposition
   (a; Easy; p. 187)

216) The amplification of an ad should contain:
   a) imagery or an attention-getting device
   b) allegory or alliteration for memory
   c) a unique selling proposition
   d) an alternative perspective
   (c; Moderate; p. 188)

217) The Good Housekeeping seal of approval is part of an advertisement's:
   a) promise of a benefit
   b) amplification
   c) subheadline
   d) proof of the claim
   (d; Challenging, p. 188)

218) Many advertisements conclude with a:
   a) promise of a benefit
   b) form of amplification
   c) major selling idea
   d) tagline
   (d; Challenging; p. 188)

219) "Like a good neighbor, State Farm is there" is an example of a:
- a) promise of a benefit
- b) form of amplification
- c) major selling idea
- d) tagline

(d; Moderate; p. 188)

220) Which is most likely to be repeated across several years of advertising?
- a) promise of the same benefit
- b) any form of amplification
- c) a headline
- d) a tagline

(d; Moderate; p. 188)

Short-Answer Questions

221) What is a leverage point?

The part of an advertisement that moves the consumer from understanding a product's benefits to linking those benefits with personal values.
(Moderate; p. 165)

222) Name the components of the hierarchy of effects' model.

- Awareness
- Knowledge
- Liking
- Preference
- Conviction
- The actual purchase

(Moderate; p. 165)

223) Name the components of the MECCAS model. What does MECCAS stand for?

1. Product attributes
2. Consumer benefits
3. Leverage points
4. Personal values
5. Executional framework

Means-Ends Conceptualization of Components for Advertising Strategy
(Moderate; p. 167)

224) How are visual elements of ads stored in the brain?

As both pictures and words.
(Easy; p. 169)

225) What are the various types of appeals that can be used in advertising and what is the primary benefit of each type?

- Fear – Increases a viewer's interest in an ad as well as recall.
- Humor – Excellent at breaking through ad clutter and getting a viewer's attention.
- Sex – Good at breaking through clutter and increasing a positive attitude toward the brand being advertised, if it is appropriate to a sexual approach.
- Music – Good at capturing attention and linking the ad to emotional feelings.
- Rational – Good for high involvement and complex products.
- Emotions – Excellent for developing the affective component of attitude and developing feelings towards a brand.
- Scarcity – Useful for marketing a product that is in limited supply or available for only a limited amount of time.

(Challenging; p. 171)

226) In the behavioral response model, what two elements should a fear ad contain?

1. severity
2. vulnerability
(Easy; p. 171)

227) Describe the sequence that occurs when a humorous ad is successful.

1) The consumer watches, 2) laughs, and 3) most important, remembers. 4) The consumer also attaches positive feelings to the product.
(Easy; p. 174)

228) What approaches to sexuality are used in advertising?

- Subliminal techniques
- Nudity or partial nudity
- Sexual suggestiveness
- Overt sexuality
- Sensuality

(Moderate; p. 176)

229) What are the major criticisms of sexuality in advertising?

They are too overt and offensive.
They overemphasize body image.
They create attention, but do not transmit information.
(Moderate; p. 180)

230) What roles can music play in advertisements?

- Incidental background
- Primary theme in the ad
- Inspire emotion
- Create favorable reactions to the ad

(Challenging; p. 181)

231) What is a scarcity ad? How is scarcity created?

A scarcity ad urges consumers to buy a product because of a limitation. They can be limited-production runs, time restrictions where products are only offered during one part of the year, or a result of deprivation, such as in the "Got Milk" campaign.
(Moderate; p. 186)

232) What are the steps in structuring an advertisement?

Create a headline, subheadline, amplification, proof of the claim, and action to take. Usually this completed using a tagline.
`(Moderate; p. 187)

CHAPTER 7
ADVERTISING DESIGN,
MESSAGE STRATEGIES, AND EXECUTIONAL FRAMEWORKS

True-False Questions

1) The AFLAC brand name has always been well-known in the insurance marketplace.
   (False; Easy; p. 196)

2) Selling a stuffed toy Pekin duck to support the AFLAC brand is an example of merchandising the advertising.
   (True; Moderate; p. 196)

3) Marketing messages travel in two ways: personal sources and impersonal sources.
   (True; Moderate; p. 198)

4) A message strategy is the primary tactic or approach used to deliver a message theme.
   (True; Easy; p. 198)

5) A message strategy and a message theme are the same thing.
   (False; Easy; p. 198)

6) The three categories of message strategies coincide with the three components of attitude.
   (True; Moderate; p. 198)

7) The three categories of message strategies are cognitive strategies, affective strategies, and brand strategies.
   (False; Moderate; p. 198)

8) A cognitive message strategy is a presentation of rational arguments or pieces of information about a good or service.
   (True; Easy; p. 199)

9) A cognitive message strategy's main message is about a products attributes or benefits.
   (True; Moderate; p. 199)

10) Cognitive message strategies include generic messages, preemptive messages, hyperbole messages, resonance messages, and action-inducing messages.
    (False; Moderate; p. 199)

11) There are five major forms of cognitive message strategies.
(True; Moderate; p. 199)

12) A generic message is a direct promotion of a good or service without any claim of superiority.
(True; Moderate; p. 199)

13) The preemptive message strategy works best for a firm that is clearly the brand leader and is the dominant company in the industry.
(False; Challenging; p. 199)

14) The "Soup is Good Food" tag line used by Campbell's Soup is an example of hyperbole in advertising.
(False; Challenging; p. 199)

15) Generic message strategies are seldom found in the business-to-business advertisements, because few firms dominate an industry.
(True; Challenging; p. 199)

16) Generic message strategies can be used to create brand awareness.
(True; Challenging, p. 200)

17) A preemptive message is designed to display a product in comparison to the competition.
(False; Moderate; p. 200)

18) A unique selling proposition is an explicit, testable claim of uniqueness or superiority.
(True; Easy; p. 200)

19) A unique selling proposition does not require support or substantiation, because it is so similar to hyperbole.
(False; Moderate; p. 200)

20) A hyperbole form of cognitive message strategy is a claim that can be tested based on some attribute or benefit.
(True; Easy; p. 200)

21) "We make the best tacos in town," is an example of a hyperbole form of cognitive message strategy.
(True; Moderate; p. 200)

22) A hyperbole message strategy is a conative form of message strategy.
(False; Moderate; p. 200)

23) A comparison ad means a product is directly or indirectly compared the good or service sold by the competition.
(True; Easy; p. 200)

24) To provide protection from lawsuits, company leaders and advertisers must be sure that any claim made about the competition using a comparative message strategy approach can be clearly substantiated.
(True; Moderate; p. 200)

25) The major advantage of comparison ads is that they often capture the viewer's attention.
(True; Challenging; p. 200)

26) The negative side of using comparative ads is in the areas of believability and consumer attitudes.
(True; Moderate; p. 201)

27) Negative comparison ads may transfer negative feelings toward the sponsor's product.
(True; Moderate; p. 201)

28) When Sprint advertising says "our reception is better than Cingular's," it is a form of negative comparison.
(False; Moderate; p. 201)

29) According to the concept of spontaneous trait transfer, when someone calls another person dishonest, other people tend to remember the speaker as also being less than honest.
(True; Moderate; p. 201)

30) In terms of attitude formation, cognitive message strategies are designed to follow the sequence of cognitive → affective → conative.
(True; Moderate; p. 201)

31) Comparison advertising is more common in countries other than in the United States.
(False; Challenging; p. 201)

32) The largest number of complaints that the FTC hears about potentially misleading advertisements are ads using the hyperbole message strategy approach.
(False; Challenging; p. 201)

33) In general, comparing a low-market share brand to the market leader does not work as well in comparative advertising as comparing two brands with approximately the same level of market share.
(False; Challenging; p. 201)

34) There are no real ethical challenges to advertising medical services.
(False; Moderate; p. 202)

35) Affective message strategies are designed to invoke feelings and emotions and match them to a good, service, or company.
(True; Easy; p. 202)

36) Affective message strategies take two major forms: emotional and hyperbole.
(False; Moderate; p. 202)

37) Affective message strategies are designed to invoke rational decisions, which lead to comparisons and purchases.
(False; Moderate; p. 202)

38) Resonance advertising attempts to connect a product with a consumer's experiences and is a form of affective message strategy.
(True; Moderate; p. 202)

39) Emotional advertising is based on feelings such as trust, reliability, friendship, happiness, and security.
(True; Easy; p. 203)

40) If a product's benefits can be presented within an emotional framework, the advertisement is normally more effective, even in business-to-business ads.
(True; Challenging; p. 203)

41) Cognitive message strategies are a common approach to develop a strong brand name.
(False; Challenging; p. 203)

42) Affective message strategies utilize the attitude formation sequence of affective → conative → cognitive.
(True; Challenging; p. 203)

43) For some products, affective ads are an effective approach because there are no real tangible differences among the brands.
(True; Moderate; p. 203)

44) Corporate advertising often utilizes an affective message strategy.
(True; Challenging; p. 203)

45) Corporate advertising promotes the corporate name and logo rather than an individual brand.
(True; Easy; p. 203)

46) Impulse buys are primarily linked to conative message strategies.
(True; Moderate; p. 204)

47) An action-inducing conative advertisement is one way to get people to make impulse buys.
(True; Moderate; p. 204)

48) Conative message strategies utilize the attitude formation sequence of conative → cognitive → affective.
(True; Moderate; p. 204)

49) In terms of the relationship between message strategies and the hierarchy of effects model, cognitive message strategies are best suited to develop awareness and knowledge of a particular product or brand.
(True; Challenging; p. 204)

50) In terms of the relationship between message strategies and the hierarchy of effects model, affective message strategies are best suited to develop awareness, liking and preference of a particular product or brand.
(False; Challenging; p. 204)

51) In terms of the relationship between message strategies and the hierarchy of effects model, conative message strategies are best suited to develop conviction and the actual purchase of particular product or brand.
(False; Challenging; p. 204)

52) An executional framework is the manner in which an advertising appeal is presented.
(True; Easy; p. 205)

53) Executional frameworks include animation, slice-of-life, dramatization, testimonial, authoritative, demonstration, fantasy, and informative.
(True; Moderate; p. 205)

54) Rotoscoping is a new, high-tech form of animation.
(True; Easy; p. 205)

55) Animation is a type of slice-of-life advertising execution.
(False; Moderate; p. 205)

56) The Pillsbury Doughboy is a form of clay animation.
(True; Moderate; p. 205)

57) Animation in the past was used only by firms that could not afford other forms of execution, but today animation is a popular executional framework.
(True; Moderate; p. 206)

58) The typical format for a slice-of-life ad is encounter, problem, interaction, and then solution.
(True; Moderate; p. 206)

59) A slice-of-life advertisement utilizes celebrity spokespersons offering expert endorsements.
(False; Moderate; p. 206)

60) The slice-of-life execution format was made popular in the 1950s by General Foods.
(False; Challenging; p. 206)

61) While the slice-of-life execution is ideal for television, it can be used in print advertisements.
(True; Moderate; p. 206)

62) The slice-of-life execution has become popular in Japan in recent years because Japanese advertising tends to be more indirect with a soft-sell approach.
(True; Challenging; p. 207)

63) The slice-of-life execution is a common strategy for business-to-business advertisements.
(True; Challenging; p. 207)

64) A slice-of-life executional framework and a dramatization are largely the same, except for the level of intensity or suspense.
(True; Easy; p. 207)

65) Dramatization ads are typically easier to prepare than slice-of-life executional framework ads.
(False; Moderate; p. 207)

66) The dramatization executional framework typically utilizes the fours steps of an encounter, a problem, the interaction, and then the solution.
(True; Moderate; p. 207)

67) Testimonial executions have been successful for many years, especially in the business-to-business and service sectors.
(True; Challenging; p. 208)

68) One major reason companies choose testimonial executions is that they offer a greater level of credibility, if the testimonies are by actual customers.
(True; Moderate; p. 208)

69) Consumers rely on word-of-mouth communications when choosing services, which makes the authoritative executional framework work well.
(False; Challenging; p. 208)

70) Authoritative ads either provide scientific evidence or use an authoritative voice to present the information.
(True; Moderate; p. 208)

71) A physician, dentist, engineer, or chemist endorsing a particular brand's advantages would typically be found in a slice-of-life execution.
(False; Challenging; p. 208)

72) Many authoritative executions include some type of scientific or survey support.
(True; Moderate; p. 208)

73) The authoritative executional framework assumes consumers and business decision makers rely on cognitive processes when making purchase decisions.
(True; Challenging; p. 209)

74) The authoritative executional framework works especially well in specialty magazines and trade journals.
(True; Moderate; p. 209)

75) Demonstration ads are suited to television because the actual product features can be clearly shown.
(True; Easy; p. 209)

76) Perfumes and colognes often use a demonstration form of executional framework, because they are easy to show in a positive light.
(False; Easy; p. 209)

77) A fantasy execution lifts the audience to a make-believe experience or beyond reality.
(True; Easy; p. 209)

78) The most common themes for fantasy executions are sex, love, and romance.
(True; Easy; p. 209)

79) An informative execution typically presents information to the audience in a straightforward manner.
(True; Easy; p. 210)

80) Informative executions work best for high-involvement products.
(True; Moderate; p. 210)

81) Consumer reports and the Good Housekeeping seal of approval are examples of support for an informative executional framework.
(False; Challenging; p. 210)

82) Celebrity endorsers are used for ads because their stamp of approval on a product can enhance the product's brand equity and create emotional bonds between the consumers and the brand being endorsed.
(True; Moderate; p. 211)

83) Using celebrities to create a "personality" for a new brand does not always work as well as for already established brands.
(True; Challenging; p. 211)

84) The loss of power by creatives in recent years has led some to move into the role of director, splitting time between commercial development and commercial production.
(True; Challenging; p. 212)

85) Creatives believe that in recent years there has been too much testing of their ideas as well as too much dependence on marketing research.
(True; Moderate; p. 212)

86) In terms of endorsers, celebrities and CEOs tend not be viewed as expert sources for product endorsements.
(True; Moderate; p. 214)

87) Paid actors or models used in an advertisement to resemble everyday people would be considered a celebrity endorsement since they are professional actors or models.
(False; Moderate; p. 214)

88) One reason companies are using more typical person endorsers is the overuse of celebrities in ads.
(True; Moderate; p. 214)

89) A spokesperson's credibility is derived from the composite of attractiveness, likeability, trustworthiness, and intelligence.
(False; Challenging; p. 214)

90) One reason for using typical persons as product endorsers is that they are more likely to possess at least an element of all five source characteristics.
(False; Challenging; p. 214)

91) In terms of source characteristics, attractiveness has two components: physical attractiveness and social attractiveness.
(False; Moderate; p. 215)

92) Advertisements using physically attractive spokespeople fare better than ads with less attractive people. This is true for both male and female audiences.
(True; Moderate; p. 215)

93) Ads work better if the audience can identify with the spokesperson in the ad. This identification is derived from both the similarity of the spokesperson to the audience as well as the spokesperson's attractiveness.
(True; Challenging; p. 215)

94) In terms of source characteristics, trustworthiness is the degree of confidence or the level of acceptance consumers place in a spokesperson's message.
(True; Easy; p. 215)

95) In terms of source characteristics, expertise can be valuable in persuasive advertisements designed to change the audience's opinions or attitudes.
(True; Easy; p. 215)

96) Celebrities normally score well in terms of trustworthiness, believability, persuasiveness, and likeability.
(True; Moderate; p. 216)

97) The potential for negative publicity caused by inappropriate actions of celebrities has led some advertisers to use deceased celebrities.
(True; Easy; p. 216)

98) A celebrity who endorses several products is building credibility as a spokesperson.
(False; Moderate; p. 217)

99) In terms of source characteristics, CEOs would appear to be trustworthy, have expertise, and maintain a degree of credibility.
(True; Moderate; p. 217)

100) Typical person sources are not ordinarily credible.
(False; Moderate; p. 217)

101) Typical person spokespeople do not have the name recognition of celebrities, and as a result, advertisers often use multiple sources within one advertisement to build credibility.
(True; Challenging; p. 217)

102) Using the creative brief, the creative should develop a means-end chain, starting with an attribute of the product that generates a specific customer benefit and eventually produces a desirable end state.
(True; Moderate; p. 218)

103) An effective advertisement accomplishes the objectives desired by the client.
   (True; Easy; p. 219)

104) Visual consistency is important in creating effective advertisements because buyers, whether consumers or businesses, spend very little time viewing or listening to advertisements.
   (True; Easy; p. 219)

105) The principle of campaign duration suggests that all advertisements should be easily recalled by viewers, but without them becoming boring or uninteresting.
   (True; Challenging; p. 219)

106) In terms of advertising campaign duration, a campaign that has utilized a higher frequency usually can be of a shorter duration than a campaign that used a lower frequency.
   (True; Moderate; p. 219)

107) Repeating a tag line is ineffective in advertising because the consumer becomes tired of hearing the phrase.
   (False; Easy; p. 220)

108) Tag lines help consumers tie an advertisement into current knowledge structure nodes that already exist in their minds.
   (True; Moderate; p. 220)

109) Wal-Mart's emphasis on low prices violates the principle of consistent positioning, which stresses quality instead.
   (False; Challenging; p. 220)

110) An advertisement should have only one selling point that is easily identifiable to the audience and that highlights one of the product's attributes.
   (False; Challenging; p. 220)

111) In advertising research studies, repetition of ads is effective in increasing recall if no competitor ads are present; otherwise repetition does not stimulate greater recall because of competitive ad interference.
   (True; Challenging; p. 221)

112) Based on the concept of variability theory, an advertisement's recall and effectiveness increases if the ad is seen in different environments.
   (True; Moderate; p. 221)

Multiple-Choice Questions

113) Selling a stuffed Pekin duck to support the AFLAC brand name is an example of:
    a) merchandising the advertising
    b) marketing the merchandise
    c) brand confusion
    d) brand equity
(a; Easy; p. 196)

114) An outline of the key ideas in an advertisement is the:
    a) message theme
    b) message strategy
    c) cognitive message
    d) generic message
(a; Easy; p. 198)

115) The primary tactic or approach used to deliver a message theme is a:
    a) message identification
    b) message strategy
    c) cognitive message
    d) generic message
(b; Easy; p. 198)

116) The broad categories of message strategies include each of the following, *except:*
    a) cognitive
    b) affective
    c) conative
    d) brand
(d; Easy; p. 198)

117) The presentation of rational arguments or pieces of information to consumers is which form of message strategy?
    a) cognitive
    b) affective
    c) conative
    d) basic
(a; Easy; p. 199)

118) A cognitive message strategy:
    a) invokes feelings or emotions and match these with the good, service, or company being advertised
    b) is the presentation of rational arguments or pieces of information to consumers
    c) is designed to lead more directly to some type of consumer behavior
    d) is the manner in which an ad appeal is presented
(b; Moderate; p. 199)

119) Which message strategy is linked with reasoning processes?
   a) cognitive
   b) conative
   c) affective
   d) resonance
(a; Easy; p. 199)

120) Cognitive message strategies include each of the following, *except:*
   a) generic
   b) preemptive
   c) resonance
   d) hyperbole
(c; Moderate; p. 199)

121) Cognitive message strategies include each of the following, *except:*
   a) unique selling proposition
   b) comparative
   c) preemptive
   d) action-inducing
(d; Moderate; p. 199)

122) The goal of which message strategy approach is to impact a person's beliefs and/or knowledge structure?
   a) affective
   b) conative
   c) cognitive
   d) resonance
(c; Challenging; p. 199)

123) Which type of cognitive message strategy is a direct promotion of a brand without any claim of superiority?
   a) generic
   b) hyperbole
   c) preemptive
   d) brand
(a; Moderate; p. 199)

124) The generic cognitive message strategy is a(n):
   a) claim of superiority based on a product's specific attribute or benefit, which cannot be made by a competitor
   b) direct promotion of product attributes or benefits without any claim of superiority
   c) explicit, testable claim of uniqueness or superiority that can be supported or substantiated in some manner
   d) untestable claim based upon some attribute or benefit
(b; Challenging; p. 199)

125) Which cognitive message strategy works best for a firm that is clearly the brand leader and is the dominant company in the industry?
   a) generic
   b) preemptive
   c) unique selling proposition
   d) hyperbole
(a; Challenging; p. 199)

126) An advertisement for Nintendo using a cognitive message strategy would probably feature which type of message strategy, because Nintendo holds 98 percent market share in the handheld game market?
   a) comparative
   b) generic
   c) preemptive
   d) unique selling proposition
(b; Challenging; p. 199)

127) The goal of a generic message strategy is to:
   a) increase brand loyalty
   b) persuade viewers of the brand's superiority
   c) make the brand synonymous with the product category
   d) preempt the competition from using a particular claim or benefit
(c; Challenging; p. 199)

128) Generic message strategies are seldom used in the business-to-business sector because:
   a) emotional strategies are more effective
   b) it is often used by competitors
   c) it does not lead to any specific action
   d) few firms dominate an industry
(d; Challenging; p. 199)

129) When Crest is featured as a "cavity fighter" in its advertising competitors aren't likely to make the same claim. This is an example of which form of cognitive message strategy?
   a) generic
   b) preemptive
   c) hyperbole
   d) comparative
(b; Moderate; p. 200)

130) Which message strategy is a claim of superiority based on a product's specific attribute or benefit, which cannot then be used by a competitor?
   a) generic
   b) preemptive
   c) unique selling proposition
   d) hyperbole
(b; Moderate; p. 200)

131) The preemptive cognitive message strategy is a(n):
   a) claim of superiority based on a product's specific attribute or benefit, which cannot be made by a competitor
   b) direct promotion of product attributes or benefits without any claim of superiority
   c) explicit, testable claim of uniqueness or superiority that can be supported or substantiated in some manner
   d) untestable claim based upon some attribute or benefit
(a; Moderate; p. 200)

132) An explicit, testable claim of uniqueness or superiority that can be supported or substantiated in some manner is which form of message strategy?
   a) generic
   b) preemptive
   c) hyperbole
   d) unique selling proposition
(d; Easy; p. 200)

133) A unique selling proposition cognitive message strategy is a(n):
   a) claim of superiority based on a product's specific attribute or benefit, which cannot be made by a competitor
   b) direct promotion of product attributes or benefits without any claim of superiority
   c) explicit, testable claim of uniqueness or superiority that can be supported or substantiated in some manner
   d) untestable claim based upon some attribute or benefit
(c; Moderate; p. 200)

134) A unique selling proposition message strategy differs from a preemptive or generic approach in that the unique selling proposition is:
   a) preemptive
   b) testable
   c) emotional
   d) comparative
(b; Moderate; p. 200)

135) A unique selling proposition message strategy is more difficult to use because of:
   a) brand parity
   b) FTC rulings
   c) potential lawsuits by competitors
   d) brand equity
(a; Challenging; p. 200)

136) Reebok's advertising claim that it is the only shoe using DMX technology, which results in a more comfortable fit, is an example of a(n):
   a) generic message strategy
   b) preemptive message strategy
   c) unique selling point message strategy
   d) comparative message strategy
(c; Challenging; p. 200)

137) An untestable claim about a product's benefits or attributes is which form of cognitive message?
   a) preemptive
   b) unique selling proposition
   c) hyperbole
   d) comparative
(c; Moderate; p. 200)

138) A hyperbole cognitive message strategy is a(n):
   a) claim of superiority based on a product's specific attribute or benefit, which cannot be made by a competitor
   b) direct promotion of product attributes or benefits without any claim of superiority
   c) explicit, testable claim of uniqueness or superiority that can be supported or substantiated in some manner
   d) untestable claim based upon some attribute or benefit
(d; Moderate; p. 200)

139) "We are Chicago's friendliest car dealer!" is an example of which type of cognitive message?
   a) preemptive
   b) unique selling proposition
   c) hyperbole
   d) comparative
(c; Challenging; p. 200)

140) Which term is least likely to be used in a hyperbole approach?
   a) best
   b) favorite
   c) lowest price
   d) highest quality
(c; Challenging; p. 200)

141) Puffery is most likely to be associated with which type of message strategy?
   a) generic
   b) preemptive
   c) hyperbole
   d) comparative
(c; Challenging; p. 200)

142) "Our product is better than brand X" is a form of:
   a) conative message strategy
   b) slice-of-life execution
   c) comparative message strategy
   d) expert authority execution
(c; Moderate; p. 200)

143) The cognitive message strategy approach that is most likely to require substantiation of claims to prevent potential lawsuits made would be the:
   a) hyperbole
   b) preemptive
   c) unique selling proposition
   d) comparative
(d; Challenging; p. 200)

144) The major advantage of using a comparative message strategy is that it:
   a) is more believable
   b) is a good at capturing attention
   c) has a positive impact on viewer attitude
   d) creates a higher level of brand equity
(b; Challenging; p. 200)

145) Most consumers think comparative ads:
   a) are less believable
   b) are more believable
   c) contain accurate information
   d) develop more favorable attitudes toward the brand
(a; Challenging; p. 201)

146) Showing greasy potato chips versus Pringles is an example of a:
   a) preemptive claim of superiority
   b) generic demonstration of product quality
   c) negative comparison ad
   d) positive comparison ad
   (c; Challenging; p. 201)

147) A negative comparison ad that leads to people not liking the sponsor brand may be due to:
   a) the preemptive claim of superiority
   b) a generic demonstration of product quality
   c) spontaneous trait transference
   d) internal cognitive consistency
   (c; Challenging; p. 201)

148) Which organization is most likely to investigate comparative advertising?
   a) Federal Trade Commission
   b) World Trade Organization
   c) Congress
   d) U.S. Postal Service
   (a; Moderate; p. 201)

149) In developing comparative ads, which of the following tends to work the best?
   a) comparing a low-market share brand to another low-market share brand
   b) comparing a low-market share brand to a market leader
   c) comparing a market leader to a low-market share brand
   d) comparing a market leader to another market leader
   (b; Challenging; p. 201)

150) In terms of attitude formation, the sequence being used with a cognitive message strategy is:
   a) affective → conative → cognitive
   b) conative → cognitive → affective
   c) cognitive → conative → affective
   d) cognitive → affective → conative
   (d; Challenging; p. 201)

151) Which message strategy is most linked to emotions?
   a) cognitive
   b) affective
   c) hyperbole
   d) conative
   (b; Easy; p. 202)

152) Which message strategy invokes feelings or emotions and match those feelings with the good, service, or company?
   a) cognitive
   b) conative
   c) affective
   d) hyperbole
(c; Easy; p. 202)

153) An affective message strategy:
   a) invokes feelings or emotions and matches these with the good, service, or company being advertised
   b) is the presentation of rational arguments or pieces of information to consumers
   c) is designed to lead more directly to some type of consumer behavior
   d) is the manner in which an ad appeal is presented
(a; Easy; p. 202)

154) Using music to build emotions surrounding a product is tied to which type of message strategy?
   a) cognitive
   b) affective
   c) brand
   d) conative
(b; Moderate; p. 202)

155) The two types of affective message strategies are:
   a) emotional and hyperbole
   b) resonance and emotional
   c) preemptive and unique selling proposition
   d) affective and conative
(b; Easy; p. 202)

156) A message strategy that connects a product with a consumer's experiences to build stronger ties with the consumer is which form of message strategy?
   a) generic
   b) cognitive
   c) resonance
   d) emotional
(c; Moderate; p. 202)

157) If a product's benefits can be presented within an emotional message strategy framework, the advertisement is normally:
   a) more affective for b-to-b products than for consumer products
   b) less affective than using a rational argument approach
   c) less affective than using a cognitive message strategy approach
   d) more effective for both consumer products and b-to-b products
(d; Challenging; p. 203)

158) Which strategy is often used to promote a strong brand name?
   a) affective
   b) cognitive
   c) conative
   d) generic
(a; Challenging; p. 203)

159) Affective message strategies utilize an attitude formation sequence of:
   a) affective → conative → cognitive
   b) conative → cognitive → affective
   c) cognitive → conative → affective
   d) affective → cognitive → conative
(a; Challenging; p. 203)

160) For products with no real tangible differences among the various brands, which message strategy is best at developing a liking and positive feelings toward a particular brand?
   a) affective
   b) cognitive
   c) conative
   d) generic
(a; Challenging; p. 203)

161) If an advertisement by Skechers is designed to create positive feelings toward the Skechers Sport brand, then which message strategy is being used?
   a) cognitive
   b) conative
   c) affective
   d) comparative
(c; Challenging; p. 203)

162) Which type of message strategy attempts to elicit powerful emotions that eventually lead to product recall and choice?
   a) generic
   b) cognitive
   c) emotional
   d) preemptive
(c; Moderate; p. 203)

163) A print advertisement for Bijan uses the picture of a typical grandmother with a testimony about the perfume and how her granddaughters now wear Bijan. This advertisement illustrates a testimonial execution with a(n):
   a) cognitive message strategy
   b) affective message strategy
   c) conative message strategy
   d) brand message strategy
(b; Challenging; p. 203)

164) Promoting a company's name and image rather than an individual brand is :
   a) generic advertising
   b) comparative advertising
   c) hyperbole advertising
   d) corporate advertising
(d; Easy; p. 203)

165) Which message strategy approach stresses the actual product the least?
   a) generic
   b) comparative
   c) hyperbole
   d) corporate
(d; Moderate; p. 203)

166) Corporate advertising often utilizes which message strategy approach?
   a) unique selling proposition
   b) affective
   c) cognitive
   d) comparative
(b; Challenging; p. 203)

167) Which type of message strategy is designed to elicit some type of behavior or action on the part of the viewer?
   a) emotional
   b) conative
   c) corporate
   d) affective
(b; Easy; p. 204)

168) Which message strategy is designed to trigger impulse buys?
   a) unique selling proposition
   b) resonance
   c) affective
   d) conative
(d; Moderate; p. 204)

169) Which conative message strategy is linked to impulse buys?
    a) unique selling proposition
    b) resonance
    c) action-inducing
    d) promotional support
(c; Moderate; p. 204)

170) Which conative message strategy is linked to promotions, such as coupons, premiums, and sweepstakes?
    a) unique selling proposition
    b) emotional
    c) action-inducing
    d) promotional support
(d; Moderate; p. 204)

171) Conative message strategies utilize an attitude formation sequence of:
    a) affective → conative → cognitive
    b) conative → cognitive → affective
    c) cognitive → conative → affective
    d) affective → cognitive → conative
(b; Challenging; p. 204)

172) In terms of the hierarchy of effects model, cognitive message strategies would be most closely tied to which stage(s)?
    a) awareness and knowledge
    b) liking, preference, and conviction
    c) actual purchase
    d) knowledge and preference
(a; Challenging; p. 204)

173) In terms of the hierarchy of effects model, affective message strategies would be most closely tied to which stage(s)?
    a) awareness and knowledge
    b) liking, preference, and conviction
    c) actual purchase
    d) awareness and liking
(b; Challenging; p. 204)

174) In terms of the hierarchy of effects model, conative message strategies would be most closely tied to the:
    a) awareness and knowledge stages
    b) liking, preference, and conviction stages
    c) actual purchase stage
    d) awareness stage
(c; Challenging; p. 204)

175) Using the hierarchy of effects model to develop awareness of a product or brand, which would be the best creative message strategy?
   a) affective
   b) cognitive
   c) conative
   d) corporate
(b; Challenging; p. 204)

176) Using the hierarchy of effects model, to develop knowledge of a product or brand, which would be the best message strategy?
   a) affective
   b) cognitive
   c) conative
   d) corporate
(b; Challenging; p. 204)

177) Using the hierarchy of effects model, to develop liking of a product or brand, the best creative message strategies to use would be:
   a) affective
   b) cognitive
   c) conative
   d) corporate
(a; Challenging; p. 204)

178) Using the hierarchy of effects model, to develop preference for a product or brand, the best creative message strategies to use would be:
   a) affective
   b) cognitive
   c) conative
   d) corporate
(a; Challenging; p. 204)

179) Using the hierarchy of effects model, to develop conviction for a particular product or brand, the best creative message strategies to use would be:
   a) affective
   b) cognitive
   c) conative
   d) corporate
(a; Challenging; p. 204)

180) Using the hierarchy of effects model, to encourage the actual purchase of a product or brand, the best creative message strategies to use would be:
   a) affective
   b) cognitive
   c) conative
   d) corporate
(c; Challenging; p. 204)

181) The manner in which an advertising appeal is presented is a(n):
   a) humor methodology
   b) rational approach
   c) conative message strategy
   d) executional framework
(d; Easy; p. 205)

182) The following are types of executional frameworks, *except:*
   a) animation
   b) fear
   c) slice-of-life
   d) dramatization
(b; Moderate; p. 205)

183) The following are types of executional frameworks, *except:*
   a) testimonial
   b) authoritative
   c) rational
   d) demonstration
(c; Moderate; p. 205)

184) The following are types of executional frameworks, *except:*
   a) fantasy
   b) informative
   c) animation
   d) hyperbole
(d; Moderate; p. 205)

185) The Pillsbury Dough Boy is an example of which type of which type of executional framework?
   a) animation
   b) dramatization
   c) testimonial
   d) fantasy
(a; Moderate; p. 205)

186) In recent years, the use of animation in advertising has:
    a) increased
    b) decreased
    c) stayed the same
    d) increased in the consumer market, but declined in the business-to-business sector
(a; Moderate; p. 205)

187) The process of digitally painting or sketching figures into live television sequences is called:
    a) digitalizing
    b) rotoscoping
    c) clay animation
    d) a fantasy execution
(b; Moderate; p. 205)

188) Rotoscoping is used in a(n):
    a) animation executional framework
    b) dramatization executional framework
    c) testimonial executional framework
    d) authoritative executional framework
(a; Challenging; p. 205)

189) When a product solves an everyday life problem, the executional framework being used in the ad is most likely to be:
    a) slice-of-life
    b) authoritative
    c) fantasy
    d) informative
(a; Moderate; p. 206)

190) Procter & Gamble was instrumental in developing and making popular which type of executional framework?
    a) animation
    b) slice-of-life
    c) testimonial
    d) authoritative
(b; Challenging; p. 206)

191) The first component of a slice-of-life execution is the:
    a) interaction
    b) problem
    c) encounter
    d) solution
(c; Moderate; p. 206)

192) The component of a slice-of-life execution that follows the encounter is the:
   a) interaction
   b) problem
   c) information presentation
   d) solution
   (b; Moderate; p. 206)

193) The last component of a slice-of-life execution is the:
   a) interaction
   b) problem
   c) encounter
   d) solution
   (d; Moderate; p. 206)

194) The slice-of-life execution includes all of the following components, *except:*
   a) encounter
   b) problem
   c) testimonial
   d) solution
   (c; Moderate; p. 206)

195) In a television advertisement, Chris is about ready to lose a girlfriend because he did not purchase the right piece of jewelry. A voice over offers a solution, the jewelry is purchased at the advertised store and the girlfriend is now happy. This illustrates which form of executional framework?
   a) slice-of-life
   b) testimonial
   c) fantasy
   d) informative
   (a; Challenging; p. 206)

196) A business-to-business ad featuring a routine business experience, a problem, an interaction, and then a company's product that provides a solution is which form of executional framework?
   a) slice of life
   b) dramatization
   c) testimonial
   d) expert authority
   (a; Challenging; p. 207)

197) In terms of executional frameworks, a dramatization is similar to, but a more powerful form of story than which execution?
   a) animation
   b) slice-of-life
   c) fantasy
   d) authoritative
(b; Moderate; p. 207)

198) A dramatization execution has a more intense story format than which execution?
   a) slice-of-life
   b) testimonial
   c) resonance
   d) conative
(a; Moderate; p. 207)

199) A credit card ad dramatically showing a consumer about to be attacked in a war-like fashion by high interest charges is most likely using which type of executional framework?
   a) slice-of-life
   b) dramatization
   c) resonance advertising
   d) testimonial
(b; Moderate; p. 207)

200) Which executional framework features someone telling about a positive encounter with a company or product?
   a) slice of life
   b) dramatization
   c) testimonial
   d) fantasy
(c; Easy; p. 208)

201) In an advertisement for the Weight Center, Casey talks about the weight she lost and how good the employees were to her. This would be an example of using which type of executional framework?
   a) dramatization
   b) testimonial
   c) authoritative
   d) informative
(b; Challenging; p. 208)

202) The key to a testimonial executional framework is:
    a) likeability
    b) negative likeability
    c) credibility
    d) visual consistency
(c; Challenging; p. 208)

203) The testimonial executional framework is effective, especially with services, because it simulates:
    a) a fantasy
    b) negative likeability
    c) a word-of-mouth recommendation
    d) visual esperanto
(c; Challenging; p. 208)

204) Which type of executional framework seeks to convince buyers that a given product is superior?
    a) dramatization
    b) ideological
    c) authoritative
    d) fantasy
(c; Easy; p. 208)

205) Expert authorities would most likely be used in which type of executional framework?
    a) testimonial
    b) slice-of-life
    c) informative
    d) authoritative
(d; Moderate; p. 208)

206) Authoritative executional frameworks suggest buyers will be influenced by:
    a) testimonies from customers
    b) action-inducing offers
    c) rational thought
    d) emotions
(c; Moderate; p. 208)

207) An endorsement by *Consumer Reports* would typically be used in which type of executional framework?
    a) slice-of-life
    b) dramatization
    c) authoritative
    d) fantasy
(c; Moderate; p. 208)

208) Authoritative executions are the most widely used in the:
   a) business-to-business sector
   b) consumer sector
   c) services sector
   d) governmental sector
(a; Moderate; p. 208)

209) The authoritative execution assumes consumer and business decision makers rely on which of the following when making purchase decisions?
   a) cognitive processes
   b) affective feelings
   c) impulse behaviors
   d) authoritative sources of information
(a; Moderate; p. 209)

210) The authoritative executional framework is best suited for:
   a) print ads
   b) broadcast ads
   c) television
   d) billboards
(a; Challenging; p. 209)

211) Of the following media, the best medium for an advertisement using an authoritative executional framework would be a:
   a) popular consumer magazine such as *People*
   b) specialty magazine such as *Brides*
   c) business magazine such as *BusinessWeek*
   d) sporting event on television
(b; Challenging; p. 209)

212) Showing how a product works is found in which type of executional framework?
   a) slice-of-life
   b) testimonial
   c) demonstration
   d) fantasy
(c; Easy; p. 209)

213) Showing how Windex makes a dirty window sparkle would be which type of executional framework?
   a) dramatization
   b) testimonial
   c) demonstration
   d) illustrative
(c; Moderate; p. 209)

214) Showing someone enjoying an exotic experience would be which type of executional framework?
    a) testimonial
    b) dramatization
    c) slice-of-life
    d) fantasy
(d; Easy; p. 209)

215) The fantasy executional framework relies on:
    a) raw sex and nudity
    b) comparisons of product features
    c) suggestiveness
    d) cognitive thought processes
(c; Moderate; p. 209)

216) Clairol's "yes, yes, yes" ads are examples of:
    a) resonance advertising
    b) action inducing advertising
    c) a fantasy executional framework
    d) rotoscoping
(c; Challenging; p. 209)

217) A dessert that is promoted as being "sinfully delicious" with a person sitting on a sandy beach is using which type of executional framework?
    a) resonance
    b) slice-of-life
    c) fantasy
    d) hyperbole
(c; Challenging; p. 209)

218) Of the following executional frameworks, which is *least* likely to be used in business-to-business ads?
    a) authoritative
    b) informative
    c) fantasy
    d) testimonials
(c; Challenging; p. 210)

219) Presenting product facts in a straightforward manner is which type of executional framework?
    a) testimonial
    b) dramatization
    c) slice-of-life
    d) informative
(d; Easy; p. 210)

220) Ads using an informative executional framework are best suited for:
    a) conative message strategies
    b) high involvement purchase decisions
    c) slice-of-life executions
    d) brand image message strategies
(b; Moderate; p. 210)

221) One of the major keys to successful using the informative execution is:
    a) using customers in the ad
    b) placement of the ad
    c) the selection of the right media
    d) the type of appeal that is used
(b; Challenging; p. 211)

222) Categories of spokespersons include each of the following, *except:*
    a) typical persons
    b) CEOs
    c) experts
    d) government personnel
(d; Easy; p. 211)

223) Celebrity endorsers are used in advertisements because their stamp of approval on a product can:
    a) enhance the product's brand equity
    b) enhance consumers' emotional bonds with the product
    c) aid in the establishment of a "personality" for a brand
    d) all of the above
(d; Moderate; p. 211)

224) New pressures of accountability have changed the role of creatives in recent years to:
    a) greater dependence on creative work from Madison Avenue agencies
    b) become more involved in the work of account executives
    c) market research-driven advertising creative design and development
    d) become involved in media planning
(c; Challenging: p. 212)

225) In response to the shift towards greater testing and research of creative ideas, creatives have:
    a) shifted more time to account executive responsibilities
    b) developed marketing research capabilities
    c) used focus groups to critique their creative work prior to presenting it to clients
    d) moved into the role of director, splitting time developing ads and producing ads.
(d; Challenging; p. 212)

226) Of the following types of celebrity endorsements, the one that would have the greatest level of credibility would be:
    a) celebrity endorsing a brand in a television show
    b) celebrity voice-over in a radio ad
    c) an unpaid celebrity speaking on behalf of some charity or nonprofit organization
    d) a dead-person endorsement of a particular brand
(c; Challenging; p. 213)

227) Dead-celebrity endorsements are often used in advertisements. According to *Forbes*, the dead-celebrity with the highest earnings is:
    a) Elvis Presley
    b) Charles Schulz (creator of Peanuts cartoon strip)
    c) Marilyn Monroe
    d) Theodore Seuss Geisel
(a; Challenging; p. 213)

228) In terms of spokespersons, expert sources would include each of the following, *except:*
    a) lawyers
    b) CEOs of corporations
    c) physicians
    d) financial planners
(b; Moderate; p. 214)

229) Rachel is an actress who plays the part of a housewife in a commercial for a new brand of furniture polish. For this type of ad, Rachel would be considered which type of endorser?
    a) celebrity
    b) CEO
    c) expert
    d) typical person
(d; Challenging; p. 214)

230) Dr. Duckworth has been paid to be in an advertisement to endorse a new brand of anti-inflammatory cream for muscle aches. For this type of ad, Dr. Duckworth is which type of endorser?
    a) celebrity
    b) CEO
    c) expert
    d) typical person
(c; Challenging; p. 214)

231) Mr. Booth owns the local Ford dealership and recently filmed an advertisement where he talks about the deals consumers can obtain at his dealership. For this type of ad, Mr. Booth is which type of endorser?
   a) celebrity
   b) CEO
   c) expert
   d) typical person
(b; Challenging; p. 214)

232) A spokesperson's credibility is derived from trustworthiness and all of the following characteristics, *except:*
   a) attractiveness
   b) intelligence
   c) likeability
   d) expertise
(b; Moderate; p. 214)

233) Which type of spokesperson is most likely to have all five source characteristics?
   a) a celebrity
   b) a typical person
   c) an expert
   d) a CEO
(a; Challenging; p. 214)

234) In terms of source characteristics, attractiveness consists of:
   a) physical characteristics of the spokesperson
   b) intelligence of the spokesperson
   c) both physical and personality characteristics of the spokesperson
   d) the expertise and likeability of the spokesperson
(c; Moderate; p. 215)

235) Identification is the ability of the audience to identify with the spokesperson in an ad. Identification is derived from:
   a) expertise and credibility
   b) attractiveness and likeability
   c) personality and charisma
   d) similarity and attractiveness
(d; Challenging; p. 215)

236) Britney really likes the advertisement by Saturn that featured an elementary school teacher, primarily because Britney is also an elementary school teacher. This identification with the spokesperson by Britney is an example of the concept of:
   a) attractiveness
   b) similarity
   c) likeability
   d) trustworthiness
(b; Challenging; p. 215)

237) When an accountant serves as a spokesperson in an advertisement for an accounting service, viewers who are also accountants find the ad to be more credible based on:
   a) attractiveness
   b) similarity
   c) likeability
   d) persuasiveness
(b; Moderate; p. 215)

238) An ad that is targeted toward stay-at-home wives, which begins with this phrase, "Since I stopped working, I have more time for my kids," is emphasizing:
   a) likeability
   b) similarity
   c) consistency
   d) continuity
(b; Moderate; p. 215)

239) Wishing to think and act rich like the spokesperson in an advertisement, is a form of:
   a) empathy
   b) intent to purchase
   c) identification
   d) attractiveness
(c; Moderate; p. 215)

240) Giving to a charity because the spokesperson in the ad is a Republican, and the viewer is also a Republican, is based on:
   a) likeability
   b) identification
   c) consistency
   d) empathy
(b; Moderate; p. 215)

241) In terms of spokesperson characteristics, which is the degree of confidence or the level of acceptance consumers place in the spokesperson's message?
   a) trustworthiness
   b) expertise
   c) credibility
   d) likeability
(a; Moderate; p. 215)

242) A physician endorsing a specific brand of medicine would have a high level of:
   a) attractiveness
   b) likeability
   c) expertise
   d) personality
(c; Easy; p. 215)

243) In terms of source characteristics, which type of spokesperson normally scores well in terms of trustworthiness, believability, persuasiveness, and likeability?
   a) CEOs
   b) experts
   c) typical persons
   d) celebrities
(d; Challenging, p. 216)

244) A danger of using celebrities as spokespersons is that their endorsement of too many products tarnishes:
   a) credibility
   b) likeability
   c) expertise
   d) attractiveness
(a; Moderate; p. 216)

245) A danger of using a CEO or other prominent official of a corporation, is the that person may not possess the source characteristics of:
   a) trustworthiness and expertise
   b) attractiveness and likeability
   c) credibility and expertise
   d) likeability and trustworthiness
(b; Challenging; p. 217)

246) Using typical persons and CEOs as spokespeople in ads are difficult because:
   a) the individuals are often perceived as not being credible
   b) do not have a high level of expertise
   c) they are not professional actors so they are more difficult to work with
   d) they are not physically attractive
(c; Moderate; p. 217)

247) In creating an advertisement, the process begins with:
   a) the leverage point
   b) choosing the message strategy
   c) choosing the appeal
   d) the creative brief

(d; Moderate; p. 218)

248) In creating an advertisement, the creative begins with the creative brief. From the creative brief, the creative should:
   a) develop a means-end chain
   b) choose a spokesperson or decide if one will be used
   c) choose an appropriate message strategy
   d) decide on the ad execution

(a; Challenging; p. 218)

249) The following are basic principles of effective advertising, *except:*
   a) visual consistency
   b) unique tag lines
   c) consistent positioning
   d) simplicity

(b; Challenging; p. 219)

250) Visual consistency is important in developing effective advertisements because:
   a) of the high cost of producing new ads
   b) it creates a higher level of brand equity
   c) buyers, whether consumers or businesses, spend very little time viewing or listening to ads
   d) it maintains ad consistency

(c; Moderate; p. 219)

251) Of the following principles used in developing effective advertisements, which helps viewers move the advertising message from short-term memory to long-term memory?
   a) simplicity
   b) consistent positioning
   c) identifiable selling point
   d) visual consistency

(d; Challenging; p. 219)

252) The duration of an advertising campaign is affected by:
   a) both the reach and frequency of the campaign
   b) the reach of the campaign, but not the frequency
   c) the frequency of the campaign, but not the reach
   d) neither the reach or frequency of the campaign

(a; Challenging; p. 219)

253) Typical ad campaigns last:
   a) less than a month
   b) one to two months
   c) approximately six months
   d) six months to a year
   (b; Challenging; p. 219)

254) "The Few. The Proud. The Marines" used in every Marine ad demonstrates:
   a) an identifiable selling point
   b) credibility
   c) campaign duration
   d) repeated tagline
   (d; Easy; p. 220)

255) Visual consistency combined with which feature can be a powerful approach to building effective advertising campaigns?
   a) campaign duration
   b) simplicity
   c) repeated tag lines
   d) identifiable selling point
   (c; Challenging, p. 220)

256) Which help(s) consumers tie an advertisement into their current knowledge structure nodes and cognitive maps that already exist in their minds?
   a) Tag lines
   b) An identifiable selling point
   c) Simplicity
   d) Brand equity
   (a; Challenging; p. 220)

257) The principle of simplicity should be carefully applied to Internet advertising primarily because of the:
   a) educational level of Internet users
   b) load time for web pages
   c) importance of creating a uniform look
   d) importance of using only one identifiable selling point
   (b; Moderate; p. 220)

258) In beating ad clutter, repetition can increase brand and ad recall, *except* when:
   a) the ads are put into different media
   b) competing ads are present
   c) a celebrity spokesperson is used
   d) the ad uses a fantasy executional framework
   (b; Challenging; p. 221)

259) Repeating the same ad does not always work, which has led advertisers to take advantage of the principle of variability theory. That means brand and ad recall are increased because the ad:
   a) has several identifiable selling points
   b) is seen by consumers in different environments
   c) uses the same tagline in every venue
   d) uses a typical person spokesperson
(b; Challenging; p. 221)

260) Adam remembered the advertising for John Deere lawn tractors because in one ad the person driving the tractor was a female wearing an attractive bikini, in another it was of a mother with two kids playing in a yard, and in a third of a man in a business suit. In this example, Adams' recall of the ad and encoding of the John Deere name into his cognitive map was enhanced by the concept of:
   a) identifiable selling point
   b) campaign duration
   c) variability theory
   d) source credibility
(c; Challenging; p. 221)

Short-Answer Questions

261) Name the five major forms of cognitive strategies.

   1. Generic
   2. Preemptive
   3. Unique selling proposition
   4. Hyperbole
   5. Comparative
(Easy; p. 199)

262) What are the advantages and disadvantages of comparative ads?

The advantages are they capture attention and are remembered.
The disadvantages are they are less believable and can foster negative attitudes.
(Moderate; p. 200)

263) What are the two types of affective message strategies? Define both.

   1. Resonance advertising connects the product with the consumer's experiences in order to build bonds.
   2. Emotional advertising ties emotions to product recall and choice.
(Moderate; p. 202)

264) What are the two types of conative message strategies? Define both.

1. Action-inducing ads lead directly to behaviors, such as impulse buys.
2. Promotional support ads work in combination with other promotional efforts.
(Moderate; p. 204)

265) Name the executional frameworks advertisers can utilize.

- Animation
- Slice-of-life
- Dramatization
- Testimonial
- Authoritative
- Demonstration
- Fantasy
- Informative

(Moderate; p. 205)

266) What is the difference between slice-of-life and dramatization?

Dramatization is more intense.
(Easy; p. 207)

267) Name the ways to present claims in authoritative ads.

- Experts
- Scientific or survey evidence
- Endorsements by independent organizations
- Satisfied customers

(Moderate; p. 208)

268) What four types of sources or spokespersons can advertisers utilize?

- Celebrities
- CEOs
- Experts
- Typical persons

(Easy; p. 211)

269) What are the principles of effective advertising?

- Visual consistency
- Campaign duration
- Repeated taglines
- Consistent positioning
- Simplicity
- Identifiable selling point

(Challenging; p. 219)

CHAPTER 8
ADVERTISING MEDIA SELECTION

True-False Questions

1) M & Ms primary spokespersons are animated figures.
   (True; Easy; p. 230)

2) A media strategy is the process of analyzing and choosing media for an advertising and promotions campaign.
   (True; Easy; p. 232)

3) A radio listener usually tunes into only three of the many stations that are available in a given area.
   (True; Challenging; p. 232)

4) Under the old advertising model the mass market existed and could be reached through effective broadcast advertising.
   (True; Moderate; p. 233)

5) Under the old advertising model, it was believed that segmentation based on demographic factors such age, income, gender, and education was sufficient to create effective ads.
   (True; Moderate; p. 233)

6) In the new advertising model, to be effective advertising agencies must choose spots for television ads, magazine placements, newspaper sections, Internet sites, and billboard locations.
   (True; Moderate; p. 233)

7) Media planning begins with a careful analysis of the competition.
   (False; Moderate; p. 233)

8) A marketing analysis is a comprehensive review of a company's fundamental marketing program.
   (True; Moderate; p. 234)

9) An advertising analysis is a comprehensive review of a company's fundamental marketing program.
   (False; Moderate; p. 234)

10) The media strategy, media schedule, justification, and summary are components of a media planning strategy.
    (True; Moderate; p. 234)

11) A media planner formulates a media program stating where and when to place advertisements.
(True; Easy; p. 234)

12) Part of a media planner's job is to gather facts about various media.
(True; Moderate; p. 234)

13) Power has shifted recently and more power is now held by the creative side of the agency than by the media planning and buying side of the agency.
(False; Challenging; p. 234)

14) Media planning now drives much of the strategic planning process as advertising and marketing campaigns are developed.
(True; Moderate; p. 235)

15) A media buyer job is to purchase space as well as to negotiate rates, times, and schedules for ads.
(True; Easy; p. 236)

16) The person who buys space and also negotiates rates, times, and schedules for ads is normally the creative.
(False; Easy p. 236)

17) The size of the advertising agency or media buying firm has an impact on the rates that a company will pay for media time and space.
(False; Moderate; p. 236)

18) A spot ad is an advertisement that is placed in a specific spot in the ad rotation in an ad series.
(False; Moderate; p. 236)

19) Reach is the number of people, households, or businesses in a target market that are exposed to a message at least once during a given time period.
(True; Easy; p. 237)

20) Frequency is the average number of times an individual, household, or business in a target market is exposed to a message at least once during a given time period.
(False; Easy; p. 237)

21) In terms of reach and frequency, the time period usually used for measurement purposes is four months.
(False; Moderate; p. 237)

22) Ads placed on CSI Miami each week for three months offer the opportunity for greater frequency as compared to placing an advertisement on the Super Bowl.
(True; Challenging; p. 237)

23) Reach and frequency are, in essence, the same thing, because they show how many people saw an advertisement over a given time period.
(False; Moderate; p. 237)

24) Frequency and effective frequency are measures of the impact or intensity of a media plan.
(False; Moderate; p. 237)

25) The number of cumulative exposures achieved in given time period is called opportunities to see (OTS).
(True; Moderate; p. 237)

26) If three advertisements are placed on a weekly television show for six weeks, the number of OTS is 18.
(True; Challenging; p. 237)

27) Gross rating points are a measure of the impact or intensity of a media plan.
(True; Moderate; p. 237)

28) Gross rating points are measured by multiplying ratings times frequency.
(False; Moderate; p. 237)

29) CPM (cost per thousand) measures the length of time an advertisement runs.
(False; Easy; p. 237)

30) If it costs $300,000 to place an advertisement on a television show that has an audience of 15,000,000, then the CPM (cost per thousand) would be $20.00.
(True; Challenging, p. 237)

31) CPRP stands for cost per rating point, which is a relative measure of the efficiency of a media vehicle relative to a firm's target market.
(True; Challenging; p. 237)

32) Rating points are a measure of the impact or intensity of a media plan.
(False; Moderate; p. 237)

33) Continuity is the exposure pattern or schedule used in an advertising campaign.
(True; Easy; p. 239)

34) A continuous budgeting plan of advertising for a perfume would include ads throughout the entire year with extra ads during special times, such as Christmas, Valentine's Day, and Mother's Day.
(False; Moderate; p. 239)

35) A pulsating budget schedule means there is a level pulse of advertisements shown all year.
(False; Easy; p. 239)

36) A pulsating budget plan of advertising for a perfume would have ads just during specific times of the year, with none during the reminder of the year.
(False; Moderate; p. 239)

37) A flighting, or discontinuous, budgeting plan of advertising for a perfume would include ads throughout the entire year with extra ads during Christmas, Valentine's Day, and Mother's Day.
(False; Challenging; p. 239)

38) Gross impressions are a measure of the impact or intensity of a media plan.
(False; Easy; p. 240)

39) If 100,000 people are exposed to an advertisement, the total gross impressions are 100,000 regardless of whether the people actually closely watched the ad or not.
(True; Moderate; p. 240)

40) The three-exposure hypothesis suggests that a buyer who is actively looking for a new CD player would need to evaluate advertisements for three different players before making a choice.
(False; Challenging; p. 240)

41) Three-exposure hypothesis states that consumers have selective attention processes as they consider advertisements.
(True; Moderate; p. 240)

42) Effective frequency is the number of times a target audience must be exposed to a message to achieve a specific objective.
(True; Easy; p. 240)

43) Effective reach is the percentage of an audience that must be exposed to a message to achieve a specific objective.
(True; Easy; p. 240)

44) If the objective of an advertising campaign is to increase brand recall, then reach is more important than frequency.
(False; Challenging, p. 240)

45) In general, an advertising campaign featuring ads in two or more different types of media has a greater effective reach than a campaign with the same number of total ads, but using only one medium
(True; Moderate; p. 241)

46) Recency theory is based on the concept of intrusion value.
   (False; Challenging; p. 241)

47) Intrusion value is the ability of media or an advertisement to intrude upon a viewer without his or her voluntary attention.
   (True; Moderate; p. 241)

48) Recency theory suggests a person must see an advertisement three times before it will have an effect.
   (False; Easy; p. 241)

49) Recency theory suggests that it is a waste of money when ads reach either individuals or a business that does not need a particular product or do not have an interest in the product.
   (True; Moderate; p. 241)

50) Recency theory would suggest that in terms of media strategy it is better to maximize frequency rather than reach.
   (False; Challenging; p. 242)

51) In the business-to-business arena, applying recency theory means that ads should appear in a number of outlets rather than a series of ads in one trade journal.
   (True; Challenging; p. 242)

52) According to a MediaVest USA survey concerning how attentive consumers were to brand messages, sampling was at the top of the list.
   (False; Challenging; p. 243)

53) Television offers advertisers the most extensive coverage and highest reach of any media.
   (True; Moderate; p. 243)

54) Television has the advantage of intrusion value.
   (True; Easy; p. 243)

55) One major advantage to television is the lack of clutter as compared to other media.
   (False; Easy; p. 243)

56) Television shows average almost 15 minutes of advertisements per half hour of programming.
   (False; Challenging; p. 244)

57) In a sequence of television commercials, advertisements placed at the beginning of the sequence have the best recall. Ads in the middle and end of the sequence have very little impact.
(False; Moderate; p. 244)

58) The rating of a television show is measured by dividing the number of households tuned into a particular program by the number of households with a television turned on.
(False; Moderate; p. 244)

59) A rating of 11.5 means that 11.5 percent of all televisions in the United States are tuned into that particular program.
(True; Moderate; p. 244)

60) In terms of a TV ratings, a share of 9 means that 9 percent of the television that are turned on were tuned into a particular program.
(True; Challenging; p. 244)

61) Nielsen ratings are used to establish rates for television advertisements.
(True; Moderate; p. 245)

62) Media planners utilize spot TV purchases because of the high cost of national ad time and because 75 to 80 percent of prime-time slots are sold during the spring, shortly after they go on the market.
(True; Challenging; p. 245)

63) The brand development index (BDI) is a measure of a market's percentage of sales of a particular brand divided by that market's share of the total U.S. households.
(True; Challenging; p. 245)

64) The category development index (CDI) is a measure of a market's percentage of sales of a particular brand divided by that market's share of the total U.S. households.
(False; Challenging; p. 246)

65) If the brand development index (BDI) for a particular brand in a selected market is 68 and the category development index (CDI) for that same market is 140, it would indicate that the brand's market share is weak in comparison to the sales of the product category.
(True; Challenging; p. 246)

66) One reason business advertisers are using television is that it has become more difficult to reach members of the business buying center through traditional business outlets, such as trade journals.
(True; Moderate; p. 246)

67) Radio advertising offers the advantage of having definable target markets based on the radio stations' format.
(True; Moderate; p. 246)

68) Radio is less likely to be a viable marketing alternative for Hispanic-Americans, who do not listen as often.
(False; Moderate; p. 247)

69) Radio has the advantage of intimacy, where the DJ talks directly to the listener.
(True; Moderate; p. 247)

70) Television is more mobile than radio, giving it better reach.
(False; Moderate; p. 247)

71) Radio is a viable medium for business-to-business ads because it can reach businesspeople while in transit to work and during office hours if they have the radio on in their business.
(True; Easy; p. 248)

72) Outdoor advertising is more than the use of billboards.
(True; Easy; p. 248)

73) Outdoor advertising has changed dramatically with the development of new technologies, such as global positioning systems, wireless communications, and digital display technology.
(True; Moderate; p. 248)

74) For local companies, billboards are an excellent advertising medium because primarily local audiences see the message.
(True; Moderate; p. 249)

75) Billboard advertising normally has a very low CPM (cost per thousand exposures).
(True; Moderate; p. 249)

76) A major drawback of outdoor advertising is the short exposure time.
(True; Easy; p. 249)

77) To counter the short exposure time of billboards and to take advantage of traffic jams, a rising area of outdoor advertising is the use of ads on the sides of city buses.
(False; Challenging; p. 249)

78) It is likely that the rise in Internet usage is reducing the number of television viewers.
(True; Moderate; p. 250)

79) A major benefit of Internet marketing is the creative opportunities available and the short lead time.
(True; Moderate; p. 251)

80) Through a technique called behavioral targeting, the Internet has the capability of targeting consumers with specific ads based on their Internet movement to various Web sites.
(True; Moderate; p. 251)

81) The use of the Internet as an advertising medium for business-to-business marketing has declined substantially in recent years.
(False; Easy; p. 251)

82) Of all the various media available to advertisers, magazines allows for tracking and measuring results better than any other medium
(False; Moderate; p. 251)

83) An interstitial ad on a Web page has significant intrusion value.
(True; Moderate; p. 252)

84) The Internet is an effective advertising medium for young, well-educated consumers with high incomes.
(True; Challenging; p. 252)

85) The Internet is the fastest-growing medium in history.
(True; Easy, p. 252)

86) One of the major advantages of magazines is the ability to advertise to specific target markets.
(True; Moderate; p. 253)

87) One of the key advantages of magazine advertisements is the short lead-time available, allowing the advertiser to react to current events.
(False; Moderate; p. 253)

88) One major disadvantage facing magazine advertisers is a decline in magazine readership.
(True; Moderate; p. 254)

89) Retailers rely heavily on newspaper advertising because it offers geographic selectivity.
(True; Moderate; p. 255)

90) Newspapers are an excellent advertising medium for local companies.
(True; Easy; p. 255)

91) Newspapers offer the best quality color print reproduction.
(False; Easy; p. 256)

92) The average overall response rate to direct mail is 2.5 percent.
(True; Challenging; p. 257)

93) The major advantage of direct mail is that it normally lands in the hands of the person who opens the mail, who usually makes a significant amount of family purchasing decisions.
(True; Moderate; p. 257)

94) Direct mail remains a favorite marketing tool for business-to-business marketers because it is an effective method of bypassing the gatekeepers in an organization.
(True; Moderate; p. 257)

95) One of the more widely used alternative media programs is called guerrilla marketing, which is a focus on low-cost, creative ways to reach consumers.
(True; Moderate; p. 258)

96) When a particular brand of product, such as Ford trucks, is displayed in a movie or television show as part of the show, it is known as product placement.
(True; Easy; p. 258)

97) Film companies now charge firms for product placement and the fee depends on if the product just appears on the show, is mentioned on the show, or is actually used by the actor.
(True; Challenging; p. 258)

98) Tiger Woods wearing a cap with the Nike name or Nike swoosh logo on it during a golf tournament is an example of product placement.
(True; Challenging; p. 258)

99) Currently, advertising tobacco and tobacco-related products is not permitted on television.
(True; Moderate; p. 259)

100) Media multiplier effect refers to the combined impact of using two or more media is stronger than using either medium alone.
(True; Moderate; p. 260)

101) In terms of the media mix, retailers tend to spend the most on newspaper advertising.
(True; Challenging; p. 260)

102) In terms of the media mix, apparel manufactures tend to spend the most on television advertising.
(False; Challenging; p. 260)

103) In terms of the media mix, restaurants tend to spend the most on billboard advertising.
(False; Challenging; p. 260)

104) Identifying the difference between consumer ads and business-to-business ads is becoming more difficult, especially in television, outdoor, and Internet ads.
(True; Challenging; p. 260)

105) The number one media used for business-to-business advertising is now television.
(False; Moderate; p. 260)

106) Ads in trade journals and other media have a better chance of being noticed by members of the buying center if the firm is either in a straight rebuy or a modified rebuy situation.
(False; Challenging; p. 261)

107) In business-to-business advertising, the majority of advertising dollars goes to print media and especially to magazines, both trade and business-related magazines.
(True; Challenging; p. 261)

108) Many of the goals of business-to-business advertisements are the same as those devoted to consumers.
(True; Challenging; p. 262)

109) In Europe newspapers are the best way to reach consumers, while in Japan television is the most effective medium.
(True; Challenging; p. 262)

110) Advertising in international markets is largely the same as in domestic markets because of globalization of the world.
(False; Challenging; p. 263)

111) While many tactics used to develop advertising campaigns in the United States apply to international advertising, differences do exist in terms of the nature of the target market, media preferences, and the processes used to buy media time and space.
(True; Challenging; p. 263)

Multiple-Choice Questions

112) Which form of spokesperson is used by M & Ms?
    a) celebrity
    b) CEO
    c) animated figures
    d) real person
(c; Easy; p. 230)

113) Which medium has long been the staple for M & Ms advertising?
    a) television
    b) magazine
    c) radio
    d) newspaper
(a; Challenging; p. 230)

114) A media strategy is the process of:
    a) investigating the media usage of a product's target market
    b) analyzing and choosing media for an advertising and promotions campaign
    c) selecting the outlets of each media that will be used for an advertising campaign
    d) choosing the proper appeal, message, strategy, and execution
(b; Moderate; p. 232)

115) The old advertising model was based on each of the following concepts, *except:*
    a) mass-markets exists and can be reached through broadcast advertising
    b) segmentation based on demographics is sufficient to create effective ads
    c) with enough repetition and reach to the mass-markets favorable impressions can be made
    d) increased clutter created a highly refined ability by consumers to tune out ads and messages
(d; Challenging; p. 233)

116) Under the old advertising model, the majority of advertising dollars was spent on:
    a) network television
    b) cable television
    c) print media
    d) newspaper and radio
(a; Challenging; p. 233)

117) The new method of advertising campaign development is based on the idea that:
   a) online advertising is better at reaching target markets than broadcast media
   b) a more integrated approach based on an in-depth understanding of the target market is essential
   c) clutter has made it more difficult to reach consumers with broadcast advertising
   d) there are more media outlets now than in the past
(b; Moderate; p. 233)

118) A media plan begins with:
   a) a careful analysis of the target market
   b) a trend analysis
   c) an examination of the competition
   d) a statement about the media mix
(a; Moderate; p. 233)

119) The part of the media plan that reviews the fundamental marketing program is a(n):
   a) marketing analysis
   b) advertising analysis
   c) media strategy
   d) media mix
(a; Moderate; p. 234)

120) The part of the media plan that spells out the media to be used and creative considerations is the:
   a) marketing analysis
   b) advertising analysis
   c) media strategy
   d) media mix
(c; Moderate; p. 234)

121) The part of the media plan that notes when and where ads will appear is the:
   a) marketing analysis
   b) advertising analysis
   c) media strategy
   d) media schedule
(d; Moderate; p. 234)

122) The part of the media plan that states measures of goal achievements and the rationale for choices is the:
   a) marketing analysis
   b) advertising analysis
   c) media strategy
   d) justification and summary
(d; Moderate; p. 234)

123) Which individual formulates a plan as to where and when ads should run?
    a) the creative
    b) the media planner
    c) the media buyer
    d) the client
(b; Easy; p. 234)

124) The issue of accountability for advertising results combined with the need to create a "return on investment" of marketing dollars had led to a shift of power to the:
    a) creative side of the agency
    b) account side of the agency
    c) media planning and buying side of the agency
    d) client
(c; Challenging; p. 235)

125) Marketing experts at companies such as Procter & Gamble and Unilever consider which activity to the heart of a communications strategy?
    a) media planning
    b) creative design
    c) appeal selection
    d) marketing strategy
(a; Challenging; p. 235)

126) Conducting research that matches the product to the media and the target market is the primary task of the:
    a) creative
    b) media planner
    c) media buyer
    d) client company
(b; Moderate; p. 235)

127) Which individual decided S.O.S Shop Pads should be advertised in magazines, because of the characteristics of the women who buy and use them?
    a) the creative
    b) the media planner
    c) the media buyer
    d) the client
(b; Challenging; p. 235)

128) The individual that negotiates rates for space on billboards and in magazines is the:
    a) creative
    b) media planner
    c) media buyer
    d) client
(c; Easy; p. 236)

129) What is the relationship between the size of an ad agency and the price it pays for spots on television or radio?
    a) the bigger the company, the more that will be paid for advertising
    b) the bigger the company, the less that will be paid for advertising
    c) medium-sized companies get the best deal
    d) there is no consistent relationship
(d; Challenging; p. 236)

130) Effectiveness in buying media time and space is dependent on each of the following factors, *except:*
    a) agency culture and track record
    b) relationship between the agency and the medium's sales representative
    c) size of the agency
    d) creativity of the media buyer
(c; Challenging; p. 236)

131) A spot ad is:
    a) a one time placement of an ad on a local television station
    b) one that is placed in a specific location in an ad sequence
    c) the placement of an ad series on a specific television show
    d) a one time placement of an ad on cable television
(a; Moderate; p. 236)

132) The number of people, households, or businesses in a target market who are exposed to a media vehicle or message schedule at least once during a given time period is:
    a) reach
    b) frequency
    c) demographics
    d) impressions
(a; Easy; p. 237)

133) Reach is:
    a) the number of people, households, or businesses who are exposed to a media vehicle or message schedule at least once during a given time period
    b) the number of people who place a particular brand into their evoked sets
    c) the number of people who purchase a product in a given time period
    d) the number of people who use a certain medium in a four week time period
(a; Moderate; p. 237)

134) In terms of measuring reach and frequency, the typical time period is:
    a) one week
    b) four weeks
    c) eight weeks
    d) one year
(b; Challenging; p. 237)

135) The average number of times an individual, household, or business in a target market is exposed to an advertisement during a specific time period is:
    a) reach
    b) frequency
    c) demographics
    d) impressions
(b; Easy; p. 237)

136) Frequency is the:
    a) number of people, households, or businesses who are exposed to a media vehicle or message schedule at least once during a given time period
    b) number of people who place a particular brand into their evoked sets
    c) number of people who purchase the product
    d) average number of times an individual, household, or business in a target market is exposed to an advertisement during a specific time period
(d; Moderate; p. 237)

137) Among the following ad campaigns, frequency would be highest for:
    a) six 15-second television spots
    b) one 45-second spot
    c) five 30-second spot
    d) four 15-second spots
(a; Challenging; p. 237)

138)	A company seeking to build brand awareness through repeated exposures to the same ads is using the concept of high:
   a)	frequency
   b)	continuity
   c)	exposure
   d)	reach
(a; Challenging; p. 237)

139)	OTS stands for:
   a)	outstanding test series
   b)	overview of theory sequence
   c)	opportunity to see
   d)	oldest time score
(c; Easy; p. 237)

140)	In media planning, instead of frequency, which is the commonly used measure?
   a)	reach
   b)	opportunity to see (OTS)
   c)	gross rating points (GRP)
   d)	cost per thousand (CPM)
(b; Challenging; p. 237)

141)	If an advertisement is placed in three different places in *Glamour* and run for five issues, the number of opportunities to see (OTS) would be:
   a)	3
   b)	5
   c)	15
   d)	depend on the gross rating points for *Glamour*
(c; Challenging; p. 237)

142)	The cumulative exposures achieved in a given time period is called:
   a)	cost per thousand (CPM)
   b)	gross rating points (GRP)
   c)	opportunities to see (OTS)
   d)	reach and frequency
(c; Moderate; p. 237)

143)	A measure of the impact or intensity of a media plan is:
   a)	cost per thousand (CPM)
   b)	gross rating points (GRP)
   c)	opportunities to see (OTS)
   d)	reach and frequency
(b; Moderate; p. 237)

144) Multiplying a vehicle's rating times the number of insertions for an advertisement calculates the:
- a) cost per thousand (CPM)
- b) gross rating points (GRP)
- c) opportunities to see (OTS)
- d) reach and frequency

(b; Moderate; p. 237)

145) Multiplying a vehicle's rating times opportunities to see (OTS) for an advertisement calculates the:
- a) cost per thousand (CPM)
- b) gross rating points (GRP)
- c) cost per rating point (CPRP)
- d) frequency

(b; Moderate; p. 237)

146) If an advertisement appears on ER three times and ER has a Nielsen rating of 12.3, the gross rating points (GRP) would be:
- a) 4.1
- b) 12.3
- c) 36.9
- d) there is not enough information to calculate the GRP

(c; Challenging; p. 237)

147) CPM stands for:
- a) cost per thousand
- b) cost per million
- c) cost of permission marketing
- d) choice of premium method

(a; Easy; p. 237)

148) The dollar cost of reaching 1,000 members of a media vehicle's audience is the:
- a) cost per thousand (CPM)
- b) gross rating points (GRP)
- c) cost of per million
- d) effective reach

(a; Easy; p. 237)

149) If the CPM for National Geographic is $16.44, it means it will cost $16.44 to reach:
- a) the selected target audience
- b) one thousand readers
- c) 1644 readers
- d) one million readers

(b; Moderate; p. 237)

150) If the cost for a 4-color print ad is $150,000 and the magazine has 3,000,000 million readers, the CPM would be:
   a) $50.00
   b) $500.00
   c) $20.00
   d) cannot be determined from the information given
(a; Challenging, p. 237)

151) CPRP stands for:
   a) cost per rotation program
   b) closest programmed ratings plan
   c) cost per rating point
   d) cumulative program for ratings points
(c; Moderate; p. 238)

152) Which of the following is a relative measure of the efficiency of a media vehicle relative to a firm's target market?
   a) gross rating points (GRPP)
   b) opportunities to see (OTS)
   c) gross impressions
   d) cost per rating point (CPRP)
(d; Moderate; p. 238)

153) Cost per rating point (CPRP) is the:
   a) number of people, households, or businesses who are exposed to a media vehicle or message schedule at least once during a given time period
   b) measure of the impact or intensity of a media plan
   c) relative measure of the efficiency of a media vehicle relative to a firm's target market
   d) average number of times an individual, household, or business in a target market is exposed to an advertisement during a specific time period
(c; Challenging; p. 238)

154) Cost per rating point (CPRP) is calculated as:
   a) cost of media buy divided by the vehicle's rating
   b) cost of the media buy multiplied by the number of viewers
   c) ratings divided by gross exposures
   d) cost of media buy divided by gross exposures
(a; Moderate; p. 238)

155) If an advertisement costs $200,000, the number of viewers is 2,000,000, and the rating is 2.0, then the cost per rating point (CPRP) is:
    a) $100
    b) $1,000
    c) $10,000
    d) $100,000
   (d; Challenging; p. 238)

156) The technique designed to find out an advertisement's cost in reaching a particular product's target market is called:
    a) effective frequency
    b) target reach
    c) weighted or demographic CPM
    d) cost per rating point
   (c; Challenging; p. 238)

157) If a magazine ad costs $500,000, total readership is 20,000,000, but only 2,000,000 fit the advertiser's target profile, the weighted (or demographic) cost per thousand (CPM) would be:
    a) $25
    b) $250
    c) $2,500
    d) $10
   (b; Challenging; p. 238)

158) The exposure pattern or schedule used in an ad campaign is called:
    a) continuity
    b) discontinuity campaign
    c) reach
    d) frequency
   (a; Challenging; p. 239)

159) Using media time in a steady stream throughout an entire year is which type of media budget schedule?
    a) continuous
    b) pulsating
    c) flighting
    d) frequency
   (a; Moderate; p. 239)

160) A company that manufactures washing machines is most likely to invest in a(n):
    a) continuous campaign
    b) flighting campaign
    c) reach campaign
    d) pulsating campaign
   (a; Challenging; p. 239)

161) The media budget schedule that maintains some minimal level of advertising at all times during the year, but increases advertising at periodic intervals is:
   a) continuous
   b) gross impressions
   c) pulsating
   d) flighting, or discontinuous
   (c; Easy; p. 239)

162) A company that advertises some all year round, but more during the holidays is using :
   a) a continuous campaign
   b) gross impressions
   c) a pulsating campaign
   d) a flighting campaign
   (c; Challenging; p. 239)

163) When advertisements are used at special intervals with none in-between, which media budgeting method is being used?
   a) continuous
   b) gross impressions
   c) pulsating
   d) flighting
   (d; Moderate; p. 239)

164) A summer camp with horse-riding trails is only open from March to September would tend to budget media using which type of schedule?
   a) continuous
   b) reach-based
   c) pulsating
   d) flighting
   (d; Challenging; p. 239)

165) Gross impressions are:
   a) total exposures of an audience to an advertisement
   b) calculated considering the percentage of a total audience who viewed an ad
   c) viewer reactions to the ad
   d) viewer loyalty to the medium
   (a; Easy; p. 240)

166) Five advertisements placed in a newspaper during a four-week period with a readership of 10,000 would create how many gross impressions?
   a) 10,000
   b) 40,000
   c) 50,000
   d) gross impressions can't be calculated with the information provided

(c; Moderate; p. 240)

167) The three-exposure hypothesis states that:
   a) ads in three different media need to be used to have the maximum impact
   b) three exposures to an ad is sufficient to be effective
   c) a minimum of three exposures to an ad is sufficient to be effective
   d) three exposures to an ad will only work if the person viewing the ad is in the market for that particular product

(b; Challenging; p. 240)

168) Many advertisers doubt the three-exposure hypothesis primarily because:
   a) the number of media now available to advertisers has increased substantially
   b) of ad clutter
   c) of the power of the Internet
   d) of the synergistic effect of using multiple media in an advertising campaign

(b; Moderate; p. 240)

169) Effective frequency refers to the:
   a) number of times a target audience must be exposed to an ad for it to be effective
   b) percentage of the audience that must be exposed to an ad to achieve an objective
   c) percentage of the audience that has seen the ad a minimum of three times
   d) degree of selective attention given by the target audience relative to the objective

(a; Moderate; p. 240)

170) The number of times a target audience must be exposed to a message to achieve a particular objective is called:
   a) gross rating points
   b) effective reach
   c) effective frequency
   d) opportunities to see (OTS)

(c; Moderate; p. 240)

171) Effective reach refers to the:
   a) number of times a target audience must be exposed to an ad for it to be effective
   b) percentage of the audience that must be exposed to an ad to achieve an objective
   c) percentage of the audience that has seen the ad a minimum of three times
   d) degree of selective attention given by the target audience relative to the objective
   (b; Moderate; p. 240)

172) The percentage of a target audience must be exposed to a message to achieve a particular objective is called:
   a) gross rating points
   b) effective reach
   c) effective frequency
   d) opportunities to see (OTS)
   (b; Moderate; p. 240)

173) If effective reach and/or effective frequency are too high:
   a) the company needs a larger advertising budget
   b) the company spent all of its advertising budget
   c) some of the company's budget may be wasted on extra exposures
   d) the company may need to choose additional media for future ads
   (c; Challenging; p. 240)

174) If effective reach and/or effective frequency are too low:
   a) the company needs a larger advertising budget
   b) the company has not spent all of its advertising budget
   c) some of the company's budget may be wasted on extra exposures
   d) the company will fail to attain its intended objectives
   (d; Challenging; p. 240)

175) If the objective of an advertising campaign is to increase brand recognition, then the emphasis should be on:
   a) the visual presentation of the product and/or logo
   b) a high level of frequency
   c) using persuasive advertising
   d) using an emotional appeal
   (a; Challenging; p. 240)

176) If the objective of an advertising campaign is to increase brand recall, then the emphasis should be on:
    a) the characteristics of the target market
    b) a high level of frequency
    c) a high level of reach
    d) both a high level of frequency and a high level of reach
(b; Challenging; p. 240)

177) The traditional three-exposure hypothesis is based on:
    a) selective attention exposure
    b) effective reach and effective frequency
    c) intrusion value
    d) media multiplier effect
(c; Challenging; p. 240)

178) Intrusion value is:
    a) the ability of an ad to capture a viewer's attention without his or her voluntary attention
    b) the degree to which an ad is involuntarily recalled
    c) the perception that an ad was effective
    d) using separate attention process
(a; Moderate; p. 241)

179) Recency theory is based on:
    a) the concept that the last ad a person sees has the greatest impact
    b) three exposures to an ad are necessary for the ad to be effective
    c) the concept of intrusion value
    d) consumers having selective attention processes
(d; Challenging; p. 241)

180) Recency theory would suggest that a member in a buying center about ready to purchase a copier has:
    a) to see at least three ads for copier machines before it is noticed
    b) an intrusion threshold for copier ads
    c) selective attention to copier ads
    d) little interest in copier ads until a copier is purchased
(c; Challenging; p. 241)

181) According to which of the principles below, one ad exposure is enough to affect an audience when that person or business needs the product or has an interest in the product?
    a) three-hypothesis theory
    b) recency theory
    c) the media multiplier effect
    d) the intrusion value concept
(b; Moderate; p. 241)

182) Based on recency theory, the best media strategy for a firm advertising lawn mowers would be to:
   a) place an ad in a few outlets, but use a high frequency level
   b) utilize broadcast media that offer the lowest CPM
   c) maximize reach through using multiple media and multiple outlets
   d) maximize frequency through using only one medium
(c; Challenging; p. 241)

183) According to a MediaVest USA survey concerning how attentive consumers were to brand messages, which of the following was at the top of the list?
   a) sampling
   b) word-of-mouth communication
   c) mass media advertisements
   d) in-store messages
(b; Moderate; p. 243)

184) Television offers the following advantages, *except:*
   a) high reach
   b) high frequency potential
   c) low cost per contact
   d) narrowly defined target markets
(d; Moderate; p. 243)

185) Television offers the following advantages, *except:*
   a) segmentation possibilities through network channels
   b) quality creative opportunities
   c) high frequency potential
   d) high intrusion value
(a; Moderate; p. 243)

186) The following are disadvantages of television, *except:*
   a) greater clutter
   b) high cost per contact
   c) channel surfing during commercials
   d) low recall due to clutter
(b; Moderate; p. 244)

187) Which of these media offers the most extensive coverage and the highest reach?
   a) radio
   b) newspapers
   c) television
   d) the Internet
(c; Moderate; p. 244)

188) An advertisement on television will have the biggest impact:
   a) at the beginning or end of a set of ads
   b) in the middle of a set of ads
   c) during an infomercial
   d) when the ad is 15 seconds rather than 30 or 45
(a; Easy; p. 244)

189) Most television ads (69 percent) are:
   a) 15 second spots
   b) 30 second spots
   c) 45 second spots
   d) 60 second spots
(b; Moderate; p. 244)

190) Which medium is *least* able to accommodate a local company at a low cost?
   a) newspaper
   b) radio
   c) television
   d) billboard
(c; Moderate; p. 244)

191) The number of households turned to a program divided by the total number of households in the United States calculates a television program's:
   a) rating
   b) recall
   c) relevance
   d) reach
(a; Moderate; p. 244)

192) Ratings measure the:
   a) relative efficiency of a media vehicle in hitting a target market
   b) percentage of a households tuned into a particular television show or viewing a medium such as a magazine
   c) quality of the vehicle relative to its promotional impact
   d) degree of clutter on a given night
(b; Moderate; p. 244)

193) A Nielsen rating of 15.3 on a particular television show means:
   a) 15.3 percent of all television in the U.S. were turned on
   b) of the televisions that were turned on in the U.S., 15.3 percent were tuned to a particular program
   c) 15.3 percent of all television in the U.S. were tuned to a particular program
   d) none of the above
(c; Moderate; p. 245)

194) Television advertising rates are primarily determined by:
   a) Nielsen ratings
   b) television share
   c) frequency and reach
   d) GRPs
   (a; Moderate; p. 245)

195) The number of households turned to a program divided by the total number of households with a television turned on calculates:
   a) rating
   b) recall
   c) share
   d) frequency
   (c; Moderate; p. 245)

196) 1.6 percent of Campbell's Soups sales occur in Chicago, the category sales of soup in Chicago is 1.2 percent, and that Chicago represents 0.8 percent of the total population. The brand development index for Campbell's Soups is:
   a) 200
   b) 150
   c) 133
   d) 50
   (a; Challenging; p. 246)

197) 1.6 percent of Campbell's Soups sales occur in Chicago, the category sales of soup in Chicago is 1.2 percent, and that Chicago represents 0.8 percent of the total population. The category development index for Campbell's Soups is:
   a) 200
   b) 150
   c) 133
   d) 50
   (b; Challenging; p. 246)

198) Business-to-business advertisers use television for each of the following reasons, *except:*
   a) it is becoming more difficult to reach members of the buying center and they do watch television
   b) increased clutter in trade journals and traditional business outlets
   c) business advertisements now use less emotional appeals
   d) a strong brand name is a growing factor in business purchases
   (c; Challenging; p. 246)

199) The following are advantages of using radio, *except:*
    a) low production costs
    b) flexibility
    c) long exposure time
    d) intimacy
(c; Moderate; p. 246)

200) The following are advantages of using radio, *except:*
    a) high segmentation potential
    b) flexibility in making new ads
    c) able to modify ads to local conditions
    d) easy national purchase procedures
(d; Moderate; p. 246)

201) Of the following, the medium that offers the most effective form of a one-on-one message by the spokesperson in the ad is:
    a) radio
    b) newspaper
    c) magazine
    d) outdoor
(a; Moderate; p. 246)

202) The primary advantage radio has that is not available in the other mass media outlets is:
    a) low cost per contact
    b) intimacy
    c) long exposure duration
    d) highly targeted market segmentation
(b; Challenging; p. 247)

203) Outdoor advertising has changed dramatically through each of the following technologies, *except:*
    a) global positioning systems
    b) wireless communications
    c) digital printing technology
    d) digital display technology
(c; Challenging; p. 248)

204) Of the following media, the one that is least able to target specific markets is:
    a) television
    b) radio
    c) magazines
    d) billboards
(d; Moderate; p. 249)

205)	The following are advantages of outdoor advertising, *except:*
    a)	low cost per impression
    b)	broad reach
    c)	short lead time to develop ads
    d)	accessible for local ads
(c; Moderate; p. 249)

206)	The following are disadvantages of outdoor advertising, *except:*
    a)	short exposure time
    b)	high cost per impression
    c)	brief message duration
    d)	little segmentation possible
(b; Moderate; p. 249)

207)	To counter the short exposure time and to take advantage of traffic jams in major cities, a new outdoor advertising methodology that has grown in popularity is:
    a)	LED billboards
    b)	global positioning systems
    c)	mobile billboards
    d)	urban billboards
(c; Challenging; p. 249)

208)	A study by Forrester Research indicated that 75 percent of the individuals in the study gave up time doing which of the following in order to surf the Internet?
    a)	watching television
    b)	eating and sleeping
    c)	listening to the radio
    d)	leisure and recreational time
(a; Challenging; p. 250)

209)	Which technique helps identify an Internet user's online patterns and reach the user with relevant ads?
    a)	rotoscoping
    b)	multiple media effect
    c)	interstitial advertising
    d)	behavioral targeting
(d; Challenging; p. 251)

210)	Of all of the various media available to advertisers, which medium allows for tracking and measuring results better than any of the others?
    a)	television
    b)	Internet
    c)	magazine
    d)	newspaper
(b; Moderate; p. 251)

211) Interstitial advertisements:
- a) are a new form of outdoor advertising using LED technology
- b) are streaming video advertisements that can be played on any computer
- c) interrupts a person on the Internet and must be clicked off to remove them from the screen
- d) utilize flash technology and provide advertisements using behavioral targeting technology

(c; Challenging; p. 252)

212) Magazines offer each of the following advantages, *except:*
- a) high level of market segmentation
- b) high level of color quality
- c) long life
- d) short ad lead time

(d; Moderate; p. 253)

213) The media which features the best quality of color in ads is:
- a) magazines
- b) newspapers
- c) billboards
- d) color quality is the same for most print media

(a; Easy; p. 253)

214) The major medium for business-to-business marketing is:
- a) the Internet
- b) trade and business journals
- c) newspapers
- d) television

(b; Easy; p. 254)

215) Of the following media, the medium with the greatest or longest life is:
- a) television
- b) radio
- c) magazines
- d) billboards

(c; Challenging; p. 254)

216) Magazine readership has declined in recent years. Research has indicated that most of these moved to:
- a) television
- b) alternative media
- c) newspapers
- d) the Internet

(d; Easy; p. 254)

217) Of the following media, the one that requires the longest lead time from ad development to ad appearance is:
    a) the Internet
    b) magazines
    c) newspapers
    d) billboards
(b; Moderate; p. 255)

218) For many smaller local companies, the most viable advertising options include all of the following, *except:*
    a) newspapers
    b) magazines
    c) billboards
    d) radio
(b; Moderate; p. 255)

219) Advertising in newspapers offers each of the following advantages, *except:*
    a) high flexibility
    b) high credibility
    c) long life
    d) longer copy or messages
(c; Moderate; p. 255)

220) Advertising in newspapers has the following disadvantages, *except:*
    a) poor national procedures
    b) short life span
    c) poor quality reproduction
    d) low credibility
(d; Moderate; p. 255)

221) In terms of media, local retailers tend to spend the most dollars on:
    a) newspaper ads
    b) radio ads
    c) television ads
    d) billboards
(a; Moderate; p. 255)

222) The major reason retailers tend to use newspapers for advertising is newspapers:
    a) are lower cost compared to the other media
    b) offer geographic selectivity
    c) have a longer life than radio or television
    d) show a preference for local retailers
(b; Challenging; p. 255)

223) Of the following advertising media, the one with the highest level of credibility is:
   a) television
   b) radio
   c) newspapers
   d) magazines
   (c; Challenging; p. 256)

224) National advertising in newspapers is growing faster than any other category of advertising primarily because of the:
   a) lower cost of newspaper compared to other media
   b) large number of national newspapers
   c) higher level of credibility newspapers offer
   d) Newspaper National Network and Newspaper First, which have been formed to make national buys in an number of newspapers
   (d; Moderate; p. 256)

225) Direct mail offers each of the following advantages, *except:*
   a) high intrusion value
   b) direct response programs are available
   c) the person who opens the mail is usually the household's main buyer
   d) the ability to target geographic market segments
   (a; Easy; p. 257)

226) The major advantage of direct mail is:
   a) low clutter
   b) geographic targeting
   c) the person who receives the direct mail and opens it is likely to be the decision maker
   d) low cost
   (c; Moderate; p. 257)

227) Direct mail remains a favorite of business-to-business marketers because it:
   a) is an effective means of bypassing gatekeepers
   b) reaches business buyers when they are making purchase decisions
   c) provides a high level of intimacy
   d) costs less than television advertising
   (a; Challenging; p. 257)

228) When a marketing team looks for unique ways to reach individuals and groups that will cause them to notice a product or company, the technique is known as:
   a) expenditure marketing
   b) marketing management
   c) guerilla marketing
   d) marketing facilitation
   (c; Easy; p. 258)

229) When a firm has its product shown in the background of a television program or film, the advertising technique is known as:
   a) practical marketing
   b) showcase marketing
   c) product placement
   d) passive advertising
(c; Easy; p. 258)

230) The use of Mercedez Benz in the most recent James Bond film is an example of:
   a) dealership marketing
   b) corporate identification
   c) decorative product marketing
   d) product placement
(d; Moderate; p. 258)

231) Seeing a Federal Express sign in the background behind a play at a sports event is a form of:
   a) event marketing
   b) continuous advertising
   c) product placement
   d) merchandising the advertising
(c; Challenging; p. 258)

232) In terms of media mix, retailers tend to spend the most (41.3 percent) on:
   a) magazines
   b) newspapers
   c) television
   d) radio
(b; Challenging; p. 260)

233) In terms of media mix, apparel manufacturers tend to spend the most (41.3 percent) on:
   a) magazines
   b) newspapers
   c) television
   d) radio
(a; Challenging; p. 260)

234) In terms of media mix, restaurants tend to spend the most (41.3 percent) on:
   a) magazines
   b) newspapers
   c) television
   d) outdoor
(c; Challenging; p. 260)

235) The media multiplier effect means:
   a) the combined impact of using two or more media is stronger than using either medium alone
   b) the combined effect of television and magazines will increase recall by at least 25%
   c) the use of both trade journals and consumer journals for business-to-business ads will have a greater impact than using either medium alone
   d) that if three different media or used, the combined impact is greater than if only two different media are used
(a; Challenging; p. 260)

236) A Millward Brown study revealed that ad awareness was 65 percent when consumers viewed an ad both on television and in a magazine, but it was only 19 percent when the ad was seen in only the magazine and 16 percent was it was viewed only on television. The phenomena is known as:
   a) guerilla marketing
   b) media multiplier effect
   c) media synergy effect
   d) media mix phenomena
(b; Moderate; p. 260)

237) In terms of b-to-b advertising, using non-business media rather than traditional media (e.g. trade journals) may help a company:
   a) build a stronger brand name
   b) reduce overall advertising expenditures
   c) define target markets more clearly
   d) generate unique or different prospect names for sales calls
(a; Moderate; p. 260)

238) Business-to-business advertising is:
   a) mostly in newspapers
   b) mostly spent on television
   c) looking more like consumer ads
   d) easier to create because of gatekeepers' screening ads
(c; Moderate; p. 261)

239) One reason for using non-business media to reach business buyers is the difficulty getting through to decision makers, users, and influencers in the buying center. This is especially true in:
   a) straight rebuy situations
   b) modified rebuy situations
   c) new task purchases
   d) both modified rebuy and new task situations
(a; Challenging; p. 261)

240) The recent shift in b-to-b advertising to more non-business media outlets is due to each of the following reasons, *except:*
    a) business decision makers are also consumers of goods and services
    b) non-business outlets are not as costly and tend to be more effective
    c) difficulty of reaching members of the buying center when they are at work
    d) clutter in traditional business-to-business media
(b; Challenging; p. 261)

241) In terms of business-to-business advertising expenditures, the most dollars (approximately 44 percent) is spent on:
    a) television
    b) the Internet
    c) trade journals
    d) business publications
(c; Moderate; p. 261)

242) Seventy percent of all business-to-business advertising dollars are spent on:
    a) television
    b) broadcast media
    c) print media
    d) Web site development and advertisements
(c; Challenging; p. 262)

243) Media buying in international settings is:
    a) similar in every country
    b) mostly performed by full-service agencies
    c) conducted by media buyers in some countries but advertising agencies in others
    d) subject to international law
(c; Moderate; p. 263)

244) In terms of media usage in Europe:
    a) television is the most dominant medium for advertising
    b) many elite European customers prefer media other than television.
    c) most ads can simply be translated into one of the European languages
    d) media buying habits are very similar to those of consumers in the U.S.
(b; Challenging; p. 263)

245) Which is the major advertising tool to reach consumers in Japan?
    a) television
    b) newspapers
    c) magazines
    d) direct mail
(a; Challenging; p. 263)

246) In terms of media buying, in Brazil and India, media time is purchased almost entirely by:
   a) full-service advertising agencies
   b) full-service media buying firms
   c) freelance media buying firms
   d) subsidiaries of advertising agencies that specialize in media buys
(a; Challenging; p. 263)

Short-Answer Questions

247) Describe the roles of the media planner and the media buyer.

The media planner is the individual who formulates the program stating where and when to place advertisements. The media buyer is the person who buys the space, negotiates rates, times, and schedules for the ads.
(Easy; p. 234)

248) Define reach, frequency, continuity, and gross impressions.

Reach is the number of people, households, or businesses in a target audience exposed to a media vehicle or message schedule at least one time during a given time period. *Frequency* is the average number of times an individual, household, or business within a target market is exposed to a particular advertisement within a specified time period. *Continuity* is the schedule or pattern of advertisement placements within an advertising campaign period. *Gross Impressions* are the number of exposures of the audience to an advertisement.
(Easy; p. 237)

249) What are the primary benefits of television advertising? The primary problems?

The benefits are: high reach, high frequency potential, low cost per contact, quality creative opportunities, high intrusion value, and segmentation possibilities through cable outlets. The problems are: clutter, channel-surfing during commercials, short amount of copy, high cost per ad, and low recall due to clutter.
(Moderate; p. 243)

250) What are the primary benefits of radio advertising? The primary problems?

The advantages are: lower cost per spot than television, low production costs, music can match the station's programming, high potential segmentation, flexibility, ability to modify ads to fit local conditions, intimacy with the deejay, creative opportunities, and it is mobile. The disadvantages are: short exposure time, low attention, few chances to reach a national audience, and target duplications when several stations in a region use the same format.
(Moderate; p. 246)

251) What are the primary benefits of outdoor advertising? The primary problems?

The advantages of outdoor advertising are that it is large and spectacular, key geographic areas can be selected, it's accessible for local ads, low cost per impression, broad reach, and high frequency on commuter routes. The disadvantages of billboards are: legal limitations, short exposure time, brief messages, little segmentation is possible, and clutter on highly traveled routes. (Moderate; p. 249)

252) What are the primary benefits of Internet advertising? The primary problems?

The benefits of Internet advertising are: creative possibilities, short lead-time to create an ad, simplicity of segmentation, high audience interest on each Web site, and it is easy to measure responses. The disadvantages are: clutter on each site, it is difficult to place ads and buy time, the ads only reach computer owners, low intrusion value, and it is hard to retain the interest of Web surfers. (Moderate; p. 250)

253) What are the primary benefits of magazine advertising? The primary problems?

The advantages of magazines are: high segmentation is possible, the audience is targeted by magazine type, high color quality, the availability of special features such as fold-outs or scratch and sniff, long life, direct response techniques, and they are read during leisure time, giving each ad more attention. The disadvantages are: long lead-time before an ad runs, little flexibility, high cost, high clutter, and declining readership of some magazines. (Moderate; p. 253)

254) What are the primary benefits of newspaper advertising? The primary problems?

The advantages of newspapers are: they give higher priority to local advertisers, coupon and special response features, high credibility, strong audience interest among readers, longer copy is possible, flexibility, and advertisers receive cumulative volume discounts. The disadvantages are: Internet competition, clutter, short life span, poor quality color, a limited audience (over 25), and some poor purchasing procedures. (Moderate; p. 255)

255) Other than media, name five other places in which advertisements may appear.

Possible answers include:
- Direct mail
- Leaflets, brochures, carry-home menus
- Carry-home store bags
- Ads on t-shirts and caps
- Ads on movie trailers (video and in theaters)
- Freestanding road signs
- Motel room ads on ash trays, towels, ice chests, etc.
- Yellow pages and phone books
- Mall kiosks
- Faxed ads
- Ads on video replay scoreboards
- In-house magazines (e.g., airlines)
- Walls of airports, subways, bus terminals, and inside cabs and buses

(Moderate; p. 257)

256) Name the challenges present in business-to-business media selection and in international media selection.

The challenges in business-to-business advertising include getting past the gatekeeper, selecting proper media, overcoming clutter, creating attention and interest in ads, identifying target markets, and spending ad money wisely. The challenges in international markets include finding out how to properly make media buys, media selection to match local audiences, tailoring ads to local communities, overcoming language and cultural barriers, and making sure ads convey the proper message.

(Challenging; p. 262)

CHAPTER 9
TRADE PROMOTIONS

True-False Questions

1) The majority of Sealy's sales of Posturepedic mattresses are sold through Sealy's own retail stores.
    (False; Easy; p. 274)

2) More than half of all marketing dollars are spent on trade promotions.
    (True; Challenging; p. 277)

3) Trade promotions are used by manufacturers and other members of the marketing channel to help push products through to retailers.
    (True; Easy; p. 277)

4) A trade promotion is a physical product sent as part of a promotional deal.
    (False; Easy; p. 277)

5) Manufacturers spend more on trade promotions than on either consumer promotions or advertising.
    (True; Easy; p. 277)

6) Sales promotions are sent to end-users and customers while trade promotions are not.
    (True; Easy; p. 277)

7) The amount spent on trade promotions grew from 38 percent of total promotional expenditures in the 1980s to approximately 54 percent today.
    (True; Challenging; p. 277)

8) A trade allowance is a financial incentive offer made to other channel members to motivate them to make a purchase.
    (True; Easy; p. 278)

9) Examples of trade allowances include slotting fees, exist fees, off-invoice allowances, and drop-ship allowances.
    (True; Challenging; p. 278)

10) An off-invoice allowance is money paid to a retailer who is willing to bypass wholesalers.
    (False; Moderate; p. 278)

11) More money is spent on off-invoice allowances than any other form of trade promotion.
(True; Moderate; p. 278)

12) Approximately 33 percent of all trade dollars are spent on slotting fees.
(False; Challenging; p. 278)

13) A drop-ship allowance is money paid to a retailer who is willing to bypass wholesalers, brokers, agents or distributors.
(True; Moderate; p. 279)

14) A company that is willing to offer money to retail stores that are willing to bypass wholesalers or other channel member is using a drop-ship allowance.
(True; Moderate; p. 279)

15) The primary disadvantage of bypassing a wholesaler or distributor with a drop-ship allowance to a retailer is that the wholesaler who is bypassed may retaliate by either dropping the manufacturer or not emphasizing the manufacturer's brand in other product areas.
(True; Moderate; p. 279)

16) The most controversial form of trade allowance is drop-ship allowances
(False; Challenging; p. 279)

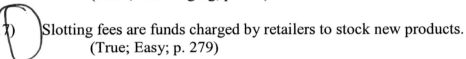

17) Slotting fees are funds charged by retailers to stock new products.
(True; Easy; p. 279)

18) The majority of major retailers charge slotting fees.
(True; Challenging; p. 279)

19) Slotting fees are utilized to cut prices on large shipments of goods to a retail chain.
(False; Moderate; p. 279)

20) One reason retailers use slotting fees is that retailers must spend money to add new products to inventories and to stock new merchandise.
(True; Moderate; p. 279)

21) Since the majority of new products fail, retailers believe charging a slotting fee forces manufacturers to weed out poor product introductions.
(True; Challenging; p. 279)

22) The average total cost in slotting fees for a nationally introduced product ranges from $1.5 million to $2 million.
(True; Challenging; p. 279)

23) Slotting fees are considered almost like extortion by manufacturers because they insist the retailer join in cooperative advertising programs.
(False; Challenging; p. 280)

24) Exit fees are funds charged by retailers to stock new products.
(False; Easy; p. 280)

25) Unsuccessful products that do not sell and are taken off the market may be charged with exit fees.
(True; Moderate; p. 280)

26) Only a small number of retailers charge exit fees compared to the large percentage that use slotting fees.
(True; Challenging; p. 280)

27) One of the disadvantages of trade allowances is that almost half of the time the retailers do not pass along the allowance to consumers.
(True; Moderate; p. 280)

 28) Forward-buying is purchasing extra inventory while it is on-deal so it can be sold later when it is off-deal.
(True; Moderate; p. 280)

29) A company that uses forward-buying is normally trying to reduce inventories at less successful stores.
(False; Moderate; p. 280)

30) Currently retailers hold the balance of power in the distribution channel.
(True; Challenging; p. 281)

31) Diversion is purchasing extra inventory while it is on-deal and shipping it to other locations where it is off-deal.
(True; Easy; p. 281)

32) A diversion is a form of exit fee where funds are transferred from failing products to successful products.
(False; Challenging; p. 281)

33) Because of carrying costs associated with forward buying, retailers tend to use forward buying less than diversion.
(False; Challenging, p. 281)

34) Trade contests encourage sales by making rewards and prizes available to brokers, salespeople in retail stores, wholesalers, and agents.
(True; Easy; p. 281)

35) Rewards given as part of a trade contest is also known as spiff money.
(True; Moderate; p. 281)

36) Spiff money takes the form of prizes paid to consumers in sales contests.
(False; Challenging; p. 281)

37) A trade incentive involves the retailer performing a function in order to receive an allowance.
(True; Moderate; p. 282)

38) A cooperative merchandising agreement is a formal agreement between the retailer and the manufacturer to undertake a two-way marketing effort.
(True; Easy; p. 282)

39) Cooperative merchandising agreements can be formed between two manufacturers seeking to jointly advertise products.
(False; Moderate; p. 282)

40) Cooperative merchandising agreements are popular with manufacturers because the retailer performs a marketing function in order to receive the allowance or incentive.
(True; Challenging; p. 283)

41) The primary benefit of trade allowances to retailers is that it allows retailers to develop calendar promotions.
(False; Challenging; p. 283)

42) A calendar promotion sets a schedule when one brand will be on-deal while others are off deal and then rotates among the brands.
(True; Easy; p. 283)

43) Offering Coke on sale one week, Pepsi the next week, and 7UP the following week can be planned out using a calendar promotion program.
(True; Moderate; p. 283)

44) While cooperative merchandising agreements benefit retailers, most retailers prefer trade allowances.
(True; Challenging; p. 283)

45) A corporate sales program (CSP) is normally offered by manufacturers selling general audience, wide distribution goods.
(False; Challenging; p. 284)

46) The corporate sales program (CSP) is a promotion across a manufacturer's total brand portfolio with products usually shipped directly from the factory in ready-to-display pallets.
(True; Moderate; p. 284)

47) A producing plant allowance (PPA) means the retailer purchases a full or half truckload of merchandise in order to receive a major discount.
(True; Challenging; p. 284)

48) When a furniture retailer offers a "truckload clearance" sale, it may be using a producing plant allowance (PPA).
(True; Challenging; p. 284)

49) A back haul allowance (BHA) means that the retailer pays the cost of shipping for a truckload of goods with a highly discounted price.
(True; Moderate; p. 284)

50) A cross dock or pedal run allowance is money paid to a retailer for placing a full truck order, which is then divided among several stores in the same geographic area.
(True; Moderate; p. 284)

51) A premium or bonus pack offers more merchandise rather than a price discount.
(True; Moderate; p. 284)

52) Manufacturers are willing to provide training for salespeople at various levels of the distribution channel because they improve the chances the salesperson will emphasize the manufacturer's brand over other brands.
(True; Easy; p. 285)

53) The two most frequently used vendor support programs are billbacks and cooperative advertising.
(True; Challenging; p. 285)

54) A billback program is one form of vendor support program.
(True; Moderate; p. 285)

55) In a billback trade program, the retailer or wholesaler bills the manufacturer for the marketing activity after the marketing activity is completed.
(True; Moderate; p. 285)

56) Cooperative advertising takes place when the consumer pays part of the advertising cost.
(False; Easy; p. 285)

57) Almost two-thirds of co-op advertising dollars offered to retailers by manufacturers go unclaimed.
(False; Challenging; p. 286)

58) Cooperative advertising money often goes unclaimed because of errors in filing for the funds or because retailers are unaware the program exists.
(True; Moderate; p. 286)

59) From a manufacturer's perspective, co-op advertising is beneficial the payments are almost always based on a certain percentage of sales.
(True; Challenging; p. 287)

60) Trade shows are the third highest expenditure for business-to-business marketing, behind only advertising and sales promotions.
(True; Challenging; p. 287)

61) From a manufacturer's perspective, a trade show offers the potential to meet customers and sell products.
(True; Easy; p. 287)

62) From a retailer's perspective, a trade show allows buyers to compare merchandise and to make contacts with several prospective vendors.
(True; Easy; p. 287)

63) At trade shows, manufacturer's representatives should concentrate efforts on attendees who are education seekers, not on attendees who are solution seekers.
(False; Challenging; p. 288)

64) In the United States, few deals are finalized during trade shows. Instead, exhibitors collect business cards and follow up later after the show is over.
(True; Moderate; p. 287)

65) A trade show participant from another country is more likely to be ready to make a buy than a domestic attendee.
(True; Moderate; p. 288)

66) Many large national and international trade shows are losing customers to niche shows.
(True; Moderate; p. 288)

67) According to the Communication Action box "Making the most of a trade show," it is recommended that trade shows be staffed with customer service personnel rather salespeople.
(True; Challenging; p. 289)

68) If the goal of attending a trade show is to enhance the firm's brand or corporate name, normally a smaller, regional trade show would be the best.
(False; Challenging; p. 290)

69) If the goal of attending a trade show is to establish a new brand or promote a new product, normally a smaller, regional trade show would be the best.
(True; Challenging; p. 290)

70) The top category of specialty gifts given by firms to their customers is writing instruments.
(False; Challenging; p. 290)

71) Specialty advertising is designed to create a feeling called reciprocation, or the desire to take advantage of someone else by getting a better deal.
(False; Easy; p. 290)

72) In selecting advertising specialty gifts, the best strategy is to make the gift item unique, but also convey the company's message.
(True; Moderate; p. 291)

73) POP is short for "Place on Page," an Internet advertising term to designate an ad placement.
(False; Easy; p. 291)

74) The store shelf and point-of-purchase display represent the last chance for the manufacturer to reach the consumer.
(True; Moderate; p. 291)

75) For products in general, the majority of purchasing brand choices are made in the store, which means Point of purchase (POP) materials can have a large impact on the decision.
(True; Challenging; p. 291)

76) Manufacturers view point of purchase (POP) displays as method to get a brand more prominently displayed before customers in retail stores.
(True; Moderate; p. 292)

77) Retailers believe point of purchase (POP) materials should either boost sales for a particular brand or draw customers to the store to purchase the brand.
(False; Challenging; p. 292)

78) Retailers prefer point of purchase (POP) materials that educate consumers and provide information.
(True; Challenging; p. 292)

79) The most common reason retailers do not use point of purchase (POP) displays furnished by manufacturers is that they are inappropriate for the channel.
(True; Challenging; p. 292)

80) To be effective, a point of purchase (POP) display must clearly communicate the price of the product.
(False; Moderate; p. 292)

81) A new trend in point of purchase (POP) displays is in integrating the display with an Internet site and the Web address of the company.
(True; Moderate; p. 293)

82) A retailer can only set up a fraction of the point of purchase (POP) displays sent by manufacturers due to space limitations.
(True; Moderate; p. 293)

83) One method companies are using to measure the impact of point of purchase (POP) displays is to utilize cash register data comparing before and after sales.
(True; Moderate; p. 294)

84) For manufacturers, the primary goal of trade promotions is to increase sales of company brands, while for retailers the primary goal is to increase market share of each store.
(True; Moderate; p. 294)

85) A pull strategy occurs when advertising and publicity cause consumers to ask about a product's availability in a retail store.
(True; Easy; p. 295)

86) A push strategy is the result of an aggressive marketing effort aimed at retailers and other channel members with the goal of getting retailers to place the product on store shelves.
(True; Easy; p. 295)

87) Trade shows, slotting fees, vendor support programs, specialty advertising, and point-of-purchase displays help a manufacturer gain a wider audience for a new product.
(True; Moderate; p. 295)

88) Trade allowances, contests, training programs, and trade incentives can assist a manufacturing in capturing and maintaining retail shelf space.
(True; Moderate; p. 295)

89) Once a manufacturer's brand has obtained retail shelf space, trade promotions are no longer needed to maintain the shelf space.
(False; Moderate; p. 295)

90) Trade promotions are rarely used to support established brands; instead they focus on new brands.
(False; Easy; p. 295)

91) To encourage channel members to increase the size of their order, a manufacturer can use trade allowances and sales contests.
(True; Challenging; p. 296)

92) One reason a manufacturer wants channel members to build large inventories of its products is that this preempts trade promotional offers the competition may offer.
(True; Challenging; p. 296)

93) Large manufacturers often have a major advantage in the area of trade promotions, compared to small manufacturers and vendors.
(True; Easy; p. 296)

94) A major concern in using trade promotions is that merchandise will not move unless a trade promotion is offered. For example, in the grocery industry, the majority of manufacturers offer some type of trade promotion to get retailers to make purchases.
(True; Challenging; p. 298)

95) If manufacturers try to quit or cut back on trade promotions, retailers often replace the manufacturer's brand with other brands or trim shelf space to allow more room for brands that are offering better deals.
(True; Challenging; p. 298)

96) Brand image is not affected by trade promotions programs since the programs are not directly connected to advertising.
(False; Challenging; p. 298)

Multiple-Choice Questions

97) What advantage does Sealy enjoy in the mattress-producing industry?
   a) lower production costs
   b) few competitors
   c) a well known brand name
   d) a reputation as the low-price leader
(c; Easy; p. 274)

98) Trade promotions are distinguished from other marketing and IMC tools in that they:
   a) involve extensive advertising
   b) retail customers are the primary target of the effort
   c) are used to entice other members of the marketing channel to make purchases
   d) are limited to activities by manufacturers

(c; Easy; p. 277)

99) Each of the following are recipients of trade promotions, *except:*
   a) end-users and consumers
   b) retailers and distributors
   c) wholesalers
   d) brokers and agents

(a; Easy; p. 277)

100) The primary role of trade promotions is to:
   a) build brand equity
   b) encourage trial purchases
   c) pull products through the channel
   d) build stronger relations with members of the distribution channel

(d; Challenging; p. 277)

101) Typically, the greatest amount of marketing funding goes for:
   a) trade promotions
   b) advertising production
   c) advertising media buys
   d) consumer promotions

(a; Easy; p. 277)

102) Offering financial incentives to channel members in order to motivate them to make a purchase is a:
   a) trade allowance
   b) trade incentive
   c) trade contest
   d) vendor support program

(a; Moderate; p. 278)

103) Trade allowances include all of the following, *except:*
   a) off-invoice allowance
   b) drop-ship allowance
   c) corporate sales program
   d) slotting fees

(c; Challenging; p. 278)

104) Financial discounts on cases or pallets of merchandise ordered are called:
   a) consumer promotions
   b) off-invoice allowances
   c) drop-ship allowances
   d) spiff money
(b; Easy; p. 278)

105) Approximately one third of all trade dollars are spent on:
   a) slotting fees
   b) vendor support programs
   c) trade incentives
   d) off-invoice allowances
(d; Challenging, p. 278)

106) Money paid to retailers who are willing to bypass wholesalers, brokers, and distributors when making prepaid orders is:
   a) a consumer promotion
   b) an off-invoice allowance
   c) a drop-ship allowance
   d) an exit fee
(c; Moderate; p. 279)

107) Of the following trade promotions, a wholesaler is most likely to be dissatisfied with a manufacturer's:
   a) off-invoice allowance
   b) drop-ship allowance
   c) slotting fees
   d) exit fees
(b; Challenging; p. 279)

108) The buyer at Target for electronic calculators has just received an offer from a large manufacturer of electronic calculators that if Target will purchase 10,000 calculators within the next 30 days, they will receive a 10% discount and the manufacturer will ship them directly to Target's warehouses. This is an example of a(n):
   a) off-invoice allowance
   b) drop-ship allowance
   c) cooperative merchandise agreement
   d) producing plant allowance
(b; Challenging; p. 279)

109) Funds paid to retailers to stock new products are known as:
    a) prepaid off-invoice allowances
    b) drop-ship allowances
    c) quantity discounts
    d) slotting fees
(d; Easy; p. 279)

110) A retailer stands to gain a direct payment from:
    a) an off-invoice allowance
    b) a drop-ship allowance
    c) slotting fees
    d) forward buying
(c; Moderate; p. 279)

111) Slotting fees are charged by approximately which percent of retailers?
    a) 25
    b) 40
    c) 50
    d) 80
(d; Challenging, p. 279)

112) Retailers use each of the following reasons to justify slotting fees, *except:*
    a) retailers must invest time and money in new products
    b) the fees help retailers finalize decisions about carrying new products
    c) the fees reduce the number of new products that are introduced each year
    d) the fees level the playing field between small and large retail outlets
(d; Challenging; p. 279)

113) The average total cost in slotting fees a manufacturer must pay for a nationally introduced product ranges from:
    a) $1.5 million to $2 million
    b) $2 million to $4 million
    c) $4 million to $6 million
    d) $7 million to $7.5 million
(a; Challenging; p. 279)

114) Manufacturers use each of the following arguments against paying slotting fees, *except:*
    a) they are a form of extortion
    b) the fees favor new companies
    c) manufacturers are forced to pay millions of dollars that could be used for advertising, sales promotions, and other marketing efforts
    d) the fees favor large manufacturers over small manufacturers
(b; Challenging; p. 280)

115) Monies paid to remove an item from a retailer's inventory are called:
   a) reverse slotting fees
   b) brokerage allowances
   c) exit fees
   d) cooperative merchandising agreements
(c; Easy; p. 280)

116) Exit fees are paid for:
   a) covering the cost of removing unsuccessful products from shelves
   b) getting a retailer to agree to limit purchases from another vendor
   c) shipping costs
   d) cooperative advertising programs
(a; Moderate; p. 280)

117) Each of the following are problems associated with trade allowances, *except:*
   a) failing to pass along allowances to retail customers
   b) forward buying
   c) diversion
   d) increased advertising costs
(d; Easy; p. 280)

118) When the price of product is reduced through a trade allowance, it is referred to as being:
   a) on-deal
   b) off-deal
   c) a side deal
   d) a slotting fee
(a; Easy; p. 280)

119) When a retailer purchases excess inventory of a product while it is on-deal to sell later when it is off-deal, the process is known as:
   a) a diversion
   b) quantity-seeking
   c) forward buying
   d) a slotting fee
(c; Easy; p. 280)

120) When a retailer stocks up on M & Ms while they are on-deal to sell them later when they are off-deal, it is called:
   a) a diversion
   b) quantity-seeking
   c) forward buying
   d) a slotting fee
(c; Moderate; p. 280)

121) Extra costs for carrying extra inventory occur when a retailer engages in:
   a) diversion
   b) exit fees
   c) forward buying
   d) cooperative merchandising agreements
(c; Challenging; p. 280)

122) The costs associated with additional inventory that is part of forward buying are called:
   a) spiff money
   b) carrying costs
   c) diversion expenses
   d) cooperative merchandising agreements
(b; Moderate; p. 281)

123) When provided with an offer of a 10% discount to purchase 10,000 electronic calculators within the next 30 days, Target buys 30,000 instead to take advantage of the price discount. Target will offer the calculator to consumers at a discount during the special sale, but then have additional calculators to sell when the sale is over. This is an example of:
   a) an off-invoice allowance
   b) cross-dock or pedal run allowance
   c) forward buying
   d) diversion
(c; Challenging; p. 281)

124) When a retailer purchases a product on-deal in one location and ships it to another where it is off-deal, the process is known as:
   a) exit forwarding
   b) a diversion
   c) a transaction alteration
   d) forward buying
(b; Moderate; p. 281)

125) In terms of trade allowances, extra shipping costs occur when a retailer engages in:
   a) slotting fees
   b) exit fees
   c) forward buying
   d) diversion
(d; Challenging; p. 281)

126) The primary disadvantage to a retailer in using diversion is:
    a) additional shipping costs
    b) additional carrying costs
    c) exit fees
    d) slotting fees
(a; Challenging; p. 281)

127) Rewards given as contest prizes to brokers, retail salespeople, retail stores, wholesalers, or agents are part of a:
    a) trade allowance
    b) trade contest
    c) cooperative merchandise agreement
    d) drop-ship allowance
(b; Easy; p. 281)

128) Rewards given to channel members such as brokers, retail salespeople, and others as prizes for winning a contest are known as:
    a) slotting fees
    b) volume incentives
    c) spiff money
    d) pay for play
(c; Easy; p. 281)

129) The primary difference between trade incentives and trade allowances is that for the trade incentive:
    a) the retailer must perform some type of function in order to receive the allowance
    b) the manufacturer must perform some type of function to encourage the retailer to accept the merchandise
    c) the retailer receives a price break if they order a specific quantity
    d) involves a price reduction being passed on to consumers by retailers
(a; Moderate; p. 282)

130) CMA stands for:
    a) cumulative money account
    b) cooperative merchandising agreement
    c) cooperative manufacturing agreement
    d) coercive marketing agenda
(b; Moderate; p. 282)

131) A formal agreement between a retailer and a manufacturer to undertake a two-way marketing effort is called a(n):
   a) alliance of capital
   b) cooperative merchandising agreement
   c) venture agreement
   d) sales promotion
(b; Easy; p. 282)

132) A retailer agrees to display a particular brand of shoes in the front of the store and on a special end-of-aisle display in exchange for a price discount by the manufacturer. This is an example of a:
   a) trade allowance
   b) corporate sales program
   c) cooperative merchandising agreement
   d) vendor support program
(c; Challenging; p. 282)

133) The following are forms of trade incentives, *except:*
   a) cooperative merchandise agreement
   b) trade contest
   c) cooperative sales program
   d) product plant allowance
(b; Moderate; p. 283)

134) The following are forms of trade incentives, *except:*
   a) back haul allowance
   b) cross-dock or pedal run allowance
   c) vendor support program
   d) premium or bonus pack
(c; Challenging; p. 283)

135) Promotional campaigns the retailer plans for customers through manufacturer trade incentives are:
   a) slotting fee programs
   b) merchandising management programs
   c) spiff money allocations
   d) calendar promotions
(d; Moderate; p. 283)

136) Which of these can be used by retailers to always have one brand on sale while others are off-deal?
   a) forward buying
   b) calendar promotions
   c) corporate sales programs
   d) trade allowances
(b; Challenging; p. 283)

137) A calendar promotion may result in a retailer using:
    a) forward buying
    b) slotting fees
    c) exit fees
    d) cooperative advertisements
(a; Challenging; p. 283)

138) A trade incentive program across a manufacturer's total brand portfolio is a:
    a) slotting fee program
    b) corporate sales program
    c) producing plant allowance
    d) back haul allowance
(b; Moderate; p. 284)

139) A pallet with ready-to-display merchandise offered to retailers at a discount is part of a:
    a) slotting fee program
    b) corporate sales program
    c) producing plant allowance
    d) back haul allowance
(b; Challenging; p. 284)

140) A pallet of automobile batteries, complete with a display shelf, offered to retailers at a price discount is:
    a) a cross promotion
    b) multi-manufacturer marketing
    c) a corporate sales program
    d) a back-haul allowance
(c; Challenging; p. 284)

141) A retailer buying a full truckload of merchandise in order to receive a major discount is taking advantage of a:
    a) producing plant allowance
    b) calendar promotional campaign
    c) corporate sales program
    d) cooperative merchandising agreement
(a; Easy; p. 284)

142) A "truckload" sale, where merchandise is sold at a major discount because the retailer obtained a special discount from the manufacturing for ordering a truck load is probably due to which of the following being offered?
   a) a producing plant allowance
   b) an effective sales contest
   c) exit fees paid by the retailer
   d) a cooperative merchandising agreement
(a; Challenging; p. 284)

143) When the shipping costs for a truckload of merchandise is paid for by the retailer in exchange for a steep discount, the trade incentive being used is a:
   a) producing plant allowance
   b) calendar promotional campaign
   c) back haul allowance
   d) cooperative merchandising agreement
(c; Challenging; p. 284)

144) The primary difference between a back-haul allowance and a producing plant allowance is in the back-haul allowance the:
   a) retailer furnishes delivery trucks or pays the shipping costs
   b) manufacturer furnishes delivery trucks or pays the shipping costs
   c) distributor furnishes delivery trucks or pays the shipping costs
   d) costs of shipping are divided equally
(a; Challenging; p. 184)

145) A cross-dock or pedal run allowance means:
   a) several manufacturers ship on one truck
   b) several distributors ship on one truck
   c) a retailer divides a shipment from one truck among several stores
   d) the costs of shipping are prepaid by the distributor
(c; Moderate; p. 284)

146) Offering additional free merchandise for placing an order is known as:
   a) a slotting fee
   b) a discount invoice
   c) spiff money
   d) a premium or bonus pack
(d; Easy; p. 284)

147) Sony is promoting a special coupon and sale on its stereos. Retail stores that purchase at least 1000 stereos during the next 30 days will receive an extra stereo, free, for each 50 they purchase over a 1000 minimum. This is an example of a:
   a) cross-dock or pedal run
   b) calendar promotion
   c) corporate sales program
   d) premium or bonus pack
(d; Challenging; p. 284)

148) The two most frequently utilized vendor support programs are:
   a) POPs and CMAs
   b) billbacks and co-op advertising
   c) premiums and bonus packs
   d) back-haul and producing plant allowances
(b; Challenging; p. 285)

149) The two most frequently utilized vendor support programs are billback programs and:
   a) point of purchase displays
   b) cooperative advertising
   c) premiums and bonus packs
   d) back-haul allowances
(b; Challenging; p. 285)

150) In most cases, a billback program takes place between:
   a) a customer and a retailer
   b) two manufacturers
   c) a manufacturer and a wholesaler
   d) a manufacturer and a retailer
(d; Moderate; p. 285)

151) A billback program means a:
   a) manufacturer will bill back a retailer for a vendor support program
   b) retailer will bill back a manufacturer for a vendor support program
   c) consumer will bill back a retailer for defective merchandise
   d) consumer will bill back a manufacturer for defective merchandise
(b; Moderate; p. 285)

152) When a manufacturer offers to pay part of the costs of a retail advertising campaign, it is known as:
   a) incentive marketing
   b) target market advertising
   c) cooperative advertising
   d) specialty advertising
(c; Easy; p. 285)

153) The "Intel inside" tag line seen in advertisements by a retail computer store or by a computer manufacturer such as Compaq is a form of:
   a) direct marketing
   b) cooperative advertising
   c) producer markup combined with retailer pass-alongs
   d) manufacturer's prerogative
(b; Challenging; p. 285)

154) Every year manufacturers offer an estimated $24 billion in coop advertising dollars to retailers, of which about how much goes unclaimed?
   a) one fourth
   b) one third
   c) one half
   d) two thirds
(a; Challenging; p. 286)

155) Co-op money is often unclaimed for every reason listed below, *except:*
   a) co-op claims are rejected by manufacturers because of filing errors
   b) retailers are unaware of a co-op program
   c) media outlets may reject a proposed ad using a co-op program
   d) purchase accruals are tracked inaccurately by the retailer
(c; Moderate; p. 286)

156) Co-op advertising programs often stipulate each of the following items, *except:*
   a) monies are accrued for purchases over time
   b) no competing products can be advertised
   c) the manufacturer's product must be displayed prominently in the ad
   d) retailers must pay the agency fees
(d; Challenging; p. 286)

157) Retailers benefit from coop advertising in all of the following ways, *except:*
   a) they can expand their advertising program at a low cost
   b) promoting a national manufacturer's brand in their ads
   c) attract new and additional customers to their store because of national brands
   d) paid in advance for the cost of producing the ads
(d; Challenging; p. 287)

158) Manufacturers benefit from coop advertising in all of the following ways, *except:*
   a) gain additional advertising exposure at reduced costs
   b) reimbursed by retailers for their share of the ad costs
   c) coop dollars are directly tied to retail sales
   d) gain prominent exposure in an ad since no other competing brands can also be displayed
(b; Challenging; p. 287)

159) In terms of business-to-business marketing expenditures, the third highest category is for:
   a) advertising
   b) sales promotions
   c) trade shows
   d) specialty advertising
(c; Challenging; p. 287)

160) From a manufacturer's standpoint, the following are benefits obtained from attending a trade show, *except:*
   a) discover new customers
   b) find out what the competition is doing
   c) strengthen relationships with current customers
   d) identify prospective vendors
(d; Moderate; p. 287)

161) From a retailer's standpoint, the following are benefits obtained from attending a trade show, *except:*
   a) compare merchandise of various vendors
   b) find out what the competition is doing
   c) negotiate special deals with vendors
   d) meet with sellers in an informal, low-pressure setting
(b; Challenging; p. 287)

162) At a trade show, narrowing down contacts to the most promising group is called:
   a) prospecting
   b) finding the power buyer
   c) closing the deal
   d) identifying participants
(a; Moderate; p. 288)

163) In a trade show, a buyer browsing and trying to learn about products from a series of competitors is a(n):
   a) education seeker
   b) reinforcement seeker
   c) solution seeker
   d) power buyer
(a; Moderate; p. 288)

164) In a trade show, a buyer seeking reassurance about a previous buy is a(n):
   a) information seeker
   b) reinforcement seeker
   c) solution seeker
   d) education seeker
(b; Moderate; p. 288)

165) In a trade show, a buyer who is trying to solve a specific problem with a product choice is a(n):
   a) information seeker
   b) reinforcement seeker
   c) solution seeker
   d) education seeker
   (c; Moderate; p. 288)

166) The following are categories of buyers that may be found at a trade show, *except:*
   a) education seekers
   b) reinforcement seekers
   c) information seekers
   d) power buyers
   (c; Challenging; p. 288)

167) Manufacturers should concentrate their efforts at trade shows on each of the following buyer groups, *except:*
   a) solution seekers
   b) buying teams
   c) power buyers
   d) education seekers
   (d; Challenging; p. 288)

168) At a trade show, manufacturers should weed out which type of buyer group because they are not interested in buying and would take up too much of the vendor's time?
   a) solution seekers
   b) buying teams
   c) education seekers
   d) reinforcement seekers
   (c; Challenging; p. 288)

169) At a trade show, the most difficult buyer group for manufacturers to identify would be which group, because they don't want to be identified yet they are a very important group in terms of ability to make purchase decisions?
   a) solution seekers
   b) buying teams
   c) power buyers
   d) reinforcement seekers
   (c; Challenging; p. 288)

170) Several differences exist when international companies attend trade shows. These differences include each of the following, *except:*
   a) international attendees tend to be senior executives with authority to make purchases
   b) international attendees want a follow-up after the trade show by a senior executive
   c) international attendees spend more time at each exhibitor's booth
   d) international attendees tend to make purchase decisions during the trade show
(b; Moderate; p. 288)

171) Large national and international trade shows are being replaced by:
   a) Internet advertising
   b) niche and regional shows
   c) promotional videos
   d) nothing, they are still the most widely used
(b; Easy; p. 288)

172) According to the Communication Action box "Making the Most of a Trade Show," the following recommendations are suggested, *except:*
   a) Do not bombard attendees with literature.
   b) Use salespeople at the booth, not customer service personnel.
   c) Follow-up leads when the trade show is over.
   d) Avoid overcrowding the booth with materials.
(b; Challenging; p. 289)

173) According to the Communication Action box "Making the Most of a Trade Show," it is recommended that exhibitors follow the MAN principle so time is spent with the right attendees. MAN stands for:
   a) money, authority, and need
   b) money, action, and notice
   c) memory, action, and need
   d) motivation, action, and need
(a; Challenging; p. 289)

174) A large national trade show would be better than a smaller, regional trade show to:
   a) create a client base quickly
   b) establish a new brand
   c) enhance a firm's brand or corporate name
   d) promote a new product
(c; Challenging; p. 290)

175) Regional or specialty trade shows would be better than a large, national trade show for all of the following goals, *except:*
   a) create a client base quickly
   b) establish a new brand
   c) enhance a firm's brand or corporate name
   d) promote a new product
(c; Challenging; p. 290)

176) In choosing a trade show, the most important criteria for an exhibitor should be the:
   a) cost relative to the number of attendees
   b) total number of attendees
   c) number of exhibitors that match the firm's target market
   d) number of attendees who match the exhibitor's target market
(d; Moderate; p. 290)

177) Giving customers items such as pens, coffee mugs, or apparel with the company's name, logo, or tagline on it is called:
   a) trade allowances
   b) trade incentives
   c) specialty advertising
   d) merchandising the advertising
(c; Easy; p. 290)

178) The following are examples of specialty advertising, *except:*
   a) calendar
   b) contest prize
   c) mug
   d) pen and pencil set
(b; Moderate; p. 290)

179) Specialty advertising is often used in each of the following, *except:*
   a) in a trade contest
   b) at a trade show
   c) in direct mail offers
   d) by salespeople
(a; Challenging; p. 291)

180) Specialty advertising is based on the concept of:
   a) specialization
   b) prospecting
   c) identification
   d) reciprocation
(d; Moderate; p. 291)

181) When you receive a gift and wish to return a favor, the process is known as:
    a) an approach-avoidance conflict
    b) an obligation
    c) diversion
    d) reciprocation
(d; Easy; p. 291)

182) Specialty advertising can accomplish each of the following goals or objectives, *except:*
    a) reinforce buying decisions
    b) as an incentive to make a purchase
    c) strengthen business relationships
    d) stimulate interest from a new, potential prospect
(b; Challenging; p. 291)

183) POP stands for:
    a) print-offer proposal
    b) publicity over protocol
    c) point of purchase
    d) place of publication
(c; Easy; p. 291)

184) Point of purchase displays work toward which activity?
    a) pull-demand strategy
    b) brand parity
    c) impulse buys
    d) reciprocation
(c; Moderate; p. 291)

185) Point-of-purchase displays include each of the following advantages, *except* :
    a) making an impression as the consumer leaves the store
    b) creating reciprocation
    c) inciting impulse buys
    d) creating tie-ins with other promotional efforts
(b; Challenging; p. 291)

186) Retailers want point-of-purchase displays that will:
    a) boost sales for the store or draw customers into the store
    b) boost sales for a particular brand
    c) generate additional prospects
    d) increase profit for the manufacturer
(a; Moderate; p. 291)

187) The most common reason retailers do not use point-of-purchase displays furnished by manufacturers is that the displays are:
    a) not customer-oriented
    b) inappropriate for the channel
    c) not effective in stimulating sales
    d) inappropriate for the product being promoted
(b; Challenging; p. 292)

188) The following are reasons retailers do not use point-of-purchase displays furnished by manufacturers, *except:*
    a) wrong size
    b) inappropriate for the channel
    c) poorly built
    d) not accompanied by consumer promotion incentives
(d; Challenging; p. 292)

189) Research has indicated all of the ingredients listed below will increase the effectiveness of POP displays, *except:*
    a) brand signs
    b) a tie-in to a trade promotion
    c) a tie-in to a movie, sport or charity
    d) an inflatable component or mobile above the POP display
(b; Challenging; p. 293)

190) The following are current trends in point of purchase display programs, *except:*
    a) larger displays with some type of motion components
    b) greater integration with Web site programs
    c) displays that routinely change messages
    d) increased ability to track results
(a; Challenging; p. 293)

191) A new trend in measuring the impact of point-of-purchase displays is to use:
    a) day-after redemption rates
    b) Internet focus groups
    c) point-of-sale (POS) cash register data
    d) behavioral observation studies
(c; Challenging; p. 294)

192) Each of the following statements about retailers and trade promotions is true, *except:*
    a) retailers are concerned about increasing market share of their retail stores
    b) retailers are not concerned about which brand sells the most
    c) retailers promote the brands that yield the highest profit for them, or generates the highest sales for them
    d) retailers prefer brands that have the highest recall
(d; Challenging; p. 294)

193) The following are typical objectives for a trade promotions campaign, *except:*
    a) increase initial distribution
    b) identify consumer buying habits
    c) obtain better shelf space
    d) support established brands
(b; Moderate; p. 294)

194) The following are potential objectives for a trade promotions campaign, *except:*
    a) build retail inventories
    b) identify members of a retailer's buying center
    c) reduce excess manufacturer inventory
    d) build wholesale inventories
(b; Moderate; p. 294)

195) A push strategy focuses on:
    a) consumers making requests for merchandise
    b) retailers being enticed to place a product on store shelves
    c) manufacturers seeking additional advertising dollars
    d) media buyers finding new ways to buy ad space
(b; Easy; p. 295)

196) A pull strategy focuses on:
    a) consumers making requests for merchandise
    b) retailers being enticed to place a product on store shelves
    c) manufacturers seeking additional advertising dollars
    d) media buyers finding new ways to buy ad space
(a; Easy; p. 295)

197) A consumer asking for a new magazine to be stocked at a newsstand is an example of a:
    a) push strategy
    b) pull strategy
    c) reciprocation strategy
    d) trade allowance strategy
(b; Challenging; p. 295)

198) A manufacturing offering a retailer trade incentives to stock a new brand of potato chips is an example of a:
    a) push strategy
    b) pull strategy
    c) reciprocation strategy
    d) trade allowance strategy
(b; Moderate; p. 295)

199) The following strategies can be used to obtain prime retail shelf space or location, *except:*
    a) trade allowances
    b) trade contests
    c) specialty advertising
    d) trade incentives
(c; Moderate; p. 295)

200) Memorex has increased their trade allowances to retail stores because one of their major competitors started offering a higher trade incentive. This is an example of the trade promotion objective of:
    a) countering competitive actions
    b) building retail inventories
    c) increasing order sizes
    d) reducing manufacturer's inventories
(a; Moderate; p. 295)

201) Of the following trade promotion objectives, offering co-op advertising dollars to retail stores would be an excellent approach to:
    a) counter competitive trade allowances
    b) obtaining initial distribution
    c) encourage retailers to build larger inventories
    d) enhance channel relationships
(d; Challenging; p. 296)

202) When sales managers find that they are not going to make their sales quota, the strategy that is often used is to:
    a) increase the advertising budget
    b) use trade promotions to boost sales
    c) use consumer promotions to boost sales
    d) use a trade contest among retailers to encourage salespeople to push the sales manager's brand
(b; Moderate; p. 296)

203) The following are potential problems associated with trade promotion programs, *except:*
    a) costs
    b) the impact on small manufacturers
    c) over-reliance on trade promotions to move merchandise
    d) inability to tie a trade promotion to a consumer promotion
(d; Challenging; p. 297)

204) Trade promotions tend to have a negative impact on small manufacturers because small manufacturers:
   a) do not have a strong brand image or brand equity
   b) cannot offer trade allowances
   c) cannot afford to spend as much on slotting fees and other trade promotions as large manufactures
   d) do not have a sufficient sales staff to reach all of the various retailers
(c; Moderate; p. 297)

Short-Answer Questions

 205) What are the four main types of trade allowances? Describe each one.

   1. An off-invoice allowance encourages orders by granting financial discounts.
   2. A drop-ship allowance is a discount offered to retailers for bypassing wholesalers and taking direct delivery.
   3. Slotting fees are funds paid to retailers to stock new products.
   4. Exit fees are monies paid to remove an item from a retailer's inventory.
(Moderate; p. 278)

206) What are the disadvantages of trade allowances?

   - Retailers may keep the allowance and not pass it on to retail customers
   - Forward buying or purchasing an excess of product when it is on-deal
   - Diversions or purchasing product on-deal in one store and shipping it to another where it is not
(Moderate; p. 280)

207) Name various forms of trade contests.

   - Agents versus agents
   - Wholesalers versus wholesalers
   - Retail stores within a chain versus each other
   - Retail store chain versus other retail chains
   - Individual salespersons within retail stores versus each other
(Moderate; p. 281)

208) Name and briefly describe the types of trade incentives that are offered.

Cooperative merchandising agreements are formed between a retailer and a manufacturer to undertake a cooperative marketing effort.

Calendar promotions are campaigns the retailer designs for customers through manufacturer trade incentives.

Corporate sales programs are those offered across a manufacturer's total brand portfolio and are shipped in ready-to-display pallets.

Producing plant allowances are full or half-truck loads of merchandise shipped to one place and granted a major discount.

A back-haul allowance is where the retailer pays the cost of shipping.

A cross-dock or pedal run allowance divides a truckload among retailers in an area.

A premium or bonus back offers additional merchandise rather than price discounts.

(Challenging; p. 283)

209) Name and briefly describe two vendor support programs.

(1) A bill-back program occurs when the manufacturer pays the retailer for a special product display by refunding the money to the retailer that bills back the amount. (2) A cooperative advertising program is where the manufacture and retailer share the costs of advertising.

(Challenging; p. 285)

210) Name and describe the five categories of buyers who attend trade shows.

1. Education seekers who want to browse and learn but not buy.
2. Reinforcement seekers who want reassurances about past purchases.
3. Solution seekers who want problems solved and are in a buying mode.
4. Buying teams who are groups ready to buy.
5. Power buyers, who are members of upper management or key purchasing agents with the authority to buy.

(Challenging; p. 288)

211) When are specialty or niche trade shows most effective?

When the goals of the vendor are (1) to establish a client base quickly, (2) establish a new brand, or (3) to promote a new product.

(Challenging; p. 290)

212) What causes a POP to go unused?

It is inappropriate for the product, does not receive consumer responses, is too seasonal, is poorly built, is the wrong size, or is inappropriate for the channel.

(Challenging; p. 292)

213) Name three new trends in POP displays.

1. Integration with Web site programs
2. Displays that routinely change messages
3. There is better tracking of results.
(Challenging; p. 293)

214) What goals or objectives are associated with trade promotions?

- Better initial distribution
- Obtain prime retail locations or shelf space
- Support established brands
- Counter competitive actions
- Increase order sizes
- Build retail inventories
- Reduce excess manufacturer inventories
- Enhance channel relationships
- Enhance the overall IMC program
(Challenging; p. 294)

CHAPTER 10
CONSUMER PROMOTIONS

True-False Questions

1) Time shares are unique because they are partly a good and partly a service.
    (True; Easy; p. 306)

2) Consumer promotions, or sales promotions, are the incentives aimed at the firm's customers.
    (True; Easy; p. 308)

3) A franchise-building consumer promotion is the same thing as a consumer sales-building promotion.
    (False; Easy; p. 308)

4) A consumer franchise-building promotion is designed to increase brand awareness and brand loyalty.
    (True; Moderate; p. 308)

5) A consumer sales-building promotion is designed to increase brand awareness and brand loyalty.
    (False; Moderate; p. 308)

6) A consumer sales-building promotion is designed to boost immediate sales.
    (True; Easy; p. 308)

7) Consumers who are exposed to franchise-building promotions tend to develop higher levels of brand awareness and stronger perceptions of brand parity.
    (False; Challenging; p. 308)

8) In the early stages of a product's life cycle, promotions should match advertising efforts designed to achieve brand awareness, create opportunities for trial purchases, and stimulate additional purchases.
    (True; Challenging; p. 308)

9) For high-image brands, if consumer promotions are used, it should be franchise-building promotions.
    (True; Moderate; p. 308)

10) A coupon is a price reduction offer to a consumer.
    (True; Easy; p. 309)

11) The majority of coupons are issued by retailers.
    (False; Moderate; p. 309)

12) The majority of coupons are sent out through print media.
(True; Easy; p. 309)

13) FSI stands for Full Standing Inventory, which means the ad campaign is complete.
(False; Easy; p. 309)

14) FSI, or Free Standing Inserts, are the most common method used to deliver coupons to consumers.
(True; Moderate; p. 309)

15) An instant redemption coupon is sent out through print media.
(False; Moderate; p. 310)

16) An instant redemption coupon may lead to a trial purchase because the customer has immediate access to the discount.
(True; Moderate; p. 310)

17) A bounce-back coupon is placed inside a package so it cannot be redeemed immediately.
(True; Moderate; p. 310)

18) Bounce-back coupons tend to encourage trial purchases of a product.
(False; Challenging; p. 310)

19) A scanner-delivered coupon is sent out by the Internet.
(False; Easy; p. 310)

20) A scanner-delivered coupon is often given for a competing brand to encourage brand-switching.
(True; Moderate; p. 310)

21) Placing a coupon for dip on a bag of potato chips is called a bounce-back coupon approach.
(False; Challenging; p. 310)

22) A cross-ruffing coupon is placing a coupon for one product on another product.
(True; Easy; p. 310)

23) A coupon for peanut butter on a jar of jelly is a cross-ruff coupon.
(True; Challenging; p. 310)

24) Coupons issued following a request by a consumer are called scanner-delivered coupons.
(False; Easy; p. 310)

25) Electronically delivered coupons are requested via the Internet, through consumers seeing a television ad, and through word-of-mouth communications from a friend.
(True; Challenging; p. 311)

26) The redemption rate of e-coupons is considerably higher than for other types of coupons.
(True; Moderate; p. 311)

27) While coupon distribution has continued to increase, coupon redemption rates have steadily declined.
(True; Moderate; p. 310)

28) African-Americans and Hispanics tend to redeem coupons more often than the population as a whole.
(False; Challenging; p. 310)

29) Mass-cutting, counterfeiting, and misredemptions are three common problems with coupons.
(True; Moderate; p. 310)

30) Customers who already have a preference for a brand redeem the majority of all coupons.
(True; Challenging; p. 310)

31) Mass-cutting is redeeming coupons that have never been submitted to a retailer as part of a sale.
(True; Moderate; p. 310)

32) The major source of counterfeiting today is copying black-and-white coupons from newspapers.
(False; Moderate; p. 312)

33) Many retailers are leery of Internet coupons because of the problem of counterfeiting.
(True; Moderate; p. 312)

34) Retailers are usually not involved in mass-cutting or misredemption of coupons.
(False; Challenging; p. 312)

35) Redeeming a coupon for the wrong size of an item is a problem called misredemption.
(True; Moderate; p. 312)

36) Premiums are prizes or gifts consumers receive when purchasing products.
(True; Easy; p. 313)

37) When a company offers a premium, consumers pay full price for the good or service.
(True; Easy; p. 313)

38) Some marketing experts believe overuse of premiums can damage a brand's image, while the use of coupons can actually enhance a brand's image.
(False; Moderate; p. 313)

39) Free-in-the-mail premiums are gifts individuals receive for purchasing products by providing some form of proof of purchase.
(True; Moderate; p. 313)

40) A free toy placed inside a package of cereal is an example of an in- or on-package premium.
(True; Easy; p. 313)

41) A sporting goods store offering a free golf bag with the purchase of three or more golf clubs is an example of a self-liquidating premium
(False; Moderate; p. 313)

42) A self-liquidating premium is one in which the consumer pays some money for the gift or item.
(True; Easy; p. 313)

43) The two major problems with premium programs are the time factor and the cost.
(True; Moderate; p. 314)

44) Compared to other types of consumer promotions, a premium tends to have a long life span.
(False; Challenging; p. 314)

45) Building a successful premium requires matching the premium to the target market.
(True; Moderate; p. 314)

46) Premiums are normally much more successful than coupons in increasing sales and profits.
(False; Challenging; p. 315)

47) The consumer is typically required to make a purchase when entering a sweepstakes.
(False; Easy; p. 315)

48) A contest requires the use of a skill while a sweepstakes relies on random chance.
(True; Moderate; p. 315)

49) In a contest or sweepstake, the extrinsic value is the value of the prize itself to the consumer.
(True; Moderate; p. 316)

50) In a contest or sweepstake, an intrinsic value is the challenge or fun in playing the game or in participating.
(True; Moderate; p. 316)

51) The three biggest problems with contests and sweepstakes are the costs, consumer indifference, and clutter.
(True; Moderate; p. 316)

52) Consumers are increasingly indifferent to many contests and sweepstakes because of the rising availability of gambling opportunities.
(True; Moderate; p. 316)

53) A major advantage of using the Internet for a contest is that individuals can participate in the contest for its intrinsic value.
(True; Challenging; p. 317)

54) To encourage consumers to continue playing a contest, the intrinsic value of prizes can be steadily increased by allowing small, incremental rewards.
(False; Moderate; p. 318)

55) The primary goals of contests and sweepstakes are to encourage customer traffic and boost brand switching behavior.
(False; Challenging; p. 318)

56) Refunds and rebates are cash returns offered to consumers or businesses following the purchase of a product.
(True; Easy; p. 318)

57) Refunds are paid on soft goods; rebates are paid on hard goods.
(True; Easy; p. 318)

58) Refunds and rebates suffer the disadvantages of costs, paperwork, and diminished effectiveness.
(True; Moderate; p. 318)

59) Many rebate programs are more effective because consumers get excited and this leads them to wait patiently until one is offered before making a purchase.
(False; Challenging; p. 318)

60) For products that have used rebates consistently, such as automobiles, many consumers will no longer purchase the product unless a rebate is offered.
(True; Moderate; p. 319)

61) A highly visible refund or rebate is less likely to be effective, because consumers get tired of hearing about them.
(False; Moderate; p. 319)

62) An effective rebate program is based on visibility, perceived newness, and impact.
(True; Challenging; p. 319)

63) Retailers tend to like refunds and rebates because the retailer earns a higher margin on the product than if no rebate or refund is offered.
(False; Challenging; p. 319)

64) In-store sampling is a program in which samples are given directly to consumers in a retail store.
(True; Easy; p. 320)

65) Direct sampling is a program in which samples are given directly to consumers in a retail store.
(False; Easy; p. 320)

66) Direct sampling a dryer sheet attached to or in a box of laundry detergent is a form of response sampling.
(False; Moderate; p. 320)

67) Instant redemption coupons are a form of direct sampling.
(False; Moderate; p. 320)

68) Shania received a sample of a new tea drink when she attended a football game in Miami. This is an example of selective sampling.
(True; Challenging; p. 321)

69) In recent years, marketers have increased their usage of free standing inserts (FSI) for the distribution of samples.
(True; Moderate; p. 321)

70) It is not possible to offer sampling programs over the Internet.
(False; Challenging; p. 321)

71) The primary disadvantage of sampling is the cost, both of producing the sample and for distributing the sample.
(True; Moderate; p. 321)

72) When one or more extra items are place in special product package, it is called a bonus pack.
(True; Easy; p. 322)

73) A bonus pack works best for current customers.
    (True; Moderate; p. 322)

74) Bonus packs can lead to brand switching if the consumer has used the brand previously.
    (True; Challenging; p. 322)

75) For ongoing products in highly competitive markets, a bonus pack is an effective method of maintaining brand loyalty and reducing brand switching at a minimal cost.
    (True; Challenging; p. 322)

76) Price-offs are excellent at stimulating sales of an existing product.
    (True; Moderate; p. 323)

77) Price-offs can encourage customers to switch brands in brand parity situations or when the consumer has a high level of brand loyalty to another brand.
    (False; Moderate; p. 323)

78) A consumer who purchases additional product because of a price-off tends to either consume more or delay a future purchase of the product.
    (True; Challenging; p. 323)

79) Retailers use price-offs to encourage brand switching and to reward current customers for their loyalty.
    (False; Challenging; p. 323)

80) To be successful, price-offs need to have a monetary appeal to consumers and provide consumers with an immediate reward.
    (True; Moderate; p. 323)

81) An overlay combines two or more consumer promotions activities into a single campaign.
    (True; Moderate; p. 324)

82) Intracompany tie-ins are the promotion of two different products from different companies using one consumer promotion.
    (False; Moderate; p. 325)

83) Intercompany tie-ins are the promotion of two different products from the same company using one consumer promotion.
    (False; Moderate; p. 325)

84) Price-sensitive consumers regularly respond to consumer promotions, such as coupons, price-off deals, and premiums.
    (False; Challenging; p. 325)

85) Brand-loyal consumers purchase only one particular brand and do not respond to consumer promotions unless it is for their particular brand.
(True; Moderate; p. 325)

86) For brand-loyal consumers, consumer promotions can be crafted to both boost sales and reinforce the firm's image.
(True; Challenging; p. 325)

87) Retailers will support a manufacturer's consumer promotion program if the program increases traffic into the retail store, boost store sales, attracts new customers, or increases the basket size of shoppers in the store.
(True; Challenging; p. 326)

88) Price-based consumer promotions are designed primarily to either attract new customers or to boost sales.
(True; Moderate; p. 326)

89) Very few sales promotions are used in business-to-business settings because of the nature of the customers involved.
(False; Moderate; p. 326)

90) Sampling is an excellent method to encourage businesses to try a new product.
(True; Easy, p. 327)

91) Price-off programs are more difficult to offer in business-to-business relationships because prices are normally fixed by contract.
(True; Challenging; p. 327)

92) It is not possible to have a totally centralized, integrated international consumer promotion program because of differences in customs, laws, and culture.
(True; Moderate; p. 327)

93) Coupons are not as prevalent in Italy as they are in the United States because redeeming them is associated with being underprivileged and poor.
(False; Challenging; p. 327)

94) Contests and sweepstakes are highly effective in the U.S., but not in other countries due to cultural differences.
(False; Challenging; p. 327)

Multiple-Choice Questions

95) Time share properties have characteristics of both goods and:
    a) prices
    b) services
    c) sundries
    d) governmental agencies
(b; Easy; p. 306)

96) When a manufacturer offers a special promotion to other companies for their use and not for resale, it is a:
    a) consumer promotion
    b) bonus program
    c) trade promotion
    d) brand awareness program
(a; Easy; p. 308)

97) One of the primary goals of a consumer promotion is to:
    a) build brand equity
    b) entice the customer to take the final step and make a purchase
    c) enhance brand parity
    d) entice the customer to try the product
(b; Moderate; p. 308)

98) The two most general categories of promotions are consumer franchise-building promotions and consumer:
    a) price-incentive promotions
    b) nonfranchise-building promotions
    c) sales-building promotions
    d) sales promotions
(c; Easy; p. 308)

99) The two most general categories of promotions are consumer sales-building promotions and consumer:
    a) price-incentive promotions
    b) franchise-building promotions
    c) sales-building promotions
    d) sales promotions
(b; Easy; p. 308)

100) Consumer promotions designed to increase awareness and strengthen loyalty to a brand are called:
  a) consumer franchise-building
  b) consumer sales-building
  c) retailer generated
  d) alternative promotions
(a; Moderate; p. 308)

101) A consumer franchise-building promotion is designed to:
  a) reduce clutter
  b) generate immediate sales
  c) by-pass the wholesaler
  d) increase awareness and strengthen loyalty to a brand
(d; Moderate; p. 308)

102) Consumer promotions designed to create immediate sales rather than brand equity or loyalty are called:
  a) consumer franchise-building promotions
  b) trade promotions
  c) consumer sales-building promotions
  d) public relations promotions
(c; Moderate; p. 308)

103) A consumer sales-building promotion is designed to:
  a) change attitudes
  b) weaken competition
  c) create brand awareness leading to new sales
  d) create immediate sales rather than brand equity or loyalty
(d; Moderate; p. 308)

104) When Colgate promotes a new tooth-whitening product using discounts to retail stores and prizes to customers to create immediate sales, the approach is primarily:
  a) franchise building
  b) sales building
  c) territory building
  d) brand-equity building
(b; Challenging; p. 308)

105) Consumers who are exposed to which type of promotion tend to develop higher levels of brand awareness and stronger perceptions of brand equity?
  a) franchise-building
  b) sales-building
  c) equity-building
  d) brand-building
(a; Challenging; p. 308)

106) If consumer promotions are used, high-image brands should focus more on:
   a) brand-building promotions
   b) sales-building promotions
   c) franchise building promotions
   d) equity-building promotions
   (c; Challenging; p. 308)

107) If consumer promotions are used, lower image brands that emphasis price should focus more on:
   a) brand-building promotions
   b) sales-building promotions
   c) franchise building promotions
   d) equity-building promotions
   (b; Challenging; p. 308)

108) Nearly 80 percent of all coupons are offered by:
   a) manufacturers
   b) wholesalers
   c) retailers
   d) Internet companies
   (a; Moderate; p. 309)

109) Nearly 90 percent of all coupons are offered:
   a) in, on, or near store shelves
   b) in, on, or near packages
   c) through print media
   d) via broadcast media
   (c; Moderate; p. 309)

110) The primary vehicle for distributing print coupons and coupons in general is:
   a) magazines
   b) newspapers
   c) direct mail
   d) free standing inserts (FSI)
   (d; Moderate; p. 309)

111) Free Standing Inserts (FSI) are found primarily in:
   a) magazines
   b) newspapers
   c) shopping malls
   d) catalogs
   (b; Easy; p. 309)

112) The following statements concerning free standing inserts (FSI) and print media distributed coupons are true, *except:*
   a) consumers must make a conscious effort to clip or save the coupon
   b) coupons create brand awareness
   c) coupons enhance brand equity
   d) using FSI and print media encourages consumers to purchase the brand on their next trip to the store, thus increasing brand name recall
   (c; Challenging; p. 310)

113) A coupon placed on a package to be used during the purchase is called a(n):
   a) free-standing coupon
   b) bounce-back coupon
   c) instant-redemption coupon
   d) rebate coupon
   (c; Easy; p. 310)

114) An instant-redemption coupon is:
   a) delivered electronically over the Internet
   b) delivered electronically at the cash register
   c) placed inside the package to be used later
   d) placed on a package to be used during the purchase
   (d; Moderate; p. 310)

115) Vanish has a $1.00-off coupon attached to the container that can be easily removed. This is an example of a(n):
   a) instant redemption coupon
   b) bounce-back coupon
   c) cross-ruffing coupon
   d) response-offer coupon
   (a; Challenging; p. 310)

116) A coupon placed inside a package to be used for a later purchase is called a(n):
   a) free-standing coupon
   b) bounce-back coupon
   c) instant-redemption coupon
   d) rebate coupon
   (b; Easy; p. 310)

117) A bounce-back coupon is:
   a) not immediately redeemable
   b) not normally distributed by a manufacturer
   c) a form of premium
   d) used at the time the product is purchased
   (a; Moderate; p. 310)

118) Bounce-back coupons are used to encourage:
   a) brand switching
   b) repeat purchases
   c) trial purchases
   d) brand loyalty
(b; Challenging; p. 310)

119) Quaker Oats has placed a $1.00 coupon inside the box of Quaker Oats. This is an example of a(n):
   a) instant-redemption coupon
   b) bounce-back coupon
   c) cross-ruffing coupon
   d) response offer coupon
(b; Challenging; p. 310)

120) When a cash register triggers a coupon for a competitor's product, it is called a(n):
   a) bounce-back coupon
   b) scanner-delivered coupon
   c) cross-ruffing coupon
   d) response offer coupon
(b; Easy; p. 310)

121) The best type of coupon to encourage brand switching is a(n):
   a) cross ruff
   b) bounce-back
   c) scanner-delivered
   d) free standing insert (FSI)
(c; Challenging; p. 310)

122) Scanner-delivered coupons are used to encourage:
   a) brand switching
   b) repeat purchases
   c) trial purchases
   d) brand loyalty
(a; Challenging; p. 310)

123) A coupon placed on a package for a different product is a(n):
   a) cross-ruffing coupon
   b) scanner-delivered coupon
   c) response-offer coupon
   d) instant-redemption coupon
(a; Easy; p. 310)

124) A coupon on a 2-liter bottle of Pepsi, offering $1.00 off on a bag of potato chips, is which type of coupon?
   a) cross-ruffing
   b) scanner-delivered
   c) response-offer
   d) instant-redemption
(a; Moderate; p. 310)

125) A coupon for $3.00 off on a package of six golf balls placed on a golf club cover is a:
   a) response offer coupon
   b) cross-ruffing coupon
   c) premium
   d) bonus offer
(b; Moderate; p. 311)

126) A coupon that is issued after a consumer request is which type?
   a) bounce-back
   b) scanner delivered
   c) instant redemption
   d) response offer
(d; Easy; p. 311)

127) An Internet request or a toll-free number that leads to the issuance of a coupon is called:
   a) bounce-back
   b) scanner delivered
   c) instant redemption
   d) response offer
(d; Moderate; p. 311)

128) Kari has called a toll free number to request a $25 coupon for a color printer she saw advertised on television. This is an example of which type of coupon?
   a) bounce-back
   b) scanner delivered
   c) instant redemption
   d) response offer
(d; Challenging; p. 311)

129) Most, approximately 50 percent, of electronically delivered coupons were requested:
   a) by telephone
   b) after seeing a television ad
   c) from the Internet
   d) after seeing a print ad
(c; Challenging; p. 311)

130) Redemption rates for e-coupons is:
   a) considerably higher than for other types of coupons
   b) considerably lower than for other types of coupons
   c) dependent on the dollar value of the coupon
   d) approximately the same as instant redemption coupons
   (a; Moderate; p. 311)

131) Coupon distribution has continued to increase. Coupon redemption rates have:
   a) also continued to increase
   b) steadily declined
   c) remained steady
   d) fluctuated widely with changes in the economy
   (b; Challenging; p. 311)

132) Of the following groups, which has the lowest record of redeeming coupons?
   a) price-conscious consumers
   b) Caucasians
   c) females
   d) Hispanics
   (d; Moderate; p. 311)

133) Coupon redemption rates tend to be lower for:
   a) Caucasians
   b) Asian-Americans
   c) African-Americans and Hispanics
   d) every minority group
   (c; Challenging; p. 311)

134) The following are disadvantages of using coupons, *except:*
   a) reduced revenues
   b) mass-cutting
   c) counterfeiting
   d) cost of distribution
   (d; Moderate; p. 311)

135) Mass-cutting of coupons is when:
   a) coupons are redeemed through a fraudulent, nonexistent retail outlet
   b) coupons are printed as e-coupons and sold in mass to consumers
   c) a coupon is copied and redeemed twice by the same store
   d) coupons are cut out of magazines for use by charitable organizations
   (a; Easy; p. 311)

136) Making a copy of a coupon and then redeeming it for cash is an example of:

   a) mass cutting
   b) counterfeiting
   c) misredemption
   d) standard industry practice
(b; Moderate; p. 311)

137) The major source of counterfeiting is now:
   a) fraudulent retail store operations
   b) charity groups cutting coupons for fake retail outlets
   c) stores redeeming coupons for products that were not sold
   d) printing and selling bogus e-coupons over the Internet
(d; Challenging; p. 311)

138) A 50-cent coupon for a 16-ounce can that is redeemed for a 12-ounce can purchase is an example of:
   a) mass cutting
   b) retail discounting
   c) misredemption
   d) coupon flexibility
(c; Moderate; p. 312)

139) Research indicates that coupons distributed via free standing inserts (FSI) are the most attractive to consumer because:
   a) the coupons have a higher face value
   b) the coupons are for products that the consumer buys
   c) consumers can choose the coupons they want to use in the privacy of their homes
   d) the coupons are for preferred brands or brands in the consumer's evoked set
(c; Moderate; p. 312)

140) A coupon for a brand that a consumer already uses regularly will be:
   a) more attractive to the consumer
   b) less attractive to the consumer
   c) unlikely to have an impact
   d) ignored due to issues of familiarity
(a; Moderate; p. 312)

141) Coupon attractiveness is influenced by each of the following, *except:*
   a) face value of the coupon
   b) distribution method
   c) whether it is for a preferred brand or one in a consumer's evoked set
   d) target market of the coupon
(d; Challenging; p. 312)

142) Research indicates that coupons distributed via which medium are the most attractive to consumers, because they can choose coupons in the privacy of their homes?
   a) direct mail
   b) FSI
   c) the Internet
   d) newspapers
(b; Challenging; p. 312)

143) Prizes or gifts that consumers receive when purchasing products are called:
   a) add-ins
   b) premiums
   c) purchase incentives
   d) giveaways
(b; Easy; p. 313)

144) With a premium, customers:
   a) receive a discount on the purchase price
   b) receive a gift or prize for making a purchase
   c) have an opportunity to win prizes or cash
   d) purchase multiple items for a reduced price
(b; Easy; p. 313)

145) Some marketing experts believe that the overuse of coupons can damage a brand's image, while the use of which of the following can actually enhance a brand's image?
   a) contests and sweepstakes
   b) bonus packs
   c) sampling
   d) premiums
(d; Challenging; p. 313)

146) The following are types of premiums, *except:*
   a) free-in-the mail
   b) in or on-package
   c) instant-redemption
   d) self-liquidating
(c; Moderate; p. 313)

147) A gift sent by mail to a customer, based on a proof-of-purchase receipt, is which type of premium?
   a) free-in-the-mail
   b) self-liquidating
   c) bounce-back
   d) instant-redemption
(a; Easy; p. 313)

148) A small gift being placed inside of a package is a(n):
   a) in-package premium
   b) retail premium
   c) store premium
   d) self-liquidating premium
   (a; Easy; p. 313)

149) A toy placed inside a box of cereal is an example of a(n):
   a) bonus pack
   b) in-package premium
   c) store premium
   d) self-liquidating premium
   (b; Easy; p. 313)

150) A gift given by the retail store when the customer purchases a product is a(n):
   a) bonus pack
   b) in-package premium
   c) store or manufacturer premium
   d) self-liquidating premium
   (c; Easy; p. 313)

151) A Star Wars action figure given when a customer buys a Whopper at Burger King would be a:
   a) bounce-back premium
   b) in- or on-package premium
   c) store or manufacturer premium
   d) self-liquidating premium
   (c; Challenging; p. 313)

152) A PDA given as a gift for test driving a car is an example of a:
   a) free-in-the-mail premium
   b) store or manufacturer premium
   c) self-liquidating premium
   d) in- or on-package premium
   (b; Challenging; p. 313)

153) Consumers must pay a small amount of money for a(n):
   a) in- or on-package premium
   b) cross-ruffing premium
   c) store premium
   d) self-liquidating premium
   (d; Moderate; p. 313)

154) The two primary problems associated with premiums are:
    a) short life spans and costs
    b) consumer indifference and clutter
    c) negative effects on brand image and brand recall
    d) perceptions of inequity in brand comparisons and lack of identity
(a; Moderate; p. 314)

155) The following statements about premiums are true, *except:*
    a) Premiums of higher quality lead to better response rates.
    b) Premiums should add value to a product.
    c) Premiums should reinforce the brand's image.
    d) Premiums should build short-term profits.
(d; Challenging; p. 314)

156) John Deere offers to each tractor dealer that orders a new tractor a vintage toy tractor that can be displayed, sold, or given to a dealer's best customers. This promotion is an example of a business-to-business:
    a) sampling
    b) bonus pack
    c) premium
    d) rebate
(c; Challenging; p. 314)

157) Each of the following are important keys to building a successful premium program, *except:*
    a) match the premium to the target market
    b) select premiums that are highly popular and current fads
    c) select premiums that reinforce the firm's product and image
    d) integrate the premium with other IMC tools
(b; Moderate; p. 314)

158) Each of the following are principles to remember when using premiums, *except:*
    a) the premium should build rational involvement in some way with the good or service
    b) the premium should build emotional involvement
    c) the premium's value should be greater than 10 percent of the cost of the product
    d) the premium must build involvement with the product, not just the premium
(c; Challenging; p. 315)

159) The sales promotion that requires the participant to perform some type of activity in order to be eligible to win prizes is a:
    a) contest
    b) sweepstakes
    c) premium
    d) price-off program
(a; Easy; p. 315)

160) In which of the following will participants register to win a prize without making a purchase?
    a) contest
    b) sweepstakes
    c) premium
    d) price-off program
(b; Easy; p. 315)

161) In which of the following do participants may win a prize without performing any type of activity?
    a) contest
    b) sweepstakes
    c) premium
    d) price-off program
(b; Easy; p. 315)

162) A "write our new slogan" event that awards a prize to the winning slogan is a(n):
    a) contest
    b) sweepstakes
    c) premium
    d) illegal activity
(a; Moderate; p. 315)

163) Each of the following statements about contests are true, *except:*
    a) participants cannot be required to make a purchase to enter
    b) probability of winning cannot easily be calculated
    c) creates intrinsic value for those who enter
    d) often requires a judge to decide the winner
(a; Challenging; p. 315)

164) Each of the following statements about sweepstakes are true, *except:*
    a) odds of winning must be published
    b) does not require a skill to win
    c) requires a purchase to enter
    d) will provide little intrinsic value
(c; Challenging; p. 316)

165) The actual attractiveness of prizes in a contest is in its:
   a) intrinsic value
   b) extrinsic value
   c) redemption rates
   d) Internet inquiries
(b; Easy; p. 316)

166) For most people, a free trip to Hawaii is an example of a prize with high:
   a) intrinsic value
   b) extrinsic value
   c) redemption rates
   d) Internet inquiries
(b; Moderate; p. 316)

167) The enjoyment of playing or participating in a contest is called:
   a) intrinsic value
   b) extrinsic value
   c) redemption value
   d) historic value
(a; Moderate; p. 316)

168) Winning a trip to Nashville to record a song based on a singing contest is:
   a) a prize with both extrinsic and intrinsic value
   b) a prize with no extrinsic value, only intrinsic
   c) a prize based on making a purchase in order to enter the contest
   d) a prize with a high extrinsic value, but little intrinsic value
(a; Challenging; p. 316)

169) Each of the following are problems associated with contests and sweepstakes, *except:*
   a) costs
   b) consumer indifference
   c) clutter
   d) low extrinsic value prizes
(d; Challenging; p. 316)

170) A major reason for Hip Cricket's success in using cell phone instant messaging for a Miller Brewing Company Icehouse brand contest was:
   a) the value of the prizes won
   b) notification of winning instantly
   c) the intrinsic value of the contest
   d) the demographic target market of the contest
(b; Challenging; p. 317)

171) Using the Internet for contests or sweepstakes has the following advantages over traditional contest methods, *except:*
    a) provide a higher level of intrinsic value
    b) provide ability to create interactive games
    c) provide a higher level of extrinsic rewards
    d) provide promoters with data-capturing capabilities
(c; Challenging; p. 317)

172) Of the following features, all are feasible strategies to improve a contest's success, *except:*
    a) tie-ins with other companies
    b) increasing the values of prizes over time
    c) increasing the number of contests per year
    d) utilizing POPs and other advertising devices to promote the contest
(c; Challenging; p. 318)

173) The two primary goals of contests and sweepstakes are to:
    a) build brand equity and boost sales
    b) boost sales and profits
    c) overcome advertising clutter and increase inquiries
    d) encourage customer traffic and boost sales
(d; Challenging; p. 318)

174) Cash returns on soft goods, such as food or clothing, are called:
    a) refunds
    b) rebates
    c) bill back programs
    d) premiums
(a; Easy; p. 318)

175) Cash returns on hard goods, such as appliances and electronics, are called:
    a) refunds
    b) rebates
    c) bounce back coupons
    d) premiums
(b; Easy; p. 318)

176) Problems associated with refund and rebate programs include each of the following, *except:*
    a) fraud and misredemption
    b) costs
    c) paperwork to process the refund or rebate
    d) diminished effectiveness
(a; Challenging; p. 319)

177) Andy will not purchase a computer unless the manufacturer offers a rebate. This is an example of which of the following problems associated with refund and rebate programs?
   a) fraud and misredemption
   b) costs
   c) paperwork to process the refund or rebate
   d) diminished effectiveness
(d; Challenging; p. 319)

178) When consumers are made aware of a refund or rebate program before purchasing the product, the program has:
   a) visibility
   b) brand equity
   c) modesty
   d) immediacy
(a; Moderate; p. 319)

179) Effective refund and rebate programs have each of the following characteristics, *except:*
   a) visibility
   b) brand equity
   c) perceived newness
   d) an impact
(b; Moderate; p. 319)

180) To be effective, rebates and refunds must have the impact on buyers' behaviors by:
   a) making them more brand loyal
   b) generating positive word-of-mouth communications
   c) either leading to a more immediate purchase or by causing buyers to change brands
   d) stimulating a trial purchase
(c; Moderate; p. 319)

181) Retailers tend to like refunds and rebates because:
   a) the manufacturer pays for the advertising of the refund or rebate program
   b) the manufacturer furnishes a POP display to be used with the refund or rebate program
   c) the retailer's margin on the product is higher
   d) the retailer maintains its margin or markup on the product since it is sold at full retail price
(d; Challenging; p. 319)

182) The delivery of a product to consumers for their use or consumption for free is a:
   a) coupon program
   b) premium
   c) bonus pack
   d) sampling program
(d; Easy; p. 320)

183) When time-share properties offer to let you stay for a night or weekend on the condition you listen to a sales pitch, they are using which consumer promotion technique?
   a) sampling
   b) a premium
   c) price-off
   d) coupon
(a; Moderate; p. 320)

184) Of the following consumer promotions, the best for encouraging consumers to try a new product is:
   a) coupons
   b) sampling
   c) premiums
   d) contests or sweepstakes
(b; Challenging; p. 320)

185) Cooking food in a grocery store and giving small pieces of the food to consumers who pass by is which form of sampling?
   a) in-store distribution
   b) direct
   c) response
   d) cross-ruffing
(a; Easy; p. 320)

186) When samples are mailed or delivered door-to-door, which form of sampling is being used?
   a) in-store distribution
   b) direct
   c) bonus pack
   d) cross ruffing
(b; Moderate; p. 320)

187) Placing a sample bar of soap in every mail box within a 10-block area is an example of:
   a) direct sampling
   b) cross-ruff sampling
   c) selective sampling
   d) response sampling
(a; Moderate; p. 320)

188) Providing a small sample of laundry detergent with the purchase of dryer sheets is called:
   a) direct sampling
   b) response sampling
   c) cross-ruff sampling
   d) media sampling
(c; Challenging; p. 320)

189) A small perfume sample placed in a magazine is a:
   a) direct sampling program
   b) response sampling program
   c) media sampling program
   d) selective sample program
(c; Moderate; p. 320)

190) A pharmaceutical company giving free samples of medicine to a physician is:
   a) unethical influence
   b) professional sampling
   c) selective sampling
   d) media sampling
(b; Moderate; p. 320)

191) Giving out samples at a site such as a state fair, parade, or sporting event is:
   a) direct sampling
   b) response sampling
   c) cross-ruff sampling
   d) selective sampling
(d; Challenging; p.320)

192) Each of the following are types of sampling, *except:*
   a) instant-redemption sampling
   b) in-store distribution sampling
   c) direct sampling
   d) response sampling
(a; Moderate; p. 320)

193) Each of the following are types of sampling, *except:*
    a) cross-ruffing sampling
    b) self-liquidating sampling
    c) media sampling
    d) professional sampling
(b; Moderate; p. 320)

194) The best method of sampling to use is largely determined by the:
    a) cost of the sample
    b) relative cost of each sampling method
    c) target market
    d) goal of the sampling program
(c; Challenging; p. 320)

195) Women tend to prefer:
    a) in-store samples so they can ask questions about the product
    b) professional sampling because they trust professionals to provide accurate information
    c) selective sampling because they can select the sample they want
    d) mail samples so they can examine them at home
(d; Challenging; p. 320)

196) Men tend to prefer:
    a) in-store or selective samples so they can ask questions about the product or obtain additional information
    b) professional sampling because they trust professionals to provide accurate information
    c) cross-ruffing samples because it reduces costs
    d) mail samples so they can examine them at home
(a; Challenging; p. 320)

197) In recent years, marketers have increased their usage of which medium for distributing samples?
    a) broadcast media
    b) free standing inserts (FSI)
    c) magazines
    d) direct mail
(b; Challenging; p. 321)

198) The primary advantage of Internet sampling to the firm providing the sample is that:
  a) it is cheaper than the other methods of distribution
  b) more expensive samples can be provided
  c) only individuals who request the sample will receive it
  d) the target market of the sample tends to have a higher educational level and higher income
(c; Challenging; p. 321)

199) The primary disadvantage of sampling is:
  a) inability to target the sample effectively
  b) diminished effectiveness
  c) lack of visibility
  d) cost of producing and distributing the sample
(d; Moderate; p. 321)

200) The key to a successful sampling program is:
  a) targeting the right audience
  b) reducing the costs of distribution
  c) gaining visibility prior to the sampling program
  d) the cooperation of retailers and other channel members
(a; Challenging; p. 322)

201) Adding an extra bar of soap to a three pack is called a:
  a) rebate pack
  b) prize package
  c) bonus pack
  d) selective sample
(c; Easy; p. 322)

202) If Colgate packages two tubes of toothpaste together to sell at a special price, it is an example of a:
  a) cross-ruffing premium
  b) rebate
  c) bonus pack
  d) self-liquidating premium
(c; Moderate; p. 322)

203) Each of the following are reasons to offer a bonus pack, *except:*
  a) increase usage of the product
  b) stimulate trial purchase
  c) match or preempt competitive actions
  d) stockpile the product
(b; Challenging; p. 322)

204) The following are reasons to use a bonus pack, *except:*
    a) develop customer loyalty
    b) attract new users
    c) enhance brand parity
    d) encourage brand switching
(c; Challenging; p. 322)

205) Each of the following statements about bonus packs is true, *except:*
    a) Bonus packs appeal to price-sensitive consumers.
    b) Bonus packs rarely attract new customers.
    c) Bonus packs can lead to brand switching.
    d) Bonus packs can pre-empt the competition.
(a; Challenging; p. 322)

206) Bonus packs can lead to brand switching if the consumer:
    a) is price-sensitive
    b) is promotion-sensitive
    c) believes the bonus exceeds 30 percent
    d) has purchased the brand previously
(d; Challenging; p. 322)

207) One method of maintaining brand loyalty and reducing brand switching at a minimal cost is:
    a) coupons
    b) bonus packs
    c) contests and sweepstakes
    d) sampling
(b; Challenging; p. 322)

208) A temporary price reducing that is marked on the product's package is a:
    a) bonus offer
    b) price-off
    c) premium
    d) bad idea, because the retail may not honor the price
(b; Easy; p. 323)

209) Price-off offers are best for:
    a) building firm image
    b) increasing store traffic and generating sales
    c) high involvement products
    d) consumers who are not price sensitive
(b; Moderate; p. 323)

210) Folks Southern Kitchen advertises in the local newspaper a special $5.99 lunch special at any of its outlets during March. This promotion is an example of a:
   a) coupon
   b) sampling
   c) premium
   d) price-off
   (d; Challenging; p. 323)

211) A price-off program:
   a) is effective for individuals that have a high degree of brand loyalty to a competing brand.
   b) has little impact on sales.
   c) usually boosts sales, but it can hurt profits.
   d) decreases price sensitivity over time.
   (c; Challenging; p. 323)

212) Each of the following statements about price-off programs is true, *except:*
   a) A price-off program can increase store traffic.
   b) A price-off program can generate sales.
   c) A price-off program has the least immediate reward compared to contests, sweepstakes and rebates.
   d) A price-off program should not target loyal users, but rather brand switchers.
   (c; Challenging; p. 323)

213) Two or more consumer promotional activities combined into a single campaign is a(n):
   a) intercompany tie-in
   b) intracompany tie-in
   c) overlay
   d) premium
   (c; Moderate; p. 324)

214) Fisher Boy has both a 55 cents-off coupon and an entry form for a sweepstakes in an advertisement. This is an example of a(n):
   a) intercompany tie-in
   b) intracompany tie-in
   c) overlay
   d) bonus pack
   (c; Challenging; p. 324)

215) When two products from the same company are promoted together, using one consumer promotion, it is called:
   a) an intracompany tie-in
   b) an intercompany tie-in
   c) an overlay
   d) a premium
(a; Moderate; p. 325)

216) When two products from different companies are promoted together, using one consumer promotion, it is called:
   a) an intracompany tie-in
   b) an intercompany tie-in
   c) an overlay
   d) a premium
(b; Moderate; p. 325)

217) An example of an intercompany tie-in promotion is:
   a) Betty Crocker with Tyson
   b) a Whopper and onion rings at Burger King
   c) Pepsi and Diet Pepsi
   d) Popcorn and a movie from Blockbuster
(a; Challenging; p. 325)

218) Tyson and General Foods developed a joint consumer promotion. This would be an example of a(n):
   a) intracompany tie-in
   b) intercompany tie-in
   c) overlay
   d) premium
(b; Moderate; p. 325)

219) The type of consumer that responds best to coupons and premiums is:
   a) promotion-prone consumers
   b) brand-loyal consumers
   c) brand-image consumers
   d) price-sensitive consumers
(a; Challenging; p. 325)

220) A consumer who only purchases his or her favorite brand is called:
   a) promotion-prone
   b) brand-loyal
   c) brand responsive
   d) price-sensitive
(b; Challenging; p. 325)

221) In terms of planning promotions, consumers can be divided into the following categories, *except:*
   a) promotion prone
   b) brand loyal
   c) price sensitive
   d) repeat purchasers
   (d; Moderate; p. 325)

222) A consumer who makes the purchase decision based on price is called:
   a) promotion-prone
   b) brand-loyal
   c) repeat buyer
   d) price-sensitive
   (d; Easy; p. 325)

223) Britney likes to use coupons and tends to purchase whichever brand of food has the best coupon offer. Britney would be classified as which type of consumer?
   a) promotion prone
   b) brand loyal
   c) price sensitive
   d) shopper prone
   (a; Challenging; p. 325)

224) Trey likes to drink Pepsi and will use a consumer promotion, such as a coupon or premium, only if it is for Pepsi. Trey would be classified as which type of consumer?
   a) promotion prone
   b) brand loyal
   c) price sensitive
   d) shopper prone
   (b; Challenging; p. 325)

225) Oscar is on a tight budget so he uses the consumer promotions that will give him the best price for products he buys. Oscar would be classified as which type of consumer?
   a) promotion prone
   b) brand loyal
   c) price sensitive
   d) shopper prone
   (c; Moderate; p. 325)

226) The primary reasons retailers give for supporting a manufacturer's consumer promotions program include each of the following, *except:*
   a) increase store traffic
   b) increase store sales
   c) increase brand sales
   d) attract new customers
(c; Moderate; p. 325)

227) Price-based consumer promotions are normally designed to:
   a) build brand image
   b) support a push strategy by the manufacturer
   c) attract new customers and to build sales
   d) motivate retailers to support the consumer promotion program
(c; Moderate; p. 325)

228) Which of the following is the most inclined to offer some type of consumer promotion to business customers?
   a) manufacturers
   b) retailers
   c) wholesalers
   d) business merchants
(a; Challenging; p. 326)

229) The best promotion at encouraging a business to try a new product is:
   a) coupons
   b) premiums
   c) bonus packs
   d) sampling
(d; Challenging; p. 326)

230) Coupons are not as prevalent in which of the following countries, because redeeming a coupon is associated with being underprivileged and poor?
   a) Italy
   b) Japan
   c) Spain
   d) United Kingdom
(d; Challenging; p. 327)

231) Of the countries listed, the lowest overall coupon redemption rate is in:
   a) Italy
   b) Spain
   c) England
   d) United States
(d; Challenging; p. 328)

232) An organization creating an international consumer promotions program should utilize an experienced:
   a) international sales promotion coordinator or manager
   b) sales promotion agency
   c) advertising agency that offers consumer promotion expertise
   d) translator
(a; Moderate; p. 326)

Short-Answer Questions

233) What are the major forms of coupons?

Instant redemption, bounce-back, scanner-delivered, cross-ruffing, response offer, and electronically delivered U-pons.
(Easy; p. 310)

234) What problems are associated with coupons?

Reduced revenues, mass cutting, counterfeiting, and misredemptions.
(Easy; p. 311)

235) How can coupons be made more attractive to consumers?

Higher face value, FSI distribution, and a preferred brand coupon is more attractive.
(Moderate; p. 312)

236) What are the four major types of premiums?

1. free-in-the-mail
2. in- or on-package
3. store or manufacturer
4. self-liquidating
(Moderate; p. 313)

237) How can a company build a successful premium program?

- Match the premium to the target market
- Reinforce the firm's image with the premium
- Tie the premium to the firm's products
- Make the premium in sufficient quality
- Integrate with the overall IMC approach
(Challenging; pp. 314)

238) What is the primary difference between a contest and a sweepstakes?

A contest requires a skill or entry of some sort. Many require purchases to enter. Sweepstakes are games of chance where consumers may enter as many times as they wish.
(Easy; p. 315)

239) For contests and sweepstakes, what is the difference between extrinsic value and intrinsic value in prizes?

Extrinsic value is the actual attractiveness of the item. Intrinsic values are associated with playing or participating.
(Moderate; p. 316)

240) What are the characteristics of effective refund and rebate programs?

Visibility, perceived newness, impact.
(Moderate; p. 319)

241) Name the various forms of sampling.

- In-store distribution
- Direct sampling
- Response samples
- Cross-ruff samples
- Media sampling
- Professional samples
- Selective samples

(Challenging; p. 320)

242) What are the major objectives of bonus packs?

- Increase product usage
- Match or pre-empt competition
- Consumer stockpiling of the product
- Develop customer loyalty
- Encourage brand switching

(Challenging; p. 322)

CHAPTER 11

PERSONAL SELLING, DATABASE MARKETING, AND CUSTOMER RELATIONSHIP MANAGEMENT

True-False Questions

1) Levi-Strauss & Company's relationship marketing program was designed to identify various types of customer groups and give them access to the company.
   (True; Easy; p. 336)

2) A consumer who has a positive purchase experience with a product will tell an average of six others about that experience.
   (True; Challenging; p. 338)

3) An unhappy customer is likely to others about the experience. On the average, 11 other people are told about the bad experience.
   (True; Challenging; p. 338)

4) Personal selling is sometimes called the "last three feet" of the marketing function because of the relationship between selling and advertising.
   (False; Easy; p. 338)

5) The two primary forms of personal selling are to retail customers and governmental customers.
   (False; Easy; p. 338)

6) Personal selling in most retail stores is a single transaction.
   (True; Easy; p. 338)

7) An order taker is someone who simply fills an order, such as a cashier at Burger King serving a walk-in customer.
   (True; Easy; p. 338)

8) In repeat transaction sales of services, the salesperson often is involved in problem-solving for customers over time, such as an insurance agent.
   (True; Moderate; p. 339)

9) Inbound telemarketing is receiving calls and inquiries from outside customers.
   (True; Easy; p. 339)

10) Outbound telemarketing is placing calls to prospective customers.
    (True; Easy; p. 339)

11) The use of outbound telemarketing programs has increased since the Do-Not-Call Registry was established.
        (False; Easy; p. 339)

12) Outbound telemarketing calls are invasive, annoying, and yet successful for many firms.
        (True; Moderate; p. 339)

13) Text messaging is a new version of outbound telemarketing.
        (True; Moderate; p. 339)

14) In the problem recognition stage of a retail sale, the representative should strongly urge the customer to focus on one product that will best resolve the problem.
        (False; Moderate; p. 340)

15) Many salespeople in single transaction settings use high-pressure tactics to make sales, which can cost the company repeat business.
        (True; Moderate; p. 340)

16) The key to successful retail sales is determining which stage of the consumer buying process a customer is at before trying to sell the store's merchandise.
        (True; Moderate; p. 340)

17) More than half of the time the final purchase decision is made by a consumer while in the retail store.
        (True; Moderate; p. 340)

18) A missionary salesperson is primarily involved in cross-selling.
        (False; Easy; p. 341)

19) A missionary salesperson is also called a merchandiser or detailer.
        (True; Moderate; p. 341)

20) Cross-selling is marketing other items following the purchase of a good or service.
        (True; Easy; p. 341)

21) Outbound telemarketers have an excellent opportunity to cross-sell products while they have the customer on the phone.
        (False; Challenging; p. 341)

22) Field sales in business-to-business occur when the salesperson visits the client at his or her place of business.
        (True; Easy; p. 341)

23) Field salespeople would be classified as order-getters.
    (True; Easy; p. 341)

24) A field salesperson for Xerox trying to sell a copier to a college would be an order-getter.
    (True; Moderate; p. 341)

25) Single transaction business-to-business sales are typically made in new-buy situations, where the buyer is making a purchase for the first time.
    (True; Moderate; p. 342)

26) Occasional transactions in business-to-business settings are similar to modified rebuy situations.
    (True; Moderate; p. 342)

27) Repeat transactions and contractual agreements often build high levels of trust between the buyer and seller.
    (False; Challenging; p. 342)

28) Trust relationships are those that move beyond contractual agreements in business-to-business selling.
    (True; Moderate; p. 342)

29) EDI stands for electronic data interchange.
    (True; Easy; p. 342)

30) An electronic data interchange or EDI relationship is more trusting than a repeat transaction relationship.
    (True; Challenging; p. 342)

31) An electronic data interchange or EDI relationship means that companies are sharing data to manage orders, purchases, and shipping information.
    (True; Easy; p. 342)

32) A strategic partnership is the most intimate business-to-business buyer-seller relationship.
    (True; Easy; p. 343)

33) The first step of the business-to-business selling process is qualifying prospects.
    (False; Moderate; p. 343)

34) The second step of the business-to-business selling process, after identifying prospects, is qualifying them.
    (True; Moderate; p. 343)

35) The third step of the business-to-business selling process, after qualifying prospects is called "knowledge acquisition."
(True; Challenging; p. 343)

36) The fifth and last step of the business-to-business selling process is the sales presentation.
(False; Moderate; p. 343)

37) The least effective method of identifying prospects is inquiries from advertising.
(False; Moderate; p. 344)

38) Qualifying prospects in business-to-business sales is the process of compiling a complete list of potential customers.
(False; Moderate; p. 344)

39) Qualifying prospects in business-to-business sales is the process of identifying the individuals or companies showing the highest potential for a sale.
(True; Easy; p. 344)

40) During the knowledge acquisition stage of a business-to-business selling prospect, the salesperson needs to determine the prospect's perception of risk in switching vendors.
(True; Challenging; p. 345)

41) Many salespeople skip the knowledge acquisition stage of selling and move directly to the sales call because this is where commissions are gained.
(True; Moderate; p. 345)

42) An intrinsic value buyer in a business-to-business sale has very little information about the product or selling company.
(False; Moderate; p. 345)

43) An extrinsic value buyer in a business-to-business sale focuses on product attributes and the solution the product can provide.
(True; Moderate; p.   345)

44) A strategic value buyer in a business-to-business sale focuses on product attributes and the solution the product can provide.
(False; Moderate; p. 345)

45) In a stimulus-response approach to selling, the idea is to fully understand the customer's needs and customize solutions.
(False; Moderate; p. 346)

46) Outbound telemarketers tend to use the stimulus-response selling approach.
(True; Challenging; p. 346)

47) In a need-satisfaction approach to selling, the idea is to discover the customer's needs and provide solutions.
(True; Moderate; p. 346)

48) In a problem-solution sales approach, the selling organization must analyze the buyer's operations.
(True; Moderate; p. 346)

49) Of the various sales presentation formats, a team selling approach would most likely be used with the need-satisfaction sales approach.
(False; Challenging; p. 346)

50) In the mission-sharing sales approach, two organizations develop a common mission and then share resources to accomplish that mission.
(True; Moderate; p. 346)

51) The primary determinant of the sales approach is the personality type of the buyer.
(False; Challenging; p. 346)

52) The need-satisfaction sales presentation approach matches well with the lower order relationships, such as single and occasional transactions.
(False; Challenging; p. 346)

53) Follow-up is often neglected by salespeople because they usually do not earn commissions on follow-up calls.
(True; Moderate; p. 347)

54) Technology makes it possible to employ fewer salespeople, which is estimated to decline by as much as 50 percent in the next decade.
(True; Challenging; p. 347)

55) With advances in technology, experts believe the number of sales channels will decline in the future.
(False; Moderate; p. 347)

56) The trend toward develop long-term relationships with vendors means buyers in many companies will utilize more suppliers for a product rather than fewer suppliers.
(False; Challenging; p. 348)

57) The trend toward using fewer vendors and stronger commitments from those vendors means many selling companies will shift more to a team selling approach.
(True; Challenging; p. 348)

58) Database development and database marketing are essentially the same thing.
(False; Moderate; p. 349)

59) Database development is the process of creating a database to support the overall company, IMC program, and total marketing effort.
(True; Moderate; p. 349)

60) The objectives and role of the database in the marketing and communications program determine much of what will take place as the data are generated.
(True; Moderate; p. 349)

61) Psychographic, lifestyle, and attitudinal information about a firm's customers is routinely purchased from external commercial database services.
(True; Challenging; p. 350)

62) A primary source of information in database development is internal customer data.
(True; Moderate; p. 350)

63) Geocoding is adding geographic codes to customer records.
(True; Easy; p. 351)

64) A data warehouse should provide the service department and customer relations department with access to customer data as they deal with customer inquiries and complaints.
(True; Moderate; p. 351)

65) Data mining normally involves building profiles of consumer groups and preparing models that predict future purchase behaviors.
(True; Easy; p. 352)

66) Direct marketing is vending products to customers without the use of other channel members.
(True; Easy; p. 353)

67) The most common form of direct marketing is over the Internet.
(False; Moderate; p. 354)

68) Direct mail is a primary tool for promoting Internet Web sites and online sales.
(True; Challenging; p. 354)

69) Digital direct-to-press is used only in business-to-business marketing due to its costs.
(False; Moderate; p. 354)

70) Many consumers believe online shopping has replaced catalogs, but research reveals that receiving a catalog is often the first step in the buying cycle for consumers.
(True; Moderate; p. 356)

71) Catalogs offer the advantages of being long lasting, low-pressure, and can be viewed at a person's leisure.
(True; Moderate; p. 356)

72) Successful cataloging requires an enhanced database that allows for targeting of recipients.
(True; Moderate; p. 356)

73) The most common forms of mass media used in direct marketing are television, radio, magazines, and newspapers.
(True; Moderate; p. 356)

74) In terms of direct marketing, ride-alongs are materials that are placed with a company's own catalog or direct-mail pieces, such as a record club's catalog.
(False; Challenging; p. 356)

75) A permission marketing program means promotions are only sent to customers that ask for them.
(True; Easy; p. 357)

76) In permission marketing, permission is normally obtained from individuals in exchange for an incentive.
(True; Moderate; p. 357)

77) An important key to success in permission marketing programs is to make sure participants have actually agreed to participate and not been tricked into participating or signed up without their knowledge.
(True; Moderate; p. 357)

78) Record and book clubs that send out monthly mailings of books and records to purchase are using a permissions marketing program.
(True; Challenging; p. 357)

79) The number one reason individuals join permission marketing programs is a chance to win a prize or cash in a sweepstake or contest.
(True; Challenging; p. 357)

80) The number one reason individuals remain loyal to a permission marketing program once they have joined is a chance to win prizes in a contest or sweepstakes.
(False; Challenging; p. 358)

81) To optimize permission marketing, the vendor firm must feature rewards during the program and not just at the beginning.
(True; Challenging; p. 358)

82) A frequency program is an incentive program designed to encourage customers to make repeat purchases.
(True; Challenging; p. 359)

83) Companies develop frequency programs for two reasons: The first is to develop customer loyalty and the second is to match or preempt the competition.
(True; Moderate; p. 359)

84) The greater the value of the reward in a frequency program, the more effort individuals will expend in the program to obtain the reward.
(True; Moderate; p. 359)

85) Moderate users of a good or service are most likely to be enticed by a frequency program.
(True; Challenging; p. 359)

86) A program designed to build long term loyalty and bonds with customers through the use of a personal touch facilitated by technology is a customer relationship management (CRM) program.
(True; Easy; p. 360)

87) A customer relationship management (CRM) program works best when customers have highly differentiated needs, highly differentiated valuations, or both.
(True; Challenging; p. 360)

88) One of the keys to customer relationship management (CRM) programs is to differentiate customers in terms of their needs and their value to the company.
(True; Easy; p. 360)

89) The lifetime value of a customer is based on the idea that customers generate revenues over their lifetimes with a company that is greater than a single transaction.
(True; Easy; p. 360)

90) The share of a customer means the potential value that could be added to a given customer's value based on their percentage of purchases of a product with a particular vendor
(True; Moderate; p. 361)

91) Customer relationship management (CRM) works best when a company can modify aspects of its goods or services to fit customers, especially when customer needs do not vary much.
(False; Challenging; p. 362)

Multiple-Choice Questions

92) Levi-Strauss & Company's database marketing program was designed to:
   a) create a new line of products
   b) understand overall consumer demand for pants
   c) identify target groups and interact with members of those groups
   d) lead to a change in brand name from Levi's to Dockers
(c; Easy; p. 336)

93) Personal selling is sometimes called the "last three feet" of the marketing function because:
   a) three feet is the approximate distance between the salesperson and the customer
   b) personal selling is the third component of the promotion mix
   c) personal selling has three major components
   d) three feet is the "social distance" between individuals
(a; Easy; p. 338)

94) The two most general categories of personal selling are:
   a) outbound sales and inbound sales
   b) retail sales and business-to-business sales
   c) distribution sales and retail sales
   d) field sales and personal sales
(b; Easy; p. 338)

95) When a salesperson assists a retail customer in a purchase, in most cases it is a:
   a) single transaction
   b) repeat transaction
   c) missionary selling approach
   d) form of cross-selling
(a; Easy; p. 338)

96) An order-taker salesperson is most likely to also be a:
   a) telemarketer
   b) business-to-business rep
   c) cashier
   d) prospector
(c; Easy; p. 338)

97) The salesperson at a discount store such as Wal-Mart would most likely be a(n):
   a) missionary
   b) order taker
   c) order getter
   d) telemarketer
(b; Moderate; p. 338)

98) Selling services often involves which type of transaction relationship?
   a) repeat
   b) stand-alone
   c) inbound
   d) single
(a; Moderate; p. 339)

99) When the same salesperson helps a customer solve various problems over time with purchases, the type of selling relationship would be classified as:
   a) repeat transactions
   b) strategic partnership
   c) trust relationships
   d) single transactions
(a; Moderate; p. 339)

100) What type of salesperson would take inquiry phone calls from prospective customers?
   a) missionary
   b) inbound telemarketing
   c) outbound telemarketing
   d) retail
(b; Easy; p. 339)

101) When a salesperson helps a customer who has called the company with a question about a product on a 1-800 line, it is:
   a) missionary selling
   b) inbound telemarketing
   c) outbound telemarketing
   d) repeat transaction telemarketing
(b; Moderate; p. 339)

102) When a company's salespeople call potential customers, it is:
   a) inbound telemarketing
   b) outbound telemarketing
   c) missionary selling
   d) cross-selling
(b; Easy; p. 339)

103) Do-Not-Call lists affect:
   a) inbound telemarketing
   b) outbound telemarketing
   c) missionary selling
   d) all forms of telemarketing
(b; Easy; p. 339)

104) Text message advertisements to cell phone users who have granted permission is the newest form of:
   a) inbound telemarketing
   b) outbound telemarketing
   c) missionary selling
   d) cross-selling
(b; Moderate; p. 339)

105) In terms of retail sales and the consumer buying process, if a customer is in the information search stage, the salesperson should:
   a) compare the features of the various brands
   b) inquire what the consumer will need and how the product will be used
   c) provide facts about models, designs, and options
   d) ask how they would like to pay for the item
(c; Challenging; p. 340)

106) In terms of the consumer buying process and retail sales, it is important for the sales clerk to:
   a) find out how much the customer can afford to spend
   b) ask questions about which brand he or she prefers
   c) provide information about all of the brands the store offers
   d) ask questions to determine which stage of the consumer buyer process the customer is at
(d; Moderate; p. 340)

107) The manufacturer's dilemma in retail selling is that most purchase decisions are made:
   a) at home
   b) over the phone
   c) late at night
   d) in the store
(d; Moderate; p. 340)

108) The manufacturer's dilemma in personal selling is that:
   a) most salespeople do not purchase the manufacturer's brand
   b) most customers base sales decisions on advertising by retailers
   c) most customers make final purchase decisions in the store
   d) most customers are strongly influenced by cashiers
(c; Challenging; p. 340)

109) To combat the lack of influence of salespeople in retail selling, manufacturers rely on each of the following strategies, *except:*
   a) the manufacturer can provide training to retail salespeople, emphasizing the manufacturer's brand
   b) the manufacturer can pay commission on sales of their brand
   c) the manufacturer can advertise its brand to both consumers and salespeople
   d) the manufacturer can hold contests and provide incentives to salespeople who emphasize the manufacturer's brand

   (b; Challenging; p. 340)

110) A salesperson whose role is to develop good will, stimulates demand, and provide training is called a(n):
   a) order-taker
   b) improviser
   c) missionary salesperson
   d) clerk

   (c; Easy; p. 341)

111) Another name for a merchandiser or detailer is:
   a) order-taker
   b) cashier
   c) missionary salesperson
   d) clerk

   (c; Moderate; p. 341)

112) Selling a second item after the purchase of the first is called:
   a) missionary selling
   b) order-getting
   c) cross-selling
   d) detailing

   (c; Easy; p. 341)

113) Selling a home equity loan following the opening of a checking account at a bank would be an example of:
   a) missionary sales
   b) trust relationships
   c) cross-selling
   d) strategic partnerships with individual customers

   (c; Challenging; p. 341)

114) A customer at a retail store just purchased a Peerless faucet. Cross-selling has occurred when the salesperson:
    a) asks the customer to fill out a customer information card for a free drawing
    b) shows the customer how to install the faucet
    c) sells the customer a water purifier to go with the new faucet
    d) contacts Peerless to make sure the faucet will work in the customer's home
(c; Challenging; p. 341)

115) Successful cross-selling requires each of the following, *except:*
    a) collecting quality customer data
    b) integrating information technology
    c) computerized decision models
    d) a direct marketing capability
(d; Challenging; p. 341)

116) When the salesperson visits the customer's place of business, it is a(n):
    a) field sale
    b) in-house sale
    c) technology-based sales
    d) strategic partnership
(a; Easy; p. 341)

117) Business-to-business salespeople who actively seek out new customers are called:
    a) merchandisers
    b) order-getters
    c) buyer-seller specialists
    d) cashiers
(b; Easy; p. 341)

118) Of the following, which involves the most face-to-face contact with customers?
    a) field sales
    b) in-house sales
    c) Internet sales
    d) telemarketing
(a; Moderate; p. 341)

119) The following are primary forms of business-to-business selling, *except:*
    a) field sales
    b) in-house sales
    c) missionary sales
    d) technology-based sales
(c; Challenging; p. 341)

120) Salespeople who work from the company's office taking phone-in orders and fax orders are involved in:
   a) field sales
   b) in-house sales
   c) technology-based sales
   d) outbound telemarketing
   (b; Easy; p. 342)

121) Which type of sale is responding to or taking an order from an established customer by telephone, a fax, or by e-mail?
   a) new buy
   b) field sales
   c) missionary sales
   d) in-house sales
   (d; Challenging; p. 342)

122) In terms of business-to-business buying situations, single transactions are normally associated with:
   a) new-buy situations
   b) modified re-buy situations
   c) straight re-buy situations
   d) missionary sales
   (a; Moderate; p. 342)

123) In terms of business-to-business buying situations, occasional transactions are normally associated with:
   a) new-buy situations
   b) modified re-buy situations
   c) straight re-buy situations
   d) missionary sales
   (b; Moderate; p. 342)

124) In terms of business-to-business buying situations, repeat transactions are normally associated with:
   a) new-buy situations
   b) modified re-buy situations
   c) straight re-buy situations
   d) missionary sales
   (c; Moderate; p. 342)

125) Making sure the price and delivery of a good or service will remain stable over time is often accomplished by:
- a) repeat transaction relationships
- b) contractual agreements
- c) modified re-buy arrangements
- d) missionary selling

(b; Moderate; p. 342)

126) An electronic data interchange (EDI) relationship is the:
- a) sharing of data
- b) sharing of sales reps
- c) sharing of telemarketing information
- d) same as a contractual relationship

(a; Easy; p. 342)

127) The most intimate buyer-seller relationship is called a(n):
- a) contractual agreement
- b) trust relationship
- c) electronic data interchange relationship
- d) strategic partnership

(d; Moderate; p. 343)

128) When a wireless phone company combines with an Internet access company to develop a plan to reach certain business customers, the relationship is a(n):
- a) electronic data interchange (EDI) relationship
- b) trust relationship
- c) joint partnership
- d) strategic partnership

(d; Challenging; p. 343)

129) The movement from a single transaction relationship to the strategic partnership begins with:
- a) a trial purchase by the customer
- b) a positive experience between the buyer and seller
- c) the customer becoming aware of the vendor's products and capabilities
- d) exchanging data

(c; Moderate; p. 343)

130) The first step in the business-to-business selling process is:
- a) qualifying prospects
- b) knowledge acquisition
- c) identifying prospects
- d) the sales presentation

(c; Easy; p. 343)

131) The second step in the business-to-business selling process, which follows qualifying prospects is:
    a) prospecting
    b) knowledge acquisition
    c) identifying prospects
    d) the sales presentation
(a; Easy; p. 343)

132) The third step in the business-to-business selling process, which follows qualifying prospects is:
    a) prospecting
    b) knowledge acquisition
    c) follow-up
    d) the sales presentation
(b; Moderate; p. 343)

133) The fourth step in the business-to-business selling process, which follows knowledge acquisition, is:
    a) prospecting
    b) qualifying prospects
    c) follow-up
    d) the sales presentation
(d; Moderate; p. 343)

134) The last step in the business-to-business selling process is:
    a) qualifying prospects
    b) knowledge acquisition
    c) follow-up
    d) the sales presentation
(c; Easy; p. 343)

135) When identifying business-to-business prospects, the least effective method is:
    a) current customers
    b) trade shows
    c) advertising
    d) cold calls
(d; Easy; p. 344)

136) Deciding which companies have the best potential to make sales purchases is called:
    a) prospecting
    b) qualifying prospects
    c) knowledge acquisition
    d) cold canvassing
(b; Easy; p. 344)

137) Placing companies into categories such as "high potential," "moderate potential," and "no potential" is an example of:
   a) prospecting
   b) qualifying prospects
   c) knowledge acquisition
   d) cold canvassing
(b; Moderate; p. 344)

138) Gathering the information needed to make an effective sales presentation is part of:
   a) prospecting
   b) qualifying prospects
   c) knowledge acquisition
   d) the sales presentation
(c; Easy; p. 345)

139) During the knowledge acquisition step of the b-to-b selling process, the following information should be collected, *except:*
   a) prospect's current vendor or vendors
   b) prospect's customers
   c) prospect's needs
   d) prospect's potential purchase volume
(d; Challenging; p. 345)

140) During the knowledge acquisition step of the b-to-b selling process, all of the following information should be collected, *except:*
   a) role of price, service, and product attributes in the purchase decision
   b) role of trade and consumer promotions in the purchase decision
   c) critical customer benefits or product attributes
   d) prospect's potential purchase volume
(d; Challenging; p. 345)

141) Intrinsic value buyers:
   a) focus on price
   b) focus mostly on product attributes
   c) seek information about new vendors
   d) seek partnerships with suppliers
(a; Moderate; p. 345)

142) From the following types of buyers, which would be most interested in price?
   a) intrinsic value buyers
   b) extrinsic value buyers
   c) strategic value buyers
   d) electronic data interchange (EDI) partners
(a; Moderate; p. 345)

143) Extrinsic value buyers:
    a) focus on price
    b) focus mostly on product attributes
    c) seek information about new vendors
    d) seek partnerships with suppliers
(b; Moderate; p. 345)

144) From the following types of buyers, which would be most interested in product attributes and the solution that a particular product can provide?
    a) intrinsic value buyers
    b) extrinsic value buyers
    c) strategic value buyers
    d) electronic data interchange (EDI) partners
(b; Moderate; p. 345)

145) Strategic value buyers:
    a) focus on price
    b) focus mostly on product attributes
    c) seek information about new vendors
    d) seek partnerships with suppliers
(d; Moderate; p. 345)

146) From the following types of buyers, which would be most interested in seeking out a partnership with suppliers?
    a) intrinsic value buyers
    b) extrinsic value buyers
    c) strategic value buyers
    d) electronic data interchange (EDI) partners
(c; Moderate; p. 345)

147) A stimulus-response sales approach is sometimes called:
    a) missionary selling
    b) order-taking
    c) a "canned" sales pitch
    d) emotive selling
(c; Moderate; p. 346)

148) Of the following types of salespeople, the most likely to use a stimulus-response sales approach would be a(n):
    a) missionary salesperson
    b) order-taker
    c) telemarketer
    d) engineers and teams
(c; Challenging; p. 346)

149) A need-satisfaction sales approach focuses on the customer's:
   a) response to a canned sales approach
   b) strategic value orientation
   c) reaction to competition
   d) desire for solutions to specific needs
(d; Easy; p. 346)

150) When the selling organization analyzes the buyer's operation to make a quality sales presentation, it is called:
   a) stimulus-response
   b) need-satisfaction
   c) problem-solution
   d) mission-sharing
(c; Moderate; p. 346)

151) A mission-sharing sales approach is most similar to:
   a) price-quality relationships
   b) joint-venture projects
   c) missionary sales
   d) modified re-buy situations
(b; Challenging; p. 346)

152) The sales approach most likely to be used in a strategic partnership relationship between the buyer and seller would be:
   a) stimulus-response
   b) need-satisfaction
   c) problem-solution
   d) mission-sharing
(d; Challenging; p. 346)

153) The primary determinant of the sales presentation approach is the:
   a) form of buyer-seller relationship that is present
   b) nature of the product
   c) buyer's personality
   d) buying situation
(a; Challenging; p. 346)

154) Which sales presentation approach is typically used in the lower order relationships, such as single and occasional transactions?
   a) stimulus-response
   b) need-satisfaction
   c) problem-solution
   d) mission-sharing
(a; Challenging; p. 346)

155)	Which sales presentation approach matches mid-level relationships involving repeat transactions and contractual agreements?
	a)	stimulus-response
	b)	need-satisfaction
	c)	problem-solution
	d)	mission-sharing
(b; Challenging; p. 346)

156)	Which sales presentation approach is normally used with strategic partnership buyer-seller relationships, and can also be used occasionally with EDI relationships and trust occasions?
	a)	stimulus-response
	b)	need-satisfaction
	c)	problem-solution
	d)	mission-sharing
(d; Challenging; p. 346)

157)	Which sales presentation approach is best for higher order relationships, including repeat transactions, contractual agreements, trust relationships, and EDI relationships?
	a)	stimulus-response
	b)	need-satisfaction
	c)	problem-solution
	d)	mission-sharing
(c; Challenging; p. 346)

158)	Extrinsic buyers would tend to respond the best to:
	a)	the stimulus-response sales approach
	b)	either the needs-satisfaction or the problem-solution sales approach
	c)	the mission sharing sales approach
	d)	any of the sales approaches
(b; Challenging; p. 346)

159)	Which is often the case in a follow-up to a business-to-business sale?
	a)	The rep has lost interest because the commission has been earned.
	b)	The company will want to re-negotiate the sales contract.
	c)	The buyer will seek out additional information about competitors.
	d)	The vendor will redefine its IMC approach.
(a; Moderate; p. 347)

160)	The following are future trends in business-to-business personal selling, *except:*
	a)	an expected increase in the number of salespeople
	b)	expansion of sales channels
	c)	greater emphasis on team selling
	d)	greater emphases on long-term relationships
(a; Challenging; p. 347)

161) The following business-to-business personal selling trends are expected to *increase, except* the:
   a) number of salespeople
   b) number of sales channels
   c) use of long-term relationships and strategic partnerships
   d) use of the team selling approach
   (a; Challenging; p. 347)

162) As technology continues to evolve, many experts expect:
   a) more sales positions
   b) fewer sales positions
   c) about the same number of sales positions
   d) more emphasis on sales training
   (b; Moderate; p. 347)

163) In addition to a sales call, potential customers of Polycom's Videoconferencing System can contact Polycom through the Internet or by calling a toll-free number. This is an example of the business-to-business selling trend of:
   a) decline in the number of salespeople
   b) expansion of sales channels
   c) increase in long-term relationships and strategic partnerships
   d) increase in team selling
   (b; Challenging; p. 347)

164) Creating a database to support the overall company, IMC program, and marketing efforts is called:
   a) database development
   b) operations management
   c) an electronic data interchange
   d) data mining
   (a; Easy; p. 349)

165) The first step in developing a database should be:
   a) determine objectives
   b) identify competitors
   c) create relationships with customers
   d) data mining
   (a; Moderate; p. 349)

166) Typical objectives for an IMC database program include each of the following, *except:*
   a) providing useful information about the firm's customers
   b) revealing contact points that can be used in direct marketing programs
   c) creating information about why customers purchase the products they do
   d) making informal contact with customers
   (d; Challenging; p. 349)

167) The following are examples of internal data, *except:*
   a) scanner data
   b) telephone numbers collected from sales contacts
   c) addresses recorded from checks
   d) commercial database service information
(d; Moderate; p. 350)

168) In developing a database, the information below would be internal data a company should have, *except:*
   a) where customers live
   b) what customers have purchased and how much
   c) how often they have purchased
   d) the products customers dislike
(d; Challenging; p. 350)

169) Each of the following is a source of external marketing data, *except:*
   a) governmental data
   b) telephone numbers and addresses collected from checks
   c) survey data
   d) commercial database service information
(b; Moderate; p. 350)

170) A data warehouse should be available for all of the following uses, *except:*
   a) target customers with a direct marketing program
   b) access by field salespeople to customer information while making a sales call
   c) provide profiles of the firm's best customers
   d) access by the service department and customer relations department in dealing with customer inquiries and complaints
(c; Challenging; p. 351)

171) Adding geographic codes to customer records to plot them on a map is called:
   a) geo-identification
   b) geo-coding
   c) finding neighborhood lifestyle clusters
   d) commercial database service analysis
(b; Moderate; p. 351)

172) With geocoding, a company can add to each customer's record:
   a) demographic information and lifestyle data
   b) total purchases made at each retail outlet in the area
   c) demographic and political information
   d) a composite analysis of his or her neighbors
(a; Challenging; p. 351)

173) The process of building profiles of customers from a firm's database is called:
   a) data warehousing
   b) direct marketing
   c) a commercial database service
   d) data mining
(d; Easy; p. 352)

174) Data mining is:
   a) collecting addresses and zip codes of customers
   b) reviewing past purchases of a product by customers
   c) building customer groups and models that predict their future purchase behavior
   d) selecting cities for data analysis
(c; Moderate; p. 352)

175) Data mining can be used for each of the following purposes, *except:*
   a) develop profiles of a firm's best customers
   b) develop profiles of customers who tend to purchase competing brands
   c) identify current customers who fit the profile of a firm's best customers
   d) identify current customers who would be good prospects for cross-selling other products
(b; Challenging; p. 352)

176) The following are examples of data mining, *except:*
   a) American Eagle studying how consumer responded to price markdowns
   b) Goody's analyzing baskets of merchandise purchased by individual consumers
   c) Target identifying what other retail stores customers use for particular purchases
   d) First Horizon National expanding its wealth management business by studying profiles of its best customers
(c; Challenging; p. 352)

177) Vending products to customers without the use of other channel members is:
   a) database marketing
   b) direct marketing
   c) indirect marketing
   d) by-pass marketing
(b; Easy; p. 353)

178) Direct-marketing programs create:
   a) one-to-one contacts with customers
   b) frequency programs
   c) re-analysis of databases
   d) new mass media messages
(a; Moderate; p. 353)

179) According to the Direct Marketing Association, about 60 percent of a typical direct marketing budget is used for:
   a) customer retention
   b) direct response advertising
   c) outbound telemarketing
   d) prospecting for new customers
   (d; Challenging; p. 353)

180) According to the Direct Marketing Association, about 40 percent of a typical direct marketing budget is used for:
   a) direct response advertising
   b) outbound telemarketing
   c) customer retention
   d) prospecting for new customers
   (c; Challenging; p. 354)

181) The most common method of direct-marketing is:
   a) mail
   b) telemarketing
   c) direct response TV
   d) e-mails
   (a; Moderate; p. 354)

182) The direct marketing technology that allows for customized printing of material is called:
   a) data mining
   b) digital direct-to-press
   c) digital computerization
   d) direct press
   (b: Challenging; p. 354)

183) The primary disadvantage of direct mail is:
   a) cost
   b) inability to target mailings
   c) response rates
   d) clutter
   (d; Challenging; p. 355)

184) Successful cataloging today requires:
   a) a companion Web site to facility purchasing
   b) an enhanced database for better targeting of catalogs
   c) data mining to determine best profiles of high catalog purchasers
   d) digital direct-to-press technology
   (b; Challenging; p. 356)

185) In terms of online sales, in many cases receiving which of the following is the first step in the buying process?
    a) package inset or ride along card
    b) e-mail
    c) catalog
    d) telemarketing call
(c; Challenging; p. 356)

186) Alternative media direct marketing programs include all of the following, *except:*
    a) infomercials
    b) package insert programs
    c) ride alongs
    d) card packs
(a; Moderate; p. 356)

187) Placing marketing materials in order fulfillment packages is the alternative form of direct marketing known as:
    a) infomercials
    b) package insert programs
    c) ride alongs
    d) card packs
(b; Moderate; p. 356)

188) Placing marketing materials with another company's direct mailing piece or catalog, which is an alternative form of direct marketing known as a(n):
    a) infomercial
    b) package insert program
    c) ride along
    d) card pack
(c; Moderate; p. 356)

189) A card pack is:
    a) telemarketing to a stack of cards containing prospects
    b) direct-marketing materials placed in mail-order fulfillment packages
    c) direct marketing materials containing business reply cards in a plastic pack
    d) a form of ride-along program
(c; Easy; p. 356)

190) Valpak is a successful direct marketing company using the alternative form of direct marketing called:
    a) infomercials
    b) package insert programs
    c) ride alongs
    d) card packs
(d; Challenging; p. 356)

191) When promotional materials are only sent to customers who have given their approval, the program is called:
   a) direct mail
   b) Internet marketing
   c) permission marketing
   d) a frequency program
(c; Moderate; p. 357)

192) The Book of the Month Club is an example of:
   a) digital direct-to-press
   b) relationship marketing
   c) direct marketing
   d) permission marketing
(d; Challenging; p. 357)

193) Response rates are often higher for permissions marketing programs because:
   a) consumers are receiving marketing material they have given permission for
   b) consumers are high-frequency purchasers
   c) consumers can reject any offer that is made
   d) consumers are contacted only by mail
(a; Easy; p. 357)

194) Each of the following statements concerning permission marketing is true, *except:*
   a) The company does not intrude with unwanted junk mail.
   b) Response rates are higher because consumers have given permission.
   c) Marketing costs are increased due to greater records that must be kept.
   d) Consumers enjoy not being bombarded with catalogs and telemarketing calls.
(c; Moderate; p. 357)

195) The highest level of involvement and loyalty occurs at which stage in a permission marketing program?
   a) when obtaining the initial permission
   b) when reinforcing the incentives
   c) when increasing the permission level
   d) when leveraging the information
(d; Challenging; p. 357)

196) Consumers often ignore marketing information sent to them after joining a permissions marketing program because:
   a) the products are too costly
   b) the marketing pieces are not relevant any more
   c) they can no longer win prizes or receive free gifts
   d) the person has moved and did not leave a forwarding address or e-mail
(b; Challenging; p. 357)

197) The number one reason, at 41 percent, consumers opt-in to an e-mail permissions marketing program is:
    a) a sweepstakes entry or chance to win something
    b) an e-mail was requested in order to access material the person wanted
    c) the person was already a customer
    d) friend recommended the program
(a; Challenging; p. 358)

198) The number one reason, at 36 percent, consumers choose to remain loyal to a permission marketing program is:
    a) to receive account status updates
    b) chance to win something through a contest or sweepstakes
    c) interesting content
    d) price bargains that are offered
(c; Challenging; p. 358)

199) To optimize permission marketing programs, firms must feature:
    a) prizes and price discounts
    b) regular newsletters
    c) entertaining content and account information
    d) empowerment and reciprocity
(d; Challenging; p. 358)

200) An incentive program designed to encourage repeat purchases is called:
    a) direct marketing
    b) permission marketing
    c) a frequency program
    d) a ride along program
(c; Moderate; p. 359)

201) Frequent flier miles in airline travel are a form of:
    a) direct marketing
    b) permission marketing
    c) frequency program
    d) ride along program
(c; Moderate; p. 359)

202) Typical objectives for frequency programs include all of the following, *except:*
    a) maintain sales, margins, or profits
    b) attract new customers
    c) increase loyalty of existing customers
    d) preempt or match a competitor's frequency program
(b; Moderate; p. 359)

203) Typical objectives for frequency programs include all of the following, *except:*
   a) build brand parity
   b) induce cross-selling to existing customers
   c) differentiate a parity brand
   d) preempt the entry of a new brand
   (a; Challenging; p. 359)

204) The following are principles for building a successful frequency or loyalty program, *except:*
   a) exclude less valuable customers through data mining
   b) design the program to enhance the value of the product
   c) calculate the full cost of the program
   d) design a program that maximizes the customer's motivation to make the next purchase
   (a; Challenging; p. 359)

205) The most likely individuals to be enticed to join a frequency or loyalty program are:
   a) light users
   b) moderate users
   c) heavy users
   d) new users
   (b; Challenging; p. 359)

206) The program designed to build long-term loyalty and bonds with customers, using a personal selling touch combined by effective technology is known as:
   a) permission marketing
   b) direct marketing
   c) customer relationship management
   d) frequency marketing
   (c; Easy; p. 360)

207) A customer relationship management (CRM) program works best when customers have:
   a) similar needs and wants
   b) profiles that are closely match the firm's best customers
   c) identifiable interest, opinions, and attitudes
   d) highly differentiated needs and highly differentiated valuations of the product
   (d; Challenging; p. 360)

208) The following are key technological underpinning to a customer relationship management (CRM) program, *except:*
    a) database technology
    b) interactivity through Web sites, call centers, or other means of contact
    c) mass customization technology
    d) ability to develop customer profiles

(d; Challenging; p. 360)

209) Building a customer relationship management (CRM) program requires each of the following steps, *except:*
    a) identification of the firm's customers
    b) have an established curriculum that can be offered over time
    c) differentiate customers in terms of their needs and value to the firm
    d) interact with customers in ways that improve efficiency and effectiveness

(b; Challenging; p. 360)

210) When differentiating customers in terms of needs and value as part of a (customer relationship management (CRM) program, which two metrics are calculated?
    a) earnings per share and markup per customer
    b) markup per sale and cost of the sale
    c) customer lifetime value and share of customer
    d) cost of permissions minus revenue per customer

(c; Moderate; p. 360)

211) Which is *false* concerning customer relationship management (CRIM) programs?
    a) they succeed nearly every time they are implemented
    b) it is crucial to change the organization to match the program in order to succeed
    c) the company must be customer, not technology driven in order to succeed
    d) the program will not succeed if customers feel they are being pressured

(a; Challenging; p. 360)

212) To calculate the lifetime value of a customer, a firm marketing team needs all of the following data, *except:*
    a) average expenditure per visit or purchase
    b) average number of purchases per month
    c) average life span for the firm's customers
    d) the cost of acquiring the customer

(b; Challenging; p. 360)

213) To calculate the lifetime value of a customer, a firm needs all of the following data, *except:*
   a) revenue generated by referrals from the customer
   b) cost of servicing the customer
   c) number of years the customer has already been with the firm
   d) cost of acquiring the customer
   (c; Challenging; p. 360)

214) In developing a CRM program, the "share" of the customer refers to:
   a) the value of the customer over his or her lifetime
   b) the share of the firm's revenue the customer generates
   c) the share of expenditure the customer spends compared to his or her total income
   d) the potential value of the customer based on the percentage of business the customer does with the a particular firm for a particular product
   (d; Moderate; p. 361)

215) In developing a CRM program, the "share" of customer term means:
   a) the potential value that could be added to a given customer's lifetime value
   b) the lifelong earning of a customer
   c) the share of a customer's income that is spent on a particular product
   d) the percentage of time spent on acquiring the customer's loyalty
   (a; Challenging; p. 361)

Short-Answer Questions

216) What are the three main kinds of retail selling?

   1. Selling in shops and stores
   2. Selling services and merchandise to accompany services
   3. Telemarketing
   (Easy; p. 338)

217) What are the stages of the purchasing process?

   1. Problem recognition
   2. Information search
   3. Evaluation of alternatives
   4. Purchase decision
   5. Post-purchase evaluation
   (Moderate; p. 340)

218) What are the three primary forms of business-to-business selling?

1. Field sales
2. In-house sales
3. Technology based telemarketing and Internet programs

(Easy; p. 341)

219) What kinds of buyer seller relationship are present in business-to-business selling? Rank them from lowest to highest.

1. Single transaction
2. Occasional transaction
3. Repeat transaction
4. Contractual agreements
5. Trust relationships
6. Electronic Data Interchange (EDI) relationships
7. Strategic partnerships

(Moderate; p. 342)

220) What are the steps of the personal selling process in business-to-business relationships?

1. Identifying prospects
2. Qualifying prospects
3. Knowledge acquisition
4. Developing a sales approach
5. Sales presentation
6. Follow-up

(Moderate; p. 343)

221) What methods are available for identifying business-to-business sales prospects?

- Current customers
- Databases
- Trade shows
- Advertising and Internet inquiries
- Consumer sales promotion responses
- Vendors
- Channel members
- Networking
- Cold canvassing

(Challenging; p. 344)

222) What are the new trends in business-to-business personal selling?

- Increased use of technology
- Decline in the number of salespeople
- Expanding channels
- More long-term partnerships
- Team selling approaches used more frequently

(Challenging; p. 347)

223) Name the steps involved in developing an IMC database.

1. Determine objectives
2. Collect data
3. Build a data warehouse
4. Mine data for information
5. Develop a marketing program
6. Evaluate the marketing program and data warehouse

(Challenging; p. 349)

224) Define permission marketing.

Sending promotional information to customers who given the company permission to do so.
(Moderate; p. 357)

225) Name two industries that use frequency marketing programs.

1. airlines
2. hotels
3. casinos (Harrah's is an example from the text)

(Moderate; p. 359)

226) What four steps are involved in creating a customer relationship management (CRM) program?

1. Identify the company's customers
2. Differentiate customers in terms of their needs and their value to the selling company
3. Interact with customers in ways that improve cost efficiency and the effectiveness of the interactions
4. Customize some aspects of the products or services being offered to the customer

(Challenging, p. 360)

CHAPTER 12
PUBLIC RELATIONS, REGULATIONS, AND SPONSORSHIP PROGRAMS

True-False Questions

1) E-Bay's response to the September 11 attacks can best be described as "business as usual."
(False; Easy; p. 370)

2) The public relations department is the unit in the firm that manages publicity and communications with other groups that are in contact with the company.
(True; Easy; p. 372)

3) The public relations department is the unit in the firm that manages items such as advertising and consumer promotions.
(False; Easy; p. 372)

4) Most marketers today support creating a department of communications that would handle all of the marketing as well as public relations activities for a firm.
(False; Challenging; p. 372)

5) A hit is the mention of a company's name in a news story.
(True; Easy; p. 373)

6) A hit may or may not be a positive news story.
(True; Moderate; p. 373)

7) One of the functions of public relations is to assess the company's reputation.
(True; Moderate; p. 373)

8) One of the functions of public relations is to audit the company's social responsibility and to develop cause-related or other types of programs to enhance the company's social responsibility image.
(False; Moderate; p. 373)

9) One of the functions of public relations is to create positive image-building activities through developing sponsorships and cause-related programs that enhance the company's image.
(False; Challenging; p. 373)

10) A stakeholder is a person or group with a vested interest in an organization's well-being.
(True; Easy; p. 373)

11) While the overall message to each stakeholder group should be the same, each message should be tailored to meet the different expectations of the various audiences.
(True; Moderate; p. 374)

12) Employees are external stakeholders and owners are internal stakeholders.
(False; Moderate; p. 374)

13) Labor unions and shareholders are internal stakeholders or publics.
(True; Moderate; p. 374)

14) It is easier for the public relations department to access internal stakeholders as opposed to external stakeholders.
(True; Challenging; p. 374)

15) The human resource department plays a vital role in preparing effective internal public relations messages.
(True; Moderate; p. 374)

16) The company has little influence on what external stakeholders think and say about a company.
(True; Easy; p. 375)

17) The key to managing external stakeholders is for the public relations department to constantly send out positive information about the company to all of the external stakeholder groups.
(False; Moderate; p. 375)

18) Most company leaders do a thorough job of understanding the corporation's reputation.
(False; Moderate; p. 375)

19) Less than half of the companies in the United States have someone assigned to monitor corporate reputation.
(True; Challenging; p. 376)

20) Assessment of a firm's reputation begins with company leaders taking the time to conduct surveys and interviews of what people think of the company.
(True; Moderate; p. 376)

21) Social responsibility is the obligation an organization has to make the highest level of profits.
(False; Easy; p. 376)

22) Social responsibility is the obligation an organization has to be ethical, accountable, and reactive to the needs of society.
(True; Easy; p. 376)

23) A code of ethics for a profession or company is one element of a social responsibility program.
(True; Moderate; p. 376)

24) The purpose of a social responsibility audit is to develop a corporate code of ethics and make sure everyone in the organization is aware of the code and is following it.
(False; Moderate; p. 377)

25) Cause-related marketing is a program that ties a marketing program in with some type of charity in order to generate good will.
(True; Easy; p. 377)

26) Cause-related marketing is an internal program working with company employees.
(False; Easy; p. 377)

27) Nearly half of all consumers have switched brands, increased their usage, or tried a new product when the brand and or company were connected with a specific cause they supported.
(True; Challenging; p. 377)

28) Cause-related marketing can reduce the problem of brand parity by helping consumers feel more loyal to a brand.
(True; Challenging; p. 377)

29) The key to cause-related marketing is to find a cause that resonates with consumers, whether or not that cause matches a particular company's business.
(False; Challenging; p. 378)

30) In choosing a cause-related program, the marketing team should focus on causes that in some manner relate to the company's business.
(True; Moderate; p. 378)

31) To benefit from cause-related marketing, companies must develop publicity about what they are doing but the amount of money spent on the publicity should not be significant.
(True; Challenging; p. 378)

32) One way Philip Morris develops positive publicity is by supporting the "We Card Program" with retailers.
(True; Moderate; p. 379)

33) Green marking is the development and promotion of products that are environmentally safe.
(True; Easy; p. 379)

34) Most consumers will buy green products even if the quality is slightly lower.
(False; Moderate; p. 379)

35) While consumers favor green marketing and environmentally-safe products, actual purchases will occur only when all things are considered equal, such as price, quality, convenience, and performance.
(True; Moderate; p. 379)

36) The consumer segment called True Blue Greens are the most likely to buy environmentally safe products.
(True; Moderate; p. 379)

37) In terms of consumer segments, both the True Blue Greens and the Sprouts are heavy users of green products.
(False; Challenging; p. 380)

38) In terms of consumer segments, the Grousers do not care about environmental issues or social issues.
(False; Challenging; p. 380)

39) In deciding on a green marketing or pro-environmental approach, a company should analyze if the company's current customers will be alienated by such an approach.
(True; Moderate; p. 381)

40) While Coca-Cola is involved in pro-environment activities, it does not widely publicize these activities because company leaders believe they will not gain more customers.
(False; Challenging; p. 381)

41) Practically every company actively promotes its environmentally safe products.
(False; Moderate; p. 381)

42) Damage control is reacting to negative events caused by a company error, consumer grievances, or when unjustified or exaggerated negative press appears.
(True; Easy; p. 381)

43) Damage control is only used when consumers are making unjustified complaints against a company.
(False; Easy; p. 381)

44) Proactive prevention strategies for damage control include entitlings, enhancements, and justifications.
(False; Moderate; p. 382)

45) Entitlings are a form of image damage prevention involving claiming responsibility for positive outcomes of events.
(True; Moderate; p. 382)

46) Showing a sports star from a team that just won a championship on the cover of a box of Wheaties is an example of using the proactive prevention strategy of enhancements.
(False; Challenging; p. 382)

47) Enhancements image damage prevention technique involves the attempt to increase the desirable outcome of an event in the eyes of the public.
(True; Moderate; p. 382)

48) Claiming that a product is low-carb, even when it has a high amount of fat and calories, is an example of using an enhancement strategy.
(True; Challenging; p. 382)

49) Reactive damage control strategies include Internet interventions, crisis management, and impression management techniques.
(True; Moderate; p. 382)

50) Internet interventions are designed to combat negative word-of-mouth communication.
(True; Easy; p. 382)

51) To spread negative information about a company or brand using the Internet, an individual can utilize e-mail, chat rooms, rogue Web sites, and Internet blogs.
(True; Easy; p. 382)

52) Crisis management involves accepting the blame for an event and offering an apology or vigorously defending the company when negative charges have been made.
(True; Easy; p. 383)

53) An apology strategy is an impression management technique that is often used by companies in reacting to negative events.
(False; Challenging; p. 383)

54) In using an apology strategy to a crisis situation, the firm must acknowledge their inappropriate behavior and make a commitment not to engage in any further inappropriate behavior.
(True; Moderate; p. 383)

55) If a company uses an apology strategy in a negative crisis situation, it will only work if the public feels the apology is sincere and heartfelt.
(True; Moderate; p. 383)

56) Impression management is the process of making an apology for a mistake.
(False; Easy; p. 384)

57) An expression of innocence is a form of impression management.
(True; Moderate; p. 384)

58) In dealing with a negative situation, if company leaders provide information designed to convince others that the company was not responsible for the negative situation, the company is using the impression management technique of excuses.
(False; Moderate; p. 384)

59) In dealing with a negative situation, if company leaders try to convince the public the firm is not responsible and the predicament could not have been foreseen, the company is using the impression management technique of excuses.
(True; Moderate; p. 384)

60) Sponsorship marketing occurs when a company pays money to sponsor a person or group involved in an activity.
(True; Easy; p. 385)

61) Sports represent the majority of all sponsorships.
(True; Challenging; p. 385)

62) FedEx uses sponsorships to build brand awareness.
(False; Challenging; p. 385)

63) Sponsoring cultural events, such as classical music groups, jazz bands, visual art exhibits, and noted painters, dance troupes, and theater performances best fits manufacturers and mass merchandising types of retail stores.
(False; Challenging; p. 386)

64) In choosing a sponsorship, it is important to match the audience profile with the company's target market.
(True; Easy; p. 386)

65) The best sponsorship programs include some method of assessment.
(True; Moderate; p. 386)

66) Beach volleyball is an attractive sport to sponsor because of the demographic profile of the fans.
(True; Challenging; p. 387)

67) Event marketing occurs when a company sponsors a specific event, such as the Special Olympics at a particular venue.
(True; Easy; p. 388)

68) A rodeo held in Dallas sponsored by Lee Jeans is an example of event marketing.
(True; Challenging; p. 388)

69) Tiger Woods' entry into the Buick Open as a representative of the company is an example of event marketing.
(False; Challenging; p. 388)

70) Event marketing is closely related to lifestyle marketing.
(True; Moderate; p. 388)

71) Cross-promotions are used with event marketing to boost the impact of the event.
(True; Easy; p. 389)

72) The difference between event marketing and sponsorship marketing is the duration of the program being featured.
(False; Easy; p. 389)

73) The Wheeler-Lea Amendment (1938) of the Federal Trade Commission Act prohibits false and misleading advertisements.
(True; Moderate; p. 390)

74) When a substantial number of people are misled by a series of commercials, it is deemed to be deceptive or misleading.
(True; Moderate; p. 391)

75) A "typical person" must believe the content of an advertisement to be false in order for the Wheeler-Lea Amendment to apply.
(True; Moderate; p. 391)

76) The Wheeler-Lea Amendment makes advertising puffery illegal.
(False; Moderate; p. 391)

77) Puffery exists when a firm makes an exaggerated statement about a good or service, while a claim is a factual statement made about a good or service.
(True; Moderate; p. 391)

78) The key difference, in terms of the Federal Trade Commission (FTC) and the courts, between puffery and a claim is that puffery is not considered to be a factual statement while a claim is considered to be a factual statement that can be proven true or false.
(True; Challenging; p. 391)

79) The Federal Trade Commission (FTC) monitors advertising on food packages and advertisements for drugs.
       (False; Challenging; p. 392)

80) A person targeted by a mail fraud campaign should contact the Federal Communication Commission (FCC).
       (False; Challenging; p. 392)

81) The Federal Communication Commission (FCC) is responsible for monitoring television advertising directed to children, in terms of how many minutes per hour is directed to children.
       (True; Moderate; p. 392)

82) For consumers who find an advertisement to be offensive, the Federal Trade Commission (FTC) would be a legitimate place to file a complaint.
       (False; Moderate; p. 392)

83) The first step a firm can take to end a Federal Trade Commission (FTC) investigation of a complaint is the signing of a consent order, if a violation has occurred.
       (True; Easy; p. 393)

84) When a consent order is signed, the company has agreed to a corrective advertising program.
       (False; Moderate; p. 393)

85) The Federal Trade Commission (FTC) can order civil penalties for violating consent orders.
       (False; Moderate; p. 393)

86) If consent agreement cannot be reached after an investigation by the Federal Trade Commission (FTC), the case would next go to the full commission.
       (False; Challenging; p. 393)

87) When the Federal Trade Commission (FTC) issues an administrative complaint and an administrative judge rules a violation has occurred, the judge would issue a cease and desist order.
       (True; Challenging; p. 393)

88) The Federal Trade Commission (FTC) can use the court system to stop unfair and deceptive advertising and communication practices without going through the normal steps of starting with a consent agreement.
       (True; Moderate; p. 393)

89) The Federal Trade Commission (FTC) has the power to order firms to prepare and disseminate corrective advertising.
(True; Moderate; p. 394)

90) If a company uses endorsers, the statements made by the endorsers must be truthful and represent their actual experiences or opinions.
(True; Moderate; p. 395)

91) In terms of substantiation of a claim in an advertisement, all claims must reflect the typical experience that a customer would expect to encounter from using a good or service, unless the advertisement clearly and prominently states otherwise.
(True; Challenging; p. 395)

92) In terms of substantiation of ad claims, the Federal Trade Commission (FTC) and the courts assume that consumers can read fine print or qualifying language that is placed in an advertisement.
(False; Challenging; p. 395)

93) In terms of substantiation of ad claims, the Federal Trade Commission (FTC) and the courts will consider the totality of evidence. If the company has one study that supports the ad claim, but a number of other studies contradict the claim, the FTC and courts will state the ad claim has not been properly substantiated.
(True; Challenging; p. 395)

94) A complaint filed with the National Advertising Division (NAD) of the Better Business Bureau regarding an unsubstantiated advertising claim would be dismissed because substantiation is not a criterion.
(False; Moderate; p. 396)

95) If a complaint concerning false or misleading advertising is referred to the Better Business Bureau, it would first be heard by the National Advertising Review Board (NARB).
(False; Moderate; p. 396)

96) Cases that are not settled by the National Advertising Division (NAD) of the BBB can be appealed to the Federal Trade Commission.
(False; Moderate; p. 397)

97) The National Advertising Review Board (NARB) seldom refers cases to the FTC.
(True; Moderate; p. 397)

Multiple-Choice Questions

98)   One reason for e-Bay's financial success is a business model featuring:
      a) low cost items
      b) no merchandise or inventory
      c) allowing multiple purchases by vendors
      d) free shipping and handling
(b; Moderate; p. 370)

99)   The program e-Bay used to respond to the September 11 attacks was called:
      a) anti-terrorism day
      b) unity day
      c) auction for America
      d) stand up and be counted
(c; Moderate; p. 371)

100)   The unit in the company that manages publicity and other communications with all groups that contact the firm is the:
      a) department of communications
      b) department of advertising
      c) department of specialty events
      d) department of public relations
(d; Easy; p. 372)

101)   The public relations department is the unit in the company that:
      a) manages publicity and other communications with all groups that contact the firm
      b) manages advertising and promotions
      c) monitors quality control and operations
      d) handles in-bound telemarketing calls
(a; Easy; p. 372)

102)   Some individuals would like to create which type of department to oversee both the public relations activities and the marketing programs?
      a) communications
      b) advertising
      c) specialty events
      d) production
(a; Easy; p. 372)

103)   In terms of goals for public relations, a hit is:
      a) an advertisement that is successful
      b) a consumer promotions' tie in with publicity
      c) mention of the company's name in a news story
      d) an advertising slogan with high recall
(c; Moderate; p. 373)

104) In terms of public relations, a mention of the company's name in a news story is called a:
   a) press release
   b) publication
   c) hit
   d) mention
   (c; Easy; p. 373)

105) In terms of measuring the impact of public relations, a "hit" can enhance:
   a) the use of a tagline
   b) brand or company awareness
   c) company or brand image
   d) stock dividends
   (b; Moderate; p. 373)

106) In terms of measuring public relations, a news story about the Ford Explorer's tire problems is an example of a(n):
   a) public relations hit
   b) event
   c) negative tie-in
   d) negative cross-promotion
   (a; Challenging; p. 373)

107) A person or group with a vested interest in a firm's well-being is a(n):
   a) stakeholder
   b) arbitrator
   c) foreign government
   d) media buyer
   (a; Easy; p. 373)

108) A stakeholder is:
   a) a disinterested third party in a negotiation
   b) a member of a foreign government
   c) a person or group with a vested interest in a firm's well-being
   d) lobbyist for a company
   (c; Easy; p. 373)

109) The following are internal stakeholders, *except:*
   a) employees
   b) labor unions
   c) shareholders
   d) customers
   (d; Easy; p. 374)

110) Of the internal stakeholders, the group that is the most critical to the success of a firm would be:
    a) shareholders
    b) employees
    c) the labor union
    d) customers
(b; Moderate; p. 374)

111) The following are external stakeholders, *except:*
    a) labor unions
    b) channel members
    c) customers
    d) the media
(a; Easy; p. 375)

112) Special interest groups would be considered:
    a) internal stakeholders
    b) disgruntled employees
    c) external stakeholders
    d) governmental stakeholders
(c; Moderate; p. 375)

113) The following are stakeholders of a company, *except:*
    a) suppliers of raw materials
    b) foreign governments for a non-international company
    c) the media
    d) contributors to a charity
(b; Challenging; p. 375)

114) Which statement below about corporation's reputation is *true?*
    a) Most corporate leaders clearly understand the reputations of their companies.
    b) It is very difficult to change in a negative direction.
    c) It is vulnerable to both internal and external negative events.
    d) In the past decade most consumers have expressed greater trust and respect for various corporations, meaning the reputations have improved.
(c; Moderate; p. 375)

115) Assessment of a corporation's reputation begins:
    a) when company leaders take the time to conduct surveys and interviews to learn what people think of the organization, both internal and external to the company
    b) with hiring a public relations firm to conduct a public relations audit of the firm's publicity
    c) by counting hits a company has received in the public press
    d) by developing a corporate image-building campaign
(a; Challenging; p. 376)

116) The obligation an organization has to be ethical, accountable, and reactive to the needs of society is called:
    a) public relations
    b) social responsibility
    c) marketing myopia
    d) sponsorship marketing
(b; Easy; p. 376)

117) Social responsibility is:
    a) less of a concern due to better quality governmental oversight of business
    b) a form of marketing based on sponsorships and events
    c) the obligation consumers have to shop from companies engaged in green marketing
    d) the obligation an organization has to be ethical, accountable, and reactive to the needs of society
(d; Easy; p. 376)

118) The purpose of a social responsibility audit is to:
    a) develop positive-image building activities
    b) develop contingency plans in case of negative events or negative publicity
    c) make sure the organization has clear-cut ethical guidelines for employees to follow and that the company acts to serve the interests of all publics
    d) uncover any unethical behavior and to develop rules and policies for enhancing social responsibility
(c; Challenging; p. 377)

119) A program that ties marketing to a charity in order to generate good will is called:
    a) cause-related marketing
    b) social responsibility marketing
    c) marketing myopia
    d) sponsorship marketing
(a; Easy; p. 377)

120) Cause-related marketing is:
- a) a type of Internet intervention
- b) a program that ties marketing to a charity
- c) the same thing as green marketing
- d) causing buyers to want to buy a product due to an effective cross-promotion

(b; Easy; p. 377)

121) When a dentist provides free services to women living in a shelter, it is:
- a) event marketing
- b) a form of entitling
- c) cause-related marketing
- d) altruism

(c; Easy; p. 377)

122) In terms of cause-related marketing, the highest percentage of Americans prefer that companies support causes that:
- a) improve public schools
- b) support dropout prevention
- c) provide scholarships
- d) cleanup the environment

(a; Challenging; p. 378)

123) In choosing a cause-related program, a company should focus on:
- a) causes that employees are involved with
- b) local community causes
- c) causes that are not supported by the company's primary competitors
- d) causes that relate to the company's business

(d; Challenging; p. 378)

124) In terms of the public relations aspect of cause-related marketing, for companies to benefit the company should:
- a) make sure the public is always aware of any cause-related marketing they support
- b) spend some money to publicize causes, but the amount should not be significant
- c) not publicize causes because the public will think any effort to do so is shameless self-aggrandizement
- d) spend approximately 25 percent of whatever is given to a cause on publicizing the cause

(b; Challenging; p. 378)

125) Developing products that are environmentally friendly is:
   a) cause-related marketing
   b) event marketing
   c) green marketing
   d) positive public relations
(c; Easy; p. 379)

126) Green marketing is:
   a) a form of cause-related marketing
   b) an Internet intervention focused on money-making
   c) developing and selling environmentally friendly products
   d) a type of apology strategy in which money is paid to the victim
(c; Easy; p. 379)

127) Biodegradable laundry detergent is an example of:
   a) cause-related marketing
   b) event marketing
   c) green marketing
   d) positive public relations
(c; Moderate; p. 379)

128) Of the following activities, the one that most Americans, 58 percent, try to do is:
   a) recycle newspapers
   b) save electricity
   c) return bottles and cans
   d) buy products from, or packaged, in recycled materials
(b; Challenging; p. 379)

129) While consumers favor green marketing and environmentally-safe products, most consumers are not willing to:
   a) purchase green and environmentally-safe products because of higher prices
   b) support companies that are not pro-environment
   c) sacrifice price, quality, convenience, availability, or performance
   d) take time to decide which causes to support
(c; Challenging; p. 379)

130) Based on U.S. consumer segmentation of consumer attitudes toward green marketing, the group that is most willing to buy green marketing products and is politically active is called:
   a) true-blue greens
   b) greenback greens
   c) sprouts
   d) basic buyers
(a; Challenging; p. 380)

131) Based on U.S. consumer segmentation of consumer attitudes toward green marketing, the group that are heavy users of green marketing products, but is not politically active is called:
   a) true-blue greens
   b) greenback greens
   c) sprouts
   d) basic buyers
(b; Challenging; p. 380)

132) Based on U.S. consumer segmentation of consumer attitudes toward green marketing, the two groups that are heavy users of green products are:
   a) true-blue greens and sprouts
   b) greenback greens and basic browns
   c) greenback greens and true-blue greens
   d) grousers and sprouts
(c; Challenging; p. 380)

133) Based on U.S. consumer segmentation of consumer attitudes toward green marketing, the group that believes in green products in theory, but not in practice, is called:
   a) true-blue greens
   b) grousers
   c) sprouts
   d) basic browns
(c; Challenging; p. 380)

134) Based on U.S. consumer segmentation of consumer attitudes toward green marketing, the group that is uneducated about environmental issues and cynical about their ability to effect change is called:
   a) true-blue greens
   b) greenback greens
   c) sprouts
   d) grousers
(d; Challenging; p. 380)

135) Based on U.S. consumer segmentation of consumer attitudes toward green marketing, the group that is cynical about green marketing and believes green products are too expensive and inferior in quality is called:
   a) true-blue greens
   b) basic browns
   c) sprouts
   d) grousers
(d; Challenging; p. 380)

136) Based on U.S. consumer segmentation of consumer attitudes toward green marketing, the group that does not care about environmental issues or social issues is called:
   a) true-blue greens
   b) basic browns
   c) sprouts
   d) grousers
(b; Challenging; p. 380)

137) Which statement is true about green marketing?
   a) It almost always is effective.
   b) It will work even when product quality is lower.
   c) It reaches every purchasing group equally.
   d) It is not always advertised or promoted by companies involved.
(d; Moderate; p. 381)

138) A company stops using Styrofoam containers because they hurt the environment and starts using recycled paper is an example of:
   a) event marketing
   b) green marketing
   c) altruistic effort
   d) cause-related marketing
(b; Challenging; p. 381)

139) The firm below that is involved in pro-environmental activities, but does not publicize the activities because of fear of alienating current customers is:
   a) Toyota's Prius
   b) The Body Shop
   c) Honest Tea
   d) Coca-Cola
(d; Challenging; p. 381)

140) The firm below that is involved in pro-environmental activities, but promoted the product's tangible benefits first with only a secondary mention of the pro-environmental impact is:
   a) Toyota's Prius
   b) The Body Shop
   c) Honest Tea
   d) Coca-Cola
(a; Challenging; p. 381)

141) Damage control is:
   a) almost always effective
   b) reacting to negative events caused by a company error, consumer grievances, or exaggerated negative press
   c) a public relations programs designed to reach every purchasing group
   d) not always advertised or promoted by companies involved
   (b; Easy; p. 381)

142) Reacting to negative events caused by a company error, consumer grievances, or exaggerated negative press is called:
   a) affirmative social responsibility
   b) acclaiming
   c) entitling
   d) damage control
   (d; Easy; p. 381)

143) Claiming responsibility for positive outcomes of events is called:
   a) affirmative social responsibility
   b) acclaiming
   c) entitling
   d) enhancement
   (c; Moderate; p. 382)

144) Believing that Wheaties may help make you a champion, since so many successful athletes have endorsed the cereal, is the result of using which proactive prevention strategy for damage control?
   a) impression management
   b) acclimation
   c) entitlings
   d) reinforcement
   (c; Challenging; p. 382)

145) The attempt to increase the desirable outcome of an event in the eyes of the public is called:
   a) affirmative social responsibility
   b) acclaiming
   c) entitling
   d) enhancement
   (d; Moderate; p. 382)

146) When Tang noted in company commercials that the product was the official drink of NASA during the first moon landing, the proactive prevention strategy approach being used was:
   a) impression management
   b) crisis management
   c) enhancement
   d) entitling
   (c; Challenging; p. 382)

147) Entitlings and enhancements are forms of:
   a) reactive damage control strategies
   b) acclaiming
   c) proactive prevention strategies for damage control
   d) crisis management
   (c; Moderate; p. 382)

148) Proactive prevention strategies for damage control include:
   a) entitlings and enhancements
   b) crisis management
   c) justifications and excuses
   d) defense of innocence
   (a; Moderate; p. 382)

149) Reactive damage control strategies include each of the following, *except:*
   a) Internet interventions
   b) entitling strategies
   c) crisis management programs
   d) impression management techniques
   (b; Moderate; p. 382)

150) If negative publicity is combated in an Internet chat room, the approach being used is called:
   a) impression management
   b) entitling
   c) enhancement
   d) Internet intervention
   (d; Moderate; p. 382)

151) Accepting blame for an event, offering an apology, or forcefully refuting the charges is:
   a) impression management
   b) crisis management
   c) an entitling
   d) an enhancement
   (b; Easy; p. 383)

152) PepsiCo reacted to negative claims about hypodermic needles being in their products with photographs and videos of the production processing showing such an event could not happen at their factories. This is an example of using which approach to managing negative publicity?
   a) impression management
   b) crisis management
   c) enhancement
   d) an apology strategy
(b; Challenging; p. 383)

153) An apology strategy is part of:
   a) impression management
   b) defense of innocence
   c) crisis management
   d) justification
(c; Moderate; p. 383)

154) An apology strategy to manage a negative publicity situation should include each of the following elements, *except:*
   a) an expression of guilt
   b) a statement recognizing the inappropriate behavior
   c) acceptance of sanctions because of wrong behavior
   d) a statement about behaviors of the competition
(d; Moderate; p. 383)

155) An apology strategy to manage a negative publicity situation should include each of the following elements, *except:*
   a) names of individuals who were responsible for wrong behavior
   b) rejection of the inappropriate behavior
   c) approval of the appropriate behavior
   d) offer of compensation or penance to correct the wrong
(a; Moderate; p. 383)

156) Apology strategies are most often used in situations in which:
   a) the violation was a major situation affecting a large number of people
   b) the violation was minor or the company cannot escape being found guilty
   c) an individual within the company has acted inappropriately, but the company itself has not
   d) charges have been filed against the company or someone in the company
(b; Challenging; p. 383)

157) The conscious or unconscious attempt to control images in social situations is:
    a) crisis management
    b) enhancement
    c) social responsibility
    d) impression management
(d; Easy; p. 384)

158) Saying, "we didn't cause this negative event to happen, it was some other company" is an example of using the impression management technique of:
    a) an expression of innocence
    b) an excuse
    c) moral ambiguity
    d) a justification
(a; Challenging; p. 384)

159) Saying, "we could not have prevented this negative event from happening" is an example of using the impression management technique of:
    a) an expression of innocence
    b) an excuse
    c) moral ambiguity
    d) a justification
(b; Challenging; p. 384)

160) In terms of using an impression management technique to respond to negative publicity, a company that makes the negative incident appear minor or trivial is using the remedial approach of:
    a) expressions of innocence
    b) excuses
    c) justification
    d) apology
(c; Challenging; p. 384)

161) Each of the following is an impression management technique, *except:*
    a) expression of innocence
    b) excuses
    c) justification
    d) entitlings
(d; Moderate; p. 384)

162)   In the Ford and Bridgestone tire incident, Ford CEO Jacques Nasser blamed
       Bridgestone/Firestone for the problem with the tires. Nasser was using which
       strategy?
           a) expression of innocence
           b) excuses
           c) apology
           d) justifications
       (a; Challenging; p. 384)

163)   In the Ford and Bridgestone tire incident, Bridgestone/Firestone blamed drivers
       for the problem with the tires saying that the tires were under-inflated.
       Bridgestone/Firestone was using which strategy?
           a) expression of innocence
           b) excuse
           c) apology
           d) justifications
       (a; Challenging; p. 384)

164)   When a company pays money to sponsor someone or some group that participates
       in an activity, it is called:
           a) public relations
           b) advertising expenditures
           c) marketing myopia
           d) sponsorship marketing
       (d; Easy; p. 385)

165)   Sponsoring a team, group, or person or a specific venue is:
           a) public relations
           b) sponsorship marketing
           c) event marketing
           d) marketing management
       (b; Easy; p. 385)

166)   Paying for entry fees into a league and uniforms for a little league soccer program
       is an example of:
           a) sponsorship marketing
           b) event marketing
           c) cause-related marketing
           d) an ineffective contact point
       (a; Moderate; p. 385)

167) Paying for an advertisement promoting a concert tour by a band and creating tie-ins with company products at the concerts is an example of:
    a) sponsorship marketing
    b) event marketing
    c) cause-related marketing
    d) musical marketing
(a; Moderate; p. 385)

168) A local race car driver who displays advertising on the car is involved in:
    a) sponsorship marketing
    b) event marketing
    c) mobile marketing
    d) cause-related marketing
(a; Challenging; p. 385)

169) Approximately $9 billion is spent each year on sponsorships and events. Which is largest category (making up 70 percent of all sponsorships and events)?
    a) causes
    b) entertainment, tours, and attractions
    c) sports
    d) festivals, fairs, and annual events
(c; Moderate; p. 385)

170) Companies that serve high-end clients have moved away from sponsoring sporting events to sponsoring more:
    a) cultural events
    b) entertainment, tours, and attractions
    c) causes
    d) festivals, fairs, and annual events
(a; Challenging; p. 386)

171) In choosing a sponsorship, it is important for a company to:
    a) choose local groups or individuals to sponsor
    b) match the audience profile with the company's target market
    c) develop a method of assessment prior to engaging in the sponsorship program
    d) choose an individual or group that is well known to maximize the sponsorship impact
(b; Moderate; p. 386)

172) Sponsorships can be used to accomplish each of the following objectives, *except:*
    a) enhance a company's image
    b) increase a firm's visibility
    c) increase sales
    d) differentiate a company from its competitors
(c; Challenging; p. 386)

173) To entice sponsors for beach volleyball, the Association of Volleyball Professionals:
   a) offered special lower-priced sponsorships
   b) provided free sponsorships to select companies
   c) advertised extensively on television and the Internet
   d) offered several event sponsorship packages that provided for different levels of sponsorships
   (d; Challenging; p. 387)

174) When a firm supports a specific event, such as the Special Olympics, it is:
   a) sponsorship marketing
   b) event marketing
   c) cause-related marketing
   d) tie-in marketing
   (b; Moderate; p. 387)

175) A Hispanic fiesta held in Houston, Texas funded by a food company is an example of:
   a) sponsorship marketing
   b) event marketing
   c) cause-related marketing
   d) a cross-promotion
   (b; Challenging; p. 388)

176) Conducting a health fair at a local hospital is an example of:
   a) sponsorship marketing
   b) event marketing
   c) cause-related marketing
   d) tie-in marketing
   (b; Moderate; p. 388)

177) The Coca-Cola booth at spring break on South Padre Island is an example of:
   a) sponsorship marketing
   b) event marketing
   c) specialty marketing
   d) a cross-promotion
   (b; Challenging; p. 388)

178) When a company advertises, develops consumer promotions, such as a contest, and develops other marketing communications as a tie-in with an event marketing program, it is called a(n):
   a) local promotion
   b) corporate promotion
   c) advertising promotion
   d) cross-promotion
   (d; Moderate; p. 389)

179) Giving out samples of Pizza Hut products in conjunction with the debut of a motion picture that was funded by Pizza Hut is an example of:
   a) sponsorship marketing
   b) event marketing
   c) specialty marketing
   d) a cross-promotion
(d; Challenging; p. 389)

180) The Wheeler-Lea Amendment to the FTC Act:
   a) regulates excessive advertising to children
   b) prohibits deceptive and misleading advertising
   c) prohibits puffery and comparative advertising
   d) sets for the substantiation requirements that an ad must meet when claims are made about a product
(b; Challenging; p. 390)

181) An advertisement or communication is deemed to be deceptive or misleading when:
   a) the misrepresentation induces anyone to make a purchase
   b) a substantial number of people make a purchase
   c) a substantial number of people or the "typical person" is left with a false impression or misrepresentation that relates to the product
   d) a competing firm makes the same claim
(c; Challenging; p. 391)

182) Puffery is:
   a) a deliberate attempt to mislead and deceive
   b) any illegal marketing activity
   c) increased product prices to cover advertising costs
   d) an exaggerated claim with no overt attempt to mislead or deceive
(d; Easy; p. 391)

183) Words such as "best," "greatest," and "finest" are examples of:
   a) deceptive advertising
   b) misleading advertising
   c) standard industry practices
   d) puffery
(d; Moderate; p. 391)

184) When McDonald's claims they have the best-tasting hamburgers, they are engaged in:
   a) a code of ethics violation
   b) misleading and deceptive advertising
   c) puffery
   d) cross-promotions
(c; Moderate; p. 391)

185) The FTC, NAD, and the courts would consider the word "better" used in an advertisement to be:
   a) deceptive and misleading advertising
   b) puffery
   c) either a or b depending on the context of the word in the ad
   d) a violation of the Federal Trade Commission Act
   (c; Challenging; p. 391)

186) The agency that monitors advertising on food packages and advertisements for drugs is the:
   a) FTC
   b) FCC
   c) United States Postal Service
   d) FDA
   (d; Moderate; p. 392)

187) If a customer is concerned about the labeling on a bag of potato chips, the regulatory agency that should be contacted is the:
   a) FCC
   b) FDA
   c) FTC
   d) BATF
   (b; Moderate; p. 392)

188) Public complaints about the amount of violence on television would be sent to the:
   a) FCC
   b) FDA
   c) FTC
   d) BATF
   (a; Moderate; p. 392)

189) The law states that advertising to children cannot exceed 12 minutes per hour during weekdays. Which organization is responsible for making sure this time limit is not exceeded?
   a) FCC
   b) FTC
   c) FDA
   d) BATF
   (a; Challenging; p. 392)

190) The agency with the greatest degree of jurisdiction over marketing and advertising is the:
   a) FTC
   b) FCC
   c) United States Postal Service
   d) FDA
(a; Easy; p. 392)

191) When the Federal Trade Commission (FTC) insists that a company stop making a false claim in an advertisement and that company agrees to stop, it is an example of a:
   a) legal review
   b) cease-and-desist order
   c) administrative complaint
   d) consent order
(d; Moderate; p. 393)

192) In terms of a judgment by the Federal Trade Commission against a company for false or misleading advertising, which of the following would come first?
   a) administrative complaint
   b) cease-and-desist order
   c) consent order
   d) court-ordered reparations
(c; Challenging; p. 393)

193) An administrative complaint is:
   a) a formal proceeding before an administrative law judge used by the FTC
   b) a formal hearing before the Court of Appeals
   c) a formal hearing before the full FTC commission
   d) used by the NARB when the NAD cannot solve a complaint
(a; Moderate; p. 393)

194) If a consent agreement cannot be reached with a company, the Federal Trade Commission (FTC) would then issue a(n):
   a) cease and desist order
   b) corrective advertising directive
   c) appeal to the Court of Appeals
   d) administrative complaint
(d; Challenging; p. 393)

195) If at the end of an administrative hearing the judge feels a violation of the law has taken place, the judge will issue a(n):
    a) cease and desist order
    b) consent agreement
    c) corrective advertising directive
    d) trade regulation ruling
(a; Challenging; p. 393)

196) If after an administrative hearing a company is still not satisfied with the ruling of the Federal Trade Commission (FTC), the next step is to:
    a) appeal the decision to the Court of Appeals
    b) hold a hearing before the full FTC commission
    c) appeal the decision to the Supreme Court
    d) hold a hearing before an administrative law judge
(b; Challenging; p. 393)

197) Companies not satisfied with the ruling of the full Federal Trade Commission (FTC) can appeal to the U.S. Court of Appeals. The danger for companies in appealing to the Court of Appeals is that:
    a) the company does not have the opportunity to present oral arguments
    b) the cease and desist orders are normally upheld
    c) a company may be ordered to pay civil penalties
    d) the decision is not binding
(c; Challenging; p. 393)

198) Occasionally, the Federal Trade Commission bypasses the normal steps and uses the court system to stop unfair and deceptive advertising and communication practices. This occurs when:
    a) a company violates a FTC cease-and-desist order
    b) a full commission of the FTC is not available to hear a case
    c) a company violates a consent order
    d) a company appeals a consent order
(a; Challenging; p. 393)

199) Occasionally, the Federal Trade Commission (FTC) bypasses the normal steps and uses the court system to stop unfair and deceptive advertising and communication practices. This occurs when:
    a) the actions of a company are so severe that immediate action is needed
    b) a full commission of the FTC is not available to hear a case
    c) a company violates a consent order
    d) a company appeals a consent order
(a; Challenging; p. 393)

200) Which agency has the authority to order corrective advertising?
   a) FCC
   b) FTC
   c) FDA
   d) BAFT
(b; Challenging; p. 394)

201) When a company must pay for ads that refute false claims it had made in previous ads, it is called a(n):
   a) consent order
   b) administrative ruling
   c) cease-and-desist order
   d) corrective advertisement
(d; Easy; p. 394)

202) A trade regulatory ruling by the Federal Trade Commission applies to:
   a) wholesalers
   b) international companies
   c) an industry
   d) retailers
(c; Moderate; p. 394)

203) The funeral industry was sanctioned by the Federal Trade Commission (FTC) in 1984 and 1994 using a:
   a) cease and-desist order
   b) consent order
   c) corrective advertising order
   d) trade regulation ruling
(d; Challenging; p. 394)

204) The substantiation test for false and misleading advertising requires:
   a) scientific tests
   b) consumer testimonials
   c) competent and reliable evidence
   d) the average person to be convinced it is not false and misleading
(c; Moderate; p. 395)

205) The Federal Trade Commission (FTC) test of substantiation is:
   a) a comparison of marketing claims made by competing firms
   b) the use of a code of ethics
   c) using reliable and competent evidence as the basis of a marketing claim
   d) normally not a component in an FTC case regarding deceptive advertising
(c; Moderate; p. 395)

206) In terms of substantiation, if an advertiser uses expert endorsements, then statements in the advertisement must be based on:
   a) legitimate tests performed by experts in the field
   b) the opinion of "typical persons" who would use the product
   c) truthful statements that represent the experts personal experience
   d) lab or engineering tests
   (a; Challenging; p. 395)

207) In terms of substantiation of claims in the advertisements, the Federal Trade Commission and courts tend to use each of the following principles, *except:*
   a) The federal government assumes consumers read ads "broadly" and do not notice details hidden in fine print.
   b) Tests have to be with the actual product or one that is considered similar.
   c) Evidence should come from individuals or companies that would be considered by experts by others in the field.
   d) The courts and FTC will consider the totality of evidence concerning a claim, not just one particular study that may support a claim.
   (b; Challenging; p. 395)

208) If a consumer wants to know if people have complained about a particular health club being unsafe or unclean, he or she should contact the:
   a) NAD
   b) FTC
   c) Better Business Bureau
   d) NARB
   (c; Moderate; p. 396)

209) The National Advertising Division (NAD) of the Better Business Bureau becomes involved in all of the following, *except:*
   a) cases of mail fraud
   b) collecting information about misleading advertising
   c) negotiating modification of ads deemed to be misleading
   d) dismissing unsubstantiated complaints
   (a; Challenging; p. 396)

210) An appeal of a decision by the National Advertising Division (NAD) goes to the:
   a) United States Court of Appeals
   b) FTC
   c) NARB
   d) FCC
   (c; Challenging; p. 397)

Short-Answer Questions

211) What are the five key public relations functions?

1. Identify stakeholders
2. Assess corporate reputation
3. Audit social responsibility
4. Create positive image-building activities
5. Prevent or reduce image damage

(Moderate; p. 373)

212) Who are the major internal stakeholders for a public relations department to consider?

- Employees
- Labor unions
- Shareholders

(Easy; p. 374)

213) Who are the major external stakeholders for a public relations department to consider?

- Channel members
- Customers
- The media
- The local community
- The financial community
- Government
- Special-interest groups

(Moderate; p. 375)

214) What are the two forms of preventive damage control measures?

Entitlings, where the company claims responsibility for the positive outcome of an event and enhancements, where the company attempts to increase the desirable outcome of an event in the eyes of the public.

(Easy; p. 382)

215) Discuss the various damage control strategies that can be used by a firm.

Reactive strategies are designed to counter the negative action that has occurred. The reactive strategies include Internet interventions, crisis management, apology strategies, and impression management tactics which include, defense of innocence, excuses, justifications, and other explanations. These are in addition to the proactive strategies of entitlings and enhancements.
(Challenging; p. 382)

216) Describe sponsorship marketing.

Sponsorship marketing occurs when the company pays money to sponsor someone or some group that is participating in an activity.
(Easy; p. 385)

217) Describe event marketing.

Event marketing is similar to a sponsorship, except that it is in support of a specific event, such as a rodeo or county fair.
(Easy; p. 388)

218) What criteria must be met to deem an advertisement deceptive or misleading?

1. A substantial number of people, or the typical person, is left with a false impression or misrepresentation that relates to the product.
2. The misrepresentation induces people or the "typical person" to make a purchase.
(Moderate; p. 391)

219) Identify the typical steps in an FTC investigation sequence from the initial complaint to a decision that is appealed to the Supreme Court.

1. Consent order
2. Administrative complaint
3. Cease-and-desist order
4. Full commission
5. U.S. Court of Appeals
6. U.S. Supreme Court
(Challenging; p. 393)

220) What is a trade regulation?

A trade regulation is a finding or a ruling that implicates an entire industry in a case of deceptive or unfair marketing practices.
(Easy, p. 394)

CHAPTER 13
INTERNET MARKETING

True-False Questions

1) Google's primary marketing advantage is the quality of the products offered on the Web site.
   (False; Easy; p. 406)

2) Google recently began advertising to build brand strength.
   (True; Easy; p. 407)

3) About half of the people in the United States (48%) use the Internet daily.
   (True; Easy; p. 409)

4) Communication via e-mail, online chat, and instant messaging are the most common uses of the Internet.
   (True; Easy; p. 409)

5) Business-to-business marketers were among the first companies to actually make profits using the Internet.
   (True; Moderate; p. 409)

6) The Internet has a major impact on sales, marketing and distribution systems.
   (True; Easy; p. 409)

7) A flashy Web site may be designed to attract attention if the primary goal of the web site is advertising.
   (True; Easy; p. 410)

8) Business-to-business marketers would design a Web site to provide sales support more frequently than would business-to-consumer marketers.
   (True; Moderate; p. 410)

9) The goal of a customer service Web site is to support the customer after the product is sold.
   (True; Moderate; p. 410)

10) FAQ stands for "frequently answered queries."
    (False; Easy; p. 410)

11) FAQ, or frequently asked questions, are part of the customer service marketing function.
    (True; Moderate; p. 410)

12) E-commerce is selling goods or services on the Internet.
    (True; Easy; p. 411)

13) The top cyber shopping category is computer hardware and software.
    (False; Challenging; p. 411)

14) To the established retail operation, e-commerce offers customers an alternative mode for making purchases.
    (True; Easy; p. 411)

15) An e-commerce catalog is designed to help shoppers find products on a Web site.
    (True; Easy; p. 412)

16) One component that is not required or necessary on an e-commerce site is a catalog.
    (False; Moderate; p. 412)

17) A shopping cart is a method of payment for an e-commerce purchase.
    (False; Easy; p. 412)

18) The three primary e-commerce components are a catalog, a shopping cart, and a point of purchase display screen.
    (False; Moderate; p. 412)

19) Some shoppers are reluctant to shop on the Internet because of fears about security and not wanting to change purchasing habits.
    (True; Moderate; p. 412)

20) Consumer fears about e-commerce security issues are based on credit card numbers being stolen, identity theft, and fraud.
    (True; Moderate; p. 412)

21) While current purchasing habits are a concern for the future success of e-commerce, security issues have the strongest ramifications for the ultimate success of e-commerce.
    (False; Challenging; p. 412)

22) Three types of incentives can be used to encourage customers to make online purchases: financially-based incentives, convenience-based incentives, and price-based incentives.
    (False; Moderate; p. 413)

23) The three incentives that must be present for consumers to consider a purchase online are financial incentives, convenience incentives, and price incentives.
    (False; Moderate; p. 413)

24) Once individuals switch to purchasing online, financially-based incentives may not be necessary to keep them as customers.
(True; Challenging; p. 413)

25) Cyberbait is a lure or type of attraction designed to bring people to a Web site.
(True; Easy; p. 413)

26) Cyberbait is a convenience-based incentive designed to bring people to a Web site.
(False; Moderate; p. 413)

27) Typically, the most effective financial incentives to encourage online shopping are free shipping with orders, free freight, and dollar discounts, such as $5 or $10 off.
(True; Challenging; p. 414)

28) 24 hour availability is an example of a convenience incentive that can be used to attract people to an e-commerce site.
(True; Moderate; p. 414)

29) Web sites, similar to displays at retail stores, can be rearranged to create excitement and interest, but basic links and location of merchandise should not be changed too often.
(True; Challenging; p. 414)

30) In terms of e-commerce, a value-added incentive is used to cause consumers to change purchasing habits in the short term, so that convenience incentives can attract them to change long term buying habits.
(False; Moderate; p. 415)

31) An example of a value-added incentive to attract people to an e-commerce site is personalization.
(True; Moderate; p. 415)

32) In business-to-business e-commerce, a company must have an effective Web site and a strong brand name to be able to compete effectively.
(True; Moderate; p. 416)

33) A growing area of e-commerce in the business-to-business sector is on-line exchanges and auctions.
(True; Easy; p. 416)

34) Many of the online exchanges and auctions are neutral companies that simply match buyers and sellers.
(True; Moderate; p. 417)

35) Cross-selling of merchandise can also occur with online purchases and b-to-b e-commerce.
(True; Easy; p. 417)

36) Cross-selling is not possible using e-commerce or the Internet.
(False; Easy; p. 417)

37) One of the advantages of e-commerce over brick-and-mortar stores is the ability to reach consumers around the globe.
(True; Easy; p. 417)

38) While the Internet makes it possible to have customers from anywhere in the world, about half of all current Internet customers turn away international orders because they do not have processes in place to fill the international orders.
(True; Challenging; p. 418)

39) For large international shipments, many companies utilize a freight forwarder.
(True; Moderate; p. 418)

40) Cultural adaptation software makes it possible to tailor a Web site to individual countries.
(True; Moderate; p. 418)

41) Software, Internet incompatibilities, and technical problems make international e-commerce more difficult.
(True; Easy; p. 419)

42) The Internet bandwidth used by countries around the world has now been standardized.
(False; Moderate; p. 419)

43) While the Victoria's Secret Internet Fashion Show associated with the Super Bowl was a major success, due to the number of people who were drawn to the site, failure to tell the IT department resulted in the site crashing because so many viewers tried to access the site.
(True; Challenging; p. 419)

44) A search engine is the primary method most consumers use to discover new Web sites.
(True; Moderate; p. 420)

45) In a survey called the World Wide Internet Opinion Survey, television and print advertising were the primary methods consumers use to discover new Web sites.
(False; Moderate; p. 420)

46) Many experts believe that traditional Internet banner ads have little influence on shoppers.
(True; Moderate; p. 420)

47) Many consumers have become annoyed or frustrated by e-mail spam.
(True; Easy; p. 420)

48) A relatively new method of promoting Web sites, brands, and products is the Web blog.
(True; Moderate; p. 421)

49) In business-to-business markets, the number of hits at a b-to-b Web site is directly related to the amount of money spent on advertising and sales promotions.
(True; Challenging; p. 421)

50) Brand image is a major factor in the success of an online company.
(True; Easy; p. 421)

51) Cyberbranding involves integrating all of the online brand tactics so they all reinforce each other and speak with one voice.
(False; Moderate; p. 421)

52) Brand spiraling is the practice of using interactive media to promote and attract consumers to an on-line Web site.
(False; Moderate; p. 422)

53) Using traditional media to promote and attract consumers to a Web site is called brand spiraling.
(True; Easy; p. 422)

54) Brand spiraling is a form of halo effect.
(False; Easy; p. 422)

55) Cookie technology allows a Web site to look into a consumer's computer to see what sites have been visited, without the consumer ever knowing it is being done.
(True; Moderate; p. 422)

56) Word-of-mouth advertising is a form of brand spiraling where consumers pass along positive information about the brand.
(False; Challenging; p. 423)

57) The number one technique used to advertise a business-to-business Web site is advertising in trade journals.
(False; Challenging; p. 423)

58) A halo effect occurs when a well-received brand leads more customers to try new goods and services being offered by the company on the Internet.
(True; Easy; p. 423)

59) Brand-name power for an online business cannot be created solely through advertising on the Internet.
(True; Challenging; p. 423)

60) Heavy users of a product are not always brand loyal.
(True; Moderate; p. 423)

61) The Internet provides the ability to establish one-to-one communication between the consumer and the firm through both e-mails and personalization of information.
(True; Easy, p. 424)

62) In terms of developing one-to-one communications with users, free shipping and handling or other promotion is extremely important in converting a visitor to a Web site to a buyer.
(False; Challenging; p. 424)

63) In communicating with customers, it is important to provide some type of promotion in order to convert the customer to a brand-loyal consumer.
(False; Challenging; p. 424)

64) The strategy of using a Webs site for information rather than for direct sales is found more often in the consumer sector than in the business-to-business sector.
(False; Moderate; p. 425)

65) Often, the most important sales support function of the Internet is in providing information about clients and products to salespeople.
(True; Easy; p. 425)

66) In terms of using the Internet for sales support, customers may also be able to go online for information about products.
(True; Moderate; p. 425)

67) In terms of using the Internet for customer service, an important function that can be provided is the ability for prospecting and qualifying prospects.
(False; Moderate; p. 425)

68) The Internet offers a cost-effective method for companies to provide effective customer service.
(True; Easy; p. 426)

69) In a recent survey, the response time to a customer request, inquiry, or complaint was a significant factor in future purchase decisions.
(True; Easy; p. 426)

70) In a recent survey, respondents stated they were significantly more satisfied with online customer service than the customer service provided by traditional retailers.
(False; Moderate; p. 426)

71) Older consumers were more satisfied with the customer service provided by online retailers than younger consumers.
(False; Challenging; p. 426)

72) To improve customer service, a company can put together discussion groups, chat rooms, and blogs.
(True; Moderate; p. 426)

73) Direct mail is the most effective tool for getting customers to investigate a Web site and place an Internet order.
(True; Challenging; p. 427)

74) The most recent trend in online direct marketing is streaming videos and high-tech graphics.
(False; Moderate; p. 427)

75) Interactive marketing is individualizing and personalizing of Web content, offers, and e-mails.
(True; Moderate; p. 428)

76) Viral marketing is a preparing an advertisement that is tied to an e-mail.
(True; Easy; p. 428)

77) When Scope sent an e-mail attachment "kiss" that also promoted the product to customers, it was a form of viral marketing.
(True; Moderate; p. 429)

78) Viral marketing is a form of interactive marketing.
(False; Challenging; p. 429)

79) A slow loading front page and too much verbal information are two typical problems that reduce the number of people willing to search through a Web site.
(True; Moderate; p. 429)

Multiple-Choice Questions

80)   Google is:
   a) a replacement for bricks and mortar operations
   b) a global marketplace
   c) slowly losing ground to Amazon.com
   d) a search engine for Internet users
  (d; Easy; p. 406)

81)   Google's business model is to:
   a) replace for bricks and mortar operations
   b) offer a global marketplace
   c) provide free access to information coupled with advertisements
   d) sell company products through various links
  (c; Moderate; p. 406)

82)   The most common use of the Internet is for:
   a) communication
   b) customer service
   c) making online purchases
   d) information searches
  (a; Moderate; p. 409)

83)   The first companies to make profits using the Internet were primarily:
   a) online retailers
   b) search engines
   c) travel web sites
   d) business-to-business marketers
  (d; Challenging; p. 409)

84)   The Internet is enticing to companies because of the potential to:
   a) reach senior citizens so effectively
   b) save 10% to 20% of sales, marketing, and distribution costs
   c) reach consumers 24 hours a day
   d) communicate more effectively with customers
  (b; Challenging; p. 409)

85)   Internet Web sites can serve all of the following functions, *except:*
   a) advertising
   b) sales support
   c) distribution
   d) customer service
  (c; Easy; p. 410)

86) Creating a flashy site that will attract attention would be a good decision when the primary goal is:
   a) advertising
   b) sales support
   c) physical delivery of a product
   d) customer service
(a; Easy; p. 410)

87) A Web site that links the buyer with a salesperson is aimed at the function of:
   a) advertising
   b) sales support
   c) physical delivery of a product
   d) customer service
(b; Easy; p. 410)

88) A web site designed to provide sales support would be used more by:
   a) online retailers
   b) business-to-consumer marketers
   c) business-to-business marketers
   d) members of the distribution channel
(c; Challenging; p. 410)

89) The goal of a web site designed to provide customer service is to support:
   a) salespeople
   b) brick and mortar retail stores
   c) the customer during the sale
   d) the customer after the sale has been made
(d; Challenging; p. 410)

90) FAQ stands for:
   a) frequently answered questions
   b) frequently asked questions
   c) frequently asked queries
   d) follow-up answer questionnaire
(b; Easy; p. 410)

91) A FAQ page supports which function on a Web site?
   a) advertising
   b) public relations
   c) customer service
   d) collecting information about customers
(c; Moderate; p. 410)

92) If a consumer were trying to discern additional information on a website, he or she may go to:
   a) the front page
   b) a banner
   c) the FAQ screen
   d) the shopping cart
(c; Moderate; p. 410)

93) When goods and services are sold on the Internet, the approach to marketing is known as:
   a) retail by e-mail
   b) viral marketing
   c) e-commerce
   d) vicarious shopping
(c; Easy; p. 411)

94) E-commerce is:
   a) retail by e-mail
   b) viral marketing
   c) selling goods and services on the Internet
   d) vicarious shopping
(c; Easy; p. 411)

95) The top global cyber shopping category, at $52.4 billion, is:
   a) travel
   b) office, home, and garden
   c) computer hardware/software
   d) apparel
(a; Challenging; p. 411)

96) The top global cyber shopping category is travel. The second highest category is:
   a) travel
   b) office, home, and garden
   c) computer hardware/software
   d) apparel
(b; Challenging; p. 411)

97) To the established retail operation, e-commerce offers customers:
   a) an alternative mode for making purchases
   b) a place to obtain additional information about a product
   c) a place to locate the closest retail store where the actual purchase will be made
   d) all of the above
(d; Easy; p. 411)

98) All of the following are necessary components of an e-commerce site, *except:*
   a) catalog
   b) shopping cart
   c) payment method
   d) shipping and handling cost chart
(d; Easy; p. 412)

99) The component of an e-commerce site is used to display the goods or services listed for sale is the:
   a) catalog
   b) shopping cart
   c) payment method
   d) video stream
(a; Easy; p. 412)

100) An e-commerce catalog is used for:
   a) displaying merchandise
   b) placing orders
   c) answering questions
   d) providing information about other companies
(a; Easy; p. 412)

101) An e-commerce shopping cart is used for:
   a) making inquiries
   b) asking questions
   c) placing an order
   d) returning merchandise
(c; Easy; p. 412)

102) The component of an e-commerce site is used to hold products that have been chosen for purchase is a:
   a) catalog
   b) shopping cart
   c) payment method
   d) video stream
(b; Easy; p. 412)

103) Besides security issues, the primary reason why some consumers do not shop on-line is:
   a) it requires a new purchasing habit
   b) fear they will be ripped off and merchandise purchased will not be shipped
   c) they don't think they can find what they want
   d) the merchandise costs more than at retail stores
(a; Moderate; p. 412)

104) Consumers are still reluctant to make Internet purchases because of:
    a) higher prices
    b) viruses and potential of identity theft
    c) security issues and purchasing habits
    d) higher shipping costs
(c; Moderate; p. 412)

105) A consumer who does not shop on-line because of fears about identity theft is expressing:
    a) security concerns
    b) reality concerns
    c) cognitive dissonance
    d) buying behavior issues
(a; Moderate; p. 412)

106) The e-commerce component most directly affected by security concerns is:
    a) interstitial advertising
    b) the catalog
    c) the shopping cart
    d) payment programs
(d; Challenging; p. 412)

107) Credit card companies, such as Visa and MasterCard, have recently created ads about:
    a) payment systems with a high level of security
    b) placing orders
    c) creating better catalogs
    d) changing purchasing habits
(a; Easy; p. 412)

108) Incentives that can be used to encourage consumers to make online purchases include all of the following, *except:*
    a) price incentives
    b) financial incentives
    c) convenience incentives
    d) value-based incentives
(a; Moderate; p. 413)

109) A reduced price, an introductory price, and e-coupons used to encourage someone to make an online purchase are:
    a) quality incentives
    b) financial incentives
    c) convenience incentives
    d) value-based incentives
(b; Easy; p. 413)

110) A financial incentive to encourage someone to make a purchase online can include all of the following, *except:*
   a) consumer promotion
   b) introductory price
   c) home delivery
   d) e-coupon
   (c; Moderate; p. 413)

111) A lure that attracts attention and brings to people to a Web site is called:
   a) cyberbait
   b) a consumer incentive
   c) a convenience incentive
   d) value incentives
   (a; Easy; p. 413)

112) Using a fantasy football league to attract individuals to a Web site is an example of:
   a) financially-based incentive
   b) viral marketing
   c) cyberbait
   d) convenience incentive
   (c; Challenging; p. 413)

113) All of the following statements concerning cyberbait are true, *except:*
   a) It is a form of convenience incentive.
   b) It can be a lottery or contest.
   c) It can be a consumer promotion tactic.
   d) It should be changed on a regular basis.
   (a; Challenging; p. 413)

114) Free shipping, free freight, and dollar discounts are examples of which type of incentive that can be used to encourage online shopping?
   a) financial
   b) consumer
   c) convenience
   d) economic
   (a; Moderate; p. 414)

115) Persuading a first-time buyer to make an online purchase is best achieved using:
   a) interstitial advertising
   b) financial incentives
   c) convenience incentives
   d) value-based incentives
   (b; Challenging; p. 414)

116) Typically, the most effective financial incentives that can be used to encourage online shopping are:
    a) percentage off price discounts
    b) contests and sweepstakes
    c) free gifts
    d) free shipping, free freight, and dollar discounts
(d; Challenging; p. 414)

117) To be successful in using financially-based incentives to encourage online purchases, the incentives:
    a) must match the target market of the web site
    b) should offer something free
    c) apply all customers, not just first time purchasers
    d) should be meaningful to those visiting the web site and be changed periodically
(d; Challenging; p. 414)

118) Access to a Web site 24 hours a day is an example of which type of incentive?
    a) financial
    b) cyberbait
    c) convenience
    d) value-added
(c; Moderate; p. 414)

119) When a business checks on the status of an order, looks up shipment information or reviews billing data, the business is taking advantage of which type of incentives?
    a) financial
    b) convenience
    c) value-added
    d) shopping
(b; Challenging; p. 414)

120) J. Crew offering an easy "how to measure" chart is an example of a web site using which type of incentive to encourage online purchases?
    a) financial
    b) convenience
    c) value-added
    d) all of the above
(b; Challenging; p. 414)

121) Value-added incentives are designed to:
   a) attract attention
   b) provide shipment information
   c) change purchasing habits over the long term
   d) change short term buying decisions
(c; Challenging; p. 415)

122) Which type of incentive is designed to change purchasing habits over the long term?
   a) financial
   b) consumer
   c) convenience
   d) value-added
(d; Challenging; p. 415)

123) A hotel knows a customer often stays for a week and offers that person a discount for booking online. This is an example of:
   a) merchandising
   b) a financial incentive
   c) a convenience incentive
   d) a value-added incentive
(d; Challenging; p. 415)

124) A financial incentive may cause a consumer to switch to e-commerce; a value-added incentive is designed to:
   a) changing purchasing habits more permanently
   b) create brand awareness
   c) substitute payment plans
   d) find new buyers
(a; Moderate; p. 415)

125) All of the following are examples of value-added incentives designed to encourage web visitors, *except:*
   a) offering merchandise on the web site that is not available in a catalog or in retail stores
   b) offering free shipping and handling
   c) offering free online educational courses
   d) personalizing products to individual consumers based on previous visits to the web site and past purchases
(b; Challenging; p. 415)

126) When Tide offers tips on how to get tough stains out of clothes, which type of incentive is being used?
   a) financial
   b) convenience
   c) value-added
   d) all of the above
   (c; Challenging; p. 415)

127) Business-to-business e-commerce requires an effective Web site and:
   a) a strong brand name
   b) financial incentives
   c) bonus merchandise
   d) cyberbait
   (a; Moderate; p. 416)

128) One major advantage of e-commerce in the business-to-business area is:
   a) wide visibility
   b) reduced costs of sales calls and commissions
   c) the ability to eliminate the sales department
   d) reduced costs at trade shows
   (b; Challenging; p. 416)

129) Business-to-business Web sites utilize all of the following incentives, *except:*
   a) financial incentives
   b) convenience incentives
   c) value-added incentives
   d) mark-up incentives
   (d; Moderate; p. 416)

130) A growing form of e-commerce in the business-to-business sector is:
   a) discount houses
   b) financial institutions
   c) online exchanges and auctions
   d) commodity trading
   (c; Challenging; p. 416)

131) When Wells Fargo developed the Commercial Electronic Office (CEO) feature on its Web site for its large commercial customers, the primary emphasis was on:
   a) direct marketing
   b) interactive marketing
   c) viral marketing
   d) cross selling
   (d; Challenging; p. 417)

132) While e-commerce can increase international orders, many are turned away primarily because the company:
    a) does not understand the culture
    b) is focused on domestic business
    c) does not have a process in place to fill the order
    d) does not have an established global brand name
(c; Moderate; p. 418)

133) All of the following are problems faced in International e-commerce, *except:*
    a) cultural differences
    b) global shipping and infrastructure deficiencies
    c) varying degree of Internet capabilities
    d) currency foreign exchange capabilities
(d; Challenging; p. 418)

134) In terms of international e-commerce, large merchandise normally is shipped by:
    a) the company selling the merchandise
    b) shipping companies like DHL, FedEx, or UPS
    c) freight forwarders
    d) the company purchasing the merchandise
(c; Challenging; p. 418)

135) Cultural adaptation software has been developed that:
    a) performs a literal translation of an English Web site into other languages
    b) adapts Web sites to new countries
    c) cross sells merchandise to major customers
    d) reduces international spam
(b; Moderate; p. 418)

136) The most difficult challenge e-commerce companies face in the international market is:
    a) a lack of companies that can ship large or bulky products to other countries
    b) the inferior infrastructure in many countries
    c) the technical side of e-commerce, specifically software incompatibility
    d) the language barrier
(c; Challenging; p. 419)

137) In terms of Web site design, an example of a cultural disaster to avoid in international e-commerce would be:
    a) using white background and graphics in Asia, Europe and Latin America
    b) a waving hand in Middle East countries
    c) showing a woman with exposed arms or legs in the Middle East on the web site
    d) using a dog as part of a company logo in France
(c; Challenging; p. 419)

138) A recent poll, called the World Wide Internet Opinion Survey, found that the primary method consumers use to discover new Web sites is:
   a) word of mouth
   b) a search engine
   c) television and print advertising
   d) Internet banner ads
   (b; Moderate; p. 420)

139) A recent poll, called the World Wide Internet Opinion Survey, revealed that the least effective method consumers use to discover new Web sites is:
   a) word of mouth
   b) a search engine
   c) television and print advertising
   d) Internet banner ads
   (c; Challenging; p. 420)

140) All of the following statements about interstitial ads are true, *except:*
   a) They are also called pop-up ads.
   b) They are controversial.
   c) They have high intrusion value.
   d) They do not work as well as traditional banner ads.
   (d; Challenging; p. 420)

141) Spamming is the Internet equivalent of:
   a) direct marketing by mail
   b) advertising on television
   c) promotion at a trade show
   d) public relations and cause-related events
   (a; Challenging; p. 420)

142) Since the Can Spam Act went into effect in January 2004, unsolicited e-mails have:
   a) decreased sharply to only about 30 percent of all e-mails
   b) steadily decreased to only 50 percent of all e-mails
   c) increased to 80 percent of all e-mails
   d) remained steady
   (c; Challenging; p. 420)

143) The luster of using e-mails to send business advertisements has worn off with over 70% of recipients saying they are receiving too many e-mail ads and 55% saying they delete the ads without ever looking at them. As an alternative, many business-to-business companies have shifted to:
    a) viral marketing
    b) interactive marketing
    c) b-to-b newsletters
    d) cyberbait
(c; Challenging; p. 421)

144) A new, non-advertising, off-beat, word-of-mouth Internet-based method of promoting a product is a:
    a) spam
    b) blog
    c) response
    d) personalized marketing message
(b; Easy; p. 421)

145) The individual most likely to read a blog is:
    a) a senior citizen
    b) a person between the ages of 18 and 35
    c) someone who watches a great deal of television
    d) someone led to the site by a magazine advertisement
(b; Easy; p. 421)

146) In business-to-business markets, the number of hits at a b-to-b Web site is directly related to the amount of money spent on:
    a) advertising and sales promotions
    b) online advertising
    c) trade shows and business publications
    d) keyword search engines
(a; Challenging; p. 421)

147) Integrating online and off-line branding tactics that reinforce each other and speak with one voice is:
    a) cyberbranding
    b) brand spiraling
    c) off-line branding
    d) viral marketing
(a; Moderate; p. 421)

148) Using traditional media to promote and attract customers to a Web site is:
   a) cyberbranding
   b) brand spiraling
   c) off-line branding
   d) viral marketing
(b; Moderate; p. 422)

149) Brand spiraling is:
   a) spamming
   b) blogging
   c) using traditional media to promote and attract customers to a Web site
   d) value-added marketing
(c; Easy; p. 422)

150) Brand spiraling is a(n):
   a) on-line advertising technique
   b) off-line advertising technique
   c) manufacturing technique
   d) technical improvement
(b; Moderate; p. 422)

151) Posting a firm's Web address on a bag used to package goods sold at a bricks and mortar store is a form of:
   a) brand reinforcement
   b) brand spiraling
   c) interactive marketing
   d) virtual marketing
(b; Challenging; p. 422)

152) All of the following are media that would be used in brand spiraling, *except:*
   a) television
   b) radio
   c) a billboard
   d) a Web site
(d; Challenging; p. 422)

153) All of the following are methods used by business-to-business firms to boost Web site awareness, but the one used the most is:
   a) advertising in trade journals
   b) registering the Web site with search engines for keywords
   c) putting the Web site address on all printed materials and promotional items
   d) buying banner ads on other Web sites
(c; Challenging, p. 422)

154) The halo effect occurs when:
   a) a well-received brand leads customers to try purchasing goods and services over the Internet
   b) people like a particular Web site and go there more often
   c) people like salespeople who are pleasant
   d) consumers only shop when the banner advertisement is enticing
   (a; Easy; p. 423)

155) When a well-received brand name leads customers to try purchasing goods and services over the Internet, it is:
   a) a halo effect
   b) viral marketing
   c) brand spiraling
   d) cyberbranding
   (a; Moderate; p. 423)

156) In terms of the relationship between brand loyalty and being a heavy user:
   a) heavy users are brand loyal
   b) a heavy user may not necessarily be brand loyal
   c) both are driven by price considerations
   d) neither is affected by emotions because they are rational choices
   (b; Moderate; p. 423)

157) In terms of Internet programs and brand loyalty, all of the following statements are true, *except:*
   a) Brand loyalty is the same as being a heavy user.
   b) Consumers believe the brand is superior.
   c) Consumers have positive affective feelings toward the company.
   d) Inferior quality products cannot develop a high level of brand loyalty from its customers.
   (a; Moderate; p. 423)

158) In terms of developing brand loyalty, the Internet provides all of the following opportunities not possible with advertising, *except:*
   a) can make the shopping experience more pleasurable
   b) ability to establish one-to-one communication
   c) can create a higher level of brand loyalty
   d) has the potential to contact niche customers
   (c; Challenging; p. 424)

159) In terms of developing brand loyalty, the Internet has the ability to establish one-to-one communication between the consumer and the firm through:
   a) e-mails and blogs
   b) Web content and personalization of web promotions
   c) e-mails and personalized advertising
   d) e-mails and personalization of shopping
   (d; Moderate; p. 424)

160) In converting customers to brand-loyal consumers, it is important to provide:
   a) rewards for their loyalty
   b) incentives to encourage diversity
   c) promotions on a regular basis to maintain loyalty
   d) regular e-mails offering special deals
   (a; Challenging; p. 424)

161) In terms of using the Internet for sales support, all of the following are common strategies, *except:*
   a) provide client and product information to salespeople
   b) provide account information for customers
   c) provide product information that can be accessed by customers
   d) qualifying prospects by sales staff
   (b; Challenging; p. 425)

162) In terms of using the Internet for sales support, the strategy of using the Web site to provide information rather than selling a product is more common:
   a) in the consumer sector
   b) with e-commerce
   c) in the business-to-business sector
   d) with international marketing strategies
   (c; Moderate; p. 425)

163) Brittney is a salesperson for a Trinity Filters, Inc. and uses the Internet to gather information about her clients and products she sells. This is an example of using the Internet for:
   a) e-commerce
   b) customer service
   c) interactive marketing
   d) sales support
   (d; Challenging; p. 425)

164) Adam is a salesperson for a General Motors, the business fleet division, and uses the Internet to gather information about prospects in order to qualify the best ones. This is an example of using the Internet for:
    a) e-commerce
    b) customer service
    c) interactive marketing
    d) sales support
(d; Challenging; p. 425)

165) Tritan Industries just purchased a new machine for their assembly line. In order to gather information about the machine, the company's engineers access the manufacturer's Web site. This is an example of using the Internet for:
    a) e-commerce
    b) customer service
    c) interactive marketing
    d) sales support
(d; Challenging; p. 425)

166) In terms of customer service, the primary advantage to customers in using the vendor's Web site for customer service is:
    a) ability to purchase additional products
    b) speed and efficiency of obtaining information and placing orders
    c) availability of FAQs
    d) the accuracy of shipping orders
(b; Challenging; p. 426)

167) In terms of customer service, the primary advantage to a business when customer's use the company's Web site is"
    a) ability to cross-sell products
    b) reduced costs and efficiency of supplying information and filling orders
    c) history of purchase behavior
    d) the accuracy of shipping orders
(b; Challenging; p. 426)

168) In terms of customer service, which is a significant factor that will affect future purchase decisions?
    a) price of products sold
    b) response time to inquiries or complaints
    c) speed of delivery
    d) speed of process orders
(b; Moderate; p. 426)

169) According to the Institute of Management and Administration (IOMA), customer service can be improved by following all of the steps below, *except:*
   a) service reps need to be knowledgeable
   b) confirm customer inquiries or orders
   c) add a personal touch to e-mails and correspondence
   d) answer inquiries within 24 hours
(d; Challenging; p. 426)

170) According to the Institute of Management and Administration (IOMA), customer service can be improved by following all of the steps below, *except:*
   a) use personalization software to customize the Web offerings for each customer
   b) offer customers the opportunity to talk to someone in person
   c) use good communication skills
   d) be aware of the customer's work habits
(a; Challenging; p. 426)

171) The most effective tool for getting customers to investigate a Web site and place orders is:
   a) direct mail
   b) word of mouth
   c) television advertising
   d) radio advertising
(a; Challenging; p. 427)

172) Interactive marketing is:
   a) individualizing and personalizing Internet messages, offers, and e-mails
   b) providing interactive games for customers to play
   c) the ability of a Web site to visually display a product, such as clothes on a person
   d) when customers give permission for marketers to send e-mails and other types of correspondence to them
(a; Moderate; p. 428)

173) Interactive marketing can be used for all of the following, *except:*
   a) personalize products the customer is more likely to be interested in purchasing
   b) personalize Web content and e-mails to customers
   c) personalize offers for merchandise
   d) personalized interstitial advertisements of the Web site
(d; Challenging; p. 428)

174) A consumer would get a personalized message from the Internet company that is using:
    a) viral marketing
    b) interactive marketing
    c) individualized marketing
    d) brand spiraling
(c; Moderate; p. 428)

175) Marketing messages attached to e-mails and sent by individuals to their friends is called:
    a) interactive marketing
    b) cyberbranding
    c) viral marketing
    d) brand spiraling
(c; Moderate; p. 428)

176) Viral marketing is:
    a) the use of non-traditional media to promote a companies Web site
    b) a form of interactive marketing
    c) preparing an ad tied to an e-mail containing an endorsement
    d) using a virus to spread a marketing message
(c; Moderate; p. 428)

177) Viral marketing relies on:
    a) a series of click-throughs
    b) use of FAQs
    c) highly visible banners
    d) word-of-mouth communications
(d; Challenging; p. 428)

178) All of the following are clues to a poor Web site design, *except:*
    a) clueless banners
    b) slow-loading front pages
    c) too many screens
    d) too much merchandise for sale
(d; Moderate; p. 429)

Short-Answer Questions

179) What basic marketing functions can be performed on the Internet?

- Advertising
- Sales support
- Customer service
- Public relations
- E-commerce

(Easy; p. 410)

180) What are the three components of an e-commerce site?

1. A catalog
2. A shopping cart
3. A payment system

(Easy; p. 412)

181) What two consumer issues must be overcome to get them to make an on-line purchase?

Security issues and purchasing habits
(Easy; p. 412)

182) What kinds of e-commerce incentives can be offered to encourage consumers to purchase products over the Internet?

- Financially-based incentives
- Convenience-based incentives
- Value-based incentives

(Easy; p. 413)

183) What IMC activities are related to Internet programs?

- Branding and brand loyalty
- Sales support
- Customer service
- Consumer promotions

(Moderate; p. 419)

184) What is brand spiraling?

The practice of using traditional media to promote and attract consumers to a Web site.
(Easy; p. 422)

185) How can the Internet be used to provide sales support for a company's sales force?

- Provide information about clients and prospects
- Provide information about products that a salesperson can relay to a potential buyer
- Provide past purchase history of current customers
- Provide information on a prospect's organization

(Challenging; p. 425)

186) What is interactive marketing?

Using the Internet to individualize and personalize Internet Web content and e-mail messages.
(Easy; p. 428)

187) What is viral marketing?

Preparing an advertisement that is tied to e-mail.
(Easy; p. 428)

188) What design issues can lead to poor Web sites?

- Clueless banners
- A slow-loading front page
- Forcing people to go through numerous screens
- Too much verbal information
- Too many technical terms
- Hard to navigate sites

(Challenging; p. 430)

CHAPTER 14
IMC FOR SMALL BUSINESSES AND
ENTREPRENEURIAL VENTURES

True-False Questions

1)   The Pasta House Co. has essentially stayed the same, as a small, single unit business.
     (False; Easy; p. 436)

2)   The Pasta House Company's frequency program is similar to a McDonald's gift certificate because the Pasta House's frequency coupon can be redeemed at any location.
     (False; Challenging; p. 436)

3)   All small businesses and new ventures are essentially the same.
     (False; Easy; p. 438)

4)   An entrepreneurship is a company being formed with the express goal of aggressive growth.
     (True; Easy; p. 438)

5)   A corporate spin-off or start up is an intrepreneurship.
     (True; Easy; p. 438)

6)   The Pasta House Co. is an example of an intrepreneurship.
     (False; Easy; p. 438)

7)   A group of medical professionals who form a company with specific objectives, such as risk management, is known as an intrepreneurship consortium.
     (False; Challenging; p. 438)

8)   A small businesses is a family-owned or consortium of professionals company with the express goal of aggressive growth.
     (False; Easy; p. 438)

9)   A set of physicians who decide to open a group practice in one location are creating a small business.
     (True; Moderate; p. 438)

10)   The difference between a small business and an entrepreneurship is that the small business has a goal of rapid growth.
     (False; Moderate; p. 438)

11) One of the first major challenges to a small business is that it is unknown in the marketplace.
(True; Easy; p. 439)

12) Customers that worry about buying from a new vendor (or purchase risk) is not typically a major problem facing a new company.
(False; Easy; p. 439)

13) A major obstacle to overcome for a new business venture is the massive amount of marketing clutter that all companies face.
(True; Moderate; p. 439)

14) To overcome the challenges facing a new, startup business, companies must develop a quality product at price that is lower than the competition.
(False; Moderate; p. 439)

15) In promoting a new company to consumers or other businesses, it is important to remember that potential customers are interested in benefits of the good or service, not attributes.
(True; Challenging; p. 439)

16) Finding a target market for a new small business requires a match of consumer needs, goods or services, and finding a unique niche.
(True; Moderate; p. 440)

17) One key to defining consumer needs for a new business is to understand which desirable good or service is not currently available to a specific group.
(True; Moderate; p. 440)

18) VIPdesk succeeded, in part, because company leaders were able to identify an unmet need, a concierge service which could be offered over the Internet.
(True; Moderate; p. 440)

19) In the market analysis, understanding and defining consumer needs must go beyond demographic information to include psychographic and purchasing behavior information.
(True; Moderate; p. 440)

20) Once a product has been clearly defined, it is important to create a brand name, logo, and other word-based marketing elements such as the company's slogan and advertising tag line.
(True; Moderate; p. 441)

21) Finding a market niche is also known as having a unique selling position.
(True; Easy; p. 441)

22) When the goal of a company is to find a way to stand alone in the marketplace, the company is seeking to identify a unique selling position.
(True; Moderate; p. 441)

23) The best way to develop a unique selling position is to compete with price.
(False; Moderate; p. 441)

24) When a child psychologist advertises that she specializes in cases of children who have experienced trauma or stress, her organization has established a unique selling position.
(True; Challenging; p. 441)

25) A company that cannot fund a highly developed market research program should examine the market for comparable goods or those sold by comparable companies.
(True; Moderate; p. 443)

26) Marketing to ethnic populations by small businesses is on the decline.
(False; Moderate; p. 443)

27) Creating a low-cost creative method to reach customers is called guerilla marketing.
(False; Easy; p. 443)

28) Guerilla marketing involves using traditional marketing tools to reach consumers with a controversial message.
(False; Easy; p. 443)

29) Guerilla marketing is a marketing method or tactic rather than an entire mindset.
(False; Moderate; p. 443)

30) Traditional marketing is more likely to require imagination and energy where guerilla marketing identifies success using sales as a measure.
(False; Challenging; p. 444)

31) The key to using a trade show to build a new business is to clearly define the goal of the trade show and follow up on any leads that are generated.
(True; Moderate; p. 445)

32) A major concern in using sponsorships for a small business is finding one that matches the company's target market.
(False; Challenging; p. 445)

33) Public relations programs are often closely tied to sponsorships.
(True; Moderate; p. 445)

34) Finding grass roots contact points, such as rock concerts, garage sales or car races, is known as lifestyle marketing.
(True; Easy; p. 446)

35) Lifestyle marketing is different from guerilla marketing because guerilla marketing does not include special events or shows.
(False; Moderate; p. 446)

36) A new fertilizer featured in a booth at a farmer's market is an example of advocate marketing.
(False; Challenging; p. 446)

37) A traditional method of helping customers reach a company is to have easy to locate and remember telephone number.
(True; Moderate; p. 446)

38) Networking is making contacts with local people to build bonds in the community.
(True; Easy; p. 447)

39) Coupons, samples, price discounts, referral discounts, free first consultations, and money-back guarantees are all ways reduce purchase risk for small businesses.
(True; Easy; p. 447)

40) A new restaurant offering $3.00 off coupon for a meal is attempting to reduce purchase risk.
(True; Moderate; p. 447)

41) Once a customer has made an initial visit, the focus of the small business should shift to repeat or return business.
(True; Moderate; p.   448)

42) Return or repeat business is vital to the long-term growth and survival of a small business.
(True; Easy; p. 448)

43) When a small business or entrepreneur venture is new, the objective of advertising should be to persuade consumers to try the new business.
(False; Challenging; p. 448)

44) Television advertising is the medium of choice for small business owners because of the ability to reach a highly defined target market.
(False; Moderate; p. 448)

45) For small businesses that want to utilize television for advertising, purchasing rotating cable spots is a cheaper than purchasing prime time network slots.
(True; Easy; p. 448)

46) One method small retailers can use to gain greater exposure from advertising dollars is to explore cooperative advertising programs with manufacturers.
(True; Moderate; p. 449)

47) Radio advertising can be relatively low cost, especially when a local DJ reads the copy.
(True; Moderate; p. 449)

48) One advantage radio advertising has is that people can transfer an affinity for a DJ to positive feelings toward a company.
(True; Moderate; p. 449)

49) The most expensive radio advertising time is during prime driving time during the morning and late afternoon hours.
(True; Moderate; p. 449)

50) For a local business with limited advertising dollars to spend, radio will allow for better targeting of an ad than would local cable television.
(True; Challenging; p. 449)

51) Newspaper advertising is normally more expensive than radio or television, but is still a vital medium for many local businesses.
(True; Moderate; p. 449)

52) For a small local business, the best medium for reaching a local geographic area is local cable television.
(False; Challenging; p. 449)

53) Newspapers is an excellent medium for a local, small business whose target market is older individuals.
(True; Challenging; p. 449)

54) Magazines are widely used to market small businesses.
(False; Challenging; p. 449)

55) Billboard advertising features a low cost per thousand exposures (CPM) along with long-term exposure.
(True; Challenging; p. 449)

56) Buying a rotating billboard advertising package allows a local company to be featured throughout a local area.
(True; Moderate; p. 449)

57)   The use of Internet advertising by local businesses is increasing.
      (True; Moderate; p. 450)

58)   A consumer who is loyal to a small business and provides word-of-mouth
      endorsements for that firm is known as an advocate.
      (True; Easy; p. 450)

59)   Database management in order to make advocates out of customers does not work
      in a small business due to the cost involved.
      (False; Easy; p. 450)

60)   If the rule of thumb that 80 percent of business comes from 20 percent of a
      company's customers, then database management can be extremely helpful in
      building loyalty in that 20 percent.
      (True; Moderate; p. 450)

61)   One of the major benefits of a database for a small business is the ability to create
      more effective ads and related marketing material.
      (False; Moderate; p. 451)

62)   According to the Direct Marketing Association, one dollar spent on direct-mail
      results in about $10 in sales.
      (True; Challenging; p. 451)

63)   Follow-up telephone calls after a direct mail almost always provides positive
      results and is an excellent method of increasing sales and developing stronger
      relationships with customers.
      (False; Challenging; p. 451)

64)   Personal selling can be emphasized by making sure employees know customer
      names and preferences, which may help turn a customer into an advocate.
      (True; Moderate; p. 451)

65)   The only useful form of consumer promotion for a small business is to distribute
      coupons.
      (False; Moderate; p. 451)

Multiple-Choice Questions

66) The Pasta House Company builds loyalty among its customers using:
    a) a frequent diner program
    b) price discounts
    c) market research
    d) guerilla marketing
(a; Challenging; p. 436)

67) When the Pasta House Company gives a coupon for free food following previous purchases, it is an example of:
    a) neighborhood marketing
    b) a frequency program
    c) incentive purchasing
    d) company altruism
(b; Moderate; p. 436)

68) A company that is formed with the express goal of becoming larger through aggressive growth is:
    a) an entrepreneurial venture
    b) an intrepreneurship
    c) a small business
    d) lifestyle marketing
(a; Easy; p. 438)

69) The type of business that is most oriented to aggressive growth is a(n):
    a) entrepreneurship
    b) intrepreneurship
    c) small business
    d) a corporate spin-off
(a; Moderate; p. 438)

70) The Pasta House Company has expanded to more than 20 locations, which is an example of:
    a) an entrepreneurial venture
    b) an intrepreneurship
    c) a small business
    d) lifestyle marketing
(a; Moderate; p. 438)

71) A corporate spinoff or start up is called:
    a) an entrepreneurship
    b) an intrepreneurship
    c) corporate altruism
    d) vertical integration
(b; Easy; p. 438)

72) Genuity.com is a wireless phone and Internet service started by a long-distance carrier, making it:
   a) an entrepreneurial venture
   b) an intrepreneurship
   c) a small business
   d) a takeover or merger

(b; Moderate; p. 438)

73) A family-owned dry cleaners that has no intention of expanding to any more locations is:
   a) an entrepreneurship
   b) intrepreneurship
   c) a small business
   d) guerilla marketing

(c; Moderate; p. 438)

74) A family-owned car dealership passed from father to son is an example of:
   a) entrepreneurship
   b) intrepreneurship
   c) a small business
   d) a spin-off

(c; Moderate; p. 438)

75) The type of business that is most oriented to providing steady income for the owner is a(n):
   a) entrepreneurship
   b) intrepreneurship
   c) small business
   d) a corporation

(c; Challenging; p. 438)

76) A common denominator for all new businesses is that they:
   a) all seek aggressive growth
   b) all try to provide a solid income for the owners
   c) are all unknown in the marketplace
   d) rarely experience purchase risk

(c; Challenging; p. 439)

77) All of the following are typical challenges to a new small business, *except:*
   a) offering goods and services that are in demand
   b) advertising and promotional clutter
   c) small budgets for marketing and advertising
   d) consumers who are not aware of the company

(a; Challenging; p. 439)

78) All of the following are typical problems for new businesses, *except:*
   a) strong brand equity
   b) advertising and promotional clutter
   c) consumers who are cautious of the new good or service
   d) worries about negative word of mouth
   (a; Moderate; p. 439)

79) In promoting a new company, it is important to remember:
   a) pricing is critical for initial success
   b) advertising is essential to build brand awareness and move the brand name into the evoked set of consumers
   c) customers are interested in benefits of a good or service, not the attributes
   d) the IMC plan should include non-traditional media to overcome clutter
   (c; Challenging; p. 439)

80) A market analysis for a new business consists of defining consumer needs, creating a clearly defined product, and:
   a) developing a unique market niche
   b) finding financing
   c) hiring employees
   d) paying taxes
   (a; Easy; p. 439)

81) The first step in starting a new company or business is to:
   a) develop a detailed integrated marketing plan
   b) obtain appropriate financing to support the new business
   c) identify the company's mission and objectives
   d) conduct a market analysis
   (d; Moderate; p. 439)

82) A market analysis includes all of the following, *except:*
   a) understand and define consumer needs
   b) develop a unique market niche
   c) establish a plan to locate customers
   d) establish a clearly defined product
   (c; Challenging; p. 439)

83) One key for a small business owner to understand and define consumer needs is to:
   a) spend time in a corporate setting first
   b) ignore demographics and concentrate on psychological tendencies
   c) identify what a particular group desires that is not currently available
   d) ignore consumer names and concentrate on demographics
   (c; Moderate; p. 440)

84) In the market analysis, understanding and defining consumer needs should include all of the following *except:*
   a) demographic characteristics
   b) psychological tendencies
   c) benefits which have not been previously obtainable
   d) what brands consumers purchase now

(d; Challenging; p. 440)

85) When creating a clearly defined product component of the market analysis, a new business owner should focus on a product's:
   a) compatibility
   b) benefits
   c) features
   d) flexibility

(b; Challenging; p. 440)

86) In terms of a clearly defined company name, the name below that is the least defined in terms of what the company does would be:
   a) Acme Products
   b) Champion Dry Cleaners
   c) Margie's Herbal Shoppe
   d) Computer Solutions

(a; Moderate; p. 440)

87) The Pasta House Company is a better name for a new business than Geeks on Call because:
   a) people like pasta more than geeks
   b) Geeks on Call suggests a 24/7 service
   c) Pasta House creates a clearer perception of what the company offers
   d) one is more creative than the other

(c; Moderate; p. 441)

88) In choosing a name for a new business, if a name is chosen, such as Geeks on Call, that does not clearly tell consumers what product is being sold, the company will:
   a) expend extra effort in defining the business so customers will know what is being sold
   b) need to develop a memorable tagline
   c) develop a more precisely defined market niche
   d) spend more money on consumer promotions to encourage customers to try the product

(a; Challenging; p. 441)

89) In developing a unique market niche component of the market analysis, USP stands for:
   a) unified sales position
   b) unusual service place
   c) unidentified safe property
   d) unique selling position
   (d; Easy; p. 441)

90) Developing a unique market niche is also known as having a:
   a) unified sales position
   b) unusual service place
   c) unidentified safe property
   d) unique selling position
   (d; Easy; p. 441)

91) A feature, which allows a newly formed company to stand alone and be distinct, is a:
   a) form of marketing myopia
   b) entrepreneurship by-line
   c) individualized selling place
   d) unique selling position
   (d; Easy; p. 441)

92) VIPdesk, a wireless concierge service, has a:
   a) brand recognition problem
   b) unique selling position
   c) corporate competitor advantage
   d) economies of scale problem
   (b; Moderate; p. 441)

93) Small business owners must match a market niche with:
   a) a large demographic population
   b) consumer needs for the good or service
   c) reducing purchase risk
   d) past purchasing patterns of heavy users
   (b; Easy; p. 441)

94) After the market analysis, a firm should create an IMC Plan that includes all of the following, *except:*
   a) locating customers
   b) making it easy for customers to reach the new company
   c) preparing a web site
   d) reducing purchase risk for customers
   (c; Moderate; p. 442)

95) One of the fast-growing market segments is:
   a) ethnic markets
   b) teenagers
   c) women
   d) Caucasians
(a; Moderate p. 443)

96) Using Spanish-speaking endorsers in advertisements for a company targeting Hispanics is an example of:
   a) lifestyle marketing
   b) guerilla marketing
   c) personalizing the product and message
   d) a generic appeal
(c; Moderate; p. 443)

97) For small businesses to effectively reach ethnic target markets, Ken Greenberg of AC Nielsen offers all of the following suggestions, *except:*
   a) hire an ethnic advertising or marketing firm to produce the marketing materials
   b) create or participate in special ethnic events
   c) utilize ethnic media
   d) review all marketing materials to make sure they are relevant and not offensive
(a; Challenging; p. 443)

98) Using low-cost, creative strategies to reach customers is known as:
   a) traditional marketing
   b) incentive marketing
   c) media planning
   d) guerilla marketing
(d; Easy; p. 443)

99) The concept of guerilla marketing was created by:
   a) Jay Livingstone
   b) Conrad Hilton
   c) the Marlboro company and Philip Morris
   d) Jay Conrad Levinson
(d; Challenging; p. 443)

100) A paintball "cat shoot" (at a painting of a cat) designed to raise funds for the local humane society while attracting attention and customers, is an example of:
   a) guerilla marketing
   b) lifestyle marketing
   c) brand recognition development
   d) poor marketing judgment due to alienating customers
(a; Moderate; p. 443)

101) Of the following marketing tactics, the one that is *least* likely to be considered a guerilla marketing tactic would be:
   a) radio spots during drive time
   b) participation in a local trade show
   c) involvement in local sponsorships
   d) use of alternative media
(a; Challenging; p. 444)

102) The goal of guerilla marketing is to find:
   a) new ways to reach consumers with a marketing message
   b) unique, unusual ways to reach consumers with a marketing message
   c) ways to reach consumers with a unique message that will cause them to take notice
   d) the lowest cost methods of marketing that effectively reach the target market
(c; Challenging; p. 444)

103) A new business owner who tries to obliterate the competition and generate sales through advertising expenditures is using:
   a) traditional marketing
   b) guerilla marketing
   c) safe marketing tactics
   d) lifestyle marketing
(a; Moderate; p. 444)

104) Which is associated with traditional marketing rather than guerilla marketing?
   a) measure success by sales
   b) measure success by profits
   c) based on psychology and human behavior
   d) aims messages at individuals and small groups
(a; Moderate; p. 444)

105) Which is associated with guerilla marketing rather than traditional marketing?
   a) measure success by sales
   b) grows by adding customers
   c) grows through existing customers and referrals
   d) aims messages at large groups
(c; Challenging, p. 444)

106) All of the following concepts are associated with guerilla marketing, *except:*
   a) requires energy and imagination
   b) designed to obliterate the competition
   c) aims messages at individuals and small groups
   d) "you marketing," based on how we can help "you"
(b; Challenging; p. 444)

107) Guerilla marketing is:
   a) the best method for locating customers for a small business
   b) not so much a method of marketing as a mentality or approach to marketing
   c) a method a small business can use to obliterate the competition
   d) based on a database marketing foundation
(b; Challenging; p. 444)

108) Typical goals for trade shows include all of the following, *except:*
   a) generating leads
   b) setting prices for the upcoming year
   c) introducing a new good or service
   d) generating awareness of the company
(b; Challenging; p. 445)

109) The primary objective of a small business sponsorship program should be to:
   a) reach a wide audience
   b) make sure the right people are exposed to the company
   c) eliminate expenses
   d) create brand parity
(b; Moderate; p. 445)

110) T-shirt and baseball cap giveaways, ads on mall kiosks, and billboards on little league baseball parks are places for:
   a) magazine advertising
   b) alternative media advertising
   c) public relations programs
   d) buyer incentives programs
(b; Moderate; p. 446)

111) A local real estate company gives away T-shirts featuring the realtor every time a piece of property is sold. This is an example of:
   a) magazine advertising
   b) alternative media advertising
   c) public relations programs
   d) buyer incentives programs
(b; Moderate; p. 446)

112) Finding grass-roots contact points for potential customers is known as:
   a) traditional advertising
   b) lifestyle marketing
   c) advocate programs
   d) billboards
(b; Easy; p. 446)

113) In terms of guerilla marketing, which of the following is an excellent method of reaching customers and also an excellent method for customers to reach the company?
    a) traditional advertising
    b) lifestyle marketing
    c) advocate programs
    d) billboards
(b; Moderate; p. 446)

114) Setting up a booth at a farmer's market or bluegrass festival to sell a related product is an example of:
    a) traditional advertising
    b) lifestyle marketing
    c) advocate programs
    d) billboards
(b; Moderate; p. 446)

115) When a new music store distributes literature and free key chains at a rock concert, the group is engaging in:
    a) lifestyle marketing
    b) an illegal act
    c) a sponsorship program
    d) public relations' activities
(a; Challenging; p. 446)

116) A furniture store setting up a special display of massage chairs at a little league baseball tournament is an example of:
    a) generating leads
    b) developing a unique market niche
    c) lifestyle marketing
    d) creating a clearly defined product
(c; Challenging; p. 446)

117) When Flip Records gives free tapes of new music to people in specialty stores, tattoo parlors, and at rock concerts, the firm is using:
    a) an incentive program
    b) targeted give-aways
    c) lifestyle marketing tactics
    d) traditional marketing tactics
(c; Moderate; p. 446)

118) Traditional methods for helping customers reach a small business include all of the following, *except:*
   a) telephone calls
   b) mail
   c) in-store visits
   d) networking

(d; Moderate; p. 446)

119) A traditional method for helping customers reach a small business is:
   a) an Internet ad
   b) having a phone number such as: 781-AUTO
   c) attending a farmer's market
   d) attending a rock concert

(b; Moderate; p. 446)

120) Attending a Chamber of Commerce meeting to find new customers is an example of:
   a) intrusive connections
   b) lifestyle marketing
   c) networking
   d) traditional marketing

(c; Easy; p. 447)

121) An attorney who is willing to give a speech about legal rights at a Rotary Club meeting and then speak with individual members of a Kiwanis club meeting is engaging in:
   a) guerilla marketing
   b) networking
   c) a sponsorship program
   d) proactive target marketing

(b; Challenging; p. 447)

122) When a customer talks to a business about the firm's products at a booth setup during a local job fair, the customer is reaching the company through:
   a) traditional methods
   b) networking
   c) lifestyle marketing
   d) brand spiraling

(c; Challenging; p. 447)

123)   A new or small business using coupons, samples, price discounts and free first visits are examples of:
    a) reducing purchasing risk
    b) expensive marketing programs small business cannot afford
    c) lifestyle marketing
    d) guerilla marketing
(a; Easy; p. 447)

124)   A small business or new business can reduce purchase risk using all of the following methods, *except:*
    a) samples
    b) coupons
    c) price discounts
    d) advertising
(d; Easy; p. 447)

125)   After a customer makes an initial visit, the focus of a new or small business should shift to:
    a) developing brand awareness
    b) developing brand equity
    c) discouraging word-of-mouth communications
    d) encouraging repeat or return business
(d; Moderate; p. 448)

126)   Because small businesses have limited advertising dollars to spend, a major temptation that is often seen in ads is:
    a) no color, only black and white
    b) using a local ad agency that has little experience in creating ads
    c) developing only one ad is using it too long
    d) putting too much information into the ad so it becomes cluttered
(d; Challenging; p. 448)

127)   For a new business that is relatively unknown, the primary objective of advertising should be to:
    a) generate leads
    b) create brand awareness
    c) persuade consumers to choose the new business
    d) remind consumers where the business is located
(b; Challenging; p. 448)

128)   One problems with television advertising for small business is:
    a) relatively high costs of ad time
    b) too many local television stations in most markets
    c) ad slots are already pre-sold
    d) cost of producing a local television ad
(a; Moderate; p. 448)

129) In terms of television advertising, the best option for a small business is:
   a) network television
   b) prime time television, but local
   c) rotated cable spots
   d) ignoring television and using other media
(c; Moderate; p. 448)

130) One problems with television advertising that small business tend to do is:
   a) too much information crammed into the ad
   b) poor grammar in taglines
   c) imprecise messages
   d) naming the competitor in the ad
(a; Moderate; p. 448)

131) One method retailers can use to increase the number of ads without spending additional dollars is to:
   a) purchase rotating cable spots
   b) say as much as possible in the ad about every company feature
   c) engage in cooperative advertising when possible
   d) name the competitor in the ad
(c; Moderate; p. 449)

132) For small, local businesses, radio:
   a) is normally more expensive than television
   b) national advertising time is readily available
   c) spots can be prepared at a relatively low cost
   d) offers special discounts to local businesses
(c; Easy; p. 449)

133) The best time for a radio spot for a small business, funds permitting, is:
   a) rotated
   b) drive time
   c) mid evening
   d) late evening
(b; Moderate; p. 449)

134) The best time for a radio spot for a small business, called drive time, takes place:
   a) mornings between 7:00 a.m. and 9:00 a.m.
   b) early afternoon, after lunch time
   c) mid evening, between 7:00 p.m. and 9:00 p.m.
   d) late evening, after midnight
(a; Moderate; p. 449)

135) The best time for a radio spot for a small business, called drive time, takes place:
    a) early afternoon, after lunch time
    b) mid to late afternoon, 4:00 p.m. to 7:00 p.m.
    c) mid evening, between 7:00 p.m. and 9:00 p.m.
    d) late evening, after midnight
(b; Moderate; p. 449)

136) Advertising in newspapers is most advisable for a small business with a(n):
    a) teenage target market
    b) Generation X target market
    c) ethnic target market
    d) baby boomer target market
(d; Challenging; p. 449)

137) Newspaper advertising will likely be the most effective for a small business when:
    a) full page ads are used
    b) the ad is on Sunday or Wednesday
    c) the ad defines clearly the new product or businesses USP
    d) the ad is tied to a consumer promotion and encourages consumer action
(d; Challenging; p. 449)

138) Of the following mediums, the one that is the *least* effective medium for advertising for a small, local businesses is:
    a) radio
    b) billboard
    c) Internet
    d) magazines
(d; Moderate; p. 449)

139) Low CPM and long-term exposure for a small business can be accomplished using:
    a) newspapers
    b) the radio
    c) billboards
    d) magazines
(c; Moderate; p. 449)

140) The local businesses, which medium an excellent method of building brand awareness as well as informing local consumers where the business is located?
    a) the newspaper
    b) radio
    c) billboards
    d) magazines
(c; Challenging; p. 449)

141) One successful key to Internet advertising for a local company is:
   a) create quality pop-up ads
   b) tie-in the Internet with coupons
   c) create links through the Chamber of Commerce or local visitor's bureau
   d) ignore it, Internet advertising doesn't work locally
   (c; Moderate; p. 450)

142) A customer advocate is:
   a) a person who is loyal to a business and draws others through word of mouth
   b) the company's attorney
   c) another name for a creative designing a small business ad
   d) a small business owner
   (a; Easy; p. 450)

143) A person who is loyal to a business and draws others through word of mouth is a(n):
   a) advocate
   b) adventurer
   c) first user
   d) liability reducer
   (a; Easy; p. 450)

144) Methods that can be used by a small business to keep customers and turn them into advocates include all of the following, *except:*
   a) database management
   b) public relations
   c) direct marketing
   d) personal selling
   (b; Challenging; p. 450)

145) Methods that can be used by a small business to keep customers and turn them into advocates include all of the following, *except:*
   a) trade and consumer promotions
   b) advertising
   c) direct marketing
   d) personal selling
   (b; Challenging; p. 450)

146) Database management, direct marketing, and quality personal selling has the potential to turn customers into:
   a) advocates
   b) allies
   c) endorsers
   d) experts
   (a; Moderate; p. 450)

147) For a new startup business, the most cost-effective method of keeping customers and turning them into advocates is through:
   a) database management
   b) direct marketing
   c) consumer promotions
   d) personal selling
(a; Challenging; p. 450)

148) All of the following statements about direct marketing are true, *except:*
   a) According to the Direct Marketing Association, each dollar spent on direct marketing yields $10.00 in sales.
   b) Direct marketing should begin with defining the goals of the program and then specifying an audience.
   c) Direct marketing is rarely viable for small businesses due to the large expense.
   d) The principles that guide direct-mail campaigns are also useful for e-mail, telephone, and fax campaigns.
(c; Challenging; p. 451)

149) Creating advocates includes database management, direct marketing, and:
   a) market research
   b) networking
   c) collective bargaining
   d) personal selling
(d; Moderate; p. 451)

150) Coupons, contests and sweepstakes, free samples and refunds are all examples of which program that can be used by small businesses to turn customers into advocates?
   a) consumer promotions
   b) networking
   c) database marketing
   d) personal selling
(a; Moderate; p. 451)

151) In regard to small businesses, all of the following statements concerning trade and consumer promotions are true, *except:*
   a) They include using specialty advertising, such as pens or calendars, to increase consumer recognition and loyalty.
   b) Trade promotions are not effective for small manufacturers.
   c) They are most effective when tied to a database program in some way.
   d) They should reflect the firm's image and position.
(b; Moderate; p. 451)

Short-Answer Questions

152) Name and describe the three most common forms of small business.

1. Entrepreneurship in which a company is being formed with the express goal of becoming larger through an aggressive growth agenda.
2. Intrepreneurship, which is a corporate spinoff or start up.
3. A small business, which is normally family owned, or is a consortium of professionals with specific goals in mind.

(Moderate; p. 438)

153) What are the common challenges new businesses face?

- Consumers who are not aware of the company
- Consumers who are cautious or wary of trying a new product, service or company
- Advertising and promotional clutter
- Small budgets for marketing, advertising, and promotional activities
- They are the most vulnerable to negative word of mouth

(Moderate; p. 439)

154) What are the three steps in analyzing a market?

1. Understand and define consumer needs
2. Establish a clearly defined good or service
3. Develop a unique market niche

(Easy; p. 439)

155) What is a unique selling position (USP)?

Some feature which allows a newly formed company to stand out and be distinct from other competitors.
(Easy; p. 441)

156) What three activities are crucial parts of an IMC plan for a new small business?

1. Locating customers
2. Making it easy for customers to reach the new company
3. Reducing purchase risk for customers

(Moderate; p. 442)

157) What is guerilla marketing? How is it different from traditional marketing?

Guerilla marketing is focusing on low-cost, creative strategies to reach the right people.

It is different from traditional marketing because the company uses energy and imagination; measures success through profits rather than sales; bases efforts on psychology and human behavior rather than experience; seeks growth through existing customers and referrals rather than by simply trying to add customers; aims messages at targeted, rather than large groups; and focuses on the customer rather than the company. Primary places to implement guerilla tactics include trade shows, sponsorship programs, public relations' programs, and by using alternative media.
(Challenging; p. 443)

158) What is lifestyle marketing?

It is a form of guerilla marketing. The goal is to locate customers in targeted places of interest that reflect their lifestyles, such as bluegrass festivals, farmers' markets, stock car races, 5k runs, and other identifiable activities.
(Moderate; p. 446

159) How can customers reach a new small business?

- Through traditional methods such as a telephone, Internet or mail address
- By managers networking in the community
- Through lifestyle marketing
- With interactions on a Web site
(Moderate; p. 446)

160) What methods are available to help a new business reduce purchase risk?

- Samples
- Coupons
- Price discounts
- Referral discounts
- Free first consultation visits
- Money-back guarantees
(Moderate; p. 447)

161) How is the Internet used in marketing a new small business?

The Internet should link the company's site to places such as the Chamber of Commerce page, city home page or visitor's bureau. All other advertisements and marketing activities should mention the company's Web site and address.
(Moderate; p. 450)

CHAPTER 15
EVALUATING AN INTEGRATED MARKETING PROGRAM

True-False Questions

1) Pretesting is normally not a cost effective method of preparing an advertisement.
    (False; Easy; p. 458)

2) In terms of a rocket analogy, correcting an advertisement in the latter stages of development is less time consuming and less costly than in the early stages of development.
    (False; Easy; p. 458)

3) When studying marketing effectiveness, the two main types of evaluation techniques are message evaluations and respondent behavior evaluations.
    (True; Easy; p. 460)

4) Messages evaluations primarily deal with visible company actions, such as making store visits.
    (False; Easy; p. 460)

5) Message evaluation programs assess both cognitive and affective components of attitude towards an ad.
    (True; Moderate; p. 460)

6) When studying marketing effectiveness, evaluation techniques that study messages are numbers-based.
    (False; Easy; p. 460)

7) Respondent behavior evaluations primarily deal with customer actions and outcomes, such as making store visits.
    (True; Easy; p. 460)

8) The method of evaluating a marketing piece should match the IMC objective for that marketing piece.
    (True; Easy; p. 460)

9) When studying marketing effectiveness, short term outcomes such as increases in sales or redemption rates are the only relevant criteria.
    (False; Moderate; p. 460)

10) Evaluating advertising and other marketing communication venues is difficult because of extraneous factors that can impact the results of the marketing communication.
    (True; Easy; p. 461)

11) Evaluation or testing of advertising communications can occur at any stage of the development process.
(True; Easy; p. 462)

12) A storyboard is a series of pictures providing an overview of the structure of a television ad.
(True; Easy; p. 462)

13) In terms of message evaluation techniques, concept testing occurs prior to the development of the ad.
(True; Challenging; p. 462)

14) In terms of message evaluation techniques, copytesting occurs prior to the development of the ad.
(False; Challenging; p. 462)

15) In terms of message evaluation techniques, recall tests occur primarily after the ad has been launched.
(True; Challenging; p. 462)

16) In terms of message evaluation techniques, recognition tests occur after the ad has been launched.
(True; Challenging; p. 462)

17) In terms of message evaluation techniques, attitude and opinion tests occur primarily after the ad has been launched.
(False; Challenging; p. 462)

18) In terms of message evaluation techniques, emotional reaction tests are typically used anytime during or after the ad have been developed.
(True; Challenging; p. 462)

19) In terms of message evaluation techniques, physiological tests are typically used anytime during or after the ad have been developed.
(True; Challenging; p. 462)

20) In terms of message evaluation techniques, persuasion analysis tests are used before an ad is developed.
(False; Challenging; p. 462)

21) Most market researchers employ more than one method of evaluation to make sure the findings are as accurate as possible.
(True; Moderate; p. 462)

22) Concept testing examines the proposed content of an advertisement and the impact that content may have on potential customers.
(True; Easy; p. 462)

23) Concept testing is important because the average cost of developing a national 30-second television ad is now over $300,000.
(True; Challenging; p. 463)

24) The most common procedure used for concept testing is in-depth interviews.
(False; Challenging; p. 463)

25) Focus groups are normally made up of 8 to 10 people who are representative of a target market.
(True; Easy; p. 463)

26) Focus groups are so reliable that it ordinarily only takes one good session to gain a solid understanding of how a communication will be viewed.
(False; Moderate; p. 463)

27) Two common testing approaches used in concept testing are comprehension tests and awareness tests.
(False; Challenging; p. 463)

28) A copytest is used when the marketing piece is finished or is in the final stages of development.
(True; Easy; p. 463)

29) A portfolio test is a display of television ads in a theater.
(False; Easy; p. 464)

30) A portfolio test is often used for copytesting.
(True; Moderate; p. 464)

31) A theater test is a display of television ads shown together in a theater.
(True; Easy; p. 464)

32) A theater test can be used to study a print ad from a billboard or the side of a bus.
(False; Challenging; p. 464)

33) When people at a shopping mall are stopped and shown an ad or coupon, a mall intercept technique is being used.
(True; Moderate; p. 464)

34) Copytesting is practically universally accepted due to its ability to incite creativity.
(False; Moderate; p. 464)

35)	While some marketing professionals do not favor copytesting, the majority think it is necessary because without it, creativity is stifled.
	(False; Challenging; p. 464)

36)	Because of the issue of accountability, agencies continue to use copytesting although many feel it may not be a good method of evaluating ads.
	(True; Challenging; p. 464)

37)	When someone is asked to remember if an ad was seen during the previous week, a recognition test is being used.
	(False; Moderate; p. 465)

38)	When someone is asked to remember if an ad was seen during the previous week, a recall test is being used.
	(True; Moderate; p. 465)

39)	In testing advertising effectiveness, DAR stands for day-after recall.
	(True; Easy; p. 465)

40)	When a person is given prompts or memory jogs during a test of recall, it is an unaided recall test.
	(False; Easy; p. 465)

41)	Unaided recall tests work best at identifying the times when an ad has been lodged in a person's memory.
	(True; Challenging; p. 465)

42)	Most researchers believe the unaided recall approach is superior to other evaluative tests.
	(True; Challenging; p. 465)

43)	Often researchers begin with aided recall tests, and then proceed to unaided recall tests and even to recognition tests.
	(False; Challenging; p. 465)

44)	When a subject provides incorrect information about the recall of an ad, the test is immediately stopped.
	(False; Moderate; p. 465)

45)	A person with a positive attitude toward advertising is more likely to recall ads.
	(True; Moderate; p. 466)

46)	An advertisement that mentions a brand name five times during the commercial usually will receive higher recall scores than ads where the brand name is mentioned only twice.
	(True; Moderate; p. 466)

47) If a person uses a brand regularly, he or she is more likely to remember an ad in either an aided recall or unaided recall test than if he or she does not use the particular brand.
(True; Easy; p. 466)

48) Institutional ads tend to have higher recall scores than brand ads because it is easier to remember a company's name.
(False; Challenging; p. 466)

49) Older people tend to more readily recall ads than do younger people.
(False; Moderate; p. 466)

50) When individuals are shown ads and asked if they seen them before, a recognition test is being used.
(True; Easy; p. 467)

51) Comprehension tests are designed to see if subjects recall seeing a marketing piece in the past 24 hours.
(False; Moderate; p. 467)

52) Recall tests are best suited to testing for comprehension of and reaction to ads.
(False; Challenging; p. 467)

53) Recognition tests help when the advertiser is more concerned about how the ad is received and what information is being comprehended.
(True; Moderate; p. 467)

54) Recognition tests results are influenced by a person's interest in a particular advertisement.
(True; Challenging; p. 467)

55) Large size ads are more likely to be recognized than smaller ads.
(True; Moderate; p. 468)

56) One difference between recognition scores and recalls scores is that recall scores do not decline over time.
(False; Challenging; p. 468)

57) Both recognition and recall help establish a brand in the consumer's mind.
(True; Moderate; p. 468)

58) Attitude and opinion studies may be used to evaluate sales promotion devices, such as direct mail pieces.
(True; Moderate; p. 468)

59)   Attitude and opinion tests can be used with both recall and recognition tests.
        (True; Challenging; p. 468)

60)   Open-ended questions narrow down a study to specific items the researcher
        wishes to test.
        (False; Moderate; p. 468)

61)   A warmth monitor is an alternative method of measuring emotions that does not
        involve a questionnaire-type of test.
        (True; Moderate; p. 469)

62)   Emotional reaction tests are self-reported instruments.
        (True; Easy; p. 469)

63)   Emotional reaction tests are a form of copytesting.
        (False; Challenging; p. 469)

64)   A psychogalvanometer measures a person's eye movements.
        (False; Moderate; p. 470)

65)   Someone with sweaty palms is having an emotional response to a stimulus, which
        can be measured using a psychogalvanometer.
        (True; Moderate; p. 470)

66)   A pupillometric measures a person's pupil dilation, because smaller pupils mean
        more emotion is present.
        (False; Moderate; p. 470)

67)   Psychophysiology is a brain imaging process designed to identify emotions based
        on electrical currents in the brain.
        (True; Moderate; p. 470)

68)   Of the three physiological arousal tests discussed in the text, the one with the
        most promise for the future in terms of advertising and marketing communication
        evaluations is the pupillometric test.
        (False; Challenging; p. 471)

69)   Persuasion analysis techniques require pre- and post-tests.
        (True; Moderate; p. 471)

70)   PACT stands for positioning advertising copytesting.
        (True; Moderate; p. 471)

71)   PACT was designed to assist in the evaluation of television ads.
        (True; Challenging; p. 471)

72) According to PACT, testing procedures should be relevant to the advertising objectives.
(True; Moderate; p. 472)

73) According to PACT, multiple measures should be used in the evaluation.
(True; Moderate; p. 473)

74) According to PACT, multiple exposures to an advertisement are essential to obtain accurate results.
(False; Moderate; p. 473)

75) According to PACT, tests should be conducted within laboratory settings and not in field settings.
(False; Moderate; p. 474)

76) Some marketers contend that the only valid evaluation criterion of marketing that should be used is actual sales.
(True; Easy; p. 475)

77) Measuring changes in sales following a marketing campaign is now easier than ever in the past because of Internet technology and the use of "cookies."
(False; Moderate; p. 475)

78) Scanner data makes it possible for companies to monitor sales and help both the retailer and manufacture discover the impact of a particular marketing program.
(True; Moderate; p. 475)

79) The impact of advertising is difficult to measure because consumers may change their minds concerning which brand to buy while they are in the store.
(True; Moderate; p. 476)

80) The impact of advertising is difficult to measure because often the impact is delayed.
(True; Easy; p. 476)

81) Scanner data can be used to measure the impact of a point-of-purchase display.
(True; Moderate; p. 476)

82) By using different toll free telephone numbers or different Internet URLs, a company can measure where a person saw a direct television ad or other direct marketing promotion.
(True; Challenging; p. 477)

83) For coupons, contests, sweepstakes, and other types of consumer promotions, the redemption rate is an effective method of measuring the impact.
(True; Easy; p. 478)

84) It is difficult, if not impossible, to measure redemption rates of coupons, premiums, and direct mail pieces.
(False; Easy; p. 478)

85) Test markets are a behavioral response method in which marketing on a small scale is used to predict the potential for marketing success on a larger scale.
(True; Challenging; p. 478)

86) Test markets can only be used to test the effects of price changes on sales.
(False; Moderate; p. 478)

87) One major advantage of a test market is that it resembles an actual market situation more than any of the other evaluation methods.
(True; Challenging; p. 479)

88) The biggest problem for a long test market is that the competition can more easily interfere with the test results more than if a shorter time period is used.
(False; Challenging; p. 479)

89) Scanner data makes it possible for results from a test market to become quickly available to managers.
(True; Moderate; p. 479)

90) A purchase simulation test is behavioral approach used to study how consumers end up making buying decisions.
(True; Challenging; p. 480)

91) Public relations activities can be measured by counting the number of times a company's name is mentioned in the media using a clipping service.
(True; Challenging; p. 481)

92) An alternative approach to evaluating public relations is measuring the number of impressions a company mention in a particular media achieved.
(True; Moderate; p. 481)

93) An alternative method of evaluating public relations is to evaluate the cost of the equivalent time or space an article or news item about a company occupied, as if it were paid advertising.
(True; Moderate; p. 481)

94) The least used, but best analysis of a public relations program is to make sure publicity matches the company's PR objectives.
(True; Challenging; p. 481)

95) The major problem with measuring marketing ROI is that marketers cannot agree on a definition of what constitutes ROI for marketing.
(True; Moderate; p. 482)

96) Even if marketers could agree on a definition of ROI for marketing, most marketers believe it would be difficult to measure, especially in the area of advertising.
(True; Moderate; p. 482)

97) Market share is one measure of success of an overall IMC program.
(True; Challenging; p. 482)

Multiple-Choice Questions

98) The two broad categories of evaluation tools are:
   a) message evaluations and respondent behavior evaluations
   b) pre-tests and post-tests
   c) attitude evaluations and sales evaluations
   d) cognitive evaluations and affective evaluations
(a; Moderate; p. 460)

99) An examination of a creative message and the physical design of an advertisement or other marketing communication pieces is called:
   a) respondent behavior evaluation
   b) pretesting
   c) message evaluation
   d) message synthesis
(c; Easy; p. 460)

100) An examination of visible customer actions including making store visits and purchases is called:
   a) respondent behavior evaluation
   b) pre-testing
   c) message evaluation
   d) message synthesis
(a; Easy; p. 460)

101) In terms of evaluation categories, which techniques utilize actual numbers and results of marketing communication pieces?
   a) message evaluation
   b) respondent behavior evaluation
   c) pre-test
   d) recognition evaluation
(b; Moderate; p. 460)

102) Which is an affective response to a marketing message?
    a) sales and redemption rates
    b) product specific awareness
    c) awareness of the overall company
    d) liking the company
(d; Challenging; p. 460)

103) Evaluating the impact of a marketing program by measuring a variable before and then after the program is called:
    a) pre and post test analysis
    b) change analysis
    c) side by side analysis
    d) response analysis
(a; Easy; p. 460)

104) A message evaluation can take place:
    a) when an ad is completed
    b) when an ad has been shown to the public
    c) when the campaign is complete
    d) at any stage of the development of an ad
(d; Moderate; p. 460)

105) A storyboard is used to outline the structure of:
    a) a radio ad
    b) a television ad
    c) an Internet ad
    d) print ads
(b; Easy; p. 462)

106) In terms of message evaluations, concept tests are mostly likely to be used:
    a) prior to any ad development
    b) in the final stages of ad development or with the finished ad
    c) after the ad has been launched
    d) anytime during or after ad development
(a; Challenging; p. 462)

107) In terms of message evaluations, copytesting is mostly likely to be used:
    a) prior to any ad development
    b) in the final stages of ad development or with the finished ad
    c) after the ad has been launched
    d) anytime during or after ad development
(b; Challenging; p. 462)

108) In terms of message evaluations, recall tests are mostly likely to be used:
    a) prior to any ad development
    b) in the final stages of ad development or with the finished ad
    c) after the ad has been launched
    d) anytime during or after ad development
(c; Challenging; p. 462)

109) In terms of message evaluations, recognition tests are mostly likely to be used:
    a) prior to any ad development
    b) in the final stages of ad development or with the finished ad
    c) after the ad has been launched
    d) anytime during or after ad development
(c; Challenging; p. 462)

110) In terms of message evaluations, attitude and opinion tests are mostly likely to be used:
    a) prior to any ad development
    b) in the final stages of ad development or with the finished ad
    c) after the ad has been launched
    d) anytime during or after ad development
(d; Challenging; p. 462)

111) In terms of message evaluations, emotional reaction tests are mostly likely to be used:
    a) prior to any ad development
    b) in the final stages of ad development or with the finished ad
    c) after the ad has been launched
    d) anytime during or after ad development
(d; Challenging; p. 462)

112) In terms of message evaluations, physiological tests are mostly likely to be used:
    a) prior to any ad development
    b) in the final stages of ad development or with the finished ad
    c) after the ad has been launched
    d) anytime during or after ad development
(d; Challenging; p. 462)

113) In terms of message evaluations, persuasion analysis tests are mostly likely to be used:
    a) prior to any ad development
    b) in the final stages of ad development or with the finished ad
    c) after the ad has been launched
    d) anytime during or after ad development
(c; Challenging; p. 462)

114) The proposed content of an ad and the impact the ad may have on potential customers is measured using:
   a) behavioral response models
   b) multiattribute analysis
   c) concept testing
   d) emotional testing
(c; Easy; p. 462)

115) Concept testing examines the:
   a) success of an IMC program
   b) media purchasing pattern the agency will use
   c) art in an ad
   d) proposed content of an ad and the impact of the content on potential customers
(d; Easy; p. 462)

116) The average cost of producing a 30-second national television advertisement is:
   a) $124,000
   b) $195,000
   c) $236,000
   d) $358,000
(d; Challenging; p. 463)

117) The most common procedure used for concept testing is:
   a) In-depth interviews
   b) focus groups
   c) day-after recall
   d) theater or portfolio procedures
(b; Moderate; p. 463)

118) Cajun Pizza's marketing team has a new idea for an advertising campaign. Before developing the ad, they would like to see how consumers react. The appropriate evaluation technique would be a:
   a) concept test
   b) copytest
   c) recognition test
   d) attitude or opinion test
(a; Challenging; p. 463)

119) When 8-10 people test an ad concept because they are representative of a target market, they are called a(n):
   a) pre- and post-test group
   b) review group
   c) ad content group
   d) focus group
(d; Easy; p. 463)

120)   Which component of marketing communication listed below is *not* studied using concept tests?
    a)   sales rates
    b)   the meaning of a message
    c)   a translation of an international ad
    d)   the value associated with a prize
(a; Challenging; p. 463)

121)   When participants are asked the meaning of a marketing communication piece during a concept test, the researcher is using a(n):
    a)   portfolio test
    b)   theater test
    c)   comprehension test
    d)   warmth test
(c; Moderate; p. 463)

122)   During a concept test, which would help a moderator understand why an intended message in an ad was not correctly understood by an individual or group?
    a)   a comprehension test
    b)   a reaction test
    c)   a behavioral response test
    d)   a translation test
(a; Challenging; p. 463)

123)   When participants are asked to express their overall feelings about a marketing communication piece during a concept test, the researcher is using a(n):
    a)   portfolio test
    b)   reaction test
    c)   comprehension test
    d)   warmth meter
(b; Challenging; p. 463)

124)   During a concept test, which would help a moderator understand why an intended message received a negative response?
    a)   a comprehension test
    b)   a reaction test
    c)   an analytical test
    d)   a psychogalvanometer
(b; Moderate; p. 463)

125) In a concept test, which test measures both negative and positive feelings about a marketing piece?
    a) comprehension
    b) reaction
    c) emotional
    d) recognition
(b; Challenging; p. 463)

126) When copytesting print ads, researchers often use which type of approach?
    a) portfolio test
    b) theater test
    c) regulatory test
    d) pupillometric meter
(a; Easy; p. 464)

127) When copytesting television ads, researchers often use:
    a) a portfolio test
    b) a theater test
    c) a reaction test
    d) the mall intercept technique
(b; Easy; p. 464)

128) In copytesting, researchers will sometimes stop people as they are shopping to solicit their opinion about ads. This approach is called:
    a) a portfolio test
    b) a theater test
    c) a reaction test
    d) the mall intercept technique
(d; Easy; p. 464)

129) The mall intercept technique can incorporate which copytesting procedure?
    a) warmth meter
    b) pupillometric meter
    c) psychogalvanometer
    d) portfolio test
(d; Moderate; p. 464)

130) In terms of copytesting, the current thought by the majority of agencies is that the test:
    a) is no longer needed
    b) stifles creativity
    c) is necessary primarily because of the issue of accountability
    d) is not really useful, but necessary because of demands of creatives
(c; Challenging; p. 464)

131) In terms of copytesting, all of the following criticisms have recently been voiced, *except:*
    a) copytests stifle creativity that is needed to produce ads that stand out
    b) copytests favor emotional approaches in advertising
    c) copytests tend to lead to ads about product benefits that are believable and understandable to a focus group
    d) members of focus groups know little about creativity and are not legitimate judges of creative advertising
(b; Challenging; p. 464)

132) When an individual is asked to remember what ads he or she saw in a given setting or time period, the test form is called:
    a) recall
    b) representation
    c) behavioral response
    d) attitudinal adjustment
(a; Easy; p. 465)

133) DAR stands for:
    a) Delivery of Advertising Response
    b) Data Analysis and Review
    c) Day-After Recall
    d) Data Analysis of Advertising Reactions
(c; Easy; p. 465)

134) If McDonald's marketing team wants to know the percentage of consumers remembered a new ad that was just launched on television, the appropriate test would be:
    a) DAR
    b) PACT
    c) POPAI
    d) test market
(a; Challenging; p. 465)

135) For recall tests, when consumers are asked which ads they viewed the previous evening, the form of test is:
    a) unaided recall
    b) aided recall
    c) concept modeling
    d) day-after recall
(d; Easy; p. 465)

136) For recall tests, when consumers are prompted about a product category, it is part of a(n):
   a) unaided recall test
   b) aided recall test
   c) concept testing model
   d) mall intercept technique
   (b; Easy; p. 465)

137) Aided recall tests mean that:
   a) the ad is shown to the consumer
   b) consumers are prompted about a product category
   c) the consumer may use a dictionary while studying the ads
   d) the research helps the consumer to find ads to view
   (b; Easy; p. 465)

138) Most researchers believe unaided recall tests are superior to other evaluation tests because they:
   a) demonstrate that an advertisement has become lodged in a person's memory
   b) indicate what percentage of respondents have a favorable attitude towards the brand
   c) indicate future purchase intentions
   d) note when a person is favorably disposed towards the brand
   (a; Challenging; p. 465)

139) Which of the following statements is true in both aided and unaided recall tests?
   a) Incorrect responses are important data.
   b) Older people recall ads more easily.
   c) They are used in conjunction with behavioral measures.
   d) They are less effective than other evaluative tests.
   (a; Moderate; p. 465)

140) When using recall tests, it is important to remember all of the following factors, *except:*
   a) a person's general attitude towards advertising impacts his or her recall of ads
   b) the prominence of the brand name impacts recall scores
   c) the gender of the respondent; because females tend to have higher recall scores than males
   d) the age of the respondent; older individuals tend to have lower recall scores
   (c; Challenging; p. 466)

141) The group which is least likely to recall an ad for a soft drink would be:
   a) children
   b) teens
   c) baby boomers
   d) senior citizens
(d; Challenging; p. 466)

142) The type of person that is most likely to recall an advertisement is:
   a) senior males (over the age of 60)
   b) senior females (over the age of 60)
   c) someone with a positive feeling toward advertising
   d) someone with an open mind
(c; Moderate; p. 466)

143) When individuals are given copies of an ad and asked if they recognize it or have seen it before, the technique is called:
   a) an aided recall test
   b) a storyboard test
   c) a theater test
   d) a recognition test
(d; Easy; p. 467)

144) Recognition tests are best suited to test for all of the following *except:*
   a) reaction
   b) price sensitivity
   c) comprehension
   d) likeability
(b; Challenging; p. 467)

145) When advertisers are more concerned about how an ad is received and what information is being comprehended, the best message evaluation test would be a:
   a) concept test
   b) recall test
   c) recognition test
   d) physiological test
(c; Challenging; p. 467)

146) For recognition tests, the ability of respondents to recognize an advertisement which would have *least* impact?
   a) the size of the ad
   b) the customer uses the product already
   c) the ad seemed interesting
   d) a regular person as the spokesperson in the ad
(d; Moderate; p. 468)

147) In terms of message evaluation, recognition tests are:
   a) used before an unaided recall test
   b) more reliable than recall tests
   c) an expression of a person's interest in a particular advertisement
   d) a test of the linkages found in a person's cognitive map
(c; Challenging; p. 468)

148) Recognition tests are impacted by all of the following *except*:
   a) if the respondent found the ad interesting
   b) if the respondent used the brand in the ad
   c) if the respondent liked the ad
   d) if the respondent had recently purchased a competing brand
(d; Moderate; p. 468)

149) The primary difference between recognition scores and recall scores is that recognition scores:
   a) do not decline over time
   b) are more reliable than recall scores
   c) tend to be lower than recall scores
   d) tend to indicate brand loyalty better than recall scores
(a; Challenging; p. 468)

150) The kind of test that can measure both cognitive and affective reactions to ads is called:
   a) recognition test
   b) recall test
   c) attitude and opinion test
   d) behavioral reaction test
(c; Moderate; p. 468)

151) Which test would tell McDonald's marketing team that consumers formed a negative impression of a sandwich after seeing an ad?
   a) a comprehension test
   b) an attitude or opinion test
   c) a recall test
   d) a behavioral reaction test
(b; Challenging; p. 468)

152) A 1 = highly favorable to 7 = highly unfavorable scale is called a(n):
   a) recognition test
   b) closed-ended questionnaire
   c) open-ended questionnaire
   d) validation test
(b; Easy; p. 468)

153) When subjects are ask whatever comes to mind regarding a product or advertisement, the form of research is called:
   a) recognition test
   b) closed-ended questionnaire
   c) open-ended questions
   d) validation test
(c; Easy; p. 468)

154) Which uses a computer joystick to test emotional reactions to an ad?
   a) a warmth monitor
   b) a psychogalvanometer
   c) a pupillometric test
   d) voice-pitch analysis
(a; Moderate; p. 469)

155) Warmth monitors and the Discover Why Internet program are examples of:
   a) emotional reaction tests
   b) recall tests
   c) recognition tests
   d) physiological arousal tests
(a; Moderate; p. 469)

156) In measuring emotions, researchers could use questions to inquire about emotional reactions to an ad. An alternative method would be to use:
   a) recall tests
   b) attitude and opinion tests
   c) warmth monitors
   d) recognition tests
(c; Challenging; p. 469)

157) Psychogalvanometers, pupillometric tests, and psychophysiology are forms of:
   a) emotional reaction tests
   b) recall tests
   c) recognition tests
   d) physiological arousal tests
(d; Easy; p. 470)

158) Emotional responses measured by instruments that are *not* self-report instruments are called:
   a) recognition tests
   b) recall tests
   c) cognitive accumulation tests
   d) physiological arousal tests
(d; Moderate; p. 470)

159) For evaluating advertisements, such as a Maidenform ad with a woman at an airport dressed only in her underwear, respondents may give what they consider to be a socially acceptable response instead of their true feelings. In such situations, the best evaluation method would be:
   a) persuasion analysis
   b) emotional reaction tests
   c) physiological arousal tests
   d) attitude and opinion tests
   (c; Challenging; p. 470)

160) Of the following evaluation methods, which of the following is *not* a self-report test?
   a) a warmth meter
   b) an emotional reaction test
   c) a closed-ended questionnaire
   d) psychophysiology
   (d; Challenging; p. 470)

161) In terms of physiological arousal tests, which measures perspiration levels?
   a) a warmth monitor
   b) a psychogalvanometer
   c) a pupillometric test
   d) a sweat meter
   (b; Moderate; p. 470)

162) In terms of physiological reactions to an ad, increased levels of perspiration indicates:
   a) greater emotions
   b) reduced emotions
   c) higher level of interest
   d) dislike for the ad
   (a; Moderate; p. 470)

163) In terms of physiological arousal tests, which measures pupil dilation to test emotional reactions to an ad?
   a) a psychogalvanometer
   b) a pupillometric meter
   c) a visualization meter
   d) psychophysiology
   (b; Moderate; p. 470)

164) Using a pupillometric meter, pupils become smaller when the subject:
   a) reacts positively to an ad
   b) reacts negatively to an ad
   c) has an interest in an ad
   d) likes an ad
(b; Challenging; p. 470)

165) Using a pupillometric meter someone who feel positively about an ad spokesperson will have pupils that are:
   a) larger
   b) smaller
   c) unchanged
   d) clearer
(a; Changing; p. 470)

166) Psychophysiology measures:
   a) impulse buying
   b) brain electricity
   c) dilation of a person's pupil
   d) perspiration
(b; Moderate; p. 471)

167) Brain-image measurement is part of :
   a) psychogalvanometer test
   b) pupillometric meter
   c) cognitive accumulation tests
   d) psychophysiology
(d; Moderate; p. 471)

168) Of the following physiological arousal tests, the one that offers the most promise in the future for advertising and marketing evaluation research is:
   a) psychogalvanometer test
   b) pupillometric meter
   c) psychophysiology
   d) warmth meter
(c; Challenging; p. 471)

169) The test used to see if an ad changed the consumer's mind about a product is called:
   a) a warmth meter
   b) a recognition test
   c) a recall test
   d) persuasion analysis
(d; Challenging; p. 471)

170) Positioning advertising copytesting was a set of principles originally designed for:
   a) evaluating television ads
   b) evaluating print ads
   c) monitoring emotional responses
   d) persuasion analysis
(a; Challenging; p. 471)

171) All of the following are principles of Position Advertising Copytesting, *except:*
   a) the procedure should be relevant to the advertising objective being tested
   b) researchers should agree on how results will be used
   c) the test should measure the degree of social responsibility
   d) researchers should use multiple measures to evaluate ads
(c; Challenging; p. 473)

172) All of the following are principles of PACT, *except:*
   a) the ad should be based on a theory of human response
   b) the ad should receive a single exposure to measure results
   c) the ads shown should be at the same stage of development
   d) the sample should represent the larger population
(b; Challenging; p. 473)

173) All of the following are behavioral evaluation measures, *except:*
   a) actual sales
   b) coupon redemptions
   c) emotional arousal
   d) Internet hits
(c; Easy; p. 475)

174) Which of the following is a short-term measure of marketing effectiveness?
   a) sales and redemption rates
   b) brand loyalty and equity
   c) product-specific awareness
   d) awareness of the overall company
(a; Moderate; p. 475)

175) Measuring changes in sales following a marketing campaign is easier now than in the past because of:
   a) commercial database services
   b) scanners and the UPC
   c) the power of retailers to control sales data
   d) Internet technology
(b; Moderate; p. 475)

176) Advertising is the most difficult part of the IMC program to evaluate for all of the following reasons, *except:*
    a) a delayed impact of the ad
    b) consumers changing their minds while in the store
    c) the consumer price index changes
    d) brand equity considerations
(c; Challenging; p. 475)

177) Of the following IMC components, the most difficult to measure in terms of effect on actual sales would be:
    a) personal selling
    b) advertising
    c) trade promotions
    d) direct marketing
(b; Easy; p. 476)

178) To measure the impact of a point-of-purchase display, retailers and manufacturers can use:
    a) response rates
    b) changes in sales
    c) scanner data
    d) number of inquiries
(c; Moderate; p. 476)

179) The best behavioral method to measure the impact of a coupon program is:
    a) changes in sales
    b) number of inquiries
    c) changes in attitude towards the brand
    d) the redemption rate
(d; Easy; p. 478)

180) The impact of all of the following marketing programs can be measured using redemption rates, *except:*
    a) point-of-purchase displays
    b) coupons
    c) sweepstakes
    d) direct-mail letters
(a; Challenging; p. 478)

181) When reactions to a small scale marketing effort are used to predict reactions in a larger area, the testing method is:
    a) emotional response
    b) PACT principles
    c) a test market
    d) a simulation model
(c; Easy; p. 478)

182) Test markets are typically used for all of the following, *except:*
    a) advertising effectiveness
    b) pricing tactics
    c) brand equity
    d) new product acceptance
(c; Easy; p. 478)

183) Test markets are used for all of the following, *except:*
    a) study promotions and premiums
    b) test emotional reactions to marketing campaign
    c) set prices
    d) study new product acceptance
(b; Moderate; p. 478)

184) The greatest danger in using a long time period for a test market is:
    a) the cost of the test market
    b) fear the competition will have time to study the test market and react
    c) the possibility of more interference from external factors
    d) changes in the economy
(b; Challenging; p. 479)

185) Scanner data is often used to measure the impact of the marketing communications in which of these programs?
    a) test markets
    b) recall tests
    c) purchase simulation tests
    d) mall intercept copytests
(a; Challenging; p. 479)

186) McCormick's marketing team wants to test three different advertisements for its new Chicken Dijon gravy before it launches the product nationwide. To measure actual market reaction, the best approach would be to:
    a) use the ads in three different markets and use DAR tests to measure the impact
    b) use different test markets for each of the three ads and compare the actual sales differences among the three markets
    c) place the three ads in a theater test and measure the audience reaction
    d) count the number of times the brand name or specific product is mentioned in the media after each ad has run
(b; Challenging; p. 479)

187) A purchase simulation test takes place in a:
   a) mall
   b) retail store
   c) laboratory
   d) theater
(c; Easy; p. 480)

188) Which statement below, concerning purchase stimulation tests, is *false*?
   a) They are performed in laboratory settings.
   b) They measure opinions and attitudes.
   c) They are a form of pre and posttest.
   d) They are designed to resemble a shopping experience.
(b; Moderate; p. 480)

189) All of the following are methods for evaluating public relations programs, *except:*
   a) counting clippings
   b) calculating the number of impressions
   c) using the advertising equivalence technique
   d) counting Internet hits
(d; Moderate; p. 480)

190) For evaluating public relations, which technique involves finding mentions of the company's name in magazines, newspapers, and journals?
   a) counting clippings
   b) calculating impressions
   c) the advertising equivalence technique
   d) the multiple exposure method
(a; Easy; p. 481)

191) For evaluating public relations, which technique involves knowing the circulation and newsstand sales of a newspaper?
   a) counting clippings
   b) calculating impressions
   c) the advertising equivalence technique
   d) the multiple exposure method
(b; Challenging; p. 481)

192) In a public relations evaluation, the advertising equivalence technique is designed to measure the:
   a) number of advertising clippings compared to news releases
   b) number of subscribers and buyers of a print medium in which the company's name has been mentioned
   c) number of calls to a toll-free number following a public relations event, coupled with an advertising campaign
   d) cost of the time and space if a story were an advertisement
(d; Moderate; p. 481)

193) The public relations evaluation method that is the least used, but probably the best method is:
   a) counting clippings
   b) calculating impressions
   c) advertising equivalence
   d) comparison to objectives
(d; Challenging; p. 481)

194) The measure or definition of marketing ROI that is the most commonly used is:
   a) incremental sales from marketing activities
   b) changes in brand awareness
   c) ratio of advertising costs to sales
   d) reach/frequency achieved
(a; Challenging; p. 482)

195) All of the following are common measures of the overall health of a company, *except:*
   a) market share
   b) level of innovation
   c) brand awareness
   d) productivity
(c; Moderate; p. 483)

196) All of the following are common measures of the overall health of a company, *except:*
   a) physical and financial resources
   b) profitability
   c) manager performance and development
   d) level of brand equity
(d; Moderate; p. 483)

197) Consumer awareness and brand loyalty are closely linked to a measure of:
   a) market share
   b) innovation
   c) productivity
   d) ROI
(a; Moderate; p. 483)

198) Which indicates a company that tries to eliminate negative activities and pursue positive programs?
   a) level of market share
   b) degree of social responsibility
   c) productivity increases
   d) greater physical and financial resources
(b; Moderate; p. 483)

Short-Answer Questions

199) What items should be identified when evaluating an advertising program?

- Short-term outcomes, such as sales
- Long-term results, such as brand loyalty
- Product-specific awareness
- Awareness of the overall company
- Affective responses, such as a positive brand image

(Challenging; p. 460)

200) What components of a marketing communications plan can be evaluated using concept tests?

- The copy or verbal component
- The message and its meaning
- The translation of copy in an international ad
- The effectiveness of peripheral cues
- The value associated with an offer or prize in a contest

(Challenging; p. 463)

201) What are the three main forms of copytesting?

1. Portfolio tests
2. Theater tests
3. The mall intercept technique

(Easy; p. 464)

202) What are the two main forms of Day-After Recall tests?

1. Aided recall
2. Unaided recall

(Easy; p. 465)

203) What forms of emotional reaction tests are available?

- Warmth meter
- Psychogalvanometer
- Pupillometric test
- Psychophysiology

(Easy; p 469)

204) What behavioral measures of advertising effectiveness are possible?

- Sales figures
- Calls to a toll-free number
- Response cards
- Internet responses
- Redemption rates of coupons and premiums
- Contest and sweepstakes' entries
- Responses to direct mail pieces

(Moderate; p. 475)

205) What makes measuring the effectiveness of advertisements more problematic?

- The influence of other factors, such as the weather
- The delayed impact of an ad
- Consumers changing their minds while in the store
- Whether or not the brand is in the consumer's evoked set
- Brand equity considerations

(Moderate; p. 476)

206) What can test markets assess?

- Advertisements
- Promotions and premiums
- Pricing tactics
- New products

(Moderate; p. 478)

207) What four methods are available for evaluating public relations' activities?

1. Counting clippings
2. Calculating the number of impressions
3. The advertising equivalence technique
4. Comparison to PR objectives

(Moderate; p. 480)

208) What objectives can be used to measure the overall IMC program?

- Market share
- Innovation
- Productivity
- Physical and financial resources
- Profitability
- Manager performance and development
- Employee performance and attitudes
- Social responsibility

(Challenging; p. 482)